One Child
Reading

MARGARET MACKEY

One Child Reading

My Auto-Bibliography

The University of Alberta Press

Published by

The University of Alberta Press
Ring House 2
Edmonton, Alberta, Canada T6G 2E1
www.uap.ualberta.ca

Copyright © 2016 Margaret Mackey

LIBRARY AND ARCHIVES CANADA
CATALOGUING IN PUBLICATION

Mackey, Margaret, 1948–, author
    One child reading : my auto-bibliography /
Margaret Mackey.

Includes bibliographical references and index.
Issued in print and electronic formats.
ISBN 978-1-77212-039-4 (paperback).—
ISBN 978-1-77212-147-6 (PDF)

    1. Mackey, Margaret, 1948- —Books and
reading. 2. Mackey, Margaret, 1948- —Childhood
and youth. 3. Reading. 4. Literacy. I. Title.

PN83.M32 2016   418'.4   C2016-900167-9
                            C2016-900168-7

First edition, first printing, 2016.
Printed and bound in Canada by Houghton
Boston Printers, Saskatoon, Saskatchewan.
Copyediting and proofreading by
Meaghan Craven.
Maps by Wendy Johnson.
Scanning by Dave Vasicek.
Indexing by Judy Dunlop.

The University of Alberta Press is committed to
protecting our natural environment. As part of
our efforts, this book is printed on Enviro Paper:
it contains 100% post-consumer recycled fibres
and is acid- and chlorine-free.

The University of Alberta Press gratefully
acknowledges the support received for its
publishing program from the Government of
Canada, the Canada Council for the Arts, and
the Government of Alberta through the Alberta
Media Fund.

This book has been published with the help of
a grant from the Canadian Federation for the
Humanities and Social Sciences, through the
Awards to Scholarly Publications Program,
using funds provided by the Social Sciences and
Humanities Research Council of Canada.

Every effort has been made to obtain permission
for copyrighted materials included in this book.
The author and publisher gratefully acknowledge
the many publishers and individuals who have
granted permission or provided letters of no
objection. The publisher will gladly address any
omissions in future reprints.

Canada   Canada Council   Conseil des Arts
          for the Arts   du Canada

Alberta
Government

Contents

Foreword

In the particular is contained the universal.

—*JAMES JOYCE, in Arthur Power,* Conversations with James Joyce

HOW DO A LITTLE GIRL'S FEET affect her literacy?
How are her reading perceptions changed while she journeys home from
the public library, carrying newly found books with anticipation but
weighed down by galoshes as she trudges through the streets of St. John's,
Newfoundland, which is grey in winter's gloom? How have St. John's
history and politics affected how she acquires literacy? When she plays
in her home on Pennywell Road, how does her imagination influence her
sense of narrative as she accepts the roles that various girls' toys in the
1950s ask her to adopt: playing, for instance, the part of mother or nurse or
teacher to her dolls and toy animals? How do the media and varied genres
she experiences—radio, television, recorded music, songs, poetry—influence her to perceive story and the rhythm of language? How does her
physical connection to the book she holds nestled in her lap affect her
cognition when she traces with one finger the relationships between
characters illustrated on the smooth, cool paper of each page?

In *One Child Reading: My Auto-Bibliography*, Margaret Mackey narrates
the story of her own multivariate acquisition of literacy. She situates her
learning within a narrative that is both about herself and about the ways
many—perhaps most—children become literate. She calls this work an
auto-bibliography because it is her self-reflection about the many texts that
have shaped her literacy. In a coda that precedes the final chapter, Mackey

identifies a paradox: "My reading story only partially mirrors everybody else's; and everyone else joins the general and abstract process in equally singular ways"; that is, every individual's literacy has emerged from elements that are almost universal and entirely unique to that individual. Mackey's auto-bibliography is also a testimony to the physicality of literacy. None of us learns to read without a body; none of us learns to read isolated from the environment in which we are living. As she puts it, all reading is "earthed"—reading always happens with a body that is always located somewhere.

Without in any way devaluing the work of the poststructuralists influenced by the "linguistic turn," whose work has dominated literary theory for the last several decades, Mackey builds on poststructuralism's emphasis on the discursive to demonstrate how the material interacts with language in the acquisition of literacy. She shows us that the materiality of literacy includes our bodies, the geographies in which we live, the media that surround us, and the artifacts with which we interact. *One Child Reading* participates in the "material turn," a movement that connects the discursive to the material (and the material to the discursive), rather than privileging discourse to the exclusion of other considerations. The geospatial theory at work here is just one example of materiality: as Mackey explores the paths, landmarks, nodes, edges, and districts of the city where she acquired literacy from 1950 to 1962, she reminds us that we have all learned language through embodied minds that are geographically situated.

Moreover, this auto-bibliography both introduces us to and elegantly employs the work of cognitive science. Mackey demonstrates by example how cognitive science helps us understand literacy. Reading fiction, for instance, requires our understanding of the subjunctive, that is, our ability to understand possibility and potential. Reading also cultivates our empathy and requires us to engage our Theory of Mind: characters challenge us to acknowledge the thoughts and feelings of other humans. Since the cognitive act of memory plays a particularly significant role in literacy, Mackey also delves into the workings of her own memory, identifying the "Murk" of pre-memories in her early childhood that undoubtedly involved her immersion into schemas and scripts in a process at once cognitive and physical. She writes about those "stereo-temporal" moments in which she experienced a *frisson* of recognition while researching this book. The embodied nature of that *frisson* testifies to the physicality of that which is remembered. Indeed, I myself experienced many such startling remembrances as I turned the pages of this volume and recognized illustrations from picture books I haven't seen since the 1960s.

One Child Reading has invited me to consider the geographies and materiality of my own literacy acquisition: how important the snug corners in which I read at home were; the apple tree I perched in as a reading getaway in my grandparents' yard; the red brick wall on the front porch that served in my young imagination as a suitable substitute for a card catalog when I played library. I also think about the materiality of my children's literacy as it emerged at the turn of this century—the most poignant exemplar being my second son holding his own Woody doll in his lap at a movie theatre and clutching in terror to ensure his own doll's arm was still intact when Woody-in-the-movie had his arm ripped off. Although he was quite young, my son knew how the narrative arc worked by that point, and the narrative of *Toy Story 2* was as material to him as the doll in his lap. His passion for the story, too, was one that motivated him to work on his reading skills, despite a variety of learning disabilities. I suspect that the word "ANDY" printed on the bottom of Woody's boot was one of the first words John ever read; certainly, "JOHN" was one of the first words my son ever wrote...on the bottom of his own Woody's boot.

Margaret Mackey lyrically narrates a story of her own literacy acquisition that reinforces the universal qualities inherent in all of our reading processes: reading is embodied; it requires us to understand the subjunctive—the "what-if" of story—and literacy is a geographically influenced process affected by landscape, history, and politics. *One Child Reading* illustrates poignantly James Joyce's point cited in the above epigraph: in the particulars of Mackey's literacy acquisition lie a host of universal issues that affect all emergent readers.

ROBERTA SEELINGER TRITES
Distinguished Professor of English
Illinois State University

Acknowledgements

THE ACKNOWLEDGEMENTS for this massive effort are both lengthy and heartfelt.

First, I thank the funders: the Social Sciences and Humanities Research Council of Canada, which provided very generous support, both to me individually and also via the publishing program. In the late stages of this project, the office of the Vice-President (Research) and the Faculty of Education at the University of Alberta also contributed.

My project is rooted in the province of Newfoundland and Labrador, and dozens of people there helped my pursuit. The libraries and archives at Memorial University of Newfoundland provided an enormous wealth of texts, photographs, maps, and other documents. I owe a particular debt to Linda White of Archives and Special Collections. Linda went to Prince of Wales College, just a couple of years behind me, and was friends with the girl who moved into 106 Pennywell Road immediately after we left. She therefore knew my home territory from a child's perspective and made connections for me that I could never have sorted out for myself. This book is very much richer for her interventions. Alison Mews in the curriculum library also offered important and knowledgeable support. The existence of the historical collection of school textbooks in that library provided an essential cornerstone of the whole project. The Centre for Newfoundland Studies was another ally, and I thank Joan Ritcey and her team. Dan Duda in the Maps Library offered imaginative and practical support, and also introduced me to Susan Kearsey, whom I thank very much for her research contributions.

The Faculty of Education at Memorial University was also very helpful, and I particularly wish to thank Alice Collins, Anne Burke, and Bobbi Hammett for providing space for me there.

At Gower Street United Church in St. John's, a variety of people went far beyond the call of duty to help me out. Rev. Guy Matthews, Rev. Marion Davis, Garfield Fizzard, Linda White (again), and James Hiller all assisted at various points in my six-year project. Parishioners Susie Noseworthy and her daughter Grace Glastonbury generously scanned a large number of Sunday-school leaflets that I was very glad to see again after many decades.

The librarians at the A.C. Hunter branch of the Newfoundland and Labrador Public Library were uniformly helpful. I particularly thank John Griffin for helping me attain usable images of some essential library documents in 2014. Similarly, at the Archives of the City of St. John's, Helen Miller and her team provided invaluable assistance. Provincial archivists at The Rooms were also supportive.

Individuals in Newfoundland were also generous beyond anything I could have imagined when I began this project. I am greatly indebted to Christopher Pratt for his permission to make use of two of his paintings that speak very profoundly to my childhood—and also for his kind words about my father. Mack Furlong gave excellent advice on aspects of the book; and Shane O'Dea kindly supplied his historical family photograph of the house on Pennywell Road—my thanks to both. Max Sheppard in Harbour Grace South let me spend a summer enjoying his copy of the 1927 Gerald S. Doyle songbook. Geralyn Christmas gave me two old Newfoundland stories, and provided many other forms of support. Marlene Creates very generously took me on a tour of the amazing landscape of her Portugal Cove property and provided a stimulating discussion on the particulars of place and literacy on the Avalon Peninsula. Charlotte Strong offered endless hospitality, intelligent recollections and confirmations, a variety of helpful book titles, and an assortment of very useful tips and introductions. To all these people and many others in St. John's and its environs, and to my friends in Harbour Grace South, I offer heartfelt thanks.

The University of Alberta provided a variety of supports. First and foremost, I appreciate the scale of the vast library collections. If I remembered an obscure children's series, the U of A Libraries invariably turned out to have holdings of a dozen different titles. At one point, a title was so obscure I had to ask the child_lit listserv for help (I thank its members, as well), but when the information came through to me, it turned out that the library had a copy in BARD—Book and Record Depository—and the book was in my hands less than twenty-four hours after I requested it.

Nobody has better faculty colleagues or better students than I do; I would not be able to do any of the work I do without all the people in the School of Library and Information Studies (SLIS), and I thank everyone who took an interest in my project. Bethany MacCallum pursued permission requests for the many images in this book with a mixture of doggedness and ingenuity that was wonderful to see. Emily Paulsen did yeoman work in checking the bibliography. Karen Willsher, initially assisted by Chelsea Murray and Angie Friesen, and subsequently working on her own with care and dedication, made video vignettes of many of the materials in this book. The SLIS office staff, as usual, have provided much practical help. My thanks also to the Department of Secondary Education at the University of Alberta for a number of helpful interventions.

The Department of Computing Science and some of the technology experts in the Department of Educational Psychology at the University of Alberta also provided very practical support, and I thank Mike Carbonaro of Educational Psychology for seeing the potential synergy and making the introductions. Eleni Stroulia in Computing Science was a huge help, not least for putting me in contact with Logan Gilmour and Parisa Naeimi. Logan's role in creating the first dedicated app of this project played a vital role in my developing sense of how multimodal materials might be incorporated into an analysis conducted for the most part in extended prose. Parisa then converted his work to a template. Later, Cody Steinke from the Department of Educational Psychology offered new insights into ways of thinking multimodally, as he created the second app. Erik Christiansen and Andrew Theobald of the Research Innovation Space in Education (RISE) have also made great contributions to my thinking and to my capacity to act on my ideas. My debt to all these people is enormous.

Homerton College and the Faculty of Education at Cambridge University provided a temporary base for me as I pursued British materials. Thanks especially to Morag Styles, who facilitated my visiting scholarship and took a generous (and hospitable) interest in the project. Victor Watson and his wife Judy provided a fabulous lunch and a tour of an equally mouth-watering collection of old annuals. Gabrielle Cliff Hodges, Maria Nikolajeva, Emma Charlton, and other members of the Places Project offered crucial intellectual pointers at an early stage of my work, and the book is much the richer for their input. Many people in Sheffield also provided early support and encouragement, especially Jackie Marsh, Julia Davies, Guy Merchant, and Cathy Burnett. As always, I thank Jenifer and Richard Allaway for their hospitality on occasions too numerous to mention.

Colleagues in Canada have also provided both moral and specific support. I particularly thank Perry Nodelman for his practical help in pinning down *The Book of Knowledge* and the audio rendition of *The Bear That Wasn't*. The Toronto archives of the United Church of Canada and the Canadian Broadcasting Corporation were both helpful. Leslie McGrath at the Osborne Collection of Early Children's Books at Toronto Public Library also made very helpful contributions, especially in assessing what might and might not be possible to retrieve. My mother's cousin, Graham Clarke, has been a valuable source of confirmation for some Nova Scotia stories, and I thank him, too.

I gratefully acknowledge the encouragement of the editors of *Children's Literature in Education*, who exhorted me to produce a series of articles on this project; and I also thank Springer for consent to redistribute the contents of these three articles and republish them here in slightly altered form. Colleagues in the United Kingdom Literacy Association and the Children's Literature Association responded constructively to very early presentations from this project, and it is impossible for me to overvalue the reinforcement they provided for my own deep instinct that, although I was talking about myself at extended length throughout this work, I was also talking about readers in more general ways. This project has entailed the loneliest research I have ever done, and such confirmation from people whose opinion I value was a crucial support.

I am also extremely grateful to everyone at the University of Alberta Press. Linda Cameron was quick to recognize the significance of what I was attempting to do, and all her colleagues at the press have offered moral and practical support along the way. Alan Brownoff's creative design and Meaghan Craven's editorial guidance have enhanced my original efforts. Judy Dunlop's sensitive work on the index has also enriched the final result. The anonymous reviewers made significant contributions to the improvement of the manuscript, and I thank them all.

As usual, the circle of my closest colleagues has provided utterly invaluable help and support. I thank Ingrid Johnston, Jill McClay, Gail de Vos,

Heide Blackmore, Anne Marquis, Elaine Jones, and especially Anna Altmann, who was the first reader for almost every chapter of this book. Everyone should be so lucky in their friends!

Finally, and most important, my family: five generations contributed to this story. My parents, my grandparents, and my three brothers all play important roles in the book that follows. Of this group, only two brothers remain alive today, and I thank both Earle and Bruce McCurdy for their enormous help. Earle, in particular, is in many ways my only witness of events that even Bruce is too young to remember; his surprised and delighted laughter at the sight of some of the materials that appear in these chapters has been a particular pleasure and encouragement. The generosity of both my brothers in answering my sometimes very obscure questions has provided some essential details in specific, and been tremendously heartening in general. They were allies then, and they are still allies today.

In very real ways, this story also incorporates those members of my family who arrived later: in roughly chronological order, my sister, Jan Horwood; my husband Terry (whose active support, intelligent interest, and ongoing patience have been exemplary); my assorted sisters- and brother-in-law, present and former; my two children, Beth and Sarah; their husbands, Dave Waldbillig and Jamie Burns; and my three grandchildren, Annabelle and Gabriel Waldbillig, and Eleanor Burns. My experiences of six childhoods subsequent to my own (those of my sister, my daughters, and my grandchildren) have undoubtedly inflected my memories of being a kid, and add their own invisible shaping to the story told here.

Literacy is a family event, a social and civic event, a historically and geographically located event—and a textual event. My acknowledgements encompass many communities, which is as it should be for a story of one person's reading life. All errors are my own responsibility, but my thanks to all the many people who helped along the way are extensive and profound. In addition, I offer retrospective thanks to all those whose work on my behalf is indirectly represented in this book: my teachers, my librarians, my Brown Owl, and all the many other individuals, unnamed here, who put in hours of voluntary labour to scaffold the developing literacy of the children around them.

This book is dedicated to the five generations of my family who partici-pated in this story, and above all to the two people who set my own story in motion, Betty and Sherburne McCurdy. It will be clear in the pages that follow that their actions and influence were crucial. Like my brothers and sister, I know how lucky I was to be their child and to grow up in the secure and loving home they created. This book expresses only a fraction of the debt I owe them.

This book presents words and still images from one child's literate experience. I continue to experiment with more multimodal forms of representation of my childhood materials, and readers interested in following such possibilities should visit my website, margaretmackey.ca, for a variety of audio, video, and interactive supplements.

PREAMBLE

1
Auto-Bibliography

An Introduction

PART I

I AM READING. My official breakfast chore is to stir the porridge, but, even though my face is hidden by my arm in the photograph that opens this chapter, there is no question where my best attention is directed: to the book in front of me. All sighted readers will recognize the invisible dotted line that connects my eyes to the words and images on the page. That virtual line, that indefinable connection between abstract representations and the live imagination of an interpreter, is the subject of this book.

Before I learned to read, my allotted morning task was to set the break-fast table. Once I could read, however, I got in everyone's way by refusing to put down my book as I carried the plates. Acknowledging an irresistible force, my parents transferred me to porridge duty, out of the line of general traffic. As is hinted by the perfunctory angle of the spoon in the photo, the porridge was often lumpy as my mind was always elsewhere.

This picture is the only visual record of my childhood passion for reading, so it is fortunate that it compresses into a single image many of the important issues I want to explore. My face does not show in this photo, but the intensity of my connection with my book is registered in my demeanour. I have vivid recollections of reading and stirring, and this photograph brings back many embodied memories of that kitchen: the sight and smell of drying laundry and of wet scarves and mittens hanging on an unseen rack behind the oil stove; the contrast between standing in that hot location and sitting in the damper, draftier area of the breakfast table beside a poorly sealed window; the angle of the light; the inevitable background chatter of the radio; the smell of porridge and toast and eggs boiling, all inflected by my huge and lifelong distaste for every kind of porridge ever invented; the bustle of my father and my younger brothers (eventually three of them), each with defined chores. (Dad did breakfast; Mum was not a morning person.)

All these associations crowd my mind as I look at this photograph. I can describe them, but I cannot make them truly accessible to anyone else. In order to understand and interpret this image, other readers will have to bring their own private and internal sense of what it means to maintain focus on an act of reading through an assortment of ordinary, daily distractions. It is part of the alchemy of how we communicate to each other that I can assume that these hypothetical others will be able to bring their own physical and psychological knowledge of the world to bear on how they make sense of this photograph and how they interpret my description of the scene it records.

In this book, I explore the full, embodied implications of being a reader, of being that reader in the photograph, in that setting, St. John's, Newfoundland, in the 1950s and early 1960s. For the most part in this project, I investigate my childish reading self by revisiting the materials I read, viewed, heard, and played. I contend that we can learn many important general truths from an in-depth singular study, and I explore as many as possible of the full set of materials with which I became literate in the 1950s and early 1960s in St. John's, the east coast capital of what was then called the Province of Newfoundland, newly joined to the country of Canada.

To create the best, most complete, shifting, contingent, plural, and multi-faceted understanding of interpretive processes that I can develop, it is worth testing the value of making a detailed, principled, and theoretically informed investigation of one interpreter's specific collection of textual materials. The texts are available for re-examination, even if elements of the experience are irretrievable; and a picture that is only partial may still offer valuable insights. In order to maximize the available text set, I work outward from my own personal awareness of what I read, saw, heard, and played.

That re-examination, of course, is also fraught with complexity. Valerie Krips (2000) comments usefully on the activity of returning to childhood texts: "Our memory—which includes memories of childhood—runs like a thread through our thinking and experiencing. In this sense, we are never free of our past. We are, however, fully capable of reimagining and renarrativizing it; thus, when we come across a book we loved as a child, we meet it from a long perspective, with the accretions of time and socialization upon us" (p. 15). But Krips does not stop with this simplistic notion that the past is just irretrievable.

> We cannot put aside our adult life and memories, our socialization and cultural expectations: we cannot read as the child we once were. In this sense, the memory we seek to revitalize seems almost certain to elude us.
>
> But books are more than the narratives they contain: they operate in the world as material objects, things in themselves. The books of childhood are in a special phenomenal relation to the world and the child's experience of it: they are very likely to be one of the objects through which the young child comes to interact with the world. In this sense, the children's book is capable of returning the past to us through its existence as an object that we remember from our earliest years, one which may come to represent that past for us. (p. 16)

Krips's observation is confirmed by Lewis Buzbee (2006), rereading books from his childhood: "The books of our childhood offer a vivid door to our own pasts, and not necessarily for the stories we read there, but for the memories of where we were and who we were when we were reading them; to remember a book is to remember the child who read that book" (pp. 36–37).

My aunt Mimi gave me a child's introduction to archaeology when I was six,
and coming upon that book now, I am taken back to my bedroom on Flood
Drive in San Jose, reading in bed at night, and the precise moment when I
understood that the written word "says" was pronounced "sez" rather than
rhyming with the plural of "hay." I can see the brown cowboy bedspread,
lariats and corrals rampant, feel the orange-tasseled fringe of it, and know
again the child I was. Find an old book from your childhood, take a good
whiff, and suddenly you're living Proust. (p. 37)

Memory is unreliable at the macro-level. Maria Nikolajeva (2014) describes our long-term episodic memory as "subjective, incoherent, fragmentary, disjunctive, random and imprecise" (p. 146). We do, mostly, kind of, know that we cannot trust our own narrative account of ourselves. We perhaps still need to take on board just how untrustworthy memory can be at the micro-level as well. Peter Mendelsund's (2014) brilliant evocation of what it means to read fiction sums up some of the problems entailed in recapping a single reading experience:

> *The story of reading is a remembered story. When we read, we are*
> *immersed. And the more we are immersed, the less we are able, in the*
> *moment, to bring our analytic minds to bear upon the experience in which*
> *we are absorbed. Thus, when we discuss the feeling of reading we are really*
> *talking about the memory of having read.*
>
> *And this memory of reading is a false memory. (p. 9)*

We imagine, says Mendelsund, that we have read a continuous sequence that unfolds rather like a movie. In reality, what we do when we read is assemble the fragments that authors make available to us. Characters, he suggests, are "collages, composed of clippings" (p. 50), rather than anything more "choate" (p. 16).

In ways that are strangely similar, fragments are all that are available to me from my own personal memory. The point of reacquiring my childhood texts is that they represent the main, indeed the only, stable element in the story of my reading past.

As I revisit the assortment of texts I have collected, I do find patchy details of my own life returning to mind. As I locate and scan these pages once more, listen to these recorded sounds again, re-encounter those moving images, in many cases after a time-lapse of half a century and more, I also find myself recalling more of my own past sensations that I initially filtered into the stories in order to make them breathe for me. Many of my private childhood experiences and atmospheres are obliquely captured in these stories and songs, and going back to the old materials restores some of the resonance of the life I lived at the time.

For this project, I have accumulated as many as possible of the resources that enabled me to become literate as a child aged one to thirteen, between 1950 and 1962, in St. John's, Newfoundland. I have cast my net as broadly as possible: picture books and chapter books, school textbooks, church and Sunday-school materials, gramophone recordings of music and audiobooks, radio and television programs, magazines for children and for adults, newspapers, movies, specialist texts such as sheet music and knitting patterns and cookbooks, museum artifacts and exhibits, songs and hymns—plus any other material I can retrieve after so many decades. My ambition has been to take advantage of a degree of particularity that I can ascertain only for myself. Establishing as much breadth as I can manage, I have aimed to create a maximally inclusive perspective on the material matrix underlying one person's development as a textual interpreter. My collection of the texts (in a range of media) that contributed to my literate childhood now fills eleven shelves, each thirty inches wide.

These childhood texts reverberate for me in telling ways, with all the biases and rhetorical tricks of any telling. My re-exploration of these materials offers potential to develop a deeper understanding of the complex internal world of reading. Trying not to make a falsely "choate" picture of the narrative of my own youth, I have focused as carefully as I can on the available materials.

One Reader among Many

This book tells part of the story of how I became a reader. But of course it also, by default, tells some of the story of who I am today. I will emphasize the importance of place to my literate development and explore how what I learned about reading was affected by my location as I learned it. What will remain invisible in this tale, unless I make a point of foregrounding it, is the importance of my place now, as the remembering adult. "Where and when we remember affects how we remember," says Harold Rosen (1996, p. 21). Who did that reading child grow up to be?

As I write these words, I remain a daughter and a sister. I am also a wife of long standing, a mother of two, a grandmother of three, and a professor of Library and Information Studies at the University of Alberta. I have spent my life working with young readers: as a big sister, as a teacher and a teacher-librarian, as a researcher, as an instructor of graduate courses, and as a parent and grandparent.

I currently spend nine or ten months of the year in Edmonton, and I pass my summers living and writing in Harbour Grace South, a small community on the Avalon Peninsula where we have owned a house since 2008. It is difficult for me to imagine how this study would have differed without that annual injection of just *being* in Newfoundland; it seems to me that some of the essential vividness that has been part of this retrospective experience would simply be missing. Certainly my capacity to walk the streets of my childhood would have been radically reduced, with many attendant consequences for my thinking.

No doubt the embodied recollections engendered by my reassembled collection of the texts of my youth will be most vividly fleshed out in my own mind, but I do anticipate that other readers will be able to extrapolate from my detailed account to a sense of their own reading childhoods. Yet that transfer of understanding between one body and another also raises problems, creates the potential for too-glib assumptions. The ease with which readers can perceive that connection between me and my book in the porridge-stirring photo may deceive them into thinking that, of course, they know what I am doing and, more generally, what reading is—it's what they do when they themselves read.

This fallacy that there is a singular act called reading is furthered by the great difficulty of explaining just what goes on inside a reader's head at any given moment. You cannot read and talk about your reading at the same time; to start talking, you must stop reading. As Mendelsund (2014) highlights, all commentary is retrospective of necessity, and the activation of cognitive and affective responses when we read is so diffuse and personal that it seems likely that all commentary is also edited from the swarming mass of associations crowding the privacy of the mind. It is as if there were a black box inside an interpreter's head, where words or images or soundscapes take on some form of mental life closed off to anyone else; that life is not itself describable and must be reduced to representations to be expressed.

After many years of attempting to record and understand behaviours of the "other reader," I am finally frustrated by the limitations of that effort. In one research project, I spent ten hours apiece interviewing nine different readers (Mackey, 2007), but although this study gave me an enormous respect for the range and variety of interpretive tastes and experiences, it left me unsatisfied with the scale of the terra incognita that these interpreters and I simply could not enter in any kind of collective way. Even after ninety hours, I had only scratched the surface of the enormous breadth and diversity of their interpretive activities. I know from the benchmark of my own private reading life that much greater complexity exists under the surface, accessible only to interior observation. Perhaps a careful and principled auto-study could fill a few gaps.

I have spent more than two decades listening to the retrospective, edited, and reduced accounts of other readers describing what happens inside their own minds as they construe the material before them. As a result, I am aware both of the limitations of this approach and also of the salutary admonition it provides about how enormously readers differ from each other. Just because we can look at a person reading and extrapolate our own experience does not certify that our mental image of what they are doing is accurate. Some aspects of reading can be observed only from inside—but, of course, our internal perspective is radically singular and does not allow for the variety that is such an essential component of the larger social achievement of interpreting texts.

The year 2014 saw a rush of publications that explore the cognitive implications of this kind of interior experience and make connections to children's development as readers. For example, Hugh Crago produced a detailed account of how story works (Crago's expertise lies in the field of counselling but he also has a background in literature and it is probably not a coincidence that he and his wife Maureen produced a uniquely detailed and specific account of a single young reader—their daughter Anna [Crago & Crago, 1983]).

Crago suggests that we experience story differently in the right and left hemispheres of our brain. His account speaks to the phenomenon I have just described: how the description of our reading experience seems to come later and to represent the full nature of a reading encounter only retrospectively and inadequately. Crago's explanation (to summarize a complex argument very coarsely) is that the right hemisphere deals in feelings and the left in words. Crago (2014) suggests:

[S]tory—as a literary form, as a particular kind of experience—originates in the right hemisphere, and offers a right hemisphere experience to its listeners, readers or viewers....[T]he left hemisphere communicates digitally, putting together words and concepts to represent experience. In contrast, the right hemisphere creates analogies to experiences—instead of talking about joy, it tells us a story that evokes joy, just as a piece of music automatically evokes sadness, elation or blissful peace. Instead of telling us, the right hemisphere shows us. (p. 13)

Stories represent "the right hemisphere's unique view of the world, a world that is whole, coherent, full of vivid sense impressions, replete with feeling, and imbued with intense significance," says Crago (p. 13). But it is the left hemisphere that is "ultimately responsible for turning shapeless, dreamlike sequences of events into strongly patterned narratives that command interest and attention" (p. 13).

Crago builds an elaborate theory of story on these foundations, an achievement too complex to be addressed rigorously in these pages. This brief representation of his hemispheric account of the storying brain at work is useful, however, in helping us account for that vivid but inchoate connection with the words on the page that we struggle to express when we talk about our reading experience to someone else.

The hemispheric vocabulary is not necessarily essential to the overall impact of this doubly staged response; Maria Nikolajeva (2014) describes the same division in terms of how our brains are wired to respond to emotional stimuli "through the very quick 'low path', short-cutting the rational part of the brain, and a slower, but more accurate 'high path' where among other things, language is situated" (p. 95). Melba Cuddy-Keane (2010) points out that terminology is a problem in discussing different components of our mental processes; she cites William James talking about the nucleus and the fringe, and David Galen talking about feature awareness and explicating awareness (p. 635). The sense of a doubled information channel feeding our cognitive assessment of the world survives all these variations of language.

However the demarcation is labelled, in this project I will not necessarily undertake to verbalize these vivid but undeveloped sensations that emanate in my own right hemisphere / low path when I read. Nevertheless, I will have at least implicit access to their potent contribution to the complete experience. Even in its raw and *unspeakable* form, such aware-ness will allow for a deeper sense of what is going on when we read; such tacit awareness will feed my analysis in considered and unconsidered ways.

A Retrievable Singularity?

I am certainly not exploring my own literary history because I think it provides a detailed template of how everyone learns to read. Far from it; I was a bookish, middle-class, straight, white girl in an isolated setting on the fringe of North American mainstream culture; and the idiosyncrasies of my experience are at least as significant as the regularities. I was not an especially interesting or adventurous reader as a child. I was simply an intelligent girl reader of the 1950s, conventional in tastes and aspirations, constrained by the gender assumptions and expectations of those times, and somewhat restricted by today's standards in the availability of books, TV shows, and movies, though with lavish access to materials by the yard-stick of earlier centuries. These limitations are part of the detailed work I propose.

Inevitably, over the years of my prior research projects, I have compared the restricted nature of the insights I could glean from participants in my research projects with my much broader, if tacit, awareness of the elaborate intricacy of my own reading experience. How could I gain the advantage of that extended knowledge locked inside my head in ways that were more disciplined than self-indulgent? What tools could I develop for probing the cumulative interpretive experiences of more than sixty years, stored some-where inside me, sometimes surfacing in random and incoherent flashes of memory?

Simply combing my mental storehouse in order to produce some kind of reading memoir would not be an adequate approach. Penelope Lively (2012) eloquently describes some of the complexities of personal recollection:

> That evanescent, pervasive, slippery internal landscape known to no one else, that vast accretion of data on which you depend—without it you would not be yourself. Impossible to share, and no one else could view it anyway. The past is our ultimate privacy; we pile it up, year by year, decade by decade, it stows itself away, with its perverse random recall system. We remember in shreds, the tattered faulty contents of the mind. (pp. 224–225)

It was clear to me that relying on "the tattered faulty contents" of my own mind would not supply a basis for a robust consideration of reading development. But reading is a partnership between the reader and the text, and the text is less susceptible to tattering and shredding. The picture of me reading as I stir the porridge contains an image of a specific book as well as a situated girl. That unidentifiable book is a permanent object that came into our kitchen from elsewhere. The local pulse of breakfast preparation in our house was counterpointed by its narrative rhythms. As Deborah Brandt and Katie Clinton (2002) point out, "literacy arises out of local, particular, situated human interactions while...it also regularly arrives from other places—infiltrating, disjointing, and displacing local life" (p. 343).

In the face of these paradoxes, my project took life. By various means over a number of years, I have reacquired many of the texts with which I sharpened my reading skills throughout my childhood. I took advantage of the 360° nature of my knowledge about my own interpretive life and assembled a more complete set of materials than is normally considered in reading histories, including texts in many media from school, home, church, Brownie pack, and much more. However faulty my memory, the books and other materials I encountered in my youth have not materially changed, and they offered the potential of one kind of reliable data set.

Furthermore, the reacquisition of the texts of my youth allowed me to establish some parallels with my previous research experience. When I have worked with other readers, I have always grounded our discussions in relation to particular texts; we have always talked about interpreting a specific something. Similarly, to explore my own development as I became a reader, I located my considerations in a material data set: the texts I read, watched, heard, performed; with which and through which I learned to make sense of a variety of formats and media. As Margaret Meek (1988) so memorably told us, "Texts teach what readers learn," and some of my own learning might still be retrievable from those materials.

The Nouns and Verbs—and Adverbs—of Reading

Interpreting texts is an activity, something we do, a verb. The materials we read, watch, hear, and play are the nouns of the event. But it was not long into this project before I realized that the adverbs of context are also vital. *I read something*—subject, verb, and object fall neatly into place, but the sentence is incomplete nevertheless. Who and what are clear, but where, when, why, how, all press for attention. For me, the where was a given: I learned to read in St. John's, Newfoundland. The *when* was almost as inflexible, but I did decide on some temporal limits for my project. I was born in Halifax, Nova Scotia, and moved to Newfoundland at the age of twenty months in August 1950. I left Newfoundland for a temporary two-year stay in Alberta in July 1962, at the age of thirteen and a half. Those twelve years were crucial to my becoming a literate person, and they presented me with a defined timespan.

The *why* and the *how* of my reading varied from one text to another, but the *when* and *where* conditions were pervasive. They localized my reading. I was not just a generic child learning to make sense of texts; I was a *placed* child. The specifics of that placing are important in themselves, and they also provide a number of metaphors that help to organize my thoughts about what is and what is not possible in a project such as mine. The physical and social situation of any reader is important. Some scientists would suggest that situation even affects how we direct our sensory apparatus; "more and more [anthropologists] are willing to argue that sensory perception is as much about the cultural training of attention as it is about biological capacity" (Luhrmann, 2014, SR6)

I hypothesize that local situation is more crucial to a learning reader because of the restricted repertoire such a reader can bring to bear on a text. My location influenced my early literacy—and eventually my literacy became strong enough to influence my awareness of my location in return.

A Local Habitation and a Time

To explore the potential of placement, I metaphorically zoom the camera back from the close-up image of a reading Margaret to the perspective of a broader picture.

I am now looking at Google Earth. The aerial image is dotted with camera icons, and when I click on one of them, I close in for a 360° photograph of a street scene. I pick a particular plot of land, and I move around its perimeter, rotating my camera-eye to see all around me. The digital detail is compelling in its familiarity, and yet there is a deep and essential strangeness to this perspective.

I am exploring the site of 106/108 Pennywell Road in St. John's, Newfoundland. The house there, which was divided into two apartments in my day, has been torn down and replaced with a gravel parking lot. There is

> *The site of 106/108*
Pennywell Road.
[© *Google Earth 2013*]

∨ *The right-hand*
gatepost, set back from
the road, bears the last
traces of "106."
[*Collection of the author*]

grass where the entrance used to be, but two cement gateposts still remain, and you can read the last traces of "106" on the right-hand post. East of this post, a row of five trees stands along a shallow, grassy rise above a low cement wall.

106/108 Pennywell Road stood on the edge of a school's athletic grounds, covering six acres of hilltop. In my time, the area incorporated two soccer pitches, a derelict tennis court, a sports pavilion, a fenced-in garden, and a large, two-apartment house. I lived in the top half of the house, number 106, the first home I can remember. I explored every corner of those six acres. I climbed the trees. I rolled, somersaulted, tobogganed down the slopes. With my brothers and friends, I played games at different locations around the site. The houses that line the opposite side of Pennywell Road and mount the slope of Linscott Street along the eastern edge of the site are still the most familiar buildings in the world to me, even gentrified as they appear today in the Google Earth images, with their new windows and vinyl siding.

My place in this world was secure; indeed I used that security to help "place" myself further in very literal and embodied ways. I have never been very good at spatial relationships and struggled for years to master left and right. For a long time, I would inscribe the number 106 with both index fingers—in the air, or inside my coat pocket. The hand that felt more comfortable with this project was my right hand; it was a mental trick that served me well for many years.

To explore this territory now, via Google's street images, is an uncanny experience. The six acres remain open. Our tobogganing hill is still there; the soccer pitches are more or less viable. The trees are bigger but stand in recognizable relation to each other. The landscape is intimately known to me. Yet at the heart of this so-familiar territory is a dominating absence. The house is missing. My exploration of this virtual landscape is on the one hand profoundly, viscerally comfortable; on the other hand it yearns endlessly toward that crucial empty space where home ought to be.

This commonplace twenty-first-century story resonates doubly with my purposes in this project of literary reclamation. The details of this setting are very significant in the story I am about to tell. And, as a metaphor, the image of the familiar territory with a *lacuna* at its heart provides an apt comparison for the degree to which I can achieve my goals.

The Gap at the Heart of the Landscape

Just as the 360° perspective in the Google street images is based from a specific point of view, so my ability to radiate outward through my own literacy materials is grounded in the core of my internal, personal perspective.

But at the centre of this project lies a gap, an absence. In part, this absence is the result of a significant decision on my part. I am interested in the particulars of my own literacy experiences, but I do not intend to create a personal memoir. My sister was born some years after my cut-off date of 1962, so her undeniable importance in my life is not represented by a role in this narrative. My parents and my three brothers, however, played a part in my expanding literacy whose significance is probably impossible to exaggerate. Yet, though I hope I acknowledge their vital roles with due justice, I am not writing a family history, either. I refer to this project as an auto-bibliography rather than an autobiography, and I have designed it as a study of materials rather than simply a personal history. Telling a purely private narrative is not the driving impetus of this work; instead, I am interested in creating a complex understanding of the three-way relationship between a particular life *and* named, specific texts *and* the theories that help us understand how reading works.

A second reason for the absence at the heart of this story is more existential and essential. Geoffrey O'Brien (2004), exploring aspects of his own life history through the framework of recorded music, expresses it well: "The age of recording is necessarily an age of nostalgia—when was the past so hauntingly accessible—but its bitterest insight is the incapacity of even the most perfectly captured sound to restore the moment of its first inscribing. That world is no longer there" (p. 16). "That world," the beginning point where we learn about how to place ourselves in space and time, is indeed "no longer there," except as it continues to live inside us, orienting us to all the remainder of the world that is *not* our starting place. Robert Kroetsch (2010) describes that loss and yet that presence of the past in two brief, simple, and eloquent lines of verse:

> *Too bad the house is gone.*
> *It's still the place where I live. (p. 11)*

This paradox of the past being inexorably gone and yet unavoidably built into our present perspectives in ways that we may never be able to perceive or describe—or erase—will necessarily inform and infuse this study. Such a paradox lies at the very heart of this project and serves as one reason for its existence. Only for myself can I attempt to register the scale and significance of what is lost—and also the power of what remains—because it is built into my own cognitive processes. I will necessarily be restricted by my own blind spots, by those memories lost through repression or simple fading away, by my unexamined ideological biases, and by my probably infinite capacity to invent myself in a more favourable light. I persist, nevertheless, *because* I believe the project offers the potential for understanding literate development in innovative and exciting ways.

There is a third kind of gap in this study, a challenge to its bibliocentric approach. Kevin Leander and Gail Boldt (2013) make a cogent case for considering literacy in terms of energy and potential, rather than in the reified terms of the text: "[L]iteracy is unbounded. Unless as researchers we begin traveling in the unbounded circles that literacy travels in, we will miss literacy's ability to participate in unruly ways because we only see its proprieties" (p. 41). Instead of pursuing the "unruly" nature of literacy, say Leander and Boldt,

> *researchers subtract. We view a scene, with an infinite number of movements, interactions, possible rhizomatic lines, and we subtract from the scene all that makes the telling of a coherent post hoc narrative difficult....* *[W]e interpret backward from texts to practices. We subtract those things that are not so clearly about texts, making texts central to any instance of practice, perhaps because they are central to us. In so doing, we risk developing contorted views of what people are up to. (p. 41)*

I find this admonishment very helpful. One reason why I want to explore as many elements of my own literate development as I can muster for investigation is to include those messy components that are usually edited out of accounts of reading. For all their deceptive neatness and stability, for the purposes of this project, I believe the texts themselves offer one route into that inherent untidiness, a route that is more reliable than simply running on recollection. At least as much as research, memory is also a single-minded tidy-upper. In both cases, I believe the villain is the narrative impulse that ruthlessly eliminates randomness in favour of a streamlined and tellable set of causal relations. As far as possible, I wish to respect a sense of unboundedness, though I know I will not be able to do it justice.

Leander and Boldt (2013) say, "[B]eginning with texts and resources misses what seems to be the centrality of practices as affective events" (p. 40). Because my personal investment in this reading story cannot be eliminated, I will begin with affective events, as I now remember them, but then turn to the texts that were involved in these events because today they represent my best and least-edited access to experiences of the past. It is a hybrid approach with many points of vulnerability and much potential for being misguided. The texts present a disciplining of the memories that has the potential to cause problems; but an undisciplined memory is also riddled with potential weaknesses. Leander and Boldt suggest that "script-like, purposeful, or rule-governed practices [are] in constant interaction with actions that [are] spontaneous and improvisational, produced through an emergent moment-by-moment *unfolding*" (p. 29). I cannot recapture all my original spontaneous unfolding, but I hypothesize that my approach to the materials today bears traces of the original impulses that animated my reading in the first place. The personal is a necessary component of this work, with all its energy and potential; the materials that I revisit today are "tinged with event" (Massumi, 2002, p. 11). Warping is inevitable, but warping is part of everyone's story of literacy. The experiment of revisiting these packages of potential, past and present, is worth trying.

The particular materials on which I happened to sharpen my literary teeth were tools, prosthetics for complex acts of cognition. They were also what Robin Bernstein (2011) calls "scriptive things" (p. 8), objects that invite particular forms of performance. Bernstein supplies a partial answer to the concerns of Leander and Boldt. We can recreate the invitation of the scriptive text, she suggests, "using archival knowledge and historical context to determine the documented, probable, and possible uses of a category of object" (p. 8). In such ways, we can recover more than might be expected of past performances of everyday life that have seemed "ephemeral and untraceable" (p. 8). My personal memories are indeed ephemeral and potentially unreliable, but the scriptive element of the materials themselves, inviting some kinds of performance and rendering others more difficult, also forms a cogent component of the data set.

The challenge of exploring acts of cognition forms the spine and theoretical core of this study. My working hypothesis is that reopening the specific texts of my youth will intensify my explicit, and perhaps especially my tacit, understanding of reading. The guiding principle of this project is that the particular provides insights into the general; even that, in some important ways, we can understand the general only as a concatenation of specifics. The singular account is risky, but the general account is also risky, insofar as it overlooks the shaping significance of the idiosyncratic and individual experience. The role of individual accidents and quirks is often crucial to developing literacy.

Theoretical Frames

Theories of reader response and cognitive poetics inform this project. These approaches focus on processes of reading much more than on textual analysis; they privilege verbs even as they try (with varying success) to take respectful account of nouns. Both perspectives highlight the role of the individual reader as an integral part of any interpretive activity, but that reader is vaguely situated at best, in a very abstract and insignificant setting. The adverbs (when, where, why, how) are effectively lost.

Once I began intensive work on this project, I realized that the "situatedness" of my childhood self as a reader constituted a specific and highly important component of my account. Much of this book is a reflection on why it mattered to my development as a reader (surely an abstract intellectual task) that I was based in St. John's in the 1950s.

My initial awareness of this priority was nebulous: a strong feeling of the significance of my feet, in action along Pennywell Road and elsewhere. This powerful sense that, in order to understand the past, I must look to my neighbourhood locations, as well as to my books and recordings, was a very early, very primitive, and very strong building block of the entire project. I interrogated this sensation, suspicious that I was simply falling into a trap of sentimentality and nostalgia. But that feeling that my early reading had been physically located in a particular place was too robust to be readily dismissed; it strengthened with each individual title I reread. I began to explore other people's perspectives on the situated element of reading.

I am not alone in valuing the particularities of the extremely local. David Barton and Mary Hamilton (1998) remind us, "Literacy events are located in time and space. Reading and writing are things which people do, either alone or with other people, but always in a social context—always in a place and at a time. To make sense of people's literacy practices we need to situate them within this context" (p. 23). Alistair Pennycook (2010) reinforces this idea by relating it to broader turns in academic thought: "The notion of the local has become an increasing significant focus across the social sciences, to a large extent as a reaction to what has been seen as broad, ungrounded theorizing throughout much of the 20th century. Rather than talk about human nature, universal cognition, or language structure, the focus has shifted towards the local, the grounded, the particular" (p. 1). Here, Pennycook is talking about language more than literacy but his points remain germane:

> *Understanding the locality of language, therefore, is not merely about accurate descriptions of language systems...but about people and place. The ways in which languages are described, legislated for and against, policed and taught have major effects on many people. In trying to develop a perspective on languages as local practices, therefore, we need to appreciate that language cannot be dealt with separately from speakers, histories, cultures, places, ideologies. (p. 6)*

Literacy in most contemporary conditions involves texts produced *somewhere*, within the contingencies of one locality (though online collaboration is beginning to nibble away at this central concept). The miracle of the preserved word, in whatever medium—print, audio text, video recording, digital exchange—means that it may transfer into new times and new places. It is then consumed in the context of that new place, taking on the accent and aura of its new local setting in novel ways, enabled and circumscribed by local decisions.

Shaun Moores (2005) raises this point as a challenge for media theories: "What we require is an understanding of how the immediate social environments of media *consumption*...contribute to shaping processes of signification" (p. 122, emphasis added). Book reading is often distinguished from other forms of "media consumption," but I think we benefit significantly from including reading under this larger umbrella. How do "the immediate social environments" affect how a child learns to become a reader? How does that child make use of understandings developed locally in order to participate in a system of literate activities that is more broadly based and largely rooted elsewhere?

By focusing on the texts available to me in my childhood, I explore that broader system of communications through the lens of the local and the vernacular. At one level, this study is a micro-local project, but my aim is also to explore how the macro-forces of contemporary national and international publishing and broadcasting filtered into that local environment through the medium of my everyday texts. The midlevel is also important; local institutional decisions by school boards, Sunday-school committees, library staff, Brownie leaders, and many more, also inflected my literate development in formative ways.

Ultimately, the internalizing of particular geography and specific history is all anyone is given when beginning to create an interpretive toolkit. My own locally assembled understanding, expanding through my youth by the day, created the repertoire I brought to bear on understanding texts. Initially, my reading was necessarily placed; I had to assemble enough scripts and schemas to make a start, and then the books could offer expansion beyond the local—but only as places and times elsewhere could be brought to life through the lens of my own home-grown awareness.

As years passed, my sense of being local and home-grown became layered more complexly with my literacies. Neil Gaiman (2013) reflects on a bookish childhood, and it is perhaps apropos that his fictional boy addresses a factor that was real in my own world: "Growing up, I took so many cues from books. They taught me most of what I knew about what people did, about how to behave. They were my teachers and my advisors. In books, boys climbed trees, so I climbed trees, sometimes very high, always scared of falling" (p. 77). My own local understanding wove in and out of my literate experiences and vice versa.

One Young Reader

Before I turn to the materials, a few words about myself as a reader may offer clues to the kinds of filters I bring to this project out of the nature of my own experiences. I do not propose an exhaustive self-study of my past readerly tricks and habits, but I can account for my reading self through some rough and ready categories. I was a child who read for momentum rather than accuracy or accountability (Chittenden & Salinger, 2001, p. 89), and I reread frequently. I was usually satisfied with a good-enough experience and was not a careful reader. I was cautious about hazarding the emotional commitment required by a new book and relatively quick to reject a title without giving it a reasonable chance. In many ways, I felt safer with rereading.

In terms of what I understand of my own cognitive processes, I have never been a "visualizer"; all my life I have created, from the words I am reading, a mental presence of what I can only describe as blurry emotional forces rather than any kind of image whatsoever. These emotional forces have no features, and their setting is vague, but I am sharply aware of their interrelationships. I am not a "listener" either, though I have always been very sensitive to cadence; the music of the text matters to me. I have never heard words in my head as I read, as some readers do, but I do "feel" the cadences of the sentences. If anything, I am a "kinesthetic" reader, responding to forces and movements and rhythms in the story. Other readers will behave differently with texts. Indeed, I hope that by describing my own cognitive activity in this kind of singular detail, I invite readers to a better understanding of the plurality of reader response, simply through consideration of how their own reading behaviour differs from mine.

Lawrence Sipe describes the kind of stance I most frequently remember as "transparent." As an external observer of young children reacting to picture book read-alouds, he was, of course, confined to commenting on what they vocalized, and, as he rightly says, it may well be that their absorbed silence was a more eloquent testimonial than anything they might have said aloud.

> *The type of literary understanding that responses in this category represent is the ability to position oneself in (or indeed, inside) the dynamics of the narrative to such an extent that the story and one's own life, for an evanescent moment, merge with and are transparent to each other....I am arguing that deep engagement in a story is in itself an aspect of literary understanding, one that has often been noted anecdotally by teachers (especially those in the primary grades), but that has not been theorized extensively or incorporated into a broader theoretical framework; the response, like many other types of response, is simply noted as one kind of interesting reaction young children display, without relating it to the complex and diverse matrix of responses children exhibit through their talk.*
>
> *Transparent response may be interpreted by some as immature and naïve: it may seem that the children are behaving as if the story were "real," and the characters were actually alive. (Sipe, 2008, pp. 172–173)*

Immature and naïve such responses may well be, but they also represent one of the most remarkable elements of fiction reading: the capacity for a reader to imagine him or herself into a different world. Just as the children Sipe studied did not necessarily articulate their intense involvement with the story, so it is all too easy for us to overlook the huge step involved in moving the psyche into a new and imaginary space.

Sipe observes that children in his project could switch very rapidly between this absorbed relationship with the fictional world and other, more detached and analytical comments (p. 173). My own reading life was largely solitary; often there was no impetus for me to separate myself from the story to assess it, and my occasional conversations about what I was reading would mainly have been with children whose responses were equally transparent. My preference, every time, was to immerse myself whole-heartedly in the world of the story, blasting through it at pell-mell speed with little pause for correction or reflection. In many ways, my reading activity resembled the experience of "flow" that Raymond Williams (1974) ascribes to the kind of television viewing that consumes one program after another through the evening (p. 86). As the viewer might accurately describe this experience as "watching television" rather than viewing a discrete program, so I was often just "reading," picking up one book after another in a continuous sequence where continuity of access to something mattered more than specific titles.

I did not worry unduly about the accuracy of my decoding and was more than content to settle for the gist of the story. I was used to large gaps between my own understanding of my local world and the conventions taken for granted in my books, so I persevered through transitory forms of incoherence in a relatively untroubled way, as long as I could make emotional sense of the story. I read vividly but carelessly.

I mention these features, though up to now they have been of no import to anyone but myself. For my purposes here, these tastes and predilections, these inveterate habits good and bad, form part of the point of view I bring to bear on my reading past. I was not "*the* reader"; I was a specific little girl whose hasty and often sloppy reading habits were daily reinforced through enthusiastic repetition. Furthermore, I usually settled for conventionally feminine tastes as deemed acceptable in the 1950s (and I do not intend to be defensive or dismissive about the degree to which I "bought into" those stereotypes of femininity). For the most part, I read to feel safe, not to take risks—or at least not beyond the limits of the thrills in my series fiction. Much of what I read was very bland.

If I had not been this reader with these preferences, I would simply bring another set of limitations, arising out of a different reading style, to bear on this project. The singularity of my focus restricts my perspective. That finite point of view is both constraint and driving force in this project. I propose to explore the specifics and particularities of one named reader's textual life in order to investigate the necessary role of specifics and particularities in any reader's textual life. The limitations are in-built and unavoidable, but they are still limitations. But restrictions are part of what makes it possible for us to become literate at all.

Revisiting the Past

I started this project with many memories of those twelve years of my early literate life, mostly represented in my mind as random and disconnected moments, intense but fleeting and not very contextualized except in general terms. When I check out what I remember and compare it with the actual materials, I find my memory fragments are largely accurate, even though the haphazard balance of what is recalled and what is forgotten is neces- sarily arbitrary. Much of what I remember about reading is pretty low-stakes stuff, and probably more reliable as a result. I am not trying to expand these gleams and glimpses into any coherent narrative; my approach is to take my flicker of memory and then turn to the remembered text for greater detail. However ephemeral or faulty my recollection, the text is constant; in physical terms, at least, it remains what it was in the past.

An example will give an idea of how mundane some memories and associations can be. In 2012 I acquired a second-hand copy of the series book *Beverly Gray's Quest* (Blank, 1942). Certain that I had read it before, I tucked into it eagerly, hoping to find traces of the child reader who had devoured it in the late 1950s. As I picked up the book, I even felt a residual memory of the cold, damp, and drafty windowseat in my bedroom.

The novel is full of incidents and adventures that seemed completely new to me, and I began to be convinced I was mistaken about having read it before. Yet at the end of the day, I know that I did read this book in my childhood—probably in the windowseat; I do trust that flash of embodied recollection.

What is my proof? It is strikingly low-key, transient, and personal. Late in the book is a throw-away sentence that I was not expecting but instantly recognized. Beverly is flying her own plane home (she did a lot of that kind of thing), and she nearly lands in the water. As the plane loses altitude, she remembers an insignificant line of verse: "Down went McGinty to the bottom of the sea!" and her mind effects a word change: "Down went Beverly to the bottom of the sea—right into Davy Jones' lap!" (p. 198). I recognized that line immediately, possibly because I do normally remember distinctive cadences. I clearly recalled being annoyed by the changed scansion of Beverly's version, compared to the original. In any case, I could hardly have made up the jolt of visceral familiarity that ran through me when I read this sentence in 2012. It is not evidence that I can demonstrate to anyone else (and indeed it is a sensation that I would not re-experience if I read *Beverly Gray's Quest* again). Nevertheless, I know that I read this book at least once, prior to my adult encounter with it.

So what? This tiny stab of recognition serves only as a prompt to observe that much of our reading experience is small and inconsequential, that our memories can be random and capricious, that our capacity for forgetting is enormous, and that much reading, in childhood or later, may do little but contribute to a general mental compost. In re-excavating these texts from my childhood, I am not always dealing with eternal truths, character-building principles, or an undeviating route from a kind of lesser childhood toward one informed by greater moral values because of my reading experiences. Nothing so straight-line occurred.

The trifles of a reading life are often the first lost to view when the researcher comes calling and readers are invited to speak about their reading experience to somebody else. Unruliness is subtracted; an economical account of an indescribably sprawling reality is carved out, edited, reduced. Yet while the nondescript reading experience is unmemorable, by definition, its role in a reading life may be highly significant in cumulative ways. One positive result of my memory flickering randomly is that it includes minor moments along with major insights. As I have perused the materials of my reading childhood, I have expanded my access to my own earlier life, sometimes vividly, sometimes vaguely, and sometimes trivially.

Situation and residue do not necessarily align in any reasonably coherent way. A reading experience that was highly compelling at the time left strange traces. When I was eight, my father was sent a sample textbook that he kept in his bedroom. I thought I was forbidden to read it, though I doubt now that anyone would have objected. I regularly sneaked in to snatch a few more pages. The book, as I recall it now, read like a temperance manifesto: In Chapter 1, Bobby is knocked down by a drunk driver. While he recuperates from his broken leg, his classmates set up a project to research the effects of alcohol on the human body. Bobby arrives back at school for their big presentation of the results (all strongly anti-alcohol) in the final chapter.

What has stuck with me over the decades, however, is neither specific information about alcohol and the body, nor any overwhelming sense of the subversive joys of illicit reading. Instead, it is the strangely strong sense of recognition I experience when I see a particular type of (usually dark green) car. "Oh, a car like the one that hit Bobby," flashes involuntarily in my mind. It is not a useful or interesting trace, nor one with any social utility what-ever, but it appears to be ineradicable. Inevitably it makes me wonder about the size of my mental junkroom and the scope of the reading castoffs contained therein. By definition, such a topic is almost unresearchable, but it remains significant to most readers.

This book will not comprise a collection of such anecdotes, however. I am not setting out to create a coherent story of my own past, if indeed I ever could. A single flash is enough if it leads to the retrieval of a text (alas, I do not remember enough salient information to locate Bobby's story). Most of the impetus encapsulated in this study comes from the texts them-selves and their "scriptive" potential for directing performance. My own life is not plotted in these pages, and I hope the project is more rather than less reliable as a consequence.

PART II

A Contingent Setting

I cannot emphasize the importance of the local without providing some context for the very distinctive society in which I happened to *find myself* (with all the literal and metaphorical implications that this phrase allows). By historical accident, I learned to read, view, listen, and reflect in Newfoundland, in the first decade of that province's Confederation with Canada.

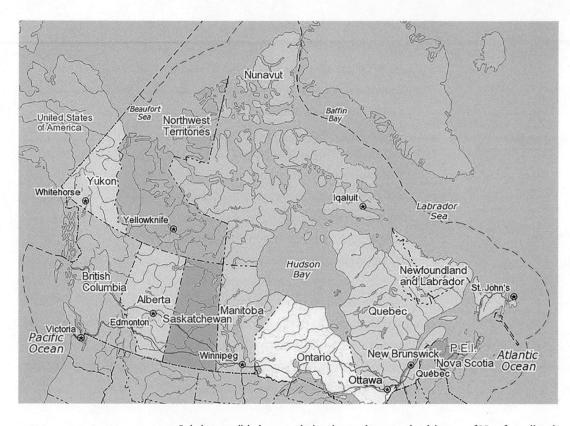

Map labels: Nunavut · Beaufort Sea · Northwest Territories · Baffin Bay · United States of America · Yukon · Whitehorse · Iqaluit · Labrador Sea · Yellowknife · British Columbia · Hudson Bay · Newfoundland and Labrador · St. John's · Alberta · Manitoba · Quebec · Victoria · Edmonton · Saskatchewan · Pacific Ocean · Winnipeg · Ontario · New Brunswick · P.E.I. · Nova Scotia · Atlantic Ocean · Ottawa · Québec

∧ *The eastern, isolated, and exposed location of St. John's is clear on the right-hand side of this map. Facing the North Atlantic, St. John's is the easternmost city in North America. The dotted line represents the two-hundred-mile limit and highlights the importance of fisheries (then) and oil resources (now) in the province's economy.*

[Map from The Atlas of Canada, National Resources Canada]

It is impossible here to do justice to the complex history of Newfoundland and Labrador, as the province has been named since 2001. Some (very) edited highlights will have to provide hints of its many idiosyncratic turns. The jurisdiction consists of the island of Newfoundland and the continental territory of Labrador. In the interests of space, I will focus mainly on the island, where my own understanding was rooted, and I will stick largely to the twentieth century.

At the start of that century, Newfoundland—with its small and isolated population largely dependent on the labour-intensive salt-cod fishery—functioned as a dominion in the British Empire, under a system of responsible government. The exploitative nature of the fishing economy manifested itself in a system of truck and barter that made the St. John's fish merchants rich while confining working families to lives of desperate poverty and debt.

The First World War irrevocably changed this society, as the horrific losses of the Royal Newfoundland Regiment in a single hour in 1916 affected the whole population. To this day, the word "Memorial" appears on many public constructions, including the university. The consequent massive war debts compounded already-existing financial problems created by the fluctuations of the fish markets. The impact of the Great Depression led to even more dire poverty—and a government declaration of bankruptcy in 1932. In 1934 elections were suspended and a Commission of Government ruled Newfoundland directly from London, with some token local representation. Acrimonious debates, two referenda, and a considerable amount of backroom negotiation, whose final impact is still disputed, resulted in the ending of direct rule from London as Newfoundland became the tenth province of Canada on March 31, 1949.

This complicated political history was an essential element of the stage I entered as a toddler in 1950. Even as a child I felt a sadness to civic life there, a elegiac acknowledgement of past sorrows, paradoxically juxtaposed to the great humour and wit that also marks public and private life in Newfoundland. My own childhood was hardly lavish, but it was secure (my parents both knew greater poverty than I ever experienced). But, along with my Newfoundland-born friends and classmates, I lived in a society that was fundamentally marked by the afterlife of three major historic events: the slaughter of the First World War; the terrible, bleak poverty of the 1930s that crippled Newfoundland physically, socially, and politically; and the acrimonious vote on Confederation. Each turning point has an eloquent spokesperson whose observations are salient to understanding and appreciating the essential cultural framework of my environment.

David Macfarlane writes of the effect of the First World War, in which the Royal Newfoundland Regiment distinguished itself at very great cost. Most famously, in about half an hour on the morning of July 1, 1916, the first day of the Battle of the Somme, 710 men were killed or wounded or went missing at Beaumont Hamel; only 68 members of the regiment responded at roll call the next morning. A society much larger than Newfoundland,whose population in 1916 stood at around 240,000 people, would have reeled from the impact of such loss ("Newfoundland," n.d.).

"[T]he greatest change the war brought," says Macfarlane (1991), in the most acute analysis of the haunting of Newfoundland that I have ever encountered,

> was one that no one could measure. It was an absence. It was marked eventually with war memorials and parades, which, by their very existence, contradicted what they were supposed to represent. July 1 is Memorial Day

in Newfoundland—the first services were held one year after Beaumont Hamel, on July 1, 1917—and what the cenotaphs and marches really commemorate is nothing. They substantiate not what had been before the war, and not what happened during it, but what never was to be, after the war was over. The best were gone by 1917, or doomed, and what the world would have been like had they not died is anybody's guess. The war left their things unfinished: enterprises conceived, projects initiated, routes surveyed, engagements announced. And that's where it ended. Their fiancées waited for them forever, their mail went unanswered, their deals never closed. Their plans were left in rough draft, their sentences unfinished. (p. 189)

As if it were not enough to suffer this agony of blanks, which Macfarlane describes as descending through the generations (as the spaces of lost brothers extended into the gaps where lost cousins would never appear), war debt crippled the Newfoundland economy and the 1930s took a terrible toll on the people.

Don Jamieson, Newfoundland broadcaster and Canadian cabinet minister, a man who had a front-row seat for much of Newfoundland's twentieth-century history, provides a sober thumbnail description of that era. Having taken a commercial class after he left school at thirteen, he worked as a stenographer for the London-based Commission of Government in the field of rural development. He travelled the island in the 1930s. In his memoirs, Jamieson (1989) confronts the unelected commission's dismissal of the population as not interested in self-government:

> [W]hile the absence of local government was undeniable, little of this situa-
> tion was due to public apathy. The widely-scattered, small population and
> the resultant social structure did not provide fertile ground for the flow-
> ering of participatory democracy. Then, too, adult illiteracy was widespread
> and much of what local leadership there was came from the churches, a
> few educators and even fewer merchants. Dispersed as they were in over
> one thousand mostly unconnected small communities, the Newfoundland
> people had their hands full with the struggle to stay alive, a grim task at
> which not all of them succeeded.
>
> When the group with which I worked began to travel around
> Newfoundland to promote the idea of self-help and greater involvement,
> the principal problem we encountered was not indifference. Rather, seem-
> ingly immutable geographic and economic circumstances frustrated even

the most industrious and best intentioned efforts to establish any form
of local organization. The degree of isolation of most communities was
appalling—no roads, a fortnightly mail service, a rudimentary and often
inoperable telegraph service and poor to non-existent radio reception.
Several villages lacked any form of schooling, and regular medical service
was unheard of. As a result of inadequate medical care and diets meager
in both quantity and quality, malnutrition was rampant, contributing to an
understandable lack of energy and enthusiasm for community betterment.
In any event, since there were rarely more than fifty families to a settlement,
frequently less, the scope for the enrichment of life was decidedly limited.

Still, there persisted in the highest circles of government an unfortunate
tendency to attribute the people's woes to their own slothfulness. Too many
policies ignored the real nature of the basic challenge: the curse of isolation
compounded by the worst economic collapse in living memory. (p. 27)

To cut a long and fascinating story short, the Second World War
provided an economic jump-start to that depressed economy, and the war
debt was repaid. Next came the debate over Newfoundland's political
future. By a narrow majority, Newfoundland wound up in Canada, whose
social-support systems relieved some of the direst local desperation. The
charismatic Joseph Smallwood (serially a journalist, a union organizer, a
radio broadcaster, a champion of the pro-Confederation forces, and the first
premier of the new province from 1949 until 1971) provided lively, though
idiosyncratic and sometimes wrong-headed, political leadership, filling the
vacuum described by Jamieson, with variable results.

But bitterness and regret over the close vote on Confederation lingered
well into my time. Marjorie Doyle (2013), writing in *The Globe and Mail* and
addressing Canadians on the occasion of the fiftieth anniversary of
Confederation, asked,

How long does it take to forget nationhood? Just for a moment, imagine
Canada is subsumed by the United States. How many years would it take
before you felt about July 4 as you now feel about July 1? How long before
The Star-Spangled Banner would stir you? And if you have children who are
15 or 20, how long before they would become true Americans. Would there
be Canadian spillage into the households they set up? Feelings don't die
because your passport changes. (p. 194)

Those feelings, still lingering in 1999, when Doyle's article was originally published, were fresh and raw in the early 1950s. Even some of those who voted in favour of Confederation, because they thought it would ease the struggles of the very young and the very old, had voted with regret. As a Canadian-born child, I took the virtues of Confederation for granted and was oblivious to the wistfulness of many in my society, but the issue was much more complex than I comprehended at the time.

These harsh memories of sacrifice and slaughter, hunger, poverty, injustice, and roads not taken, always augmented by the physical and emotional hardships entailed in battling the North Atlantic Ocean for a living, lingered in the social framework in ways that were perhaps nebulous but that demanded respect, even as Confederation announced changing times. It would not be possible to describe the social framework of my developing literacy without evoking something of this social and cultural sense, both regretful and proud, of *looking back*.

Today Newfoundland has experienced some relative prosperity. Offshore oil has temporarily made big differences, and tourism thrives. The pulp and paper industry is dead and the fisheries are crippled. But Newfoundland confidence is high, and the artistic output of this small society is dazzling. Some old memories still rankle, but many positive developments have taken root. A child learning to read there today would acquire very different local knowledge and perspective.

The Incomers

In the early stages of Confederation, our family arrived in Newfoundland, moving into a turbulent social, economic, cultural, political, and emotional landscape.

I was twenty months old when we moved to St. John's from Halifax in August 1950. I do not remember ever living elsewhere. My classmates, however, born in 1948 like me, represented the last cohort born as Newfoundlanders rather than Canadians. They were extremely proud of this fact, even as children, and I was part of a very small minority coming from elsewhere, a status I registered from early childhood onward.

The cultural ethos of Newfoundland prizes family connections and genealogical background very highly. It ensured I was always pegged as "Canadian." My name, too, marked me as an outsider; McCurdy is a common surname in Nova Scotia but almost unknown in Newfoundland before our arrival. In many essential ways, I participated in local life as an immigrant—the word is not too profound for the experience. Indeed, my parents in their first years in St. John's had to collect Christmas parcels from Halifax at the "foreign mail" wicket (McCurdy & McCurdy, 2010/2002, 13). Yet, like many other very young immigrants, I knew no other "home" landscape but that of my adopted city.

The fact that I grew up in Newfoundland at all was actually a consequence of my Canadian roots. All public education was denominational in Newfoundland in the 1950s; there were no secular state schools. Prince of Wales College (PWC) in St. John's was a United Church school system that covered Kindergarten to Grade 11—the province could not afford Grade 12—and inherited the august mantle of the Wesleyan Academy, the flagship school of Newfoundland Methodism, founded in 1860. After Confederation in 1949, the PWC Board of Governors decided that it was time to revisit their long-standing tradition of always hiring a British principal for the college. New times called for new mores, and they went recruiting at Dalhousie University in Halifax to find a Canadian to run their school system. There they selected my father, a young man of twenty-six, with wartime military experience in the Royal Canadian Air Force but with no teaching background. He brought his Canadian credentials to the job and was my own school principal for all the years covered by this study.

The social, historical, and political details of how a dominion gradually transformed into a province thus also affect this project. It is impossible to isolate my literacy story from this unique cultural setting. Yet I do not believe uniqueness is a drawback to my ambition to tell a general story; every child lives in a particular relation to a specific culture, and I am sure the great majority do not find themselves seamlessly aligned with either the real or the textual worlds in which they find themselves. Learning to read *with*, they also learn to read *against* and also to read *comparatively*, and they are probably better off in a variety of ways for learning to cope with this challenge, however it manifests itself.

Naming a Culture

In Newfoundland (to this day, to some extent, and most definitely in the 1950s), a strong strain of nationalistic pride mingled with and/or contested an assortment of allegiances and connections to Great Britain, the United States of America, and Canada. This distinct cultural climate was formalized in certain school textbooks, and in museum exhibits, radio programming, provincial holidays, and the like.

For the most part, however, the texts I encountered mostly bore no relation to this world. *Captains Courageous* (Kipling, 1897), an unsuccessful Christmas gift one year, was the only novel I saw that even mentioned the word Newfoundland; unfortunately, I detested it. Even Canadian literature for children was very thin on the ground, and I valued L.M. Montgomery all the more fervently as a result.

Fiction writer Bernice Morgan (2003), who is a few years older than I am and who grew up in a Newfoundland outport, describes her childhood experiences of never meeting her own culture rendered in print or any other artistic form:

> *I grew up without it ever occurring to me that Newfoundland had a culture, without even thinking that the place I lived in could be the subject of novels, or art, drama or poetry. In school essays I used the word "village" rather than "outport." Outports did not exist either in the printed world or in the world of my imagination. The Newfoundland Museum had been closed during the Depression. There were no art galleries and I knew of no Newfoundland artists. No local plays were being written or performed. Anyone who walked on stage in St. John's—even born and bred Newfoundlanders—spoke with English accents, as did radio announcers and almost everyone in authority. (p. 374)*

To people who have never lived in circumstances where all available forms of both imagined past and imagined present belong *elsewhere*, those who identify the hollowed-out nature of such a colonized culture must sound like whiners or professional victims. Yet there is a hard reality to being invisible on every page you ever see, as post-colonialist projects have clearly established. It would not have occurred to me as a child that any book plot could possibly be worked out on my own ground. And, as an immigrant child, and unlike Bernice Morgan, I had little family access to Newfoundland's legendary oral culture to flesh out, at least partially, the meagre institutional forms of record I encountered.

At the same time, although its own distinctive individuality in that era was not recorded or transfused into many permanent artistic forms, the isolated city of St. John's was also a recognizable North American urban centre of the 1950s. Many norms and conventions of civic life on that continent applied to us. Furthermore, I was a member of an orthodox, white, middle-class family; our lives, though marked by frugality, followed daily routines and established disciplinary expectations that I would certainly recognize in the books I came to read. We went to school and church and Sunday school in highly normative ways; I joined Brownies and visited the library and the local museum. Like most children of the 1950s, my brothers and I played outdoors and were allowed to roam freely as long as we remained within earshot of the whistle my mother blew to summon us home to meals. Our family of four children resembled every other family I knew and also resembled characters on page and screen. The distinctive components of our own lives and culture were not reflected in our literature, but we were easily able to recognize the conventional elements.

Almost all of my recreational reading was American or British—I sampled both literatures widely, if not always well. From the time I was eight, my friend and I made a weekly trip to the children's branch of the Gosling Memorial Library at the conclusion of our Saturday morning Brownie meeting. We owned only a few books at home, so the librarians' selections were my selections for the most part. School prizes, the occasional Christmas present, some tattered children's annuals and Sunday-school awards surviving from my mother's youth, all supplemented our library choices. My father remembered titles from his childhood (Henty and Alger for the most part) and often enthused about them, but he didn't actually own any of the books, and his recommendations often fell on deaf ears. (I do recall standing by a bookshelf in the library to dip into a Henty book and being repelled by its derring-do.) Hand-me-downs from family friends completed the domestic supply; and it was a motley collection, to put it mildly. I out-read my three brothers, but they outnumbered me, so there were boys' books as well as girls' books to be had—and I tried everything.

The Newfoundland Museum opened in 1957 and was located on the top floor of the library building. I had just turned eight that year and was luckier than Bernice Morgan in that it was a perfect age to start museum visiting. Every couple of months my friend and I would head upstairs after a library visit and browse the exhibits before returning home. To my recollection, they changed very little over the years, and made their own contribution to my developing understanding of my environment.

While I find on a reassuringly regular basis that my figments of memories are confirmed when I track down the appropriate material, I know that I can never recreate my own childhood perspective on the challenges and joys of reading. To re-explore and reinterpret the broad variety of materials that were available to me is a task that is possible, fascinating, and, I am convinced, useful. To re-immerse myself completely in a child's world from the early days of Confederation in Newfoundland can never be achieved. Inexorably I bring the sensibilities of an adult and the perspectives of the twenty-first century to bear upon the materials I have acquired. The gap at the heart of this project must simply be acknowledged; the child's view of that world is no more restorable than the vanished house in the street-scene image.

Reading the City

Even from the earliest days of listening to stories at bedtime, I was preoccupied with learning to make sense of my own environment. I was a recognizably "normal" urban child, even though I lived in an idiosyncratic city. So it is perhaps not entirely surprising that a classic study of the patterns of urban life provides a key both to my own early understanding and also to my current project; it has shaped my thinking, and it has shaped this book.

In 1960 Kevin Lynch produced a seminal study on "the apparent clarity or 'legibility' of the cityscape. By this," he says,

> *we mean the ease by which its parts can be recognized and can be organized into a coherent pattern. Just as this printed page, if it is legible, can be visually grasped as a related pattern of recognizable symbols, so a legible city would be one whose districts or landmarks or pathways are easily identifiable and are easily grouped into an over-all pattern. (pp. 2–3)*

Many educational toys for young children invite activities of grouping, clustering, associating like with like, and recognizing patterns; they are key intellectual developments. Lynch does not consider the significance to children of learning to read their urban environment, but I find it productive to explore the connection between myself learning to read the patterns of my own city and myself learning to comprehend the stories that were offered to me, both before and after I learned to read. The city was *there*, it offered daily raw material for my developing awareness and provided practice in script- and schema-building.

Lynch suggests that we make use of five categories for structuring our sense of a city. I report these categories in detail because I make double use of them, and I edit Lynch's more extensive descriptions to serve my own purposes most precisely.

A city, says Lynch, may be analyzed through the following elements:

1. **Paths.** *Paths are the channels along which the observer customarily, occasionally, or potentially moves....People observe the city while moving through it, and along these paths the other environmental elements are arranged and related.*

2. **Edges.** *...They are the boundaries....These edge elements, though probably not as dominant as paths, are for many people important organizing features, particularly in the role of holding together generalized areas, as in the outline of a city by water or wall.*

3. **Districts.** *Districts are the medium-to-large sections of the city, conceived of as having two-dimensional extent, which the observer mentally enters "inside of," and which are recognizable as having some common, identifying character. Always identifiable from the inside, they are also used for exterior reference if visible from the outside....*

4. **Nodes.** *...They may be primarily junctions,...a crossing or convergence of paths, moments of shift from one structure to another. Or the nodes may be simply concentrations, which gain their importance from being the condensation of some use or physical character....*

5. **Landmarks.** *...They are usually a rather simply defined physical object: building, sign, store, or mountain. Their use involves the singling out of one element from a host of possibilities. (pp. 47–48)*

By Lynch's standards, St. John's is a particularly legible city, even more so in the 1950s. Its *edge* is definitive: nothing less than the North Atlantic Ocean stretching uninterrupted to Ireland. Its main *landmarks* (Signal Hill, the Southside Hills, the Roman Catholic Basilica, and the harbour) are visible from many perspectives. The streets of the older part of town are often steep and angled, so the *paths* through the city are distinctive rather than anonymous, the *districts* are individual and idiosyncratic, and the *nodes* where paths intersect may involve complex five- or six-way junctions. Novelist Wayne Johnston (2014/2013) declares St. John's

∧ *St. John's as seen from Signal Hill, July 2010.* [Collection of the author]

> *Me on Signal Hill, either September 1952 or spring 1953.* [Collection of the author]

[t]he City of Chaotic Traffic because of the number of purposeless one-way streets, dead ends, sharp turns, all-but-vertical cul-de-sacs, intersections that were remnants of streetcar lines that criss-crossed in ways so random they could keep you going in a circle or a square for minutes with no clue from a road sign as to how you might escape. (p. 17)

Not all paths and nodes are invariably productive, however memorable they render a city.

St. John's also has the advantage of offering multiple perspectives on the elements that compose it. Even as a very small child, I loved to go to Signal Hill, from which vantage point I could look down on my own little network of paths, nodes, and districts. Thus I knew my own paths both by journeying along them and by perceiving, from above, their relation to each other.

A pair of domestic photographs illustrates the legibility of this city for me. In the first, taken by my grandfather, I am standing on the landmark of

Signal Hill, aged around four. Behind me is the mighty edge of the Atlantic Ocean.

I do not possess a contemporary image of the vista I was contemplating in this snapshot. A 2010 photo of that view, however, succeeds in demonstrating the perspective on paths, nodes, districts, and other landmarks. In this picture, Signal Hill is in the foreground. The straight lines of the harbour front are recent and artificial; in the early 1950s the waterfront would have jutted with wharves and finger piers. Many buildings are new, though the two towers of the Basilica still dominate the middle right of the photo. Even anachronistically, the photo conveys Signal Hill's unchanging affordance of overview.

My own walk to school provided examples of all five of Lynch's elements. The path I took, eastward down Pennywell Road, gave a clear sighting of the major landmark of Signal Hill with Cabot Tower at its summit; as I neared the school, my perspective included that definitive edge of the view out to sea. Various junctions provided nodes along the way, and at the far end of my mile's walk stood school, church, and library, all within a stone's throw of each other and each providing its own district identity.

The photograph that highlights my daily walk to school (see pages 42–43) shows a view eastward down Pennywell Road from the node of the junction with Linscott Street, and includes the landmarks of Signal Hill and Cabot Tower in the background. The street was unpaved until sometime around 1958. Prior to the huge event of the paving operation (a sensation that brought out every local kid as spectator), the sidewalks consisted of packed-down dirt. The north-side sidewalk wound up and down over the roots of the trees on the left of the picture. When the new, flat sidewalks appeared, I was nine or ten and instantly nostalgic for the old, winding, and "unimproved" path.

That walk to school is also represented in an aerial photograph of the city, taken in 1951, a shot that gives some idea of the complexity of the network of paths and nodes involved. The Ayre Athletic Grounds is the rhomboid in the lower left of the image, and the white curve of the gravel driveway can just be discerned on the east side of the house. We walked toward the upper right, where school, church, and library clustered within the same quarter-mile radius. (Note how finger piers fringe the harbour's edge; the city was an active fishing port in those days.)

The details of these photographs matter to the development of my case. I devote much attention to the instantiation of Lynch's elements in my own environment for two reasons. First, I believe that learning to read my environment contributed significantly to how I learned to read my books, an idea I have explored elsewhere (Mackey, 2010a, 2010b, 2011, 2012) and to which I will return later. Second, Lynch's ideas provide a helpful organizing structure for the book that follows.

Reading the Project

Some years into this study, and despairing of ever finding a way to manage the scope and scale of its cross-referential and ever-expanding dimensions, I was suddenly struck one day by the potential of Lynch's organizing taxonomy for presenting the patterns of my own project. His schema develops an interrelationship between local and general, and allows for a singular and moving perspective, useful for marshalling a large and unwieldy data set.

After two chapters establishing theoretical frameworks, therefore, this book is organized on "Lynchian" lines, adapting his order of presentation for my own purposes.

1. **Paths** *provides the most chronologically and developmentally ordered account of my own progress as a reader, from early childhood through to the age of thirteen. In this section I explore ways of understanding important details of cognitive development for the growing reader.*

2. **Landmarks** *looks at the literacy of special occasions: the landslide of literate markers that accompanied my birth, the impact of a one-time-only summer vacation, the ritual literacies of Christmas.*

3. **Nodes** *offers a look at the same years through the perspective of exploring junctions where paths crossed and I moved between and among different media, formats, social contexts, and so forth. The contrast is perhaps best described as the difference between a forward-moving video and the sweep of a 360° street scene where the viewer is able to linger, look around, make connections, and compare and contrast. I attempt to tease out the learning bound up in these "knotty" cross-connections and to explore some of the personally significant themes that I pursued through a variety of different text forms.*

4. **Edges** *explores the impact of the boundaries of my own known world, both in Newfoundland and to a lesser extent in Nova Scotia, where my family roots are intricately entwined and where we took occasional family holidays. It lays out and then disrupts the limits of my local*

Home

< The view eastward down Pennywell Road, as recorded in 2010.

[Collection of the author]

∨ Detail from a 1951 aerial photograph of St. John's. My route to school is marked by white dots.

[Reprinted by permission of the Government of Newfoundland and Labrador]

*understanding, conceived through direct experience and also through an
assortment of textual filters.*

5. **Districts** *investigates the institutional "neighbourhoods" where
my literacy was enabled and sometimes constricted: school, church,
library, museum, movie theatres, bookstore, radio and TV stations, and
more. These institutions were also placed, located in the terms of their
own historical and geographical situations. I cannot do justice to the
complexity of their history, but to ignore them would be to overlook the
important fact that my literacy was not simply a romantic accident but
rather a response to a world of texts shaped by active and deliberate
decisions by many people, both in my own society and farther afield.*

Finally, this book's **Coda** returns to the theoretical perspective, with the
aim of drawing together a widely disparate, yet individually focused set of
materials and experiences.

The first three sections focus on my own life and the texts that informed
it. The sections entitled Edges and Districts present a stronger emphasis on
the environment in which my literate development occurred. Both components contribute to an account of the essential localness of literacy, no
matter how universally distributed are the texts involved.

The Paths section establishes the forward-moving perspective of
chronological development, relating journey to map for the first time. The
subsequent sections recross the territory, revisiting the first map and
creating new ones. Perhaps as a consequence, they operate on the basis of
a different kind of impetus, possibly recalling Johnston's higgledy-piggledy
City of Chaotic Traffic from time to time (a helpful reminder that learning
to be literate is not a linear process). Just as a topographical map and a
street map provide different kinds of essential information, so these varied
sweeps across the same territory offer important perspectives on a highly
complex intellectual challenge. Readers may find they need to adjust their
pace in different sections of this book.

A pedestrian in Lynch's city can alternate attention between paths,
nodes, and the rest. By marking my sections so strongly, I hope to enable
cross-references between and among them, while still providing a coherent
framework for my complex content.

Reading this Book

My retracing of my journey toward literacy is set in an individual context. If I achieve my ambition, the singular nature of these particularities will offer a better understanding of literate development than can be supplied through generalities alone. Although my story is analogue, its mapping draws on contemporary digital sensibilities: "[N]ow we each stand, individually, at the center of our own map worlds. On our computers, phones and cars, we plot a route not from A to B but from ourselves ("Allow current location") to anywhere of our choosing; every distance is measured from where we stand, and as we travel we are ourselves mapped" (Garfield, 2013, p. 19).

As with comparisons of GPS locators, readers may find that the most appropriate response to my "maps" is to substitute recollection of their own particular histories into some of the specifics I offer here; other people's singularities may validate my own, or I may be contradicted. I offer the particularities of my own case as one way of shedding oblique light on more general understanding. Readers supplying different specifics from their own childhood memories and texts will field test my hypotheses on the same basis of particularity in which they were developed, though details will be different.

In short, I ask my readers to read the acts of cognition that made reading possible for me, to read "through" the details of my grounded circumstances and text set to the description of reading itself that I have developed through the vehicle of my own particular auto-bibliography. As Barton and Hamilton (1998) tell us in the opening sentence of their book, "Literacy is primarily something people do; it is an activity, located in the space between thought and text" (p. 3). The text is public; the thought is private; the complex act that links them is specific and singular. Readers of this book should move past these singularities to explore the performance of cognition involved.

Before we begin this complex journey, however, I offer a word about the mechanisms of this project, the acquisition of the data set on which this study is based. How trustworthy is my selection as a representative of a large and often random text set?

Retrieving the Past: Finding, Buying, Borrowing

I started this project with a major advantage—being the oldest child of a woman with the instincts (though not all the tools) of an archivist. My mother believed in preserving domestic records, and, for reasons of time and energy, her capacities were most fully engaged with her first child. A daughter of the Depression, she also saved books. I retrieved many familiar titles from her shelves when she moved into a nursing home. Another large batch came (on long-term loan) from my brother Bruce; he was for ten years the youngest child in the family and thus the natural heir of a miscellaneous collection of series books that no grown-up would bother to retain. Thornton W. Burgess and Enid Blyton feature large in his box, and the books display a beguiling mix of children's signatures and assorted assertions of provenance (school and Sunday-school prizes, Christmas and birthday gifts, and so forth).

But not everything survived at home, and I remembered many titles I had to reacquire. In terms of obtaining the physical artifacts of the 1950s, today is the right time to be trying. When I first set out to establish if this project was even achievable, the Internet was my earliest ally. Tracing and purchasing second-hand books is easy today, and the smallest fragment of memory can often be enough to facilitate the rediscovery of a lost artifact. Where online catalogues could not muster enough information to allow identification, digital communities stepped in. The collective intelligence of the child_lit listserv, for example, took less than half an hour to provide one lost book title for me on the strength of a single remembered chapter heading. To a surprising degree, if I have been able to remember a book, I have been able to lay my hands on it.

The popularity of nostalgia television means that many of the programs I watched from the age of seven onward can now be acquired on DVD. YouTube fills in some of the remaining gaps. The archives of television and radio stations are also very helpful.

I have listed my obligations to a variety of institutions in the Acknowledgements and will not repeat them here, except to stress how much constructive work is made possible by the care and hard work of librarians, archivists, and local historians. This project would not be possible without the intelligence and dedication of many people.

Perils and Pitfalls

This study is strictly limited in its nature, both by design and by necessity. My collection of materials provides the first constraint. I have reacquired many, many titles, but I do have to remember them first. Obviously the basis of this work makes it inevitable that I have no idea what is missing.

The second limitation involves space and time. Although I have tried to be expansive only where it seems helpful, there is not room, even in this large book, to encompass the miscellaneous literacy moments of a complete life. Some random examples: my understanding of typography immediately enlarged the day Dad came home with a lead slug for each of the four of us kids, bearing our names in reverse typography. Our stamped names appear on many endpapers of the books still in family possession. My understanding of the power of images to tell a potent story, on the other hand, expanded as Dad began to travel for meetings of the Newfoundland Teachers Association in the late 1950s. Mum kept picture-diaries (now lost, alas) chronicling the events of each day entirely in stick-figure sagas, labelled at most with initials. And so forth. The texture of daily life was woven through with tiny literate details. It is impossible to capture the scale (large and small) of our many connections with texts of all kinds.

The third limitation is more intangible: the nostalgia trap. I have tried to curtail the impact of my own emotional investment in this project through my determined focus on the materials—but of course, they will never be neutral to me. And, much as I try to investigate and inhabit the younger Margaret looking forward, I can never be rid of the older Margaret looking back—even as the senior Margaret is unable to dismiss all traces of the junior version. It is simply a condition of this work.

Stepping Out

My mother, like many parents, took a ritual photograph each year on the first day of school. If she had deliberately set out to create a metaphor for the journey that lay before me as I began to work on this project, it is hard to think how she could have improved on the image she recorded on my first ever morning of school.

Nearly five years old, I am standing on the gravel driveway that circles my house. In the upper left of the photograph is the gatepost that says "106" on its street side. Beside me, in a metaphorically satisfactory way, stands the foundation of my home. As soon as the photograph is safely

recorded, I will turn around and head out the gates onto Pennywell Road, past Mr. Walters' paint store in the background of this snapshot, and off to school. On the brink of a major step toward the huge challenge of becoming a literate person, I am very specifically placed, grounded, located. My home base will serve as core to the literate understanding of the world I develop. I will position myself in the world through that number 106. My feet are still steady on known ground for the moment of the picture shoot, but I will have to find ways of carrying that security with me into the imponderable world of the Kindergarten classroom. Somehow I must tuck my sense of myself, my known world, and my developing awareness of texts into my blazer pocket along with the pencil case already in my hand. I am Margaret McCurdy of 106 Pennywell Road, and I am going to learn to read.

2
Reading the First Place

Theories of the Local

I HAVE ONLY ONE COMPREHENSIVE IMAGE of the first home I can remember. We lived in the top half of the house, and the side door facing the camera in the photograph was our main entrance; from a little porch, stairs rose directly to our hall. The middle dormer window at the front of the house was in my little bedroom, sandwiched between the living room and my parents' room.

My room was small and crowded. At the foot of my bed was a dolls' bed, alongside a toybox, the lid of which served as a step to the window seat set into the dormer. Leaning at an angle backward into the room from that perch, I could reach the books stored on the shelf above the closet. The window was arched and the blind covered only the lower rectangle; I could see the sun or the fog through the semicircle of bare window at the top before I got out of bed in the morning.

This room was the first place in the world that I remember coming to know. My brothers occupied a communal bedroom, but mine was just for me. I only partially shared their interests, and when I got bored of their boisterous games, I would go into my room, shut the door, and play with my dolls or paper dolls or scrapbooks, or the assortment of miscellaneous junk that passed as toys in the toybox; once I learned how to do it, I would also read by the hour. The flat was spacious but drafty and very ill-heated; it was often extremely cold. Sometimes I had to abandon my solitary play and sit by the oil heater in the hall because my fingers were icy and stiff.

As I explore these far reaches of memory in as much detail as I can sustain, my first guide is Paulo Freire. "Recapturing distant childhood as far back as I can trust my memory, trying to understand my act of *reading* the particular world in which I moved, was absolutely significant for me," he says (Freire & Macedo, 1987, p. 30).

> *The old house—its bedrooms, hall, attic, terrace (the setting for my mother's ferns), backyard—all this was my first world. In this world I crawled, gurgled, first stood up, took my first steps, said my first words. Truly, that special world presented itself to me as the arena of my perceptual activity and therefore as the world of my first reading. The* texts, the words, *the* letters *of that context were incarnated in a series of things, objects, and signs. In perceiving these I experienced myself, and the more I experienced myself, the more my perceptual capacity increased. I learned to understand things, objects, and signs through using them in relationship to my older brothers and sisters and my parents. (p. 30)*

In such terms, Freire literally merges the reading of the world and the reading of the word that develops out of this environmental understanding.

David Malouf makes much the same point in different words, talking about the "first place" that shapes our view of the whole world:

> *If you grow up in the kind of wooden house that I grew up in, and if your first sense of space is that house and the way its rooms are laid out, and if your first sense of dimensions is developed there, then that really is your first reading of the world and you go on to apply that to whatever else you look at. In one part of my mind, every city is a city of hills like Brisbane: where you go up and down and where, when you get to the top of the street, you see something new....An Adelaide friend tells me that he grew up thinking cities were flat. He really did think that if you looked down a street you ought to be*

able to see all the way to the end of it....I can't believe that we are not deeply
determined by such factors. (quoted in Hodgins, 2001, pp. 73–74)

Malouf (1985) describes his "first place" as "the only place I know from inside, from my body outwards" (p. 3).

Without a doubt, my first place was that little bedroom. It represented a form of "mixed reality information space" (Nardi, 2008). In mastering the complexity of this compact universe, I acquired an awareness of some subtle distinctions.

My mattress and pillow, my blankets and my hairbrush represented one form of reality, whose relation to the physical world was very clear-cut. My clothes were a bit more complicated. I participated enthusiastically in the material culture of femininity in the 1950s. Good clothes expressed class-based regulation of decorum and display. Play clothes were worn to shreds, tighter and shabbier by the season. Underwear had its own set of rules. School uniform manifested allegiance, not just to a school system but also to a religious affiliation, since all education was denominational in Newfoundland at that time.

Even with all this semiotic freight, however, my clothes belonged to the physical world as I was learning to understand it. They related in recognizable ways to the weather outside my dormer window, for example. The dolls and the toys lived in another ontological territory altogether, the dolls possessing their own personalities in my eyes, the toys more inert. The dolls, in particular, were what Robin Bernstein (2011) calls "a 'scriptive thing,' an item of material culture that prompts meaningful bodily behaviours" (p. 71). Bernstein's examples are socially and historically complex, but at this point I am interested in the prior stage of what is perhaps the doll's initial invitation to performance: my dolls called on me to pretend, to invest in the performance of social and human relations, of caregiving and care receiving, even though only one of us in the relationship was a living human being.

Even allowing for the inherently astonishing nature of this achievement of pretending, the dolls and toys were defined by the limits of my own imagination. My books allowed someone else's mind into the room, and again, I think the commonplace nature of this fact often blinds us to the scale of its significance. Both the dolls and the books that were read to me at bedtime gave me practice in responding to the way that scriptive objects "hailed" me to join in "encounters in the material world: dances between people and things" (Bernstein, 2011, p. 77). As Bernstein points out, "Things script behaviour not only through determined actions that are required for function but also through *implied* or *prompted* actions" (p. 77). Learning to "read" these implications and prompts—indeed even learning that such a response is possible at all—is an early lesson in engaging with the world.

Once a year, my bedroom was transformed into a more liminal space. My parents loved Christmas. Trees were plentiful in the countryside and free for the chopping, so every year we put a small evergreen with coloured lights in each of the three front dormer windows. My room, in that Christmas light, was utterly magical to me. The resonance of expectation and excitement is almost impossible to describe. Everything about the room changed, and a different reality altogether infused my modest belongings for those few days before and after Christmas—especially beforehand, when anticipation made every detail of daily life more glamorous.

The soundscape of that bedroom was variable. We kids talked, played, pretended, bickered, planned, in the normal way of daily life; and there were more formal oral texts as well. At the end of most days, my brother and I would sit on the window seat, watching for our father's returning figure and singing a home-grown and highly ritualized little ditty that celebrated two securely known facts:

> *Daddy will soon be home,*
> *Daddy will soon be home.*
> *It will soon be suppertime,*
> *And Daddy will soon be home.*

Once Dad did come home, either the radio or a record was likely to be playing. I would shut the door against the boring radio but open it for music. Usually a parent read a bedtime story and sang a lullaby or two, and I said my nightly prayer.

There are almost no photographs of this room but my mother snapped a picture of my brother and me as we sat in the window in April 1952 (she wrote the date on the back of the photograph; we were three and two years old). She won a prize for the image in a contest held by Tooton's camera store (and spent the winnings of $25 on the rare luxury of theatre tickets for herself and Dad—plus babysitting costs—so that they could take in

∧ *Me and Earle,*
April 1952, sitting
on my bedroom
window seat.

[Collection of the author]

a sequence of plays presented by the London Theatre Company). This photograph reveals the only record I possess of the view out my window. Through the alleyway between the two houses across the street we could see Dad walking up the hill and know he would be home in five minutes. Although it is April in this snapshot, grimy snow still lingers and the street is wet with rain or sleet; as was often the case, his walk would not have been pleasant that evening.

Within the space of this room, I learned to interpret many levels of my physical reality as it fed into and shaped my psychological identity. Playing hide-and-seek with my brothers, I hid under the bed and in the closet (when not pre-empted by clutter). I folded my body into the dimensions of the unyielding window seat to read or look out at the world. I sat on the bed with my brother, snuggled up to a reading parent, to follow the adventures of Winnie-the-Pooh (Milne, 1957) or Chatterer the Red Squirrel (Burgess, 1943), detecting ontological distinction between a fictional toy animal and a fictional real animal (one equipped with powers of speech, admittedly, but still not a toy). I knelt beside the bed for the inexorable cadences of "Now I Lay Me."

I had as many as half a dozen baby dolls with plain, sensible names like Jane and Susan; I stacked them in the top corner of my bed against the wall, selected one to cuddle every night, and learned to sleep around its hard body and poky fingers, breathing its rubbery odour. Snuggled up with my doll in the darkness, I pondered the givens of my universe, including the unquestioned perception that, even camouflaged by night and blankets, I could at any moment be observed by God or Santa Claus. It was a highly complex little world.

Bedrooms as Sites of Literacy

Nowadays, children's bedrooms may be highly commodified. Claudia Mitchell and Jacqueline Reid-Walsh (2002) suggest, "Given the signifi-cance of the bedroom as a play and creative space in contemporary culture, it should not be surprising that children's bedrooms might be read as texts of popular culture in and of themselves" (p. 131). My bedroom was not so developed an artifact. With its built-in furniture, homemade out of plywood, it was an efficient but relatively nondescript little chamber. Nevertheless, there was much to read in the structure of that room.

Gender was a primary organizer. The toy box contained whatever I had most recently raided from the collective pool and its chaotic contents were relatively neutral. The adjacent dolls' bed, however, was a hotbed of baby femininity. (I missed Barbie by a couple of years.) Waiting in the closet, my school clothes, church clothes, play clothes all performed highly specified and gendered identity roles. It was cold enough that I often wore trousers in winter, but I almost invariably wore a skirt as well and took off the pants when I reached my destination. I had one shelf of books, and many of them were collectively owned by all of us, but my library books, usually piled on the desk, were most often written for and marketed to girls. My craft supplies, always much humbler than my aspirations, were neutral enough: crayons, little bits of scrap paper, blunt scissors, occasionally a pad of construction paper or a scrapbook; on very rare occasions a few pipe cleaners, a couple of doilies, or some Plasticine. My creations were singu-larly domestic: I made household interiors out of shoe boxes; cut sofas and tables out of old catalogues to furnish scrapbook pages (one page per room with accoutrements of wildly variant scale); made valentines as frilly as the supply system would permit. Many of the elements of that room—like most other ingredients of my daily existence—were utilitarian rather than dainty; nevertheless, it was imbued with a presiding sense of the feminine as I understood it in those days. I liked paper dolls with elegant dresses and crinolines (one set that I remember with great affection even ran to fur bonnets and muffs); I preferred colouring books that contained floral details and flourishes. I could be a thuggish (and very bossy) little girl in asserting my rights as the oldest child (my theory of primogeniture did not admit any gender considerations; "oldest" was an absolute term to me), and much of my play was vigorous and physical. In that room on my own, however, I became introverted and peaceful.

In short, the mixed realities of my little world had a surprisingly singular focus, as I recall them today. My notion of the feminine was highly nurturing; I looked after my dolls, created and organized a variety of virtual nests (an activity that never inspired me to tidy the real bedroom), and read about girls doing the same things. In real life, especially by the time I had three younger brothers, I was often recruited for nurturing of one or more of the actual little boys. I took much less kindly to this activity, though I certainly loved my brothers; the babies did not obligingly close their eyes when laid on their backs, as my dollies did. But to a child, caring for children is an occupation whose status and importance is immediately obvious. My parents both valued this role, and I did, too.

Looking back now, it is easy to see the gestational aura of this compact little room. Literacy enabled me to pass many more hours within its cozy confines. There was a playroom behind the kitchen, but I rarely conde-scended to join the many games of Dinky cars or table hockey that took place there. I rejected most opportunities to build with our modest sets of TinkerToys, Meccano, and Minibrix. Instead, I retreated. In a very real way, regardless of the content of what I was reading, the act of reading itself domesticated me. The summer I was eight, a kind friend passed on two large cartons of books her daughter had outgrown. I had many fights with my mother that year, about being allowed to stay indoors on sunny days to read my way through this treasure trove; and I well remember sneaking up the back stairs of the flat in order to get back to my lair. Reading was an interior occupation in all senses of that word.

Gestation, of course, provides time and space for growth, and my bedroom offered me the chance to engage in all kinds of physical and

mental exploration within a safe space. Much of what I learned there would feed the developing awareness that made reading possible.

Out the Window

The window, with its inviting seat (unfortunately not softened by the kind of bedizened cushion I admired in picture books) offered a frame on the outside world: beyond our gateposts I saw the unadorned front aspects of a few houses, a paint shop, an alleyway, and a street (Franklin Avenue) angling up to Pennywell Road—an expansion of my "first place." The houses across the street butted right up to the sidewalk, so I did not look out onto any gardens; our own was off to the side, out of my range of vision. The buildings were painted in the deep, gaudy, clashing colours that today are recognized as St. John's vernacular; I recall garnet red and turquoise, and maybe a deep forest green. I also saw weather: fog, drizzle, blizzard, gale. It was much rarer for me to sit and contemplate a sunny day; from a very young age, I internalized the rule that if it was even a little bit nice, you went outside.

Off to the east stood Signal Hill and Cabot Tower; if I stretched, I could see hilltop and tower from the window but never the horizon that lay beyond, out to sea. In Malouf's sense, however, the particular contour of that hill adjoining the flat line where ocean meets sky is my "first shape" of the world. Even in my little south-facing bedroom, I oriented to that eastern presence of hill and sea. An undated photo shows the old fishing wharves and finger piers that lined the harbour in my childhood and that have since been replaced by Harbour Drive. But it is that curve of land and flat horizon that really speaks to me of my situation in the world.

Every St. John's child learns early that hill and tower are always there even though you often cannot see them, as they are obliterated by fog or cloud on a remarkably regular basis (a sort of meteorological game of the baby's peekaboo pastime, *Fort/Da*). From a few vantage points in the city, it appears that the hills are continuous and enfold the land in a sheltering circle. In reality, and from most perspectives, the city is always open to the sea via the Narrows, the entrance to the harbour. In Malouf's terms, that perforation of the shelter and that exposure to wind and fog and driving rain or snow are part of my own sense of "first place."

I emphasize these details, including those framed by the window, because I think Freire and Malouf are right; I learned my first powers of reading in processing the details and functions of that room and its view of the outside environment. It gave me a core set of physical and ontological understandings of the world that would be essential in learning to make sense of the virtual universes of the different texts I encountered. Malouf (1985) phrases it strongly and romantically: "The place you get is always, in the real sense, fortunate, in that it constitutes your fortune, your fate, and is your only entry into the world" (p. 3). In many ways, I was extremely "fortunate" in my first place.

Moving Outside

From the very beginning of this research project, my reflections on my early literate life invoked the flavour of walking—exploring the six acres of the school athletic grounds on which our house stood; walking the streets of St. John's to school, church, library, and home again; trekking through the little forest path that led to our favourite picnic site on the edge of the city at Leary's Brook; climbing down the zigzag route into Beachy Cove on the Conception Bay side of the Avalon Peninsula; picking my way across innumerable rocky beaches.

Especially in the early days of this project, I would leave our summer house in Harbour Grace South and go into St. John's on a research outing, intent on visiting an archive or a library. Very often, however, no matter how interesting the files, I would be impelled to put down my notes and go outside to walk the old streets of my childhood once again. I was thinking deeply about my earliest reading experiences and the walking was an equally profound imperative. On every return visit after leaving home for good in 1970, I have felt one overwhelming sensation about being back in the city: *my feet are happy here*. It may not be a scientific connection (though see below), but the sensation that reading is related to that walking experience is so intense to me that I must pay heed.

Attending almost involuntarily to the activities of my feet, I began to explore the implications for reading of how a child learns to know her first place. One result was an early article reporting on this project, "Reading from the Feet Up" (Mackey, 2010b), in which I investigate samples of children's literature that involve some kind of thoughtful reflection on learning to read (they are surprisingly rare). Sure enough, Ramona Quimby and Rufus Moffat moved through their known worlds on new paths that were explicitly associated with their unfolding literacy. Christopher Robin imported new schemas into his first place in the reflection on schooling that ends *The House at Pooh Corner*.

Cuddy-Keane (2010) draws an explicit connection between physical and mental way-finding in her account of the "thinking body": "Embodied cognition is a crucial component in human spatial navigation, or 'way-finding': finding our way through and about places involves the body's exploratory navigation of its environment, in addition to the conscious learning of landmarks and signs. While the moving body thus contributes directly to conscious knowledge, it may also be devising non-conscious strategies for spatial navigation that indirectly activate similar schema for the navigation of mental space" (p. 685).

A child figuring out what is reliable and what is random in her known world is equipping herself to understand virtual worlds, as well. In later chapters, I will return to questions of what we know about how the brain learns to map, schematize, and orchestrate the world around it and how these developments might apply to a growing understanding of literature. In this section, I want to consider briefly that sense of moving through the world that was so potent to me as I began to work on exploring my own past literacies.

Tim Ingold (2004) draws our attention to the importance of the work of the feet in helping to create our sense of the world:

> It is almost a truism to say that we perceive not with the eyes, the ears or the surface of the skin, but with the whole body. Nevertheless, ever since Plato and Aristotle the western tradition has consistently ranked the senses of vision and hearing over the contact sense of touch....[A] more literally grounded approach to perception should help to restore touch to its proper place in the balance of the senses. For it is surely through our feet, in contact with the ground (albeit mediated by footwear), that we are most fundamentally and continually 'in touch' with our surroundings. (p. 330)

Rebecca Lloyd (2011), drawing on Ingold, discusses the significance of cultivating a connection to the natural world that "has the potential to shape the quality of our lives in the simplest yet profound act of walking and the motile possibility of leaving, reading and being moved by one's trace" (p. 87).

In St. John's in the 1950s, I navigated an urban landscape, sorting out paths, nodes, and districts, orienting myself with landmarks and edges. At that time, I left much more of a trace on my setting than the urban dwellers of Ingold's city, who press their shod feet on paved ground and leave no mark. Pennywell Road was unpaved until I was nine years old. The sidewalk was made of pressed-down dirt, which turned muddy or snowy as the seasons changed. My own feet were variably shod—in light summer sandals, in heavier school oxfords, in patent-leather Sunday shoes, in foot rubbers tugged on over the shoes in spring and fall, in the much-despised winter galoshes that we hauled over our shoes and buckled on the side. In summer we went barefoot some of the time, wincing across the gravel of the driveway into the dew-wet grass of the garden. In all seasons, we learned to keep our balance as we clambered over the irregular rocks of Newfoundland's beaches. We tried to learn to swim with our feet weighted down by bathing slippers, which aimed to prevent us from cutting ourselves on the stony bottoms of ponds and ocean. The ongoing regime of changing footwear made me frequently conscious of my footing, and although I appreciate the more sophisticated shoes and boots available today, I do sometimes miss that feeling of flying that came on the first spring day we graduated from boots to rubbers or from rubbers to shoes. The sense of "walking on air" was overwhelming, and an indissoluble link between time, space, and our own bodies was incarnate in our liberated and rejoicing feet on those memorable occasions.

By and large, says Ingold (2004),

> studies of haptic perception have focused almost exclusively on manual touch. The challenge is to discover special properties of pedestrian touch that might distinguish it from the manual modality. Is it really the case for example, as intuition suggests, that what we feel with our hands, and through the soles of our feet, are necessarily related as figure and ground? In other words, is the ground we walk on also, and inevitably, a ground against which things 'stand out' as foci of attention, or can it be a focus in itself? (p. 330)

An understanding of "figure and ground" offers one way of exploring our sense of real and fictional environments. A "horizon of expectations" (Jauss & Benzinger, 1970, p. 12) is a different concept, but it similarly conveys the idea of a gestalt of the world that enables us to read that world *into* a fiction created by words on a page. In that notional place, the world is only an abstraction until breathing life is imported into the words through the response of a reader.

The humble example of "footwork" offering the ground to the figure of our "handwork" (or, more explicitly, the more specific attention we address to what we hold in our hands) may supply one way of exploring the acquisition of relevant experience as we learn to become readers. Hans Jauss and Elizabeth Benzinger (1970) point out that "[t]he interpretive reception of a text always presupposes the context of experience of aesthetic perception" (p. 13), without addressing the question of where the initial aesthetic experience might come from. No infant starts from a position of literary experience ahead of life experience; at some point we must begin importing our worldly understanding into our aesthetic understanding.

For the most part, how we developed our most preliminary understanding of that world is a topic not available for conscious recollection or reconstruction. The capacity to abstract from perception (perhaps particularly vision, touch, and a sense of one's own movement as Jean Mandler [1992, p. 591] suggests) is surely a continuing component of learning. It seems reasonable to hypothesize that as my world and my own powers expanded, so the abstractions from perceptions became rather less primitive but continued to play a potent and generative role in my understanding. The abstractions I thus created were more portable than the explicit perceptions, and so were available to inform and vivify my experiences of fiction through listening and later reading, but they were grounded in the specifics of my own first place.

Moving in Space and Story

Notions of space and movement were themselves important in my ability to learn to follow a story. Tim Wynne-Jones (1998) provides a description of reading that highlights such issues:

> The deep-read is when you get gut-hooked and dragged overboard down and down through the maze of print and find, to your amazement, you can breathe down there after all and there's a whole other world. I'm talking about the kind of reading when you realize that books are indeed interactive....I'm talking about the kind of deep-read where it isn't just the plot or the characters that matter, but the words and the way they fit together and the meandering evanescent thoughts you think between the lines: the kind of reading where you are fleetingly aware of your own mind at work. (pp. 165–166)

Wynne-Jones's account features dragging and breathing and meandering; it involves motion through the text. Mary Thomas Crane (2009) goes one step further and suggests, "We can only think about abstract things because we can understand them in terms of concrete spatial experience" (p. 80). To a degree, such concrete spatial experience is generic: humans learn to stand upright and to move on two feet, with consequent impact on their perspectives on the world. But it is also, as Crane says, specific. I learned to perceive and to abstract from my perceptions in a particular environment, located in space and also in time.

Richard Wagamese (2014) describes a farm kid coming to know his world, his first place: "[H]e knew the feel of time around those eighty acres like he knew hunger, thirst, and the feel of coming weather on his skin" (p. 26). So I inhabited my own six acres of the school athletic grounds and took possession of the surrounding streets. Time was shaped to the contours of space, and space inflected time. On a sunny day, the soccer pitch became a subtly different place when you suddenly caught a sharp whiff of fog out to sea; if you could smell it, it was on its way. The timeless charm of that sunshine instantly vanished and became something restricted, something shadowed with the sorrow of losing that carefree infinity of summer delight. Similarly, the space of the field immediately acquired an aura of foreshadowing the *closing in* that fog inevitably entails. We often take weather for granted, but it occupies our space; it is durational; it merges our sense of space and time in ways that even a young child learns to process. And it is undeniably local.

My particular environment was complex. It was not a generic space where movement could be construed as taking place between Point A and Point B. It was not a set of experiences boiled down to the most simple elements that an infant could record and process. It was a complicated, dynamic world with its own priorities, problems, abundances, and hardships—with its own details. I sampled, processed, made what sense I could out of more and more of it, and rendered my understanding abstract and therefore portable enough that I could carry it into my stories. At the same time, being located in my specific surroundings meant that, very early on, I also learned the colonial lesson about processing fiction: there are concepts and understandings that you do not carry into your texts because they do not work there. Both kinds of learning influenced me in very profound ways.

To explore this world from today's vantage point, I will engage, at least metaphorically, in what Todd Presner, David Shepard, and Yoh Kawano (2014) call "thick mapping," layering my individual reference points and my set of materials over the specific site of my early literacy. Presner and his colleagues suggest,

Thickness means extensibility and polyvocality: diachronic and synchronic, temporally layered, and polyvalent ways of authoring, knowing, and making meaning....By eschewing any kind of universalism, it is a kind of analysis that is intrinsically incomplete, always under contestation, and never reaching any kind of final, underlying truth. Thick mappings, like thick descriptions, emphasize content and meaning-making through a combination of micro and macro analyses that foster a multiplicity of interpretations rather than simply reporting facts or considering maps as somehow given, objective, or complete. (pp. 18–19)

This description of a digital map that can never be labelled as complete serves as a lively metaphor for the kind of project I am undertaking with this study. The affordances of a digital map make room for readers to insert their own details, corroborative or contradictory, into the argument I am building here. "In essence," say Presner, Shepard, and Kawano, "thick maps give rise to forms of counter-mapping, alternative maps, multiple voices, and on-going contestations" (p. 19). My project opens such a "thick map" invitation to readers.

The Larger World

My own contribution to this thick map, of course, is ineluctably singular and specific, and arises from more than five years of exploring the artifacts of that remembered world. Some of the complexity of my mediated world in St. John's in the 1950s is accessible to me today through the texts with which I attempted to make sense of it at the time. Because of the miracle of recording, many materials can be retrieved a half-century later and explored anew. I cannot recreate my own initial forays into making sense of these texts, but I can recover some of the ingredients that invited and fed into those processes.

Environmental *print* is well recognized as a source of emergent literacy, but even more than fifty years ago, I was also cutting some of my literacy teeth on more multimodal input. Print was highly important to me, and I will return to its essential role in my early childhood again, but before I do that I want to consider the media of my youth.

Radio

During most days as a preschooler, I listened to *Kindergarten of the Air* on the radio. In St. John's, it was scheduled late in the afternoon, but the content of the program itself is very insistent on its morning venue. The show lasted fifteen minutes and was a fixture of CBC Radio for many years with very little change in format. The CBC Radio Archives in Toronto hold just six recordings, two from 1949 and four from 1961. In 2009 I listened to all six. The format barely changes over those twelve years, and I am reasonably secure that the family resemblance to the actual programs I heard in the early 1950s is strong. Certainly I recognized many of the repeating elements.

Kindergarten of the Air was designed for preschool "training," and it focuses substantially on discipline of the body (Dixon, 2011, p. 4). "Cross your feet and sit down with your hands in your lap" is a recurring instruction. Each of the surviving shows mentions the days of the week. The goodbye song that concludes the program emphasizes time in a different way:

> *The clock goes round so quickly.*
> *See how the minutes fly.*
> *Our Kindergarten's over*
> *And it's time to say goodbye.*
> *Goodbye until tomorrow.*
> *Goodbye until tomorrow.*
> *Keep smiling and be happy.*
> *Goodbye, goodbye, goodbye.*

In the programs I heard in 2009, there is significant emphasis on family life and a relentless construction of the little listener as highly obedient. I regret that I simply cannot remember whether or not my brother and I crept, hopped, or bounced to the music, according to the instructions of the presenter. Certainly we would have done our fair share of sitting with our feet crossed and our hands in our laps. I think we sang along when invited to do so.

But *Kindergarten of the Air* also gave us an early sense of how the realities of Newfoundland may contest the frame established by a text. No tapes from the 1950s still exist, but the recording of April 19, 1949, is extremely firm about the time of the program, clearly scheduled for the morning: the opening song (sung to the tune of "Happy Birthday") is "Good Morning to You." The St. John's radio schedules accord with my own memory, placing the timing of the program at 5:45 every weekday afternoon. It is a hard feeling to pin down, but that sense, not exactly of disorientation but of needing to make a deliberate effort to ignore aspects of the text, of writing it off as not relevant, strikes a chord in my memories of listening to the little program.

I composed these words in Newfoundland in July 2011, a summer of a significant and lengthy heat wave in central Canada but unseasonal gloom and chilliness in both east and west. Reading a central Canadian newspaper full of tips on coping with the heat when you are cold and disgruntled provides a similar kind of textual disconnect (a more irritable one; my memories of listening to *Kindergarten of the Air* are more benign. Shrugging off the discrepancies was just part of a person's normal repertoire for responding to texts). So *Kindergarten of the Air* "trained" us (in the language of the program's introductory comments) to be ready for school. It also taught us an early lesson in the "yes, but..." assent that marked much of our literacy—yes to the text, with the necessary caveats for local discordances.

It could be argued that Newfoundland makes a point of being a special case, that the exceptionalism is so ubiquitous and extreme that my situation does not really speak to the position of other young children learning to read from within the framework of the mainstream. Certainly the number of ways in which Newfoundland in the 1950s did not conform to the norms of other places and other texts was very large and included fundamental elements like time on the clock (though it was not the unavoidable half-hour discrepancy of the time-zone difference but rather a deliberate scheduling decision that threw our experience of *Kindergarten of the Air* out of kilter. It is possible that the tape had to be transported to St. John's for airing, but I do not know).

In reality, Newfoundland's outlier status simply makes visible a factor that is influential in the lives of young literates in many different situations. In the 1950s (as now), many beginning readers were poor, or non-WASP, or aligned with an immigrant culture rather than or as well as the North American mainstream, or not Christian, or not straight, or not white, or otherwise outside the standard established in our textual materials. I am sure many of these readers learned, as I did, that literacy came with a switch-off button: *normal daily understandings do not apply in this text*. Eventually such experience might develop into forms of resistant reading, but in my case at least, the first response was simply closer to a detached observation of disconnection: *book conditions apply from here on in*. The example of *Kindergarten of the Air* reminds us that such disjunctures were not exclusive to print. And we do well to remember that not every child is as eager as I was to join the literacy club (Smith, 1987). Many young readers will reasonably and logically choose to dismiss the world of the text rather than switch off their own experiences.

Recordings

Our audio experience expanded beyond radio to a limited extent. We had a few brittle 78s and extended-play children's recordings. I remember many songs but have no idea of any album title and have not so far been able to relocate the earliest records we owned. One featured two songs that entered the lullaby repertoire of all five of us children and many further descendants in our family: "Winkum, Winkum, Shut your Eye," and "Snail, Snail, Come Out and be Fed." These songs have intertwined into many of our most intimate domestic moments over a period of more than fifty years and four generations; they are now lullabies for my grandchildren.

I had never seen the words written down until I went looking for them online as part of this project. A simple search for the opening words turned up a plethora of web entries, especially for "Winkum" but also for "Snail, Snail" as a singing game. Not surprisingly, there are variant versions; what shocked me was how jarring I found them. The words I remember are these; I have not found an exact replica so far.

> *Winkum, winkum, shut your eye.*
> *Sleep my baby, lullaby.*
> *For the dews are falling soft,*
> *Lights are flickering up aloft,*
> *And the moonlight's peeping over*
> *Yonder hilltop, capped with clover.*

In my head, the rhythm then inexorably changes to a much jauntier tune, the song that our parents always sang next:

> *Snail, snail, come out and be fed,*
> *Put out your horns and bend your head,*
> *And your papa and your mama*
> *Will give you boiled mutton.*
> *Ting-a-ling-a-ling-ling,*
> *Ting-a-ling-a-ling-ling,*
> *Ting-a-ling-a-ling-ling,*

Ting-a-ling-a-ling-ling,
Ting.

"Winkum" at least offers some alliance between form and function; its soporific melody and rhythm introduced me almost from babyhood to formal words like "yonder," "flickering," and "aloft." But, as far as I was concerned, "Snail, Snail" might as well have been sung in Sanskrit for its complete absence of any kind of link between denotation and connotation. More than any nursery rhyme (although those certainly reinforced the idea), "Snail, Snail" introduced me to the idea that words making perfectly good individual sense could nevertheless constitute nonsense.

At least one of our recordings needed a stronger form of reworking to keep us safe on the streets. A little single (source unknown) offered a recorded traffic safety song:

Green means go, red means stop.
Be your own little traffic cop.
Don't cross streets until you've seen,
The traffic light has turned to green.

Our walk to school entailed only one major junction and one traffic light. This crossing involved a six-way junction. Crossing Harvey Road to Long's Hill, we could physically see only the Harvey Road signal and therefore had to cross on the red light. As was so often the case, we "parked" our conventional knowledge from the song in order to negotiate our own daily world.

Singing and Piano

There was other, home-grown music, and in some ways it bore no greater relation to our own reality. My mother played the piano; my father sang. Sometimes after we had gone to bed, they would perform together from their small supply of sheet music. Stephen Foster was a favourite; what did I learn from hearing "All de darkies am a-weeping:/ Massa's in de cold, cold ground"? (Hear it for yourself on YouTube.) Dad also performed an eloquent version of "Crossing the Bar" by Alfred, Lord Tennyson (1889), a song that manages to be lugubrious while actually inveighing against such a state:

Twilight and evening bell,
And after that the dark!
And may there be no sadness of farewell
When I embark.

My research on YouTube did not recover a version featuring the melody Dad sang. My sister, whose piano bench is a repository of a certain kind of family history, investigated its depths and dug up a photocopy of the title page and the first page of notation, but she could find no more. The scan included here is not clear, but this humble photocopy is redolent of family life; at the top of the title page is my grandmother's name in her handwriting, and some young child has attempted to copy the name of Wegenast. This writing could have been done by any of the fourteen children who comprise these sets: my mother and her five siblings, her own five offspring, and my sister's three children; any of them could have practiced their w s on this songsheet at some point over a span of about seventy years. The photocopy itself was obviously a late development in the history of this score. My literacy was set in the kind of family that saves sheet music in piano benches, both a class marker and a feature of a family dynamic favouring thrift and care with belongings.

I was seven when I first saw television, eight when we acquired our own (and I will return to this medium of my middle childhood later in this study). Before TV, throughout my early childhood, after we had gone to bed, my parents listened to the radio or entertained themselves at the piano in this time-tested fashion. Although the arrival of the television set did not kill these activities outright, it certainly reduced their frequency. A family story recounts my father's first encounter with a gramophone, as a mesmerized four-year-old in 1926. The mediation of sheet music and the importance of domestically produced music go back many generations further, however, in my own family and in others. I am glad my childhood included this experience.

Developing Musical Awareness

A few recordings contributed more actively to my musical education. For example, *Peter and the Wolf* helped to disentangle the various elements of the orchestras that played in the background of many daily moments in our classically tuned lives. We also had a little set of coloured vinyl singles that provided songs for each instrument of the orchestra; a few of

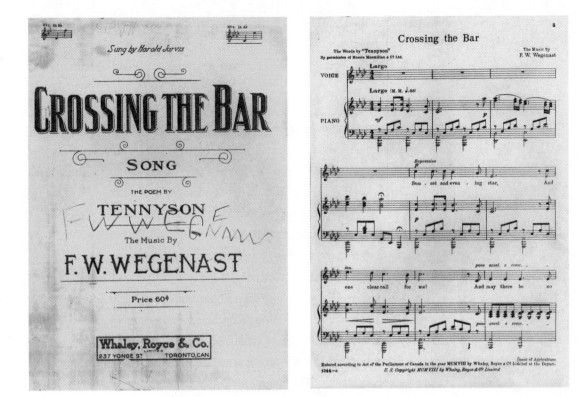

∧ Music sheets of
"Crossing the Bar,"
Tennyson and Wegenast,
1908. [Collection of the author]

the inane lyrics remain in my head to this day. I have been unable to locate our specific recordings but I did find a contemporary rendering of "The Instrument Song" (Moon, 2005) that includes a number of the little tunes. Some ditties were simply onomatopoeic; for example, "The clarinet, the clarinet/Goes doodle doodle doodle doodle-det" (Moon, 2005). The personified world of Mort, which may have been freestanding and not part of the larger set, was more listener friendly:

> Important Mort, the pianoforte,
> Is still a very friendly sort
> So you can call him Piano for short. (source unknown)

The disentanglement of the orchestral sound into individual components contributed to a version of early musical intelligence, a form of literacy. Initially we developed such discernment only through sound; later in my childhood, a series of TV programs featuring the Chicago Symphony Orchestra augmented my orchestral understanding with visual input. At the age of ten, I was taken to a season of community concerts in Pitts

Memorial Hall, but I found them long and opaque, despite the scaffolding of so much recorded classical music at home and the instilled discipline of sitting still for extended periods of time that I acquired in school and church.

Colour

The equivalent intelligence concerning colour came in the more tactile form of crayons with their exotic names, both evocative and estranging at the same time: burnt sienna, ultramarine, red ochre. I loved these mysterious labels, and I loved the subtleties of shade they represented. The sight, the feel, the smell of a set of crayons could be augmented by the sound of these rich words as you said them aloud: "Pass me the apricot and the periwinkle." (I'm pretty sure I also know what a crayon tastes like, a very distant memory.) Crayola dominates the marketplace today, but my school crayons were a different brand, with slightly variant names. The power of these labels is manifest in Wikipedia, which features nostalgic tables of Crayola crayon names, date adopted, and date retired; the evocative lure of the nomenclature does not die with the retirement of the crayon.

Whole studies could address crayon labels and their relationship to place and culture. In 1958, at the request of teachers, Prussian blue was renamed midnight blue. Purple mountain's majesty testifies to a rampant and sentimental form of American nationalism in 1993; the introduction of fuzzy wuzzy brown in the United States as late as 1998 implies a parochial labelling system that is oblivious to the racial overtones such a label would hold in Britain, for example. And, of course, the imperial and racist assumptions packed into the crayon marked "flesh" (changed to "peach" in 1962) are now obvious to us. It is a fascinating little corner of cultural presuppositions, internalized by the smallest citizens in very unquestioning ways.

Many names are redolent of broader worlds. "Commercial trade names," says Briony Fer (2008), "expand color's geography beyond that suggested by traditional artist's colors like Raw Sienna or Burnt Umber (so called because it came from Umbria)" (p. 36). The resulting palette represents "not just the geographical distances but the leaps and expanses traveled in a mental atlas, the sudden proximity between unlike things and places and colors" (p. 35). Those obscure and random leaps were always part of the gorgeousness of colour for me.

By the 1950s we were heirs to the revolution in colour that came in the nineteenth century when colour was transformed "from handmade product to synthetically manufactured, standardized, and commercially packaged commodity" (Temkin, 2008, p. 17). Without question, our crayons came out of an industrial system. Yet, as Fer (2008) usefully reminds us, "Just because the color chart is rooted in a desire to rationalize and standardize, it does not follow that its aesthetic effects are either rational or standard" (p. 35).

We learned to mix colours with skinny brushes in our little tin palettes of watercolours with their tiny rectangles of paint; we occasionally lucked into finger paints (though we always seemed to run out of the special shiny paper before we could use them all up); and as we grew older, we dabbled in little tubs of oil paint with our paint-by-numbers kits. Mucilage was cheap, and we did a lot of gluing; a pad of construction paper was a common and welcome birthday present. I always yearned for more. My life as a craftsperson was inevitably more limited than my tastes and aspirations, but there was enough of a range of tools to teach some sense of material distinctions. Crayons, however, were always the most readily available tool; everything else had a certain aura of "special occasion." Crayons were the most familiar to my hands and the simplest to use.

The Situated Learner

From my early years, therefore, out of a variety of media, developed both the seamless texture of my daily existence and also the first primitive analytical tools I acquired, relating both to language and also to more direct encounters with certain categories of mediation. Thus equipped, I began to make sense of the world as it presented itself to me through the lens of my place and time.

Margaret Laurence, a writer who became important to me as an adult reader, acknowledges the potency of situation to a child. She writes of growing up in a small prairie town, "Because that settlement and that land were my first and for many years only real knowledge of this planet, in some profound way they remain my world, my way of viewing. My eyes were formed there" (2003, p. 169). My own eyes were "formed" in St. John's, and that formation is an irrevocable part of this study as well as an inextricable element of my childhood learning. Even as I bring outside perspectives to bear, the power of the first place lingers in my analysis as well as in my affections, extending and limiting what I am able to perceive.

3
Other Places, Other Times
Theories of Trajectories

ALTHOUGH I HAVE NO DOUBT about the "firstness" of
that house on Pennywell Road, it was never my "only" place. We visited
our family in Nova Scotia four times over the twelve years between 1950
and my cut-off point in 1962, and we always knew that we were "from"
Nova Scotia. The one identity did not diminish the other, and I am grateful
to the work of geographer Doreen Massey for supplying a theory of space
and time that enables me to think about these relationships with much
greater clarity.

First, though, an explicit literacy memory. It was the summer of 1954,
and we were in Nova Scotia, visiting my father's parents, who lived just
outside of Truro. One rainy August afternoon, we left my grandparents'
farmhouse in Old Barns and drove a short distance into Beaver Brook, to
see my mother's uncle, famous in our family as the man who introduced my
parents to each other. At that time he was living in the farmhouse that had

previously been owned by his father, my maternal great-grandfather; my mother had many memories of visiting her own grandparents in that house. My parents had met each other here.

To the best of my recollection (and I was only five at the time), the house was set back from the road. A stream coiled in front of it and pooled into a swimming hole. There was a roofed verandah or woodshed on one side of the house. In this space was propped an old, small blackboard, and, because it was raining, I was sent out there to amuse myself with a piece of chalk. I have vivid recollections of attempting cursive writing. A loop or two looked authentic, but if I wrote a whole row of loops it ceased to resemble real writing. Likewise with a row of "u"s; too much repetition destroyed its effectiveness. I was not interested in making meaning with this writing. I wanted to produce a surface facsimile that simply looked like cursive. I could do some basic printing at that point, having just completed Kindergarten, but I knew that real power lay in joined-up writing, and I was eager to gain access to that power.

Umberto Eco says, "We can think of writing as an extension of the hand, and therefore as almost biological. It is the communication tool most closely linked to the body" (Eco & Carrière, 2011, p. 7). My whole body was determined to make that chalk produce a facsimile of real writing; I still recall the intensity of my focus.

In fact, I remember many details of this small interlude very clearly. For the rest of my life, I have felt a *frisson* of overwhelming security any time I stand under a roof looking out at summer rain. I knew that this little area of Nova Scotia was profoundly familiar to my parents; my father grew up here, and my mother visited often as a child. The Old Barns cemetery is filled with my relations, on both sides of my family. I loved my kind Uncle John and was glad to be visiting him. I had the blackboard and the chalk all to myself with no sharing required (a rarity in my life), and I had an absorbing challenge to address. It is an entirely satisfying memory, and the details of that particular day have grounded my sense of becoming literate for six decades.

My relationship to a kind of abstraction of "home" always included a strong Nova Scotia component. My growing awareness of the *represented* world was also embedded in schemas that my mother developed out of that particular house and other homes she knew well. A habitual doodler, she often decorated the end papers of our picture books with a little pencil drawing, usually of a house (to my great regret, none of these books has survived). She never drew the building I lived in but always a house from her own childhood. Many of them looked a bit like the drawing that I produced from memory (see page 74), but my mother was a much better draftswoman than I am, and her houses were considerably neater, snugger, better proportioned, and more cozy and inviting than mine.

Sometimes the verandah at the front of the house was roofed, but such an image is beyond my meagre talents. I dimly recall that sometimes she drew the farmhouse where I stood that day with my chalk, complete with the stream running past it, and if that recollection is accurate, it would accord well with the overwhelming aura of fitness that surrounds my memory of that rainy afternoon. Along with a mother tongue, I thus inherited from this idiosyncratic habit of hers what might be called some *mother schemas* of domestic space. Certain components were invariant: the door handle was obligatory, the chimney always included smoke, and the lattice-work under the verandah was a schematic necessity.

To my great delight, late in this project, long after I had toiled to produce this clumsy facsimile of Mum's snug domiciles, I found an old family picture of Mum's earliest house at 19 Sherwood Street, Halifax. It was a thrilling discovery: my mother's own first place! It has fewer windows along the side than my drawing (maybe Mum's did too; I do not guarantee every detail of my reproduction), but there is the verandah out the front with that essential diagonal latticework underneath. No doubt the door has a door-knob, but I am sorry there is no smoke coming out the chimney.

More came out of that maternal first space than content for doodles; the impact of my mother's childhood resonated in my own. My uncle, Philip Clarke Jefferson, in a genealogical history of his mother's ancestors, the Clarkes, includes a sidelight on the family romance. Grandmother was one of the first women in Nova Scotia to graduate from university, at King's in 1918. She met my grandfather there and wanted to marry; her father was opposed to any wedding, "saying that she needed to teach, and that he hadn't paid all that money out for her to marry and have babies" (Jefferson, 2002, p. 46). Grandmother did teach for a couple of years, but my grandparents married in 1920. Uncle Phil offers this insight into what happened next: "Belle was determined to show her father that a good education could be equally used in child rearing as in teaching. So there was great emphasis on helping with homework, correcting

grammatical speech, having lots of books in the house, and finding time to read to children and arrange for music lessons" (p. 46). Unlike her mother, Mum, who was a child of the Depression, did not get the chance to go to university, but she certainly inherited these priorities, and we were second-generation beneficiaries of this old family dispute.

On the particular occasion of my blackboard session on Uncle John's verandah in Beaver Brook, the location of my efforts at writing was a significant element of the situation. I was vaguely aware that the farm had belonged to my family for a long time and that different ancestors had inhabited the local space. Further, I identified the vernacular architecture with schemas that, even when I was only five, had been embedded in my awareness for as long as I could remember, through my mother's little doodles.

Now is a good moment to consider the role of schemas and scripts in a child's developing awareness of how the world may be organized. There are many definitions of these terms, but my own are relatively standard. A schema is a generalized mental structure that establishes a conventional framework for a concept or an understanding, a way of grouping expectations together. It may supply a set of default values and may be more or less fluid in its make-up. I know of little work that considers the implications of discrepancies at the cognitive level of schema, but I am certain many people are familiar with this phenomenon. In my simple case of clashing schemas for domestic buildings, between the luxurious architecture of Nova Scotia and the more Spartan housing of St. John's, I could make a comparison to a child growing up bilingual; the idea of multiple possibilities for categorization is challenging but can also be taken for granted in some very basic ways.

A script is a schema for an event, a mental outline of the socially appropriate and canonical way to behave in a particular situation. Deviation from a script is always possible, but when that happens the behaviour is usually marked. Even at the age of five, I would have had a well-established script for "visiting elderly relations" in Old Barns, entailing much dullness and good behaviour; one reason I remember this verandah incident so joyfully is that it marked an attention to child priorities that was almost never part of the standard script.

Schemas and scripts deal with the build-up of conventional expectations out of specific accumulations of experience. Yet Ron Scollon and Suzie Wong Scollon (2003) suggest that the *locatedness* of words is also foundational and can never be completely extracted from the making of meaning: "*Geosemiotics* is the study of the meaning systems by which language is located in the material world. This includes not just the location of the words on the page you are reading now but also the location of the book in your hands and your location as you stand or sit reading this" (p. x). Location, as my example shows, can also include its own potent emotional resonance.

Whose Space is it Anyway?

Location itself is more complex than it initially appears. Doreen Massey (2005) explores relations of space and time via the standard framework: "spatial framing is a way of containing the temporal. For a moment, you hold the world still. And in this moment you can analyse its structure" (p. 36). She challenges this stance and offers an alternative:

> Conceiving of space as a static slice through time, as representation, as a closed system and so forth are all ways of taming it. They enable us to ignore its real import: the coeval multiplicity of other trajectories and the necessary outward-lookingness of a spatialized subjectivity....

> *Conceptualising space as open, multiple and relational, unfinished and always becoming, is a prerequisite for history to be open and thus a pre-requisite, too, for the possibility of politics. (p. 59)*

Massey offers a new account of space as "the contemporaneous existence of a plurality of trajectories; a simultaneity of stories-so-far" (p. 12). Gabrielle Cliff Hodges, Maria Nikolajeva, and Liz Taylor (2010) explore the utility of this perspective as an approach to literary events, and their explication of Massey's definition is helpful:

> *Trajectories refer to the irreversible temporal and spatial "journeys" people or things have made to get to a particular point, and those that they will make in the future. So each one of the living and non-living things which, together, comprise a place, has come from somewhere and is going to somewhere, albeit over a range of temporal and spatial scales. Places are situated on a web of historical and contemporary interconnection, and that interconnection usually entails a power dimension. The close connection of space and time in Massey's work raises parallels with Mikhail Bakhtin's idea of the chronotope (Bakhtin, 1981), though the ideas arise from very different projects. (p. 191)*

Massey's fluid account of space makes room for the migrant's sense of location in ways that deepen and intensify the value of thinking through the notion of situated literacy. (The concept of the chronotope is also useful, and I will develop it in Chapter 6.)

Let us return to that vignette of the pre–Grade 1 Margaret, labouring over cursive writing on the ancestral verandah in Beaver Brook, Nova Scotia, in the summer of 1954. For me, it is a rare memory of a literate event explicitly situated in the province of my birth and my only recollection of being on my great-grandparents' farm. If I could create a thick map of my experience that day at that location, what might it contain beyond a happy five-year-old and a blackboard?

The trajectories intersecting on that verandah were multiple, indeed. Some branches of my family had, at that point, been living in Nova Scotia for about two centuries. Yet I was there both as heir to this relatively lengthy (for Europeans) sojourn in Nova Scotia and also as incomer from Newfoundland, a double trajectory. It seems possible that my ancestors were involved in the expulsion of the Acadians, and they and the Acadians alike participated in the oppression of the Aboriginal population. Local histories name my family members and establish that the house I remember was the oldest home in Beaver Brook and had been previously owned by a branch of my father's family (Beaver Brook, 1959, p. 5). The kind of genealogical connections I could never establish in Newfoundland flourished in Old Barns and Beaver Brook.

Despite the historic movement in and out of this region of First Nations inhabitants, colonizing Acadians, and subsequent incomers from the British Isles and from America, by the first half of the twentieth century, Old Barns was profoundly homogeneous in many ways. My father was fourteen years old before he knowingly laid eyes on a Roman Catholic, for example; and although Truro had its own small community of African-Canadians, my aunt told me that the Old Barns children of her era never attended school with these children and that they actually laid eyes on a black person only on the very rare occasion when one came to the farm-house door looking for work as a hired man. Relationships with local Aboriginal people seem to have been even more exiguous. However they acquired the land, the occupants of Old Barns, Beaver Brook, and Lower Truro appear to have done a good job of keeping it to themselves for the first half of the twentieth century. Yet to me as a young family member, they were always exceptionally kind and welcoming, and I loved them.

That the space on which I stood brandishing my chalk might ever have been contested was, of course, far beyond my awareness or understanding as a five-year-old. The little corner of Old Barns and Beaver Brook was then and remains today one of the areas of the world to which my connection is deep and intimate. In emotional terms, I have always felt that I "own" and am "owned by" Old Barns. I am "explained" by it, having been shaped by many of its geographical, historical, social, cultural, and religious elements. No matter what the historical foundations of this relationship might have been, or what power relations they expressed, my sense of belonging to Old Barns was certainly reified and extremely real to me, even before that very young Margaret picked up the chalk. And the understandings I developed in this community throughout my childhood still inform aspects of my literate awareness.

Massey's notion of space as a plurality of trajectories and a simultaneity of stories-so-far provides a way of thinking about my relationship to that place in the world that makes room for other perspectives, other people's sensations of "ownership," other stories. My story does not take priority over other versions—but it matters to me, and it is a little part of the history of that land. In significant and substantial ways, my relationship to that territory is built into my schemas, my developing understanding of literacy, and my own sense of identity. No matter who else has a story bound up in that place, its role in the genesis of my own literary capacities, imagination, and identity is fundamental and non-negotiable. There is no reason for my relationship with Beaver Brook to be exclusive, and there are many reasons to acknowledge plurality as part of its essential nature. At the same time, it is vital to beware the perils of complacency. We are not talking about equal-opportunity trajectories, and my own was highly privileged.

Texts move through space and time, as well, and the swarm of inter-secting trajectories of any given place includes the texts that are "passing through." Jauss and Benzinger (1970) point out that works of art published at the same time may represent differential stages of genre development and, in any case, are yoked together differently at the point of reception:

> If simultaneously appearing literature—seen from the point of view of the aesthetics of production—breaks down into a heterogeneous variety of the unsimultaneous, that is, of works formed by the different moments of the "shaped time" of their genre (as the apparently present starry sky moves apart astronomically at very different rates), then this variety of literary works moves together again for readers who perceive them as works of their present and relate them to each other in a meaningful unity of a common horizon of literary expectations, memories, and anticipations. (pp. 29-30)

Certainly the texts that temporarily occupied the focus of my attention over the years of this study moved at differential rates through the time and space of my world. Although they were of varying ages and pedigrees, I certainly regarded them all as "works of [my] present" and yoked them together through the filter of mattering to me.

A Shared Place

Space as a bundling of trajectories is a concept that illuminates my rela-tionship to St. John's and Newfoundland, as well. In some cases, I have established the nature of these trajectories only as an adult working on

∧ *Undated photograph of*
Coady's Farm, later
106/108 Pennywell Road.

[*Courtesy Shane O'Dea*]

this project. For example, the house on Pennywell Road that so illuminates all my early awareness of life in books has its own trajectory. I do not know a great deal about its past, but I have learned that it was a farmhouse belonging to the Coady family in the nineteenth and perhaps early twentieth century. Mr. Coady was a cooper as well as a farmer; he made storage barrels for salt fish, partridge berries, and butter (Murray, 2002, p. 168). A descendent of the Coadys, Shane O'Dea, has sent me an old, undated photograph of the house.

The house embodies the architectural style that Joan Rusted (2011) describes as "the most representative of St. John's architecture during the time when most of the city had to be rebuilt after the 1892 fire" (p. 41). Rusted says, "J.T. Southcott, the first trained architect in Newfoundland, introduced the mansard roof to St. John's. The Southcott style is Second Empire, typified by a concave-shaped mansard roof with rounded bonnet-shaped dormer windows, bracketed eaves, and bay windows on the ground floor—built mainly in the period from 1870 to 1900" (p. 41). The match is exact, though it does not help to pin down the house's date beyond what is already suggested by the clothing of the people in the picture.

This photo, which would have both enchanted and spooked me if I had seen it as a child, strikes me simultaneously as uncannily strange and profoundly known (my brother, Bruce, describes it as "familiar on a cellular level"). There is even some resemblance to my mother's little drawing (especially in the obligatory latticework underneath the small verandah). By my time, however, many of the strongest similarities had been erased: the bay windows, the verandah, the latticework surround, and the transom over the front door had all vanished, and it was a much more utilitarian building. In any case, I never actually thought of it as a *house* like the ones my mother lived in and drew. We lived in the upstairs flat. We didn't really have a front door; we used the side door and immediately mounted a set of stairs. In very many ways, our domestic arrangements did not match up with any schema ever presented to me. I learned those standard schemas, but, again, I also learned a kind of reality override that was equally important in my developing awareness of clashes between my stories and my own personal setting.

Trajectories and Maps

Massey's dynamic model of space makes room for transient schemas, but the pleasures of fixing a particular set of relationships on a map still provide cognitive and affective appeal. "It was thus, then," is perhaps an even more potent statement when we consider space as something always in transition.

My place, my home on Pennywell Road, was recorded in an insurance map of 1946 that outlines a specific point in time: after the farm fields had been converted to a school athletic grounds, but before our play space was curtailed sometime around 1955. The house is the building shaped like a jigsaw puzzle piece in the lower right quadrant of this map. In 1955 the school board opened a skating arena alongside the ground that on the map is marked as the tennis court, and as part of that operation, they fenced off our domestic area. We soon scrabbled a passage through the dirt underneath that chain-link fence and continued to take advantage of the whole grounds, but it was never quite the same. In the glories of the prelapsarian world before that fence arrived, we were free to roam all over this space, and we set our games up in particular sites. Games of cowboys, for example, were always played along the foot of the slope that divided the house from the football pitch. The "tennis court" was completely dilapidated, and no one ever managed a

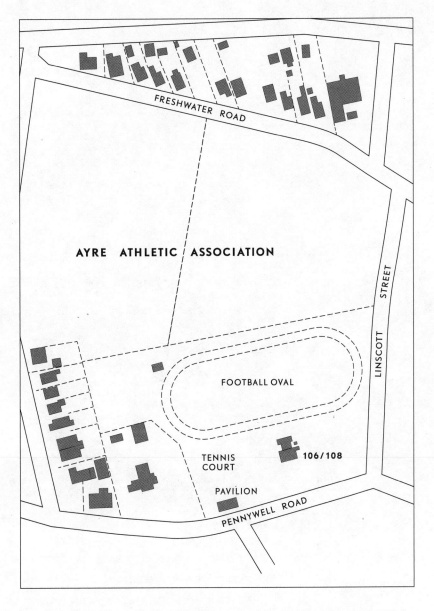

> *The Ayre Athletic Grounds with 106/108 Pennywell Road in the lower right-hand quadrant, below the Football Oval.*
>
> [*Based on City of St. John's, Newfoundland, July 1946 Insurance Plan*]

game of tennis around the potholes, but we used the space for playground games. Likewise there were spaces that we earmarked for running games or hopscotch or skipping. The strong territorial element of our play fed into my literate understanding in ways that I will develop more extensively in following chapters.

The Coady farmhouse picture presents the space still probably more familiar to me than any other place in the world; space over which I walked, ran, galloped, rolled, somersaulted, and otherwise explored with all my body. It represents this space in a guise that I do not recall but its *known-ness* is still palpable to me. The insurance map offers a stylized rendition

of this space that I recall so acutely; the portrayed relationships among the elements of the map dominated my early years in this space.

A third image shows the four of us McCurdy kids playing a game of road construction on a very particular site on this landscape in 1957. We are at the western edge of the circular driveway. Behind us are the chain-link fence and the pavilion; the tennis courts are invisible to the right, beyond the limits of the photograph. My brothers played such road-building games all the time, but it was rare for me to join in. I vaguely remember this occasion as one marked by the serenity of a common endeavour. I am sieving dirt, apparently in the cause of making a smooth floor for some kind of amphitheatre at my feet. Earle is managing a couple of diggers, and Bruce is driving his Dinky dump truck. David's demeanour, with his back turned,

suggests that he, too, has a digger at his disposal. We are calmly making our marks on our landscape; the aura of peaceful busyness is unmistakable and probably what sent our mother to find her camera.

Even as early as 1957, this spot bore traces of a lost segment of our own local history, an absent trajectory through the landscape. Before the fence went up, the path where we are playing in this photo was the dedicated site for playing Old Mother Witch. Since this game involved running from the pavilion to the driveway (while making a great deal of noise), the construction of the fence eliminated it from our repertoire; I don't recall that it ever occurred to us to play it somewhere else.

I did not see the photograph of the old Coady farmhouse until I began work on this project, nor did I encounter the insurance map or any other interesting representation of my own territory. I did myself, however, produce three records of this known world whose very dullness makes a statement. At the end of 1957, at the age of nine, I was given a little Brownie camera for Christmas. It did not have a flash attachment, so I could only take outdoor shots, but very early on I set about making a record of my world.

Three pictures from early 1958 mark my territory, one taken from the top of the hill leading to the soccer pitch and two from the boys' bedroom window. These pictures are not only boring; they are also naïve, and it seems clear to me that no adult would ever have taken them. The contrast is poor, and there is no real focus of attention, despite the soccer game that the boys are playing. Yet these mediocre photographs constitute one of the few statements I made about my own territory as a child; to me, at least, they express some sense of marking limits, and I wish I had taken more. They include the fenced-in garden area we called the Green Gate, the wilder zone called the Thistle Yard, and, at least by implication, the tobogganing hill.

The insurance map testifies that I could have had a great deal of fun making my own maps of this world. I did catch a glimpse of the allure of maps in the Grade 3–4 geography book, *Visits in Other Lands* (Atwood & Thomas, 1943). I read about the exotic doings of Bunga of Malaya, Netsook and Klaya of the Arctic, and Simba of the Congo with only moderate interest, but I do remember the little section on mapping with considerable affection. It comprised a total of two pages, but these pages fired my imagination in a way that was unusual for me in my school experience, and my pulse quickened when I saw them again.

Doubled Maps

The lure of maps for me, however, was usually expressed fictionally. I did not attempt to plot my known world. Instead, in Shaun Moores's (2005) terms, I "doubled" my landscape and overlaid fictional worlds upon the actual one: "Media situations 'overlay'...local physical settings, with symbolic materials from the one being appropriated for 'affiliation' purposes...in the other" (p. 100). The cartography that excited me involved delineations of fictional space.

The map that spoke to me most potently was that of Swallowdale (Ransome, 2001/1940), and I spent hours creating my own concatenation of caves and valleys. More physically, I paced out the delineations of my own abbey and stately home on some empty ground, building a virtual representation of the universe of the Abbey Girls (Oxenham, 1914, 1959) in my mind's eye.

Such doubling, overlaying a fiction upon a known landscape, is an act of some cognitive sophistication. In a modest way, it incorporates some of the energy embodied in Leander and Boldt's "unfolding" (2013, p. 29). Reports

About Plans and Maps

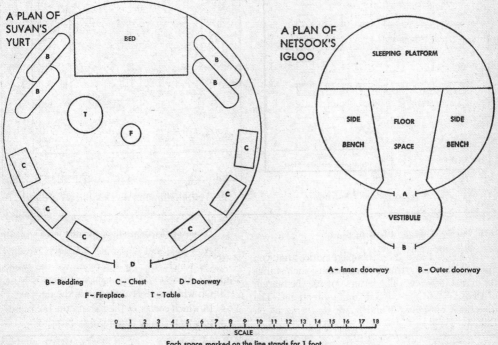

A PLAN OF SUVAN'S YURT

BED

B

B

B

T

F

C

C

C

C

C

D

B – Bedding   C – Chest   D – Doorway

F – Fireplace   T – Table

A PLAN OF NETSOOK'S IGLOO

SLEEPING PLATFORM

SIDE   FLOOR   SIDE

BENCH   SPACE   BENCH

A

VESTIBULE

B

A – Inner doorway   B – Outer doorway

0 1 2 3 4 5 6 7 8 9 10 11 12 13 14 15 16 17 18

. SCALE

Each space marked on the line stands for 1 foot.

Suvan's Yurt and Netsook's Igloo

You have learned that Suvan's yurt is round like the main part of Netsook's igloo, but that it is larger. Here is a way for you to find out how much larger it is.

Each drawing is the kind that we call a *plan*. Under the plans is a line marked off into equal spaces. This is called the *scale*, and it gives you a way of measuring the igloo and the yurt. Be sure to read what is printed under the scale.

Lay the edge of a strip of paper along the line marking the front of the sleeping platform in the igloo. Put two pencil marks on the paper, one at either end of the platform. Now lay the strip of paper along the scale with the left pencil mark at 0. Count the number of feet that the space between your two pencil marks stands for. About how many feet across is Netsook's igloo?

Now measure the yurt. Lay the edge of a strip of paper so that it goes through the middle of the fireplace, and put a mark at the wall on either side. Use the scale as you did before, to find out how many feet the space between your two pencil marks stands for. How many feet across is Suvan's yurt? How much larger is the yurt than the igloo?

65

∧ > *Images from* Visits in Other Lands (*Atwood & Goss, pp. 65–66, 1943*). [*Collection of the author*]

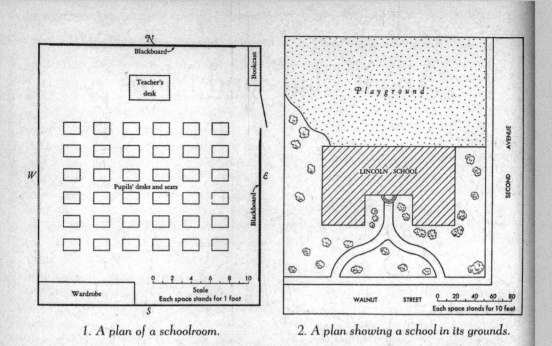

1. A plan of a schoolroom.

2. A plan showing a school in its grounds.

Three Plans to Study

On Plans 1 and 2 on this page notice that you are told the scale; that is, what each $\frac{1}{8}$ inch stands for in real distance. The letters outside the margin of Plan 1 stand for the four main directions. The directions on Plans 2 and 3 are the same as on Plan 1.

Answer these questions about Plan 1:

1. How long and how wide is the schoolroom?
2. On which sides of the room are the blackboards? Answer with the names of directions.
3. On which side of the room is the door?
4. In which corner of the room is the bookcase?
5. In which corner is the wardrobe?

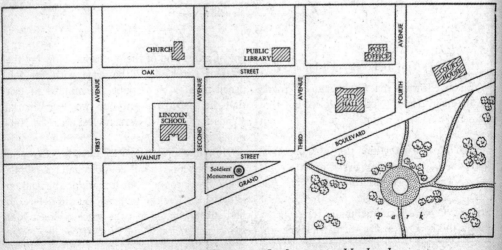

3. A plan showing the same school in its neighborhood.

66

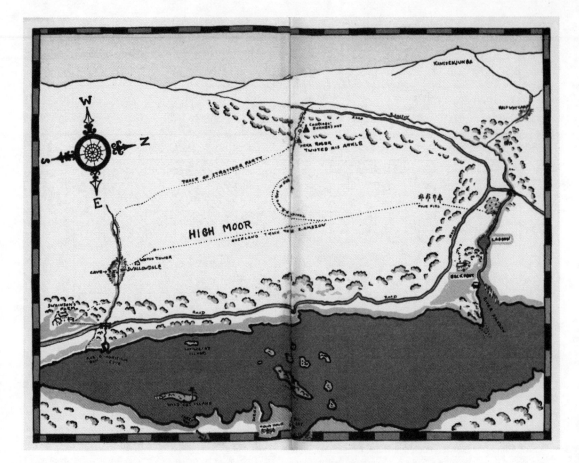

of such behaviour among young children are commonplace. Accounts of children reacting to the works of Laura Ingalls Wilder, for example, bring this capacity to life. Sara Schwebel (2011) says, "After being introduced to Laura Ingalls Wilder's series as a third-grade read-aloud, I spent weeks reenacting parts of *The Long Winter* with friends. We gathered berries on the school playground and tied bundles of pine needles together to approximate the hay Pa used to heat the family's Dakota Territory cabin" (p. 3).

Wendy McClure (2012) was a bit more uncertain about the boundaries between her own world and Laura's:

> From what I could tell, the places where the Ingalls family lived were either mythical nowhere, like the Big Woods and the Prairie, or else impossible to find: Where, on a map of Minnesota in one's parents' 1970 encyclopedia set, would one even begin to look for the unnamed town in On the Banks of Plum Creek? And De Smet, South Dakota, where the family had settled at last, was

in one of those big empty states at the top of the map, as remote, it seemed, as the moon. I knew that some kind of actual there *existed from the books, but somehow I never considered that any of them could be reached from where I was. (p. 7)*

Nevertheless, McClure invested in her own imaginary doubling, overlaying one world onto another. She simply imported Laura into the contemporary landscape:

As for me, I wanted to take Laura to North Riverside Mall. In my mind, I ushered her onto escalators and helped her operate a soda machine. I took her with me on car trips and reassured her when the station wagon would pull onto the expressway ramp and accelerate to a speed three times faster than the trains she rode, faster than she would have ever imagined a human could travel. It's okay, Laura, *I'd tell her. (p. 9)*

Sometimes the role of the fictional landscape assisted with editing the real-life world to make it cleaner or more interesting. Alice Munro (2011) describes this phenomenon in an autobiographical account of her own childhood on a fur farm:

There was quite a lot of killing going on, when I come to think of it. The horses had to be turned into meat and the fur-bearing animals culled every fall to leave just the breeders. But I was used to this and could easily ignore it, constructing for myself a scene that was purified to resemble something out of the books I liked, such as "Anne of Green Gables" or "Pat of Silver Bush."...There was always fresh manure around, but I ignored it, as Anne must have done at Green Gables. (p. 42)

Sometimes my mental mapping was more metaphoric, my setting more generic and universal, rather than merely local. For example, one summer I stayed with a friend at Lawrence Pond, now a part of the conglomerate community of Conception Bay South but then regarded as in the country. My friend and I slept (using the word loosely) in a tent in the yard and read each other the short stories of Edgar Allan Poe by flashlight. We were twelve. The name and location of the lake are not important; reading "The Pit and the Pendulum" in a tent by flashlight at the age of twelve creates its own essential and appropriate world, somehow. But such feelings of attaining a universal experience were the exception for me, rather than the rule.

For the most part, it seems clear that physical and fictional landscapes can inform each other in porous ways. But the daily reality of life in St. John's sometimes interfered with a smooth transition.

Schema-Shifting

From the Coady farmhouse to the set of two flats that housed a sequence of school principals and their families to the gravel parking lot of today, our house had its own history. Like our predecessors in the flat, those earlier British school principals, we were incomers to St. John's, but we were Canadian, not English, so, although we had points in common, our trajectories did not mirror theirs. By the nature of Newfoundland society, all the friends who came to play also came from families that had at some point lived elsewhere, though many of them would have known only St. John's for their own lifespans. Every family moved into St. John's at some historical moment, from communities round the bay or directly from elsewhere. In such a scenario, it is more precise to say that I became literate while moving *through* this space; that element of fluidity makes it easier, actually, to comprehend my strong attachment to the space and time that I knew.

The loss of the archetypal front verandah and associated latticework from the building that became my home represents one small example of the ways in which my inherited and literary schemas did not match up to my daily life experience. A 2010 view of the houses I saw from my bedroom window shows Pennywell Road row houses attached to each other with flat roofs, facing directly onto the street—no verandah, no steps, no front garden. Only the bay windows provide any sense of that opulent security that marks so many suburban homes, but they could equally well speak to the practical necessity of maximizing light in the rooms of a terraced house in a grey climate. In my time, the exterior paint colours were deep and gaudy.

These tiny details of one particular schema embody the sense of *discrepancy* that marked so much of my literate understanding. I was not the only person who found the idiosyncrasies of St. John's architecture startling. Leslie Yeo first visited St. John's from Britain in 1947. He returned many times and set up the successful London Theatre Company. Here he describes his first sighting of St. John's, which was also his first encounter with any North American community. His expectations were severely upset.

After a photo session at Torbay Airport, we motorcaded into the city, eager
for our first look at built-up North America with its dinky white picket
fences, broadloomed lawns and sunporches with cushioned hammocks
where the paperboy tosses the morning edition from his bike as he rides
whistling by.

Your first shock is that there isn't a single picket poking through the
snow and not enough porch to stop stray dogs from peeing on the morning
paper. Every front door you pass is a single step up, right off the sidewalk.
The houses are in rows, but they're not row houses as we understand them
because no two of them are exactly alike. Built entirely of wood, they stand
tightly shoulder to shoulder like an Elizabethan man-o'-war broadside on
to the worst that the Atlantic gales can throw at them. They are strangely
all about the same height, as if everybody had run out of money at the
same time, with the result that the line of rooftops ripples into the distance
in perfect synch with the contour of the road which is undulating. Then
you think about it and find you aren't shocked at all because what you are
looking at is really rather beautiful. (Yeo, 1998, p. 85)

I don't think I ever reached Yeo's stage of detached evaluation. As far as I was concerned, St. John's just *was*. Yet it was clear it didn't fit most of the imagery of my reading and viewing material.

Today I regard that lack of coherence in representation that featured in my early literacy as an intellectual advantage in terms of developing an early sense of skepticism and detachment, but at the time (although I never would have articulated this conclusion to myself until long after the era covered by this study) it drove me to compartmentalize my brain, mostly to the disadvantage of daily life. In many ways, the experience that was shown in my books, magazines, and television programs seemed infinitely more significant and satisfying to me. A part of me relaxed on the few occasions when I was in Nova Scotia; I felt I was somehow closer to the mainstream of *real* real life.

In interesting ways, St. John's has become much more self-confident about its vernacular architecture since my childhood; and I strongly suspect that contemporary children are much less defensive than I was in their sense of relationship to the mainstream images of their culture. The gaudy clapboard row houses are now a tourist attraction, and the cityscape of the older parts of town has been raided in order to create new and local schematic representations, often cast as souvenirs. Numerous paintings and fabric arts such as quilts and hooked rugs celebrate local street scenes. I even own four Christmas tree ornaments, each of which presents the distinctive buildings of St. John's in a different medium. There are several published histories of the city. Above all else, contemporary Newfoundland fiction abounds, and St. John's is now imagined and evoked in words in multiple ways. It would be impossible today to perceive this city as unrepresented in textual form.

It is challenging now for me to place myself back in that world where so many of the textual representations in my life were so significantly different from the schemas of my daily working experience. The risk of exaggerating, of wallowing in the martyrdom of a perceptual colonization, is a real threat. And of course there were also major areas of overlap between my own and my represented worlds. My Christmas schemas, for example, mapped isomorphically onto those of my fictions, and I always found Christmas reading restful. To a large degree, we followed North American sports, and so I understood the frameworks of hockey and baseball (though soccer replaced all versions of North American football in Newfoundland culture).

As I grew older, St. John's began to sprout its own neat and placid suburbs, and I met people who had grown up in ways that more closely resembled the images I encountered in my texts.

An Alien Moral Geography

But that aura of separateness is still important in Newfoundland, and it is not simply a matter of topography or political history. Susan Brooker-Gross (1981) discusses the idea of a "moral social geography" as manifested in children's popular fiction, drawing particularly on the *Nancy Drew* books. Brooker-Gross suggests that landscape stereotypes in popular fiction, especially children's series, may offer insight into how societies see themselves. She suggests that the *Nancy Drew* books value a landscape that is pastoral (neither too urban nor too wild) and romantic (featuring some kind of history of heroic events). "The pastoral setting—natural but managed—is Nancy's haven, her respite from the dangers of cities. Even more, it is a sanctuary from the uncertain treacheries of the wilderness. Wilderness implies an absence of human management and an uncertainty of events" (p. 60).

A person who does not "manage" his or her environment in a *Nancy Drew* book is always suspicious. An unpainted house, an unweeded garden is a sure pointer to a miscreant. It is all, of course, in the eye of the beholder. Without ever specifying it to myself in such terms, I viewed my society as unpastoral and unromantic. The history of Newfoundland has very many heroic elements to it, but they did not speak eloquently to a little girl cutting her literary teeth on the stereotypes and moral frameworks of series fiction.

Nouns in a Void and the Affect Link

My own geography mattered to me as a reader in more specific ways. Christopher Collins (1991) has written in very interesting terms about the "poetics of the mind's eye," and he explores the significance of the visual repertoire we bring to the word on the page: "When we enter the imaginary space of a [written] text, we don't know where we are. We orient ourselves only in reference to the few landmarks we are given—nouns situated in a void....Not having actually perceived this scene ourselves, we have no peripheral field in which to detect and target an object as our next image" (p. 151). What we do, he suggests, is provide our own peripheral field to fill in for what is missing on the page. No book can supply every detail, and the merging of the author's perspective with the reader's is one of the elements that make every reading unique. However, when her own landscape repertoire is disqualified by authorial sneering (or by a more passive closing down of options), a reader may struggle.

It should have been a straightforward matter to insert Nancy into the landscape that surrounded me, but somehow it was not that simple. I moved into Nancy's world, but I left many of the corroborating daily details of my own world behind as I did so. Nancy may have been a noun in a void, but she was a noun with attitudes that were not always easy to fit into the world I inhabited.

Nancy lives in a highly conventional society and shares its highly conventional views. Those readers who could not step right into the perspectives taken for granted within Nancy's assemblage of stereotypes would have to learn to read as if they could do so. Reading becomes a double game of pretend. I pretend I am moving through Nancy's fictional world, and I also pretend that I know how to interpret Nancy's world through the authority of my own world. I read as if I can be the implied reader—and, of course, reading in that way makes it at least partially possible. For me, in St. John's in the 1950s, I was making believe (a phrase that is potent in its precision) on two fronts at once.

The "nouns" of Collins's account exist in a visual and also an emotional void. As abstract marks on the page, they are not imbued with inherent emotions in the ways that images or sounds may be. We supply these feelings from our own local repertoires.

Sometimes a set of bundled emotions can be very precisely specified within a known landscape. When I was about five, a school sporting event on the Ayre Athletic Grounds required a concessions tent on the old tennis court. As this tent was struck late in the day, my friend and I hung around to watch. My friend persuaded me that she could hear noises in behind the canvas—suspicious, even sinister noises. Soon she had a theory to account for them: the Killer Ducks were on the rampage, avid for victims.

It did not occur to me to suspect her of duplicity, still less of simply joking. I was as terrified as I have ever been in my life and ran screaming—across the tennis court, round the back of the house underneath the clothesline, in our side door, and up the stairs like a rocket. Both my parents were in the kitchen, but it took them some time to calm me down enough to extract the source of my abject panic. When they finally got the story out of me, I am sorry to say they laughed uproariously, and they teased me about Killer Ducks for years afterward. I was glad not to be about to die a horrible death at the, well, beaks, I suppose, of the Killer Ducks, but I did not like being made a fool of, and I was mutinous about my parents' lack of sympathy. Additionally, the condensed experience that I now remember includes the aura of a cooled-off friendship that never really recovered from this joke.

The whole incident offered a heady bouquet of sensations. Any time I summon a fragment of that experience to help me understand a character in similar emotional turmoil (usually no Killer Ducks are involved, I admit, but affective sensitivity is highly transferable), some trace of that specific landscape is part of the package. And the emotions are *in* motion—terror yielding to resentment over a short period of time. No doubt in my high-speed traversal of the territory I had created a trajectory of my own, one that would inform certain fictional experiences for the remainder of my reading life. The voids surrounding certain nouns are filled with specifics of territory as well as emotion.

David Gelernter (1994) talks of "affect linking" (p. 6), the apparently arbitrary connections between one life event and another that are made through the mental "tag" of the nuanced emotions that relate similarly to each event. What seem like random mental leaps can often be explained through this affective connection. This concept strikes me as a powerful component in how we bring texts to life. We draw on a bundled set of nuanced emotions from a life experience (those threatening Killer Ducks, those heartless parents) to enliven a fiction bearing similar emotional characteristics.

Located Reading

Into the bundle of trajectories that constituted my place in St. John's with its own affective charges came the alien trajectories of *Nancy Drew* and other books that made little room for me to supply my own visual and cultural references as a working repertoire. My experience was far from unique. Many readers import very alien text into their imaginary worlds; they then may turn these imagined texts into filters on how they perceive their own experiences. Readers need a robust commitment to the fiction in such circumstances; the emotional connections created by affect linking may play a vital role.

As an apprentice reader and interpreter of the world at large, I learned to cope with discrepancies between the represented world and my own familiar life. In effect, I had access to a plural sense of moral geography. I inhabited St. John's as a real little girl. Nancy inhabited St. John's as a fictional heroine to the degree that she possessed my own and my co-readers' imaginations. I mapped my own understandings to Nancy's world and mapped Nancy's cool attitudes to my own surroundings to the best of my ability.

What I did learn was how to start that process of mapping. Nicholas Burbules (2006) describes how our bodies join an imagined space: "When watching a film or hearing a story, our posture, body tension, and startle responses—or, to take another example, our relaxation, rhythmic movement, and kinesthetic sensations listening to music—are a key dimension of the quality of immersion that makes the virtual seem or feel "real" to us at the moment it is happening" (p. 42). In that physical and embodied way, my fictions dwelt where I happened to be when I encountered them. We are in very complex territory here—grounded in place and time but donating our physical and emotional responses to an abstraction, and drawing on our personal experience of place and time to help us navigate an invented world.

The clashing of trajectories through the known places is often a fruitful element of a reading life. Initially I may have had only limited and local expectations to draw on (rendered somewhat more plural by my Nova Scotia experience). The new ideas and assumptions introduced by my books, even those as shallow and dismissive as Nancy Drew's suburban snobbery, also moved through my space. The act of reading and listening to stories in itself changed and expanded my horizon of expectations.

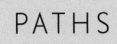

PATHS

"PEOPLE OBSERVE THE CITY while moving through it,"
says Kevin Lynch (1960, p. 47). He also says that for most of the people
interviewed for his project, "paths were the predominant city elements"
(p. 49).

Michel de Certeau (1984) draws a direct comparison between walking
the city and speaking a language; he refers to "walking as a space of enunciation" (p. 98). In an intriguing reference to our need to *place* ourselves both
physically and linguistically, de Certeau observes, "In the framework of
enunciation, the walker constitutes, in relation to his position, both a near
and a far, a *here* and a *there*" (p. 99). Children coming to fiction need to
establish that their own *here* is only "part of the story": the characters will
inhabit a different *here*, and it is the listener-reader's responsibility to move
into that alien *here*.

Childhood is often observed and recollected in motion. Whatever else
children are up to, they are ineluctably growing every day, and many of our
memories involve that sense of transit through a particular phase.

Reading also involves motion, both physical and metaphorical: the
reader is always "heading" somewhere. The pages turn; the eyes flicker.
The person who pauses is, in some senses, no longer reading (though what
Sven Birkerts [1994] calls "the shadow life of reading" [p. 95], the contem-
plative half-life that maintains the fictional or reflective trance, may well
still be in effect). There is motion between the books that a person reads, as
well; one follows another in a chronological sequence, although the content
of the reading may be higgledy-piggledy and nonlinear.

So it is perhaps not surprising that the Paths section of this book is the
longest and in many ways the core section. Moving sequentially from a
prereading awareness of story to relative fluency took me several years (still
an astonishingly short time, given the complexity of the challenge). This
section undertakes to explore the chronology of those early reading years.

At the same time, however, this map cannot simply move from one year to the next, recording the full 360° picture for 1953, 1954, 1955....I have had to collect my thoughts and present some thematic findings. The first three chapters of this section do move more or less along a timeline. The final chapter is, in some ways, more spatial than temporal in terms of organization; it discusses some of the reading material that casually lay about the house, an ecology of texts crossing several generations and constantly available to me over all the years presented here. Without the essential miscellaneousness introduced in the final chapter of this section, my "paths" would be much too neat and orderly to represent my reading life with any validity.

Navigating this section bears a basic resemblance to creating a sketch map while in motion, marking crucial turns in the road and charting readerly growth. The lay of the land is marked out in this first section; later chapters will return to the lines of the territory that are initially established here.

4
Out of
the Murk
Emerging

I DO NOT REMEMBER THE TIME when I did not understand how stories work or know there was a boundary between fictional and daily worlds. Of course, such a time existed, but I have no access to it now.

My earliest memory is of dust gleaming in sunbeams after my father took up the floorboards in the main hall of the Pennywell Road flat. This event probably occurred in the summer of 1951; I was two and a half. I was entranced by the bright motes, a bit unnerved by the strangeness of the revealed floor joists; but the memory contains no narrative element— no before or after. If I wanted to compose an account of that recollection, it would have to take life as a poem rather than a story, a lyric moment of perceiving the normally invisible: the structures beneath the floor, the atoms in the air. It was an observation that was temporal only insofar as it was fleeting.

No doubt like all children, I developed schemas and scripts that helped me to make sense of my daily life. I was undoubtedly assisted in this project by the orderly routines of our day and our week. I would have gained some grasp of the regular sequencing of certain customary events.

The Murk

I had written the words above when, in a Newfoundland novel, I came upon a precise description of the period in our lives that comes before memory but is intensely attuned to learning. By the time we begin to have some conscious understanding of the world, our mental joists have already been laid and are actually covered by the flooring of customary and remembered life. This cover-up of "normality" occurs before we are even aware of any cognitive work occurring. It seems only fitting to discover that this pre-time of our lives has been acutely and eloquently delineated by a man who grew up on the edge of St. John's, not many years after I did. In *A World Elsewhere*, Wayne Johnston (2011) describes this foundational period of our lives that he calls the Murk,

> the interval between your "commencement screech" and the first moment of your life that you remembered....No one really knew what went on in your mind throughout the Murk, what caused it or what its purpose was. While you were in the Murk you learned things that you remembered when you left, but you did not remember learning them....
>
> You emerged from the Murk knowing the names of things. It was not possible, even in retrospect, to tell where the Murk left off and your memory began. You didn't burst from the Murk. You left it gradually. Memory didn't dawn on you. It came and went, came and went, the Murk breaking, then re-forming, memory like the sun behind a threadbare cloud. The Murk lifted until you could nearly see through it, but then closed in again. And so it went, a seesaw flux of memory and Murk. (pp. 35–36)

It is exactly in this way of clouds flickering back and forth in front of the sun that I know the basic structures of my literate life were put in place, day by day, night by night—but I have no access to that knowledge now, except backward into the Murk. It must have happened because of what I knew when I first remember knowing. As Johnston points out, your caretakers can tell you some things about what you did and what you said during your time in the Murk, but their accounts are external, and they entail "misremembrance, embellishment and outright fiction" (p. 36). So, in that "mix of sun and cloud" as the weather forecasters put it, with a flash of sunshine literally illuminating my first memory, I begin to collect fleeting recollections of early events of my childhood. Because of what was completely customary and taken for granted by the time of my first coherent memories, I know that literacy was at work even back before my *aware* life began. And very, very early on came the bedtime story.

Bedtime Routines

There must have been a first bedtime story. Did I ever have that ritual all to myself? My oldest brother is thirteen months younger than I am, and, at the time my memory begins he was inextricably part of the bedtime script. We were always in my bedroom, I recall, initially because it was possible to sit on the side of my grown-up bed but not on his cot, and later because one subsequent baby or another was already asleep in the boys' room.

The rhythms of bedtime included storytime and inexorably added prayers on our knees at the bedside. At first, we said only the first four lines of the children's prayer:

> *Now I lay me down to sleep,*
> *I pray the Lord my soul to keep.*
> *If I should die before I wake,*
> *I pray the Lord my soul to take.*

Essentials thus taken care of, we moved through the litany of family blessing, adding boys' names to the list as they came along. "And make Margaret a good girl," and make however many brothers "good boys" was the final appeal before the amen.

At some point—after the Murk dissipated, because I clearly remember it—we graduated to the next two, substantially more optimistic lines of the prayer:

> *If I should live for other days,*
> *I pray the Lord to guide my ways.*

Perhaps my parents themselves learned later about this addition. The first printed appearance of the eighteenth-century prayer in the *New England Primer* included only four lines ("Now I Lay Me," n.d.).

Like the repeated chorus of a song, therefore, the rhythms of this little prayer punctuated every bedtime story, and the security of my nighttime routines included these markers of mortality and of effortful striving to be better. It just was. It was already there when I emerged from the Murk of my earliest childhood, a literate and spiritual plank nailed into place under the flooring of my daily life. Before I knew about knowing, I knew about God and Baby Jesus, I knew I was a girl and appeared in a different list from my brothers, and I knew something about stories.

Despite this essential focus on endeavouring to be good that made its nightly appearance in our prayer, not every bedtime story was entirely sunk down with morals. I suspect my parents had a sneaking preference for the more anarchic options. They hugely enjoyed the *Pooh* stories and we often had a chapter from *Winnie-the-Pooh* or *The House at Pooh Corner* (Milne, 1957). The Thornton W. Burgess books about animal lives were also constants, and the dog-eat-dog morality of those sagas was certainly taken for granted (though the guaranteed survival of any character fortunate enough to have a name mitigated the randomness to an extraordinary degree).

My brother and I, in contrast, greatly prized a Wonder Book called *Mr. Bear Squash-You-All-Flat* (Gipson, 2000/1950). Its ethic was rather more Manichean, and I thoroughly resonated to its black-and-white assessment of character and virtue.

This book is the only title in this entire project that I discussed retrospectively with my parents. I learned about its reissue in November 2006 and acquired a copy for them and one for myself, a few months before my mother's speech-destroying stroke and a year before my father died. My parents laughed when they saw it and described how much they detested it, especially during the period when we insisted on hearing it, night after night. It was very apparent that they still looked at it with no affection in 2006.

The plot of this book involves the eponymous bear, who sleeps badly when the moon is full and, consequently cranky, sets out to squash things by sitting on them. "He especially liked to squash the houses of other animals, because he was too lazy to build a house for himself and had to live out of doors all the time." Serially, he squashes the homes of a little grey mouse, a chipmunk, and an orphaned baby rabbit. The tables turn when

> *Image from* Mr. Bear
Squash-You-All-Flat
(*Gipson*, 2000).

[*Used by permission from
Purple House Press*]

**Mr. Bear stood up and looked at the tire. There it was,
the same as ever, and not the least bit squashed.**

these refugees team up and create a new home inside a large rubber bus
tire. When Mr. Bear Squash-You-All-Flat jumps on the bus tire, it not only
resists being squashed but also bounces him so high he hits his head on
an overhanging branch. He is moved to see the error of his ways and never
squashes anything again.

In 2000 Purple House Books rereleased this book with an afterword
by cartoonist Gary Larson. Larson also loved *Mr. Bear Squash-You-All-
Flat*, and his mother was similarly less enthralled. When he was three, she
read it to him every morning: "'Gary, this was *every* morning,' she emphasized, then adding, 'and it went on for a long, long time!'" (Larson in Gipson,
2000/1950, n.p.).

Larson also explores the Murk, trying to ascertain what it was in that
book that so appealed to his three-year-old self: "Through the skewed lens

of adulthood, could I look into my early childhood and find the thing in this story that, according to family legend, so gripped my imagination?" (n.p.).

Larson locates a sneaking admiration for the bear. "Like all bears, he may seem comical at times, but we know he is also a force to reckon with—in the end, a force that beckons us" (n.p.). It is certainly possible my brother and I shared a similar respect for the bear's powers. For sure he was licensed to be as mean and cruel as he liked, in ways that far exceeded the limits of our own tame little lives.

But what we particularly enjoyed was the retribution. I can see our fingers (small on the page) tracing the imaginary dotted line of Mr. Bear's bounce into the overhanging branch. We gloated over his comeuppance, night after night.

In fact, that virtual line can be traced only on a single page of the book, the one reproduced in this chapter. The images by Angela cunningly frame the tire so that the overhanging branch is invisible on most openings. A child who knows that a tire is bouncy (a fact we gleaned exclusively from its properties in this book) might muster a bit of foreshadowing, but there is almost no pictorial hint of that arboreal deus ex machina until late in the story.

Critical readings often favour the adventurous parts of a story, but my own tastes, from my earliest memories onward, ran to the domestic, peaceful, and secure. Here, I suspect that, in addition to sating my delight in vengeance, I also warmed to the concept that it is possible to have a completely safe home. My own sense of security, tested every night when the lights went out, was just about absolute, to a degree I find remarkable to contemplate now. But my personal feeling of being in an utterly safe space did not make me braver; instead, it made me want equal safety for everyone I read about. Throughout my childhood, I privileged the domestic; even in glimpses back into the Murk, I detect this abiding passion for home. Other priorities might have lead to a more audacious reading life; I can account only for my own preferences, and they were very clear-cut.

But there were also other sources of appeal in *Mr. Bear Squash-You-All-Flat*. Richard Gerrig (1993) speaks of the concept of anomalous suspense, of the way we read ourselves back into a story's open world of possibilities even when we already know the outcome (p. 158). I have vivid memories of enjoying the grief and fear of the little animals throughout the duration of the story, in the sure knowledge that they would win in the end, both engaging with the anomalous suspense and overriding it at one and the same time. Nobody would call this book sophisticated, yet, more than any other early story, it inculcated me inside that bubble-world of the subjunctive mode of make-believe. By the time I had mastered *Mr. Bear Squash-You-All-Flat*, an event that mostly happened inside the Murk, I knew a thing or two about fiction.

Learning about the Literary

What goes on in our minds as we process a story, either by reading or by listening to it (and is it different if the heard story is read aloud from an invariant text as opposed to being composed or recreated on the spot)? The answers to this question, incomplete as they undoubtedly are, offer us insight into our own mental toolboxes.

The best brief account I know of how stories affect us is Jerome Bruner's 1986 exploration of the subjunctive mode, a concept I will explore briefly here and then reconsider more substantially at the end of the book. Bruner's insights may be supplemented by findings from the field of cognitive poetics. In ideal circumstances, our cognitive toolbox is already under assembly by the time we emerge from the Murk.

I will draw on these theories, on the information about reading that is inherent or implied in my first storybooks, and on what I know I must have learned before my memories begin. Out of these ingredients, I will attempt to structure my exploration of the pre-remembered (as opposed to the more garden-variety unremembered) stages of my literate life. Some technical ingredients will feed into my account: theory of mind, the subjunctive, deictic shifting, figure and ground, the implied reader, and possible worlds. (I include more detailed work on scripts and schemas on pages 78–79 and 178.) In addition, I will attend to the role of adult scaffolding. All these recondite terms will be applied to a set of particular books aimed at the young child, a juxtaposition that may seem ridiculously unbalanced on first sight but that I hope will prove helpful.

Theories of Mind

Mr. Bear Squash-You-All-Flat may have offered the first mediated hint in my Murky world that not everyone thinks alike or shares the same motivation. Certainly the book made it clear that malevolent bears and orphaned baby rabbits do not hold many priorities in common. Knowledge that other people do not operate from your own exact frame of reference comes very early to children. This awareness is given the grand title of Theory of Mind, and babies begin to develop it before their first birthdays. Jerome Bruner (1986) observes that "young infants followed an adult's line of regard to search for an object on which to fixate, such search being contingent on the adult and child first being in eye-to-eye contact" (p. 176). Knowing that the adult's eyes are focused elsewhere on something that may be deserving of attention marks a major step forward into social learning.

Bruner suggests that "human mental activity depends for its full expression upon being linked to a cultural tool kit—a set of prosthetic devices, so to speak" (p. 15) and recommends that "we are well advised when studying mental activity to take into account the tools employed in that activity" (p. 15)—a challenge I take up in this project and particularly in this chapter, where the tools are my main source of information.

We manage our theory of mind in many ways. One major tool is language and one major subtool of language is *deixis* (the use of a small set of words, sometimes called "shifters," that require situational knowledge of the context of utterance for full interpretation—words such as "me," "yesterday," and the like). If I know that your perspective is not identical to mine, it is a relatively small step to establish that your "now" may be my "then," your "here" may be my "there." In reading fiction, I must learn the specific necessity of making the transposition to lend my own sense of "nowness" to the narrator's "now." Erwin Segal (1995) writes,

> *The center from which the deictic terms derive is more than just the point of origin for the deictic terms. This deictic center (DC) contains all the elements of the here and now, or the phenomenal present for the user of the deictic terms. Deictic Shift Theory states that in fictional narrative, readers and authors shift their deictic center from the real-world situation to an image of themselves at a location within the story world. (p. 15)*

Somehow we have to accomplish this transfer from the deictic zone explained by our own surroundings to a different one. Lost in the Murk, the memory of how I first learned to make this shift is not available to me now, and it is difficult for external studies to gain access to the toddler mind as it masters this huge challenge. So I will buttress my exploration of this enormous achievement from two different angles, investigating both the role of the text and also the role of the helper (Lev Vygotsky's [1978] well-known "adult or more capable peer" [p. 86] who enables the learner to perform at a higher level than can be achieved alone).

Stories transport us out of our own now into someone else's—that of a bear, a rabbit, or some other protagonist. We move into the now of the Other, which, as part of its essential nature as *now*, contains a future as yet unknown. We learn to react to this now as if it were our own, which it is not. All kinds of outcomes are possible in that fictional future. In Bruner's (1986) terms, describing the role of the subjunctive mode of the *as if*, we are "trafficking in human possibilities rather than in settled certainties" (p. 26). Deictic shifters are one tool for conveying that we have moved into the frame of an open future. Even if the ending of the story appears in the first sentence, there is almost always a point in the story when the *characters* do not know it will happen, and at that point, sharing their deictic centre, in important ways *readers* also do not know.

Bruner elaborates further on the forms of discourse that allow us to create a subjunctive space. The first is "*presupposition*, the creation of implicit rather than explicit meanings" (p. 25), a feature that allows readers freedom to fill in the details left undelineated by the tacit nature of the given. The second is "*subjectification*: the depiction of reality not through an omniscient eye that views a timeless reality, but through the filter of the consciousness of protagonists in the story" (p. 25). Thirdly there is "*multiple perspective*: beholding the world not univocally but simultaneously through a set of prisms each of which catches some part of it" (p. 26). Such means allow discourse to keep meaning "open or 'performable' by the reader. Together they succeed in *subjunctivizing reality*" (p. 26).

Mr. Bear Squash-You-All-Flat, simple as it is, draws on all these discursive approaches. Many infilling details of the story are left implicit; young readers must, for example, infer the importance of home to those little animals whose dwellings the bear destroys, in order to gain some measure of the desolation Mr. Bear metes out. The relationship between a poor night's sleep and a grumpy disposition the next day is made explicit, but little listeners must draw on their own life experiences of being tired in order to instantiate the details of Mr. Bear's perspective. The narrator is reasonably omniscient, and from time to time he moves inside the heads of both Mr. Bear and his victims. The story is told via these shifting perspectives between characters—both in words and in the illustrations, where we see the contrast between Mr. Bear on a good night, sleeping peacefully with a benevolent expression on his face, and Mr. Bear after a bad night, frowning ferociously and looking for someone to hurt. Sometimes the pictures take over the story altogether. The verbal story tells us that the mouse "looked sadly at all that was left of his house," and that the chipmunk "gave one low little groan when he saw what had happened to his house" (Gipson, 2000/1950, n.p.). The reaction of the baby rabbit, however, is not mentioned in the words, only conveyed by the picture, where we see him weeping many tears.

A story opens up a future operating from the base of the hypothetical now of the fiction. We learn to hope, dare, dream, fear, expect, dread what *might* happen in that future. Even if we already know what *does* happen (Mr. Bear hits his head and retires from squashing), when we begin the book anew, we return to the moment of the open fictional present when other eventualities still *might* occur.

Children develop theory of mind out of early instinct, but they need more help to grasp the invitation and the challenge of a shaped fiction. Who helps them? Clearly the tellers (author, illustrator, oral storyteller, app designer) create that opening to an as-if world, but children also and necessarily look for scaffolding from those around them. To accept the address of the story, they must shape themselves to its demands; must, to a greater or lesser extent, become the implied reader.

Mediating between Real and Implied Readers

Marilyn Cochran-Smith offers an illuminating account of how the person who reads a story aloud helps to inculcate child listeners into a reading culture. She points out that writers must address a fairly abstract version of the reader.

> [R]eaders actively and continuously participate in the creation of meanings by bringing their own life and literary experiences to bear upon texts.
>
> Writers, however, have no way of knowing specifically what their anonymous and distant readers bring to texts. Furthermore, since there is no face-to-face interaction between authors and readers during the actual reading, there is no opportunity for writers to repair misunderstood passages or offer further explanations where needed. (Cochran-Smith, 1984, p. 176)

The writer summons up and then addresses a schematic reader who possesses sufficient repertoire to process the story being told. The writer needs readers to know how to align their own life understandings with the implied reader that is shaped by the way the story is written. *Mr. Bear Squash-You-All-Flat* creates an implied reader who rejects Mr. Bear's cruelty to small animals and rejoices in his comeuppance, but Gary Larson's (2000/1950) reaction establishes that different affiliations with the story are also possible, even simultaneously:

> *Mr. Bear's scariness—far, far removed from the transparent evil of, say, the Big Bad Wolf—is so softened by Morrell Gipson's gentle humor, that a greater sense of him is fostered. And that is awe. I know I felt it then, I feel it even now. Nothing is more exciting than when Mr. Bear comes "loppety-lop" down some moonlit path. Like all bears, he may seem comical at times, but we know he is also a force to reckon with—in the end a force that beckons us.*
>
> *Truth is, as much as I rooted for the other animals in this story (despite what you're thinking), I don't think I wanted Mr. Bear to go away. He, too, belonged in this forest. And I just wanted him to come back. Day after day.*
>
> *Read it again, Mom. (n.p.)*

Larson here evokes some of the subjunctive qualities of the story: the excitement created by that astonishing power of the book to return Mr. Bear right back into the forest from which he is invariably ejected by the end of the story; the shifting of perspectives between the antagonists of the plot; the strength of implicit understanding that Mr. Bear is both comical and awe inspiring, contradictory though these qualities may seem.

Larson's mother and my own parents seem not to have shared the pleasure of moving into the subjunctive world of this particular story. Nevertheless, these adults took on a mediating role, making connections between the social and emotional understanding of the listeners and the inscribed world of the text, what Cochran-Smith (1984) describes as "the one-way or unilateral sense-making by the writer as he fictionalizes a reader in the work" (p. 177). The storyreader, says Cochran-Smith, transforms the printed story "from a unilateral to a joint sense-making process" (p. 177). Drawing on transcripts of read-aloud sessions, Cochran-Smith outlines a complex process.

[The adult reading aloud to the children] continuously monitored the match between the reader implied in the text and the real reader/listeners who sat before her, listening to the text.

To help them make sense of texts, the storyreader guided the listeners to take on the characteristics of the readers implied in particular books. To shape real reader/listeners into implied readers, or whenever a mismatch between the two seemed to occur, she overrode the textual narrator and became the narrator herself, annotating the text and trying to establish some sort of agreement between real and implied readers. The storyreader mediated by alternating between two roles—spokesperson for the text and secondary narrator or commentator on the text. (p. 177)

In order to mediate, the storyreader had to continuously assess and interpret both the text—its lexical and syntactic structures, the story-line, temporal and spatial sequences, the amount and kind of information carried by the pictures and by words, and the interrelationships of these two kinds of information—and the sense that the listeners were making of it all (Cochran-Smith, 1984, p. 177).

These commentaries combine to create a surprisingly clear illumination of that scene in the Murk. The text sets up a fiction by means of its verbal and pictorial entry into the subjunctive mode of a deictically shifted now, inscribing an implied reader, who applies life and textual understanding to the spaces created by that subjunctive. A learning reader is supported and scaffolded in this enterprise by the storyreader, who also shifts—between what the story expects and what the listener or reader is able to bring, mediating between the two in the cause of creating a shared understanding. Sometimes the storyreader conceals his or her own lack of interest in the characters and their interactions.

The explanatory potential of *Mr. Bear Squash-You-All-Flat* is probably exhausted. I will turn to another important bear of my childhood: Winnie-the-Pooh.

Reading *Winnie-the-Pooh*

In 1958, when I was ten, our aunt and uncle gave us a Christmas present of a single-volume edition of *Winnie-the-Pooh* and *The House at Pooh Corner* (confirmed by the inscription they wrote on the front page of our volume of *The World of Pooh* [Milne, 1957]). The end papers of this book comprise

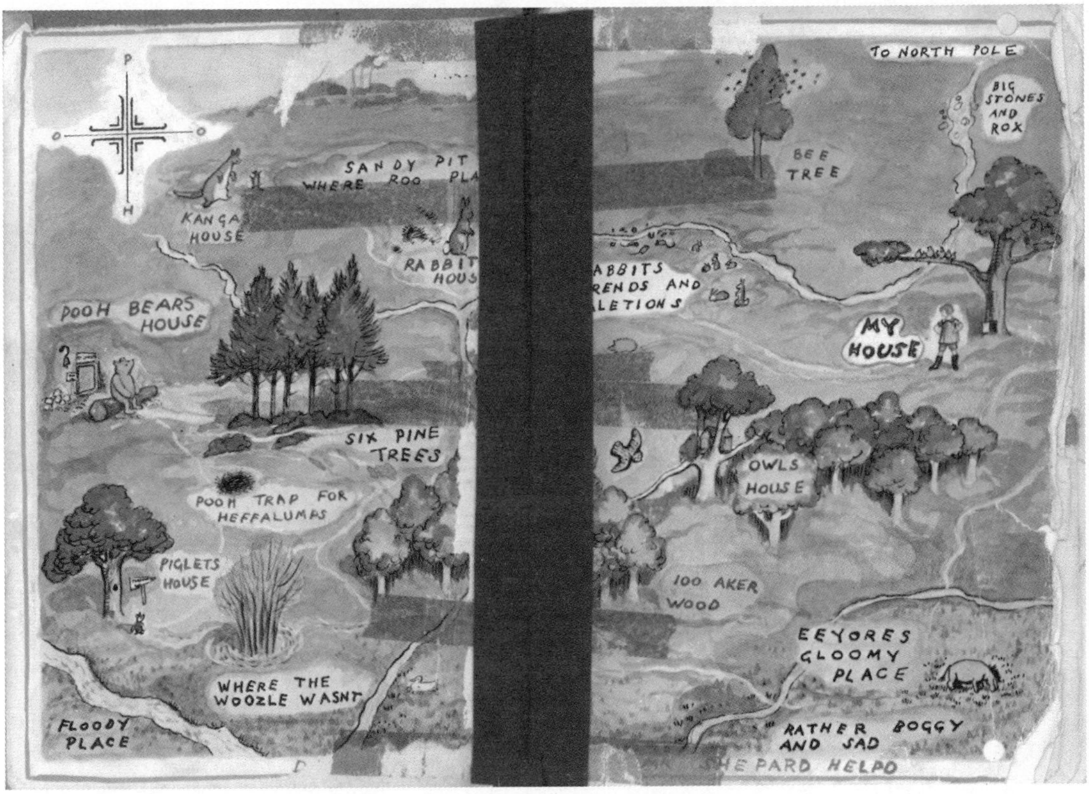
TO NORTH POLE
BIG STONES AND ROX
BEE TREE
KANGA HOUSE
POOH BEARS HOUSE
MY HOUSE
SIX PINE TREES
OWLS HOUSE
POOH TRAP FOR HEFFALUMPS
PIGLETS HOUSE
100 AKER WOOD
EEYORES GLOOMY PLACE
WHERE THE WOOZLE WASNT
FLOODY PLACE
RATHER BOGGY AND SAD

^ *The map of 100-Aker Wood in* The World of Pooh (*Milne, 1957*).
[*Courtesy Penguin Random House*]

a lavish, full-colour map of Pooh's world. I recall admiring this map wistfully, since, at my advanced age, I perceived the world of Pooh to be firmly located in my past. The map gives the flavour of the appealing landscape. The book itself is now held together by both Scotch tape and duct tape, and it is plastered with crayon drawings by a younger sibling. More than fifty years of family life have taken a toll.

I very clearly remember that elegiac moment of Christmas 1958. My earliest memories of *Winnie-the-Pooh*, however, are located in what Johnston (2011) calls "the seesaw flux of memory and Murk" (p. 36). I certainly do recall being read these stories, but I know I am not remembering the first reading of them because, in that in-and-out-of-the-Murk way, in my recollection, the stories are already familiar.

There is a route still open into that Murk, however: the text itself.

What were my brother and I learning about negotiating fiction through hearing these stories repeated? *Winnie-the-Pooh* gives many answers to that question. Milne actually plays complex games with the deictics of the opening chapter in this book. Christopher Robin is both audience and character in the first chapter, addressed both in third and second person. Even Pooh gets to comment on his own story in this early chapter. By the end of the chapter, however, readers are introduced to the switch to more conventional forms of third-person narration.

> *"Is that the end of the story?" asked Christopher Robin.*
> *"That's the end of that one. There are others."*
> *"About Pooh and Me?"*
> *"And Piglet and Rabbit and all of you. Don't you remember?"*
> *"I do remember, and then when I try to remember, I forget." (Milne, 1957, p. 23)*

I sympathize very strongly with Christopher Robin's sentiment: I, too, remember, and then when I try to remember, I forget. It is the very nature of the Murk. Yet I do have a few true memories of reading this book. Both my parents took great pleasure in Pooh's rhymes and declaimed them with great attention to their rhythmical strengths, even when the substance of the words was nonsensical. Quotes from the stories became family catchphrases, a shorthand that expressed both the content and connotation of the story *and* a form of family "glue" composed out of the real intimacy of those readings.

The subsequent chapters of *Winnie-the-Pooh* make no use of the second-person address, and I was pleased about that development. I was not familiar with the idea of "archness" as a critical term, but I detected some over-elaboration; and furthermore, I found it very difficult to follow the pronouns in Chapter I. Maria Nikolajeva (2013) disagrees with my childish assessment: "[T]he frame is essential since it governs interpretation. It is a story told by an authoritative adult to an ignorant child; the narrative voice is stronger than the purported child perspective. This exercise of power adds to the other entangled power hierarchies in the book" (p. 203). I think it possible that this opening chapter also contributes to the power hierarchies in-built in the bedtime reading ritual, but it would be too simple to say I disliked the direct address because it reminded me that I was also an ignorant child. To the best of my recollection, I took my own lack of knowledge and skills for granted and did not worry much about what I could not understand.

Once the second-person voice is left behind, the subsequent chapters do major deictic and subjunctive work in a third-person way. One particularly hardworking story is Chapter III, "In Which Pooh and Piglet Go Hunting and Nearly

Catch a Woozle," and an exploration of this chapter offers much suggestive insight into the process of learning to comprehend how stories work.

Hunting the Implied Reader

The audience for Milne's story was complex. The initial listener was a real boy who was also a character in the story. But this boy also seems to have served as an embodied placeholder for the implied reader, which may explain why Milne's books provide such excellent scaffolding for children who are learning about story.

The chapter about the Woozle offers many fine examples of such scaffolding at work. The pictures play a crucial role. Even as Pooh and Piglet puzzle over the mysterious beasts leaving footprints in the snow, working themselves into a state of some anxiety, the pictures explain perfectly clearly (in my edition on pages 38, 39, 40, 41, and 43) that Pooh and Piglet are themselves making the tracks. Viewers are inculcated into a game of figure-and-ground: are Pooh's footprints in the snow part of the background scenery or should we be mentally foregrounding their significance? What is the connection between Pooh's foot and Pooh's footprint? Talk of the Woozle distracts us from the otherwise obvious answer to this question. For me, real-life experience of walking in snow stood me in good stead as I explored the possibilities.

Little listeners with access to the pictures, especially once they learn the trick of shifting their foreground and background attention, may experience double satisfaction. They can move themselves into the subjunctive world of Pooh and Piglet's fears about the potential hostility of these creatures, shifting their deictic centre to the point of view of the two friends. Yet all the time they know better from the perspective not so much of the omniscient narrator (the puzzle is not solved verbally until page 43, when Christopher Robin draws Pooh's attention to his own contribution to the tracks) as of the omniscient illustrator. Listeners can savour Pooh's (and especially Piglet's) suspense without having to be overly frightened.

The words, in fact, never make the explanation entirely explicit. Young listeners need to complete the sense of these sentences:

> *Christopher Robin came slowly down his tree.*
>
> *"Silly old Bear," he said, "what were you doing? First you went round the spinney twice by yourself, and then Piglet ran after you and you went round again together, and then you were just going round a fourth time—"*

"Wait a moment," said Winnie-the-Pooh, holding up his paw.

He sat down and thought, in the most thoughtful way he could think. Then he fitted his paw into one of the Tracks...and then he scratched his nose twice, and stood up.

"Yes," said Winnie-the-Pooh.

"I see now," said Winnie-the-Pooh.

"I have been Foolish and Deluded," said he, "and I am a Bear of No Brain at All."

"You're the Best Bear in All the World," said Christopher Robin soothingly.

"Am I?" said Pooh hopefully. And then he brightened up suddenly.

"Anyhow," he said, "it is nearly Luncheon Time."

So he went home for it. (pp. 43–44)

As young listeners, one each side of the reading parent, we would have seen the evidence of the pictures for ourselves and possibly been ahead of Pooh at this point. The leisurely layout of Pooh's remarks to himself as he gains enlightenment across three paragraphs probably did not mean a lot to us except as it informed the pacing of how our parent read the lines aloud. Milne conspicuously does not say, "Then he fitted his paw into a Track and found that it matched his own foot perfectly, which meant that Pooh and Piglet must have made the Tracks themselves." He lets three dots do the work, aided by Mary Shepard's very clear illustrations. The storyreader may help listeners make the connections, but once children are initiated into the mystery of the Woozle, they can enjoy the ellipsis as much as any other reader. Pooh's words now certainly encourage them to feel superior to him, even if, up to this point, they have been fully caught up in the suspense of hunting the Woozle.

This little passage embodies all three of Jerome Bruner's (1986) elements of the subjunctive space: "presupposition" (p. 25) in Pooh's dawning realization of how he has misled himself, which is never articulated directly to readers and listeners; "subjectification" (p. 25) as Pooh gradually figures out his error; and "multiple perspective" (p. 26) in Christopher Robin's bird's eye view from the tree, Pooh and Piglet's terrified fantasies of Woozles, and the down-to-earth (literally!) evidence of the footprints in the illustrations. Listeners also learn that when the storyreader says "I," the meaning is "Pooh" because Pooh is fictionally pronouncing that "I"—and further, that

Pooh's subjective perspective expressed through that "I" may be misleading. Pooh draws his conclusions; young observers work from the *drawn* conclusions toward a subjunctive awareness of Pooh's misunderstanding of his own deictic centre. The audience comes to realize that Pooh has been bamboozling himself throughout the whole story and that the Woozle is Pooh himself. Not bad for a little bedtime reading.

The sophistication of the narrative work achieved in *Winnie-the-Pooh* is clarified when we compare it to another bedtime regular of ours, the animal stories of Thornton W. Burgess. To compare and contrast, I picked a chapter at random from *Old Mother West Wind's Animal Friends* (Burgess, 1912), "The Stranger in the Green Forest." It turned out to be a story about fear and fearlessness, surely a fine training ground for developing subjunctive understanding, and a useful parallel to the Woozle story.

The plot of "The Stranger in the Green Forest" is relatively straightforward. The Merry Little Breezes spot a stranger and rush to tell the animals. The first one they meet is Reddy Fox, who pretends to know all about it, to the disappointment of the Breezes.

> Now, Reddy Fox had not told the truth. He had known nothing whatever of the stranger in the Green Forest. In fact he had been as surprised as the Merry Little Breezes would have wished, but he would not show it. And he had told another untruth, for he had no intention of going down to the Smiling Pond. No, indeed! He just waited until the Merry Little Breezes were out of sight, then he slipped into the Green Forest to look for the stranger seen by the Merry Little Breezes. (Burgess, 1912, p. 17)

This little passage contains elements of deception (or false belief) and of intentions, but Burgess names them rather than leading children to infer or inhabit them. In Bruner's (1986) terms, explicitness annuls the reader's degrees of interpretation (p. 25). Contrast this approach with the layers of inference that are scaffolded as Pooh and Piglet follow the tracks of what they perceive as three animals:

> So they went on, feeling just a little anxious now, in case the three animals in front of them were of Hostile Intent. And Piglet wished very much that his Grandfather T.W. were there, instead of elsewhere, and Pooh thought how nice it would be if they met Christopher Robin suddenly but quite acciden-

tally, and only because he liked Christopher Robin so much. And then, all of
a sudden, Winnie-the-Pooh stopped again, and licked the tip of his nose in a
cooling manner, for he was feeling more hot and anxious than ever in his life
before. There were four animals in front of them! (*Milne, 1957, p. 41*)

Like Reddy Fox, Piglet is now frightened into deception, but Milne presents his fibs more subtly, leaving more work to the reader.

"I think," said Piglet, when he had licked the tip of his nose too, and found
that it brought very little comfort, "I think that I have just remembered
something. I have just remembered something that I forgot to do yesterday
and shan't be able to do tomorrow. So I suppose I really ought to go back
and do it now."
    "We'll do it this afternoon, and I'll come with you," said Pooh.
    "It isn't the sort of thing you can do in the afternoon," said Piglet quickly.
"It's a very particular morning thing that has to be done in the morning, and,
if possible, between the hours of——What would you say the time was?"
    "About twelve," said Winnie-the-Pooh, looking at the sun.
    "Between, as I was saying, the hours of twelve and twelve five. So really,
dear old Pooh, if you'll excuse me——" (p. 42)

Piglet's story itself is hardly subtle, but Milne's scriptive offer to his young readers delicately invites them to step into the subjunctive. Twice in these two little passages the narrator combines the mental state of nervousness with the motor action of licking the tip of the nose (an activity that belongs to animals but that children could imitate to a certain degree). The whole act of walking around a bush in the snow and leaving footprints would activate motor responses as well, needless to say. His subjunctive exchanges are equally adroitly managed. In this story, three sets of partial understanding scaffold each other. Piglet is gullible about the Woozle and easy to frighten, but he possesses the minimal amount of cunning needed to fabricate his very unconvincing story about the urgent errand. Pooh may be too naïve to see through this flimsy excuse (it's not quite clear if he believes it), but he is able to follow Christopher Robin's explanation of the tracks. Christopher Robin is the final arbiter and point of security through this and other adventures, but even his understanding is that of a child.

Even the non-existent Woozles are granted powers of possible intention ("Hostile") in this little extract. Milne demonstrates that even being a complete fiction created within the confines of another fiction need not stop you from having a subjunctive life.

Burgess instructs his child readers directly, telling them exactly what the characters are up to. Milne, in contrast, invites his readers to take on the subjunctive as his characters do and to participate in the ways in which they structure each other's understanding. Piglet's errand and the significance of the footprints are both made-up stories, though arising from different motivations (the latter a simple misunderstanding, the former a deliberate deception). Milne's words do not delineate the fictional nature of either story; he does not directly explain the Woozle any more than he challenges Piglet's lies. His readers are simply (maybe not the right word here) expected to shift between the layers of make-believe—initially *along with* Pooh and Piglet but with the potential of moving up to the comparatively sophisticated level of Christopher Robin. That authoritative narrative voice from Chapter I is much more reticent here, with listeners and readers invited to reach their own conclusions (a condition of mind that also directly inhabits the subjunctive: I *believe* that, I *guess* that).

As a child, I engaged intensely with these books, absorbed in the delight of the stories but also intrigued by the cognitive challenge. Even as a small girl, I liked to have my wits working. *Winnie-the-Pooh* taught me a great deal about direct and indirect narrative information, about inference, and about ellipsis, although of course no such vocabulary occurred to either me or my parents. Other titles opened different doors for me, sometimes as part of the bedtime scenario and sometimes at odd times during the day when I would browse through our picture-book collection.

A Small Sampling of Genres

We did not own many books when we were young, and the titles of some are lost in the Murk so I have not been able to relocate them. I have assembled a restricted set of those picture books I can recall, however, and I want to look very briefly at the different messages they gave me.

Not all the books told a story. *Prayer for a Child* by Rachel Field (1944), illustrated by Elizabeth Orton Jones, won the Caldecott Medal for 1945. That book was effectively a figure-and-ground manual for me. Many pages contain close-ups of particular items that can later be seen in the background image of the child's room. I loved being able to find the items featured in close-up located in their proper places in the room; that back-and-forth game was my favourite element in that book and the first thing I looked for when I found it again as an adult, many decades after I last put it down as a child.

Orton Jones also illustrated *Small Rain* (1949), a collection of Bible verses chosen by Jessie Orton Jones. This book offered many pleasures, though consecutive, absorbed reading was not one of them. The group of children featuring in its pages is at least modestly multicultural, and certainly much more so than in my normal lily-white reading material. The varied use of frames and white space to surround both words and images is exemplary in its capacity to draw attention to the cadence of the words and the frozen motion of the pictures. I loved the figure-and-ground game of *mise en abyme* that is encapsulated in the image where children are reading a book featuring a picture of themselves on the cover. The ache in my brain that I felt when I tried to pursue that picture into smaller and smaller incarnations was intriguing and pleasurable. Beyond the many tacit lessons I learned about the aesthetics of the picture book and the aesthetics of the prose of the King James Bible, there was the reassurance of the content itself. Accompanying images of a boy in prayer at the side of his bed and a girl asleep surrounded by stars, the words of the final two pages, read as follows:

> The Lord is thy keeper.
> The eternal God is thy refuge,
> ...and underneath are the everlasting arms. (Jones, 1949, n.p.)

Who would not be comforted?

Other books offered different pleasures. Kathryn Jackson's *Nurse Nancy* (1958/1952) supplies images of a child life much more affluent than my own, but easily imaginable. Nurse Nancy's three brothers are older, and they occasionally are gracious enough to allow her to play medical games with them (not that one! their games mainly involve the application of bandages to scraped knees). The story is pedestrian, and the two real bandages that came with the book quickly disappeared, to my ongoing disappointment. What I really liked about the story were the background illustrations of Nancy's dolls and accessories: so many dolls' beds (one so

Suffer the little children to come unto me, and forbid them not:
For of such is the kingdom of God.

She had a fine doll hospital, complete with lots of bandages and handy candy pills.
But she had no one to play with her.

Just then, ding-a-ling, came a telephone ring.
Nurse Nancy answered.
"Hospital," she said.
"There's been an accident," she heard a voice call.
"Down at the big tree."

∧ *Images from* Nurse Nancy, *illustrated by Corinne Malvern (Jackson, 1958/1952).*
[Courtesy Golden Books]

lavish that it features a bed skirt), and that appealing bookcase with its mix of books and toys. Nancy's dolls never jumbled together in a single cot. I did not yearn particularly for the nurse's uniform, but that bedroom enchanted me. With *Nurse Nancy*, I learned that a reader can choose to read for ground rather than figure. Certainly my predilection for enjoying the daily background details of the lives of book characters more than the adventures that fuel their plots got a healthy start with this anodyne little book.

Not all my stories were as readily accessible to my domestic imagination. Two books excluded me for different reasons, though I kept reading them because the choices were so limited at home. *Ameliaranne and the Green Umbrella* (Heward, 1972/1920) was a baffling book, even though its emotional core was legible enough. Ameliaranne is the eldest daughter of a poor washerwoman. Her five younger siblings are ill and cannot attend the squire's Christmas tea. Ameliaranne takes the big green umbrella and hides her own tea inside it with a view to taking treats home to her brothers and sisters. She is discovered by the squire's mean spinster sister, but the kindly squire has noticed that Ameliaranne ate nothing for herself and sends home a lavish tea for everyone.

> *Image from*
Ameliaranne and the
Green Umbrella,
*illustrated by Susan
Beatrice Pearse*
(Heward, 1972/1920).
[Courtesy Hodder & Stoughton]

Squires and footmen and maids and the rags Ameliaranne wears in
her hair for days to make curls for the party were all very unfamiliar
to me (though I did learn a thing or two about curlers as I grew older).
Additionally, I truly did not believe you could store cakes in an umbrella.
Most alienating of all, however, is the way Ameliaranne talks. Here is her
reply to the squire:

> *"Oh, sir," cried Ameliaranne, uncovering her face, "I'm glad you saw, 'cos
> I didn't take a bit more'n what I could easy 'ave ate; and the five of them's
> got colds in their 'eads, and when I left them they was all howlin' somethink
> horful, and I couldn't bear to go home and tell them everything and them not
> 'ave a bite, as you might say." (Heward, 1972/1920, n.p.)*

Whether or not Constance Heward intended this dialogue to sound as condescending as it does (I could find out almost nothing about her), I know I was repelled by it. When I look at the book now, I can still distinguish its past aura for me of "just barely better than nothing at all to read." It is important to remember from my current vantage point of plenty that this meagre virtue still ranked as positive in my eyes. I still cannot like the book very much, and the fact that such old-fashioned values were still being published in 1920 does not improve it in any way.

A different form of estrangement arose with *Babar and Father Christmas* (de Brunhoff, 2008/1940). Here the story made perfectly good sense to me, but in our copy all the text was presented in a cursive font, and I could not decode it, even though I could read by the time I remember this book. I knew the story from having it read to me, but the book was frustrating, and I spent most of my time ogling the lavish cut-away view of Father Christmas's subterranean kingdom.

Domestic coziness is a feature of most of these texts, but the ideological freight of my picture books was not just safe and pretty. Babar, of course, has been accused of being an elephant stand-in for imperialists (Kohl, 1995); the class lessons of Ameliaranne's world favour noblesse oblige and knowing your place. Neither interpretation is particularly attractive.

Some books were even less subtle. *Mr. Bear Squash-You-All-Flat* at least represented an external threat. One title that I now find quite horrifying to read (though I loved it as a child) offers a lesson in punishment and exclusion inside the family, a possibility that we seem to have simply taken for granted then but that might classify as abusive today. The book is *Seven Diving Ducks* (Friskey, 1940), and the moral of the story is an oppressive conformity. Six of the ducklings in the family take to swimming and diving as expected. The seventh duckling is not so sure, and his life is made a misery as a consequence—by his father in particular.

The book introduces a family with six ducklings and says boldly on the third opening, "There was also a seventh little duck. But he wouldn't dive, so they didn't count him" (Friskey, 1940, n.p.). This little duckling, unlike the others, is clothed in ignominious orange bloomers. When the other ducks learn to swim, he sticks close to shore so he can keep one foot on the bottom. We see him wearing a life belt that is attached to a nail on the beach. Father Duck is not impressed.

> That night, after supper, all the little ducks were very tired. Six of them went to bed.
>
> The seventh little duck was very tired, too, but he could not go to bed. Father Duck, who had watched the swimming lesson, made him stay up and practice swimming on the piano stool.
>
> "I won't have any sissies in my family," said Father Duck sternly. "You might just as well go and live with the chickens if you can't learn to swim."
>
> The seventh little duck was very unhappy. He worked hard. One, two. One two. (n.p.)

The little duck learns to swim but fails again when the new challenge is to dive. He is afraid to put his head in the water. Father Duck puts his threat into action.

had watched the swimming lesson, made him stay
up and practice swimming on the piano stool.

*"The time has come," said Father Duck to the seventh little duck, "for you to
swim across the pond and live with the chickens. Go!"*

*The seventh little duck, who was very forlorn indeed, went down to the
pond to swim away.*

*All the six, unhappy, little diving ducks, who were very fond of their timid
little brother, lined up on the shore to watch him go. (n.p.)*

Fortunately, as he swims sadly across the pond, an apple falls from a tree
onto his head and knocks him forward into a perfect dive. He even catches
a fish.

*"Well done," said Father Duck. "You weren't really afraid to dive at all. You
were just afraid to try." Father Duck smiled proudly. (n.p.)*

In the final picture and on the back cover, the seven little ducklings are
identical; the seventh one is indistinguishable—a happy ending.

I, too, was deadly afraid to put my face in the water, so I am not sure why I liked this nasty little story—perhaps because of Lucia Patton's charming illustrations (the book was also published with different pictures, but I was not aware of any alternative). It may be that I appreciated the fact that the duckling was saved despite the fact that he never worked up the nerve to submerse himself, since, like him, I could never see myself taking that step readily.

Or it may be that I simply liked stories in an indiscriminate way, liked how complications resolved themselves, liked living briefly in the ducklings' world of water and apple trees, liked being read to. My response to this story lives largely in the Murk.

I have much stronger recollections of *The Story of Margaret Field-Mouse*, "written and drawn by Cam" (1950/1946). Cam turns out to be Barbara Mary Campbell; I was surprised when I looked her up because I had always thought of the author as a man. My parents bought this book— even though they couldn't really afford it—because of the heroine's name, of course, and because they were beguiled by its delightful illustrations. I was captivated by Margaret, to the point that my copy now has to be held together with an elastic band. Whether Margaret was responsible for setting my preference for domestic coziness in place or whether she just represented the apotheosis of an already appealing hominess in a book is now not clear to me.

Today, everything about this ragged object speaks to me of home. There is my mother's labelling of the book as mine. There are the shreds of the deeply familiar bookstore label on the inside of the front cover.

The Story of Margaret Field-Mouse features a highly conservative plot. Margaret lives with Crocus the Frog, and she hates spring cleaning. One day she spots a circus passing by and is inspired by the elephant. She ascertains from a sparrow that elephants never do spring cleaning and wishes she could become one. Right on cue enters Fairy Pimpernel; she cannot turn Margaret into an elephant but can make her as big as one.

> AT *first Margaret was very happy,* BUT *when she went to see her friends they were all frightened and ran away. Even the people in the village put up notices offering a reward to anyone who could capture her. Poor Margaret was so upset that she went away and hid—and that's why you can't see her in the picture. And she became* TERRIBLY *hungry. (Cam, 1950/1946, n.p.)*

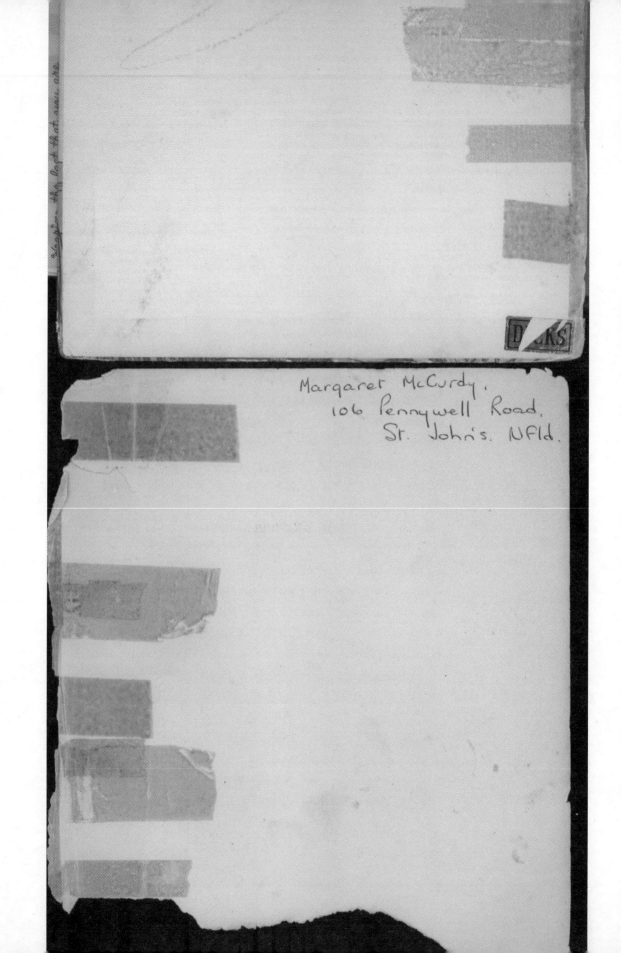

Margaret McCurdy,
106 Pennywell Road,
St. John's, NFld.

> ALL this time poor Crocus had been sitting at home, lonely and miserable. The spring cleaning wasn't finished, the fire was out, there were cob-webs every-where, and the beetles came and danced on the hearthrug. But all of a sudden Crocus heard a rushing noise outside, and then someone jumped down—down the stairs — AND there was — MARGARET

The words in capital letters are printed in red for extra emphasis. To cut a long story short, Margaret is recruited as a freak in the circus, where she is utterly miserable. Luckily Fairy Pimpernel returns and shrinks her back to normal size, and Margaret races home. She is so glad to be home that she never complains about spring cleaning again.

The double-page spread of Margaret's homecoming contains two of the most satisfying pages in all of English literature—at least so I thought as a child and, at some level, I have never really changed my mind. That opening contains many reading lessons for a young listener—probably especially for a young listener who is aware that that last word in the red caps actually speaks her name.

The illustrations also taught me about reading picture books. In the double image presented in this chapter, there are not two Crocuses, but one character portrayed at different points in time. The action between the two images is implied by the knocked-over stool, and the time lapse is at least long enough for Crocus to replace her tears with a welcoming smile and demeanour. As for the radiance of Margaret, flying down the stairs back to her home and her partner, I possessed all the repertoire needed to make very deep sense of this image.

There are continuity gaps in this opening. The stack of plates perseveres across the gutter, but the angle of perception from which Crocus is portrayed actually changes. When I look closely today, I see that the rug under the stool appears at both the right side and the left side of the picture. These small shifts are just jarring enough to indicate that it cannot be exactly the same space because it is not the same time.

My parents reading aloud took their cue from the red capital letters, and perhaps from the pleasure of the small child at their side, and always read "AND there was—MARGARET" with the utmost expression of delight. My love for this story was egocentrically wholehearted. Its origins lie in the Murk, but my pleasure in its pages was great enough that more memories survive.

Learning to Read

As with most people, my memories of learning to read for myself are also largely Murkbound. One family story, however, serves as an elegant segue from the bedtime story to the schooled achievement. At the start of Kindergarten, we were told that we would learn to read after Christmas. I took this promise very seriously, and on the last night of the Christmas holidays, settling down for our nightly story, I said grandly to my brother, "Tomorrow night, *I'll* read to you."

Alas, it was not so swift or straightforward. We laboured over the dreary doings of Dick and Jane and Baby Sally, one word at a time. "Look" was the first word, and after a while we could read, "Oh look." The big book version was propped at the front of the classroom.

Poet Billy Collins (2002) calls Dick and Jane "the first characters/the boy and girl who begin fiction" (p. 39). I already knew fiction was more interesting than anything Dick and Jane got up to, but I can resonate to the final stanza of Collins's poem, "First Reader":

They wanted us to look but we had looked already
and seen the shaded lawn, the wagon, the postman.
We had seen the dog, walked, watered, and fed the animal,
and now it was time to discover the infinite, clicking

Text in image: Oh, oh, oh. / Oh, Dick. / See Sally.

∧ *Unnamed Prince of Wales students mastering* Dick and Jane, *date unknown.*

[*Courtesy Clarence Button Collection, Archives and Special Collections, Memorial University of Newfoundland*]

permutations of the alphabet's small and capital letters.
Alphabetical ourselves, in the rows of classroom desks,
we were forgetting how to look, learning how to read. (p. 39)

Collins obliquely captures the intensity of young children's focus on the words as they laboriously figure out how the codes work ("forgetting how to look"). Most of this experience is lost to me now, but I do have one substantive memory of my progress through the little books. I distinctly recall the day we learned to read the word "said." It was sometime in late-ish Grade 1, so we had been at these labours for more than a year. I remember looking at this word and thinking, "*That's* what the trouble has been. No wonder these stories are not so good. Now I can read 'said,' I can read some proper stories." The memory stops there, but, to the best of my awareness, the next memory in this sequence of spaced-out fragments of time involves the early chapter books by Helen Louise Thorndyke about Honey Bunch, and I suspect that sometime soon after learning "said," my reading did indeed take off.

I have a further reading memory, one that arises from one of those *Honey Bunch* books: encountering the word "Europe" and toiling to remember its pronunciation. I knew "EE-rope" was wrong, and when I could (rarely) remember the correct pronunciation, I did know it was right. But holding it in my head was hard, and I have a sharp recollection of my frustration.

One last Honey Bunch memory concludes my little bouquet of memories from the era during which I did actually master the process of decoding print. Honey Bunch looks at some diamonds, and I put down my book to ask my mother what they were. She showed me the very small diamond in her engagement ring and told me to ask my grandmother to see hers, next time we met, as hers was more impressive. I actually remembered to raise the question when that opportunity arose, and my grandmother took her marginally less-modest ring to the window to flash it off the sun. A small satisfying moment in my path toward becoming a fledged reader but hardly a major turning point.

For most people, the actual process of learning to read is lost in the Murk. When I trot out my pitiful little set of reminiscences, many people are actually impressed at "how much" I do remember. The pivotal moment of learning "said" is the most interesting to me. I even have some background understanding of how the word "said" came to my attention in our bedtime reading. A family friend one night read us a bedtime story from a Thornton W. Burgess story. In some of his books, this author prefaces each chapter with a sage little utterance from the eponymous hero. In this example from *Billy Mink*, Chapter 1 opens thus:

> *The stranger and the unknown must*
> *Be always looked on with distrust.*
> Billy Mink (*Burgess, 1924/1919, p. 1*)

Our parents read these words as written, but our guest reader added an editorial flourish, concluding, "Says Billy Mink." Ever sensitive to cadence,

I liked the rhythm of this addition. This small event is linked in my mind to the learning of "said" in school, but I have no idea if the two occasions fell close together in time.

Such tiny fragments, but my archaeology of learning to read must be built out of them. Incontrovertibly, at the end of the process I could read. It did not take me long to shake off the dust of Dick and Jane; in comparison, even Honey Bunch presented complex prose. But for a year and more of my life, the doings of Dick and Jane were big news. In and out of the major events of Kindergarten and Grade 1—the end-of-year school picnic, the 1954 summer visit to Nova Scotia, the Hallowe'en party, the Christmas concert, and much more—through all this time, my day job was Dick and Jane. It is frustrating to be able to remember so little of what was effectively a major literary relationship, but there is no point in pretending I recollect more than I do.

But whether I remember it or not, I was mastering a complex challenge. Reading, says Stanislas Dehaene (2009),

> is a sophisticated construction game—a complex cortical assembly line is needed to progressively put together a unique neural code for each written word....[C]onscious reflection is blind to the true complexity of word recognition. Reading is not a direct and effortless process. Rather it relies on an entire series of unconscious operations....The entire word recognition process, from retinal processing to the highest level of abstraction and invariance...unfolds automatically, in less than one-fifth of a second, without any conscious examination. (pp. 92–93)

Maryanne Wolf (2007) points out that as we gradually master the process Dehaene describes, we move through

> a very special world where mother rabbits and loving hippos illuminate words and feelings, dragons convey concepts and syntax, and nursery rhymes and scrawled approximations of letters teach an awareness of sound and print, as well as a dawning awareness of their relationship. Reading in such a world is the sum of five years spent developing highly complex cognitive, linguistic, perceptual, social, and affective abilities, all of which flourish best in rich environmental interactions. (pp. 101–102)

So much of this effortful work is not recoverable through an act of memory. In my case, however, the laboriousness entailed in reaching this level of automaticity is preserved in at least one record. My mother kept my school exercise book from one of these years—from the internal evidence, I suspect it is a Kindergarten notebook, and it may indeed have been the first school notebook I ever had. Here, I present the first two pages of this book. As far as I can tell today, the bold letters are from the teacher's red pencil and the rest is my effort to copy. The work involved can perhaps be inferred from the way the pencil marks fade in the movement down the page, an effect that is even more noticeable on the second page.

To my eye, the sheer labour of the enterprise of learning to read and write is represented in these inexpert lines with a clarity that no amount of published text can convey. It may be the hardest work I have ever done.

Through the Bottleneck

During my preschool years, I learned a lot both about story itself and about how different stories could expand my sense of the world. The universe of Dick and Jane was a narrow one. There was almost no satisfaction in the stories themselves, but the slow achievement of reading competence was rewarding in a limited way.

The take-off once I achieved critical mass in word recognition, however, only served to emphasize the plodding nature of that year of learning laboriously. I do not remember ever sitting on the windowseat with Dick and Jane in hand, but once I graduated to reading about Honey Bunch and the Bobbsey Twins, I perched there for hours at a time. I wish I could remember more about this second stage of learning to read, but it is even more profoundly lost in memory than the initial achievement. I do vaguely recall making connections between the sleepwalking scenes in *The Bobbsey Twins* (Hope, 1950) and those in *Heidi* (Spyri, 2002/1880–81). I remember wondering about those diamonds. The rest shades into a late eruption of the Murk. It is too bad, because that escalating success of developing skill and confidence through the daily practice of enjoyable reading obviously entails an intriguing process. It would be fascinating to have better internal access to it.

5
Stereotypes and Series Books

Scaffolding

HUGE SWATHES OF MY CHILDHOOD reading time were devoted to series books, both those manufactured by the Stratemeyer Syndicate and those written by dedicated single authors. I read for character as much as for plot, and it is fair to say that Judy Bolton (Sutton), Beverly Gray (Blank), the Abbey Girls (Oxenham), and the various youngsters in the Blyton adventures taught me a lot about life and also about reading.

The series books provided an important stepping stone between having books read to me and being able to take on more complex literature. Catherine Sheldrick Ross (1995), a longtime champion of series reading, describes the impact of being able to master these thrilling stories:

> In Nancy Drew *and the* Hardy Boys *books, I encountered for the first time motifs and plot devices that seemed resonant and compelling: coded*

*messages, letters left in a hollow oak tree, a moss covered mansion, moldy
attics and secret caves, an unclaimed inheritance, a hidden box of treasure,
a stolen legacy, a mistaken identity. This repertory of storytelling devices
may seem formulaic to jaded adults, but not to the apprentice reader who
is reading for the first time about lost gold mines and fresh footprints.
The problem for all of us is that it's hard to recover the first experience of
enthrallment, of being caught up in the world of the story, of not being in
your bedroom reading but being* right there *with the hero or heroine. (p. 202)*

Elizabeth Bowen (1986) suggests that children are most successful in
"being *right there.*"

> *The child lives in the book; but just as much the book lives in the child. I
> mean that, admittedly, the process of reading is reciprocal; the book is no
> more than a formula to be furnished out with images out of the reader's
> mind. At any age, the reader must* come across: *the child reader is the most
> eager and quick to do so; he not only lends to the story, he flings into the
> story the whole of his sensuous experience which from being limited is the
> more intense....When the story, as so often happens, demands what has
> not yet come into stock, indefatigable makeshifts are arrived at. (pp. 51–52,
> emphasis added)*

Stereotypes serve a useful role in building up these "makeshifts." They
are often not detailed and can be fleshed out with materials to hand. They
assist the "coming across" through lack of substance; no impediment is
created by detail or individuality.

Much of what I read was not new fiction. The collection in the boys' and
girls' section of the library was respectable but not lavish. Some of the
comparatively newer series that I read did come from the library, for example
the *Betsy* books by Carolyn Haywood, published between 1939 and the 1960s.
Other material was hybrid. The *Abbey Girls* series by Elsie J. Oxenham was
published up to 1959, but the first book appeared as far back as 1914. I alter-
nated current with older titles, though in the case of the *Abbey Girls*, and
many other long-running series, the ethos of the stories was very old-fashioned so the publication date is perhaps misleading in any case.

My library acquisitions were augmented by a few materials at home,
many of which, whether owned or borrowed, also represented a time warp.

I would love to pursue the question of whether children today, with their personal domestic libraries of bright paperbacks, still draw on elderly household supplies and loans (I don't rule it out).

Ross, in a series of interviews with avid readers, suggests that the role of series reading is at worst benign; in all likelihood it is much more positive, despite the fears of librarians, teachers, and parents. In the 1950s, many gatekeepers ruthlessly dismissed all such material as rubbish. Yet, reporting on interviews with 142 people identified as avid adult readers, Ross (1995) says, "Out of 142 readers, 88 (62%) mentioned reading series books. More female readers reported reading series book (57 out of 85 or 67%) than did male readers (31 out of 57 or 54%)" (p. 217). This percentage is probably an underestimate, Ross says, because participants in her study were in no way prompted to talk about series books, and some may simply have thought them not worth mentioning.

But Ross is clear that she is describing a phenomenon of considerable significance in establishing a reading habit:

> Series books, together with books that had previously been read aloud, were frequently mentioned as the first "real books" that readers succeeded in reading on their own. This shouldn't surprise us when we consider that starting with something familiar makes the transition easier to reading on one's own. Psycholinguists point out that reading is more than a process of decoding sounds. Reading involves making sense out of the black marks on the page by using the "behind-the-eyes" knowledge of how stories work (Smith, 1978, p. 5). The more readers know about the story already, the less they have to rely on the words in front of them. It is therefore easier for beginning readers to read a series book with a familiar plot and characters or to read a book that has been read aloud than it is for beginning readers to get into a totally new book. (pp. 218–219)

Series books certainly provided such an essential stepping stone for me. They also offered new ways (however hackneyed) of understanding the pleasures of reading, and new notions (however clichéd) of the larger world outside my own experience.

Stereotypes and the New Reader

Charles Sarland (1991) raises important points about the significance of series books and popular novels in the developing awareness of young readers, discussing "the ways in which fiction is a source of cultural information and the ways in which young people read for cultural information" (p. 63). He investigates reader responses to popular culture and "the ways in which these forms offer sites of cultural typification and definition" (p. 63).

"Popular fiction," says Sarland, "constructs generalities, values, and views of relationships which the young can use in order to begin to understand the world and their place in it" (p. 67). He is clear that stereotypes have the potential to provide some initial mapping of the world for young people:

> Such essential *relationships are, of course, sites of cultural generalization and typification and as such constitute particular ideological formulations. Young people, in the negotiation of their own individual courses through the culture, need some signposts against which to chart their own directions. 'Marriage', 'love', 'normal sexuality', 'normal relationships', 'right', 'wrong', 'order', 'chaos', are all cultural constructs. If we want to know how such categories are currently constructed by the culture, then the first place to go will be the primary means of cultural communication—the popular arts: television, video and popular literature. (p. 68)*

Perry Nodelman addresses a similar topic from a slightly different angle. He talks about the different relationships between reader and characters in Paula Fox's *The Slave Dancer* and Paula Danziger's *The Cat Ate My Gymsuit*:

> *Since Jessie's life [in* The Slave Dancer] *is so different from our own, we are forced to stand at some distance from him. The novel demands that of us, even in requiring our interest in the detailed operations of a business venture most of us know only vaguely. Furthermore, it requires us to stand back from Jessie and understand who he is simply because we know enough about him to know that he is not like ourselves.* The Cat Ate My Gymsuit *prevents our consciousness of otherness. In fact, we cannot possibly understand the story unless we fill in its exceedingly vague outlines with knowledge from our own experience. Marcy Lewis has no life unless we give it to her; her town and her school have no physical substance unless*

we provide it. The book demands, not distance, but involvement. (Nodelman, 1981, p. 180)

My reading life on Pennywell Road was full of stories that offered me access to stereotypes of typical children and young adults (100 per cent of whom lived somewhere else, thus introducing me to stereotypes of cultures not directly my own). Here, I will explore some of the characters whose existence resembled the kind of colouring-book outline that Nodelman has described here; in the next chapter I will look at the impact on my reading life of literary characters with radically more individuality.

The distinction Nodelman draws between the vague and typical characters and the detailed and individual characters is very helpful. I am not entirely convinced, however, that we simply fill in the vague outlines with "knowledge from our own experience," at least not to any greater degree than we do with other kinds of reading. In my own case, my personal experience did not offer the requisite raw material with which to infill the details of what I perceived as sophisticated character life. Very often what child readers do, I suspect, is invest these sketches with their growing knowledge of stereotypes. Sarland is probably right that many readers benefit from moving into the use of this kind of shorthand in their early days of learning to behave like readers.

On the other hand, even at the age of six, as I started to read chapter books, I did have a modest repertoire of life experience to bring to bear. Looking back at the series I encountered, I find it interesting to interrogate them in terms of how they might have overlapped with my own sensory, social, cultural, and intellectual understanding of life, augmented by a growing set of stereotypical assumptions that gradually informed the new ways in which I began to imagine myself into the world.

Deborah Britzman (1995), in her discussion of reading straight and reading queer, cogently reminds us, however, "that there are no innocent, normal, or unmediated readings and that representations drawn upon to maintain a narrative or a self as normal, as deviant, as thinkable, are social effects of how discourses of normalization are lived and refused" (p. 164).

To a degree, what I lived and what I refused in my reading of these banal little series books reflected my own time and place. The 1950s were famous for an oppressively enforced normativity, and St. John's seemingly imported and then reinforced the most repressive elements of its

Irish, English, and North American connections. At the same time, like all Canadians, I learned almost from my very first exposure to media, that I was *not American*, so some norms did not apply. Additionally, my own Canadian identity in the newly Canadian surroundings of Newfoundland was highly ambivalent. My developing schemas only partially served an obedient reading practice. What my *times* reinforced, my *place* contradicted.

Britzman describes the need to address the unthinkable, to stretch the boundaries of pedagogy. "Reading practices might well read all categories as unstable, all experiences as constructed, all reality as having to be imagined, all knowledge as provoking uncertainties, misrecognitions, ignorance, and silences....[P]art of what is at stake when discourses of difference, choice, and visibility are at stake is the capacity of the educational apparatus and its pedagogies to exceed their own readings, to stop reading straight" (1995, p. 164). Britzman writes abstractly, but my own concrete experience helps me interpret the very large issues she raises.

In 1962 I moved for two years to Edmonton, Alberta. It was a big change, and I was very homesick, but I vividly recall being explicitly aware that there were ways in which I could actually relax because I was living in a culture that much more closely resembled many of the stereotypes I had laboriously learned to import into my reading and viewing. My clear memory of that mental shift from the isolated and idiosyncratic experiences of St. John's reminds me that, in Britzman's terms, I was active up to the age of thirteen in processing unstable categories, constructed experiences, imagined reality, and knowledge that provoked uncertainties and silences. Through the lens of comparative "normality" during my Edmonton years, I can reach back to the duality of my existence in St. John's, as I acquired the stereotypes that manifestly made sense of my books but made rather less sense in my daily life. "Uncertainties, misrecognitions, ignorance and silences" abounded in my reading experience. In Edmonton, I read "straighter," as it were—a mixed blessing.

Being a Canadian Newfoundlander in the 1950s was one route to living in a world of unstable categories and the rest. There were and are many other ways of being at odds with the prevailing stereotypes. Race, class, sexuality, and immigrant status will all unsettle a person's connection to the norm; and there are many forms of rural, urban, and/or national life that do not match the world of series books. Playwright Alan Bennett (1995/1994), for example, provides a trenchant commentary on class misalignment in a short memoir tellingly entitled, "The Treachery of Books":

> *The families I read about were not like our family (no family ever quite was). These families had dogs and gardens and lived in country towns equipped with thatched cottages and mill-streams, where children had adventures, saved lives, caught villains and found treasure, before coming home, tired but happy, to eat sumptuous teas off chequered tablecloths in low-beamed parlours presided over by comfortable pipe-smoking fathers and gentle, aproned mothers, who were invariably referred to as Mummy and Daddy.*
>
>   *In an effort to bring this fabulous world closer to my own, more thread-bare, existence, I tried as a first step substituting "Mummy" and "Daddy" for my usual "Mam" and "Dad", but was pretty sharply discouraged. My father was hot on anything smacking of social pretension. (pp. 4–5)*

The emotional resonances of that descriptor of "threadbare" could also be applied to the raw and foggy austerities of St. John's as I perceived them in the 1950s. Bennett is acute also on the disconcerting recognition that even information books were discrepant:

> *Had it been only stories that didn't measure up to the world, it wouldn't have been so bad. But it wasn't only fiction that was fiction. Fact too was fiction, as textbooks seemed to bear no more relation to the real world than did the story-books. At school or in my* Boy's Book of the Universe *I read of the minor wonders of nature—the sticklebacks that haunted the most ordinary pond, the newts and toads said to lurk under every stone, and the dragonflies that flitted over the dappled surface. Not, so far as I could see, in Leeds. There were owls in hollow trees, so the nature books said, but I saw no owls—and hollow trees were in pretty short supply too. (p. 5)*

As an urban child, I, too, saw little in the way of rabbits, squirrels, and other child-sized animals. The modest animal kingdom of Thornton W. Burgess might as well have been science fiction for all our ability to relate it to our own surroundings. Owls were as remote a prospect in St. John's as in Leeds, though there were surely some hollow trees. It seemed all our books, fictional or factual, were grounded in an alien landscape.

Is the generic sameness of the series books an asset to a child reading outside of his or her personal context? To what extent do the unspecified outlines that Nodelman describes allow us to tweak the normativity of the series story toward the lived details of our own experiences? Alternatively, does the series book's lack of particularity allow us to escape from questioning our own categories and assumptions as we find ways to come to terms with its standard plot, setting, and characters? Does it allow us to explore the pleasures of reading vaguely?

I read my brothers' books much more than they read mine and was therefore familiar with the sleuthing Hardy Boys (Dixon, 1927 and ongoing), with baseball player Johnny Madigan and his team of Blue Sox (Decker, 1947, 1958), and with teen sports stars Bronc Burnett (McCormick, 1951) and Chip Hilton (Bee, 1949). In general, however, I concentrated largely on girls' books, and many of the stereotypes and working assumptions I imbibed were associated with gender identity. The relatively rigid boxes into which the sexes were sorted in the 1950s at least made for an uncomplicated route into learning to comprehend my series books. They also provided a collection of working assumptions that connected with my own life, where girls' and boys' universes were also dichotomized. That clear-cut set of stereotypes also allows me today to explore one strand of the ways in which I absorbed and applied the assumptions that made it possible to become a reader.

(It is necessary at this point to distinguish between the stereotypes that fuelled books for female children and those that motivated books for adolescent girls. The children's clichés are in many ways less pernicious; heroines are more autonomous [within limits] and less inclined to internalize the idea that what matters most is a boy's opinion of them. In Ramona Quimby's famous phrase, child heroines and girl readers alike want to "win at growing up" [Cleary, 1988/1984, 155], and the books I read that were aimed at little girls took some cognizance of this fact, even if shades of the prison house of passive adolescent femininity were looming on the horizon.)

I acquired stereotypical knowledge of the world through accretion, a process that I will now explore through a set of analytical categories, including the following:

- *embodied stereotypes* that I understood via my own physical experience;

- *working stereotypes* that I learned from my books and then put to use over and over again in successive reading encounters;
- *recurring stereotypes* that appeared in one book after another without needing more than to be simply encountered;
- *subliminal stereotypes* that lurk in the basement of my mind unvisited, and provide a disconcerting subtext to my reading activities even today; and
- *transient stereotypes* that I forgot very quickly.

Learning the Ropes

My earliest recollections of reading independently outside of the *Dick and Jane* books involve Thorndyke's *Honey Bunch* series. In many ways, I used my own life knowledge to reject the books with some contempt. Even at the age of six, I sneered at Honey Bunch's naïveté and rolled my eyes at her saccharine nickname. She was really Gertrude Marion Morton but was called Honey Bunch because her daddy declared, "'Bunch of Sweetness,' is too long to say every day....So let's call her 'Honey Bunch'" (Thorndyke, 1923a, p. 7). Perhaps my first foray into literary criticism was my critique of the following passage from *Honey Bunch: Her First Visit to the City* (1923b):

> [*Honey Bunch*] *counted her pairs of socks—Honey Bunch counted by colors, not numbers; she wasn't old enough to count by numbers, but she could say, "white, blue, tan, black"—and helped her mother so much that Mrs. Morton said she didn't know what she should do without her.* (p. 11)

I completely missed the wink to the reader in Mrs. Morton's comment. Instead, I ranted that if Honey Bunch could identify a pair of matching colours, she could certainly count to two. As a fellow child, I did not want to be fixed in an amber of faux cuteness, and Honey Bunch's resistance to developing competence annoyed me greatly.

More often, however, I read less resistantly. Honey Bunch rubbed me the wrong way, but I followed her tame adventures regardless. I also accepted other equally bland heroines and learned to read the markers that substituted for individual character development. When my own experience could infuse the relationship with forms of lived response, so much the better.

Some recurring motifs of my series books resonated with me in meaningful ways, and some did not matter to me. It is perhaps simply a personal idiosyncrasy that left me cold to many of the ingredients of the heroes' adventures; I was always more committed to the domestic details of daily life than to the gypsies and kidnappers and sinister strangers who haunted so many of my books. Maybe I was simply unadventurous, or maybe I responded more strongly to details that I could infuse with some recognition. Maybe I was just behaving like the girl reader described by Shirley Foster and Judy Simons (1995): "The importance of domestic interiors, suggesting both enclosure and security, the recurrent references to private or secret places, and the linkage between the heroine and the natural world, have been read by both cultural and psychoanalytic critics as having a specially feminine resonance, and carry significant implications in reading the narratives of escape (whether overt or covert) which are intrinsic to juvenile literature" (p. 29). I suspect these psychological and cultural elements were all relevant to my tastes. At a minimum, in Mary Leonhardt's (1996) useful distinction (pp. 112–113), I read for insights into relationships rather than for action and adventure. This very clear-cut preference has always dominated my reading life.

A suffocatingly conventional emphasis on gender roles ruled the world of St. John's in the 1950s, as it did elsewhere, even though Newfoundland's social and economic welfare have always depended on the work of tough, strong women. I attended the only co-educational school system in the city, and the Methodist tradition my school inherited certainly expected scholarly diligence from its girls as much as from its boys. Nevertheless, even before I learned to read, I was being inculcated into many ways of being a socially acceptable girl. Ironically, it felt like territory in which I could exercise some autonomy. I could not imagine myself as living in the conventional geography or society described by many of my texts, but I could certainly imagine myself relishing the standard tropes of girlhood as encountered in my books. I have always genuinely enjoyed babies. I loved my dolls and paper dolls. I became a champion knitter at the age of nine and learned to make bread at eleven. I did not want to play many of the games my brothers enjoyed. I was well on the way to scoring a conventional bull's eye in this aspect of my existence, and there was little incentive for me to resist—except to the limits that heroines like Anne, and Katy, and Jane Moffat resisted. In this arena, where I could move into the stereotypes and let the stereotypes move back into me, I was a player! Given the many ways in which I felt excluded from the world of my books, this ability to perform the limits and constrictions of my heroines was oddly liberating.

Embodied Stereotypes

My tacit knowledge of girlness both enabled my reading and was reinforced by it; in this major structural category, there was little discrepancy between my life and my books. This coherence informed my reading in large ways, but it also provided a detailed entry point into many stories. For example, my delight in pretty clothes was shared by almost every heroine I encountered, and it provided one profoundly embodied route into inhabiting and animating the stereotypes of my books. Here was a route by which my own physical and cultural understanding could transfer into the abstractness of the words on the page—"from my body outwards" (Malouf, 1985, p. 3). I was indifferent to any ways in which a party dress restricted me; I was restricted anyway, and a pretty dress gave as much sense of power as it took away.

Dressing Up

Early exposure to Honey Bunch gave me my first access to the mutable detail and enduring significance of girls' clothing in series fiction. Being able to wallow in these accounts was one pleasure of learning to be an autonomous reader. Bedtime stories did not include extended descriptions of frocks (in part because the world of heroes involved in our evening stories was heavily male, a fact that escaped me at the time).

I was interested in girls' apparel from a very early age; something about "dressing up" and "good clothes" appealed to me from toddlerhood onward (as a last resort, I am told, my mother would occasionally dress me in my Sunday garments; she swore that my behaviour improved, at least temporarily). Colour, texture, pattern, drape, detail—everything about a pretty dress called to me (perhaps in part because most of what I wore was so stripped of such interest, so functional, utilitarian, and repetitive). I cut pictures of dresses out of the mail-order catalogues and glued them into scrapbooks (I especially liked "Big and Little Sister" ensembles). I lovingly accumulated paper dolls and their wardrobes. I dressed and redressed my own dolls and, once I learned how to knit, I made outfits for them. And I lavished a profoundly embodied form of attention on the garments of many fictional heroines.

Alice Major (2011) points out that we derive some of our understanding of the world through a "shared body plan" (p. 14) with others: "Our capacity for mapping the actions of other bodies in our own brains ultimately gives us a basis for assessing how well another has succeeded. Because we are designed for empathy, we have a basis for assessing differences" (p. 15).

Honey Bunch's little dress, described in considerable detail below, was entirely recognizable to me. The physicality of trying on a dress, the emotional surge of nice clothes, made sense to me at a very intimate and embodied level.

> Upstairs there were charming dresses for little girls and Honey Bunch tried on some while Mother and Aunt Julia watched her. The very prettiest of all was a blue linen, just the color of Honey Bunch's blue eyes. It was made with a little round white yoke which was hemstitched to the dress and the hem was hemstitched, too. Just above the hem were embroidered white daisies. (Thorndyke, 1923b, pp. 126–127)

Nobody would call Helen Louise Thorndyke a mistress of prose, but even banal writers can strike evocative notes, and, for me, Honey Bunch was only the first in a long line of literary heroines with highly specified wardrobes. Often the clothes themselves were mysterious to me; I could comprehend Honey Bunch's embroidered daisies, but what was I to make of Marjorie's motoring outfit?

> The children all had new motor coats of pongee, which they could wear over other wraps if necessary. The girls also had fascinating little hoods of shirred silk, Marjorie's being rose color, and Kitty's blue. They greatly admired themselves and each other in these costumes, and Marjorie declared it gave her a trippy feeling just to look at them. (Wells, 1911, p. 33)

What is pongee? What does it look and feel like? Is it stiff or slippery? Why were their hoods separate from their coats? Why special clothes for "motoring" in any case? The lure of the rose and blue silk (shirred for extra tactile and visual appeal) was real, but the rest was exceedingly strange. To me, the aura of "exotic but baffling" still lingers around some of these words; for decades, I remembered their bewildering allure.

Clothing did not have to be glamorous to be intriguing. Margaret Sidney's (1955) five little Peppers in their hardscrabble way almost never wore interesting clothing, but Polly's button boots were at least mysterious:

> Everything had gone wrong with Polly that day. It began with her boots. Of all the things in the world that tried Polly's patience, the worst were the troublesome little black buttons that adorned those useful parts of her clothing and that were fondly supposed to be there when needed. But they never were. The little black things seemed to be invested with a special spite, for one by one they would hop off on the slightest provocation, and go rolling over the floor just when she was in her most terrible hurry, compelling her to fly for needle and thread on the instant.
>
> For one thing Mrs. Pepper was very strict about—and that was, Polly should do nothing else till the buttons were all on again and the boots buttoned up firm and snug. (p. 255).

Polly's boots are a trial to her, as much of my own clothing was to me— the heavy winter coat that was more often wet than dry, the ugly galoshes that weighed down my feet, the dreary navy-blue bloomers whose absence would get me in trouble at school (in an all-girls class we could have bloomer inspection, standing by our desks and flipping up our tunics to the modest extent necessary to demonstrate we were wearing our bloomers over our regular underpants; hard to imagine today, perhaps, but it happened every week). But I had also an affective repertoire of how the best clothes could turn you into a different, more accomplished and complete person. Such knowledge deeply informed my reading of one of the most famous "dress" scenes in all my reading: the Christmas in *Anne of Green Gables* when Matthew gives Anne a dress with puffed sleeves.

> Anne took the dress and looked at it in reverent silence. Oh, how pretty it was—a lovely soft brown gloria with all the gloss of silk; a skirt with dainty frills and shirrings; a waist elaborately pin-tucked in the most fashionable way, with a little ruffle of filmy lace at the neck. But the sleeves—they were the crowning glory! Long elbow cuffs and above them two beautiful puffs divided by rows of shirring and bows of brown silk ribbon. (Montgomery, 1975/1909, p. 168)

I had no idea what a puffed sleeve looked like, but I knew why it was important. The essential and important glory of that gloria was entirely transparent and comprehensible to me from the moment I first encountered it at the age of nine.

The sensory appeal of the clothing in these stories was vivid even when the particulars were mystifying. The visceral call of these literary dresses intrigues me; I think at least a partial explanation can be found in contemporary neuroscience.

> *Brain scans are revealing what happens in our heads when we read a detailed description, an evocative metaphor or an emotional exchange between characters. Stories, this research is showing, stimulate the brain and even change how we act in life.*
>
> *Researchers have long known that the "classical" language regions, like Broca's area and Wernicke's area, are involved in how the brain interprets written words. What scientists have come to realize in the last few years is that narratives activate many other parts of our brains as well, suggesting why the experience of reading can feel so alive. Words like "lavender," "cinnamon" and "soap," for example, elicit a response not only from the language-processing areas of our brains, but also those devoted to dealing with smells. (Paul, 2012, n.p.)*

Sandra Weber and Claudia Mitchell (2004) suggest that clothes are evocative for many women, and that talking about dresses is very meaningful for them:

> *Ask women to talk or write about dresses, and without much prompting, they will regale you with detailed snippets from their lives, anecdotes that start out ostensibly about clothes, but end up being about so much more— events, family, community, relationships, body-image, feelings, aspirations, attitudes, beliefs and thoughts about all sorts of things. In the telling or writing of these autobiographical stories, an item of clothing becomes a springboard, an axis of rotation, or a structural grounding for a detailed account of life events. (pp. 3–4)*

I suggest that just as the word "cinnamon" may activate areas in my brain associated with smelling (and with affective connotations of the odour of cinnamon), so some of these details of clothing linked me into at least part of that network of associations and relationships that Weber and Mitchell describe so vividly. Dresses connect profoundly with notions of "identity, body, and culture" (Weber & Mitchell, 2004, p. 4). They are also very physical and tactile, and have high proprioceptive salience. Their texture against the skin, their flow and drape around the body, the sounds of swishing skirts, the feel of fabric sliding under the fingers, the colours delighting the peripheral vision, these sensations and many more are instantly available in my brain for activation on meeting a evocative word. Our phrase for the *hand* of a fabric is significant: to be able to grasp and manipulate colour and pattern is deeply appealing in highly aesthetic ways—and that tactile pleasure is stored in the brain, waiting to be activated by relevant words on the page. The cultural and social appeal of wearing a dress that flatters you is also deeply embedded in many psyches, ready to be tapped at the first hint of description. Even flat on a hanger, a dress carries with it an aura of embodied and social experience that seeps into at least my own reading about clothing to this day. The sexual allure was an underground feature initially, but I suspect some of my earliest latent notions of such appeal came through wearing and reading about dresses.

That sense of the potency of the pretty dress haunted my reading, and I have no doubt a number of elements in my brain lit up when I encountered a fictional heroine with a completely satisfactory frock. To the embodied understanding was added an awareness of acute social status considerations and of the significance of fitting in or standing outside the norm. These elements in my stored understanding of the world would have been ready for activation as I read words about girls' clothing.

Dresses were important in many of the books of that era. It was not my only route to fluency, but understanding the dress—physically, socially, emotionally, and semiotically—was one means by which I learned to enliven my reading in the most literal sense, to animate it, inhabit the stereotypes, and bring them to life in my mind. It is, of course, a highly transferrable skill. Once you learn that your own experience can vivify the words in front of you, you have taken a major step to becoming a reader.

Working Stereotypes

The literary role of the dress, though not universal in its acquired meaning, was certainly accessible to me through the vehicle of my own lived experience. Other forms of understanding I acquired in one book and transferred to others, by means of a kind of intertextual bootstrapping. Certain basic images became available to me in their most stereotypical format, and I made heavy use of their transferrable qualities.

Making Sense

One important example of how I learned some very basic stereotypes comes from the *Betsy* books, especially the first in the series. These books, by Carolyn Haywood, provided a sequence of very domestic adventures featuring Betsy and her friends as they went to school in a very ordinary (if affluent) way. An online biography of the author suggests that Haywood was creating what might be described as "a beginner's guide to stereotypes" with some deliberation: "Harcourt Brace's juvenile department editor, Elizabeth Hamilton, met the young Haywood and gave her the direction of her literary career: 'Write something about little American children doing the things that little American children like to do'" (Ford, 2005, n.p.).

Haywood obliged, and the results, for me, served as a kind of Rosetta Stone to help me to translate American school customs into something I could process through my own experiences. Some of it was very familiar:

> *Betsy was alone now in a strange new place. What a big room it was!*
> *One whole side of the room was made of windows. They were the biggest*
> *windows Betsy had ever seen. The walls seemed so far away and parts of*
> *them were black. In some cases there was writing on the black walls. And*
> *the ceiling—how high it was! It looked way, way off. So this was school! This*
> *great big room with the black walls and all the little desks was school. This*
> *was where she would have to come every morning. Betsy blinked her eyes to*
> *keep back the tears.* (Haywood, 1939, p. 10)

Other passages provided basic information that stood me in very good stead over many years. One example is a description of American Thanksgiving that even a beginning reader (one who is destined to read very many references to American Thanksgiving over the next few years) can comprehend and store away:

Then Miss Grey told the children about the first Thanksgiving which was
hundreds of years ago. She told them about the people who had come
to America from away across the ocean, and how they had to cut down
the trees to build their houses and dig big rocks out of the ground before
they could plant their seeds. Miss Grey said that these people were called
Pilgrims. The Pilgrims were so thankful to God for His care that they decided
to have a special day just to say thank you to Him. "And that is the reason,"
said Miss Grey, "that we have a Thanksgiving Day every year." (p. 78)

Miss Grey's account of Thanksgiving could hardly be more Eurocentric, but, even misleading as it is, it served a utilitarian purpose for me, as I read about Thanksgiving in my November issues of *Jack and Jill*, came across references to it in television shows, and encountered more detailed descriptions in historical novels. Canadian Thanksgiving comes in October and does not represent any grand pioneer narrative at all, being rather a mutation of the harvest festival in the church year. I would have been considerably more perplexed about the fancier American version without this early primer to supply me with that instant grasp of the stereotype.

When I located *"B" is for Betsy* in 2012, I discovered that it also helpfully provides a beginner's guide to the circus. Even amusement fairs, let alone full-fledged circuses, rarely visited St. John's, simply because the transport costs were so horrendous. I did not see a real circus until I lived in Edmonton as a teenager.

My beloved picture book, *The Story of Margaret Field-Mouse*, gave me my first oblique glimpse of the circus; Margaret was unhappily caged up as part of the freak show after Fairy Pimpernel made her enormous. But that book assumes that even picture-book readers have some life experience to bring to bear on the concept of circus life. Haywood is more helpful; the obliging Miss Grey asks her class to talk about what they know of the circus. If she had said, "Now children, the readers of this book need some working stereotypes to be getting on with," she could hardly have elicited a more useful account:

Nearly all of the children had seen the circus the last time it had come to
town. So they had a long talk about the circus. First they talked about the
barker. Billy said that the barker is the man who stands outside of the big
tent and tells the people what they will see inside.

Betsy told about the bare-back rider [which she had learned about
earlier in the chapter] and Ellen told about the trained seals that play ball
and bounce the ball right on the tips of their noses.

They talked about the elephants and the lions, the clowns and the trained
dogs. Christopher said, "I always buy a balloon from the balloon-man."
(Haywood, 1939, pp. 128–129)

There is much more. As a working kit for an isolated reader who would wait
a long time for the real thing, this description was little short of miraculously cogent. My inveterate habit of constant reborrowing from the library
and rereading any book I enjoyed meant that there was a good chance
I would encounter this description both before and after meeting other
accounts of the circus, and the definitional value to me of Haywood's plain
and unpretentious description would be reinforced.

Unlike the descriptions of pretty dresses, which I understood physically
as well as culturally, these social schemas and scripts were simply supplied
in one book and applied in others. Yet where I could, I read my own body
into the text. Betsy's account of the far-away windows and ceilings and the
blinked-back tears on the first day of school had real emotional meaning for
me and grounded some of the more unfamiliar descriptions.

Recurring Stereotypes

I read about girls like Betsy, but I also read about young women, and I drew
on some of their experiences to inform my expectations about growing up.
Most women in my life were mothers, or else middle-aged and unmarried.
I knew few young women. As a result, I felt my series heroines provided
insight into the challenges of moving into society as an adult, a process
otherwise almost completely opaque to me.

Reading about girls and their dresses gave me some authority as a
reader; I could bring my own active repertoire to bear on the process.
When it came to reading about girls and their jobs and their boyfriends,
I was on much more tenuous ground and had to take the author's word
for most of what transpired. Nobody will be surprised to learn that the
romances leaned toward the vapid, and the career prospects tended to work
out within a very restrictive framework of possibilities. I suppose some
compensation was that the lives of my series heroines did not seem entirely
out of reach to me, although Nancy Drew with all her advanced competence

and capabilities never did appeal to me as much as the heroines who manifested a few more vulnerabilities.

Growing Up

I preferred characters who grew older, branching out into new adventures. I also liked series worlds that added new characters but did not necessarily abandon the old. And I was always enchanted if I read a reference to a prior point of a character's history and could identify the reference from a book read previously. That delight was rare because of my spotty, random, and nonsequential access to series titles.

Thus, I preferred Judy Bolton (Sutton) and Beverly Gray (Blank) to Nancy Drew (Keene), who, however talented and successful she may have been as a teen detective, was actually a failure when it came to growing up. I liked the two nurses, Sue Barton (Boylston) and Cherry Ames (Wells), for the same reasons of increasing maturity and competence.

The stories of the Abbey Girls (Oxenham) and, to a lesser extent, the ballet stories of Sadler's Wells (Hill) similarly pleased me, but their British context, compounded in the ballet stories by a completely alien dance culture, made them stranger. The *Abbey* books, however, milked the pretty-dress motif at a high level; one after another of the main characters became May Queen at the girls' school, chose colours and a flower, and adorned herself in regal robes and a floral crown. These books also offered a very romantic take on British history; one of the heroines owned a ruined abbey (destroyed by Henry VIII) that sat picturesquely in the grounds of the stately home owned by another character, her identical cousin. When they weren't parading in their royal robes, the girls made a point of discovering artifacts of the old abbey, buried underground by the monks to save them from Henry VIII, or hidden under piles of Tudor detritus.

The Abbey Girls also aged, married, and had children who eventually turned into new heroines of the series (Oxenham published these books over a period of about forty-five years). Nevertheless, it was the accumulating history of the abbey rather than the ever-proliferating crowd of youngsters that gave this series its narrative arc. This plot element, though it pleased me greatly, reduced the ability of the Abbey Girls to serve as possible models for adult life; they were too foreign and exotic (and, in good British fashion, they inherited and/or married into most of what made their lives so appealing; Oxenham pays lip service only to the idea of earning the good life through hard work). I could, and did, imagine myself an Abbey

Girl, choose my regal flower and colours (they varied), and mark out the territory of my own abbey in the grass—but that was the end of it. No matter how well I exercised my imagination, I could not mentally conjure up romantic Tudor artifacts beneath a Newfoundland field.

But imagining myself as a nosy journalist (Beverly Gray) or a sleuthing secretary (Judy Bolton) was more or less within my range of make-believe potential. What I particularly admired about them, at the time and in memory, was the nonchalant way they took on the requirements of adult life. With my inveterate preference for relationships, I was hooked by the network of friends and lovers that surrounded each of these heroines, regarding the mystery component of the novel as a kind of temporary framework on which the essential ongoing story was supported. It was the backstories that I remembered in every case; clichéd as they certainly were, they represented new news to me in middle childhood.

Judy Bolton was my favourite. Although she settled for secretarial life and married her lawyer boss (and old playmate), Peter Dobbs, I read her as a more fully realized character than most of the others. It is said of Nancy Drew that she combines the best of being "feminine" and being an achiever, but Nancy Drew's femininity is radically less nurturing and affectionate than Judy Bolton's. As a child, I appreciated the loving commitment to her family and friends that Judy manifests so clearly; in many ways it is highly limiting, but I knew how to make sense of a life constrained by domestic commitments. And the idea that Judy could grow up (we first meet her in high school), fall in love, get married, and *continue detecting* was immensely liberating to me, feeble as that insight may sound in the twenty-first century. Much of my literature presented marriage as the signal for retirement from interesting life; Judy was revolutionary.

Beverly Gray offered a different kind of breakthrough. Determined to make her own way in New York City, she turns down her parents' offer of an allowance after she graduates from college:

> "I'm—I want to do everything myself. I don't want money coming in just as though I didn't—need a job. I'm going to make my own living myself! Don't you see? I want to have to depend on myself—not somebody else!"
>
> Her mother smiled sympathetically, "I understand." (Blank, 1935, p. 21)

Obtaining a job as a journalist, Beverly lives a glamorous life in New York, sharing an apartment with several chums and (daringly) being in love with two different men over the course of the series. She was engaged to the second man by the time of the latest book I read, but still detecting.

Nurses Sue Barton and Cherry Ames highlighted a quality shared by many of my series heroines: a dedication to being maximally competent within their field of expertise. The restrictions placed on young women, so notorious a component of female life in the 1950s, were limitations on the number of fields open to them. Within this constrained range of possibilities, however, these heroines exerted themselves to excel. Sue and Cherry studied hard, took their responsibilities seriously, and appreciated that it was possible for them to make the world a better place through their own dedication.

I was very familiar with this ethos. At home and at school, the expectation was that girls must work hard and do their very best. The limitations (and they were certainly real) did not let me off the hook for achieving my utmost, at least for the phase of childhood that I cover in this study. It was largely in adolescence that I, like countless other girl readers, began to incorporate the restraints of being a girl into my own sense of myself; as a child, I was conscious of few such restrictions. My mother certainly wanted me to observe the decencies, and she occasionally saw the need to inculcate some notions of feminine decorum—don't turn somersaults in your nightie, sit with your knees together when wearing a dress, and the like. But such chidings were passing annoyances and did not absolve me from ambition.

I am less interested in my own experience, however, than I am in addressing how stereotypes of one kind of femininity or another enabled the reading of these books. What did girl readers learn that they could transfer from one book to another? What are the stereotypical patterns that could help them to decipher these plots and characters?

Issues of competence do loom large. Sue Barton is a good nurse both technically and humanly, from her very earliest experiences onward. In a scene from *Sue Barton: Student Nurse*, she assists with the removal of Miss Coleman's stitches:

> *Miss Cameron's instructions rang in her ears as she turned the bedclothes down to the patient's waist and laid the sterile towel containing the surgical instruments on the folds, exactly as she had been taught. She removed the safety pins from the dressing, opened a package of gauze sponges, and dropped them on the opened sterile towel....*

She laid a warm, reassuring hand on Miss Coleman's thin one. For an instant Sue felt that she was not herself but Miss Coleman. She could feel the weight of the bedclothes on her feet, the smoothness of the sheet beneath her, the tiredness of lying in bed for a long time, and the stir of apprehension at the thought of stitches, and she looked down at the woman with such a warmth of understanding that Miss Coleman's fingers tightened gratefully about her hand. (Boylston, 1939, p. 73)

Proficiency was not confined to nurses. The dancers who make it to school at Sadler's Wells operate on the same ethos of competence fuelled by hard work and a kind of imaginative investment in the final result that indicates how well worth doing it truly is. Veronica yearns to get to the Wells, even though stuck in remote Scotland; she diligently keeps up her practice:

Don't think I forgot about my dancing in all this. I practised faithfully every morning before breakfast, and often again before we went out....

[Fiona] watched me doing pliés, grands battements, *and* développés. *Once Sebastian came, but I think he considered it rather on the dull side—all those exercises and no real dancing at all—but he was too polite to say so. Or perhaps he realized that my* pliés *and* battements *were like his scales and exercises at the piano—dull but necessary. (Hill, 1988/1950, pp. 125–126)*

As with Sue Barton, the professional vocabulary aids the sense of being an insider in a complex world. And as with Sue Barton's imaginative investment in her patient's well-being, so Veronica occupies her dancing imaginatively as well as physically:

I walked out into the wings and rose sur les pointes. *The first notes of Tchaikovsky's music were falling on the air like drops of ice tinkling into a crystal goblet. I saw in my imagination the snowy woods round Bracken Hall on a winter's day—the fir trees standing motionless, like enchanted princesses, their frosted arms outspread. I heard in my mind the church bells sounding thin and unreal in the cold, blue air. All this I thought of as I executed the crisp, clear-cut steps of that wonderful dance of the Sugar-Plum Fairy. I was a maiden of the ice; a snow queen; a frosted fairy of pink and silver, with a brittle crown of frozen dewdrops on my head. All this I tried to express in my dancing. (pp. 157–159)*

I make no case for this passage as a piece of writing. What I do argue is that the stereotype of the girls' series heroine as represented in these books is more complex than our own current stereotypes *about* these books. The heroines are certainly "feminine" in many conventional 1950s ways: they are attractive, dainty, girlish, and many other diminishing adjectives. Nevertheless they strive for their own version of excellence through passion, study, practice, and hard work—and they recognize the achievement of that excellence through a form of imaginative transformation. Their limits lie in the restriction of fields open to them, externally rather than internally imposed.

This pattern shows up in series after series, manifesting itself in different ways. Nancy Drew, as usual, gets a few shortcuts; we never see her in the effortful acquisition of expertise, though she is not afraid of hard work. In her first appearance in *The Secret of the Old Clock*, she is driving a boat whose engine suddenly fails: "Nancy studied the engine doubtfully. Like most girls, she had never interested herself in the mechanics of what made wheels go around" (Keene, 1930, p. 115). Yet by the next page she has become impatient with waiting to be rescued and miraculously fixes the engine.

> *For want of other occupation, Nancy turned her attention again to the engine. When the sun sank into the water several hours later, she was still bending over it, a determined look in her eyes.*
>
> *"There!" she muttered as she straightened up. "I've certainly done enough to it. If it won't go now, it never will."*
>
> *She gave the wheel a vicious swing, and, to her astonishment, the engine began its steady roar as unconcerned as though it had never stopped.*
> *(pp. 116–117)*

Not for Nancy the labours of the hospital classroom or the practice barre, nor does she put in Beverly Gray's unceasing hours at the typewriter keyboard. Nancy achieves with a lesser investment of sweat equity. Yet Nancy, perhaps more than any of the others, represents a line summed up by a young male reader: "I just like being good at it" (Smith & Wilhelm, 2004, p. 454). Michael Smith and Jeffrey Wilhelm (2004) explore "the importance of competence in boys' literate lives" (p. 454) but are at pains to point out that they did not investigate girls so cannot say whether or not it matters for girls, too. The evidence of these books suggests that girls, too, like to be good at things.

As a working stereotype, this kind of character is purposeful and action-oriented, and I certainly recall feeling invigorated by proxy as I read these predictable stories—an embodied sensation in itself. As I became knowledgeable about the pattern itself, I was increasingly able to pride myself on being good at reading as well.

Subliminal Stereotypes

All girl detectives had preposterous adventures, but Beverly Gray's were probably the most ridiculous. When I revisited these books, I was surprised at the ludicrousness of the plots (Mackey, 2006). Gypsies, insane hermits, wild animals, and numerous swarthy and sinister ethnic villains (including cannibals and head shrinkers) dog her every step. Over the years, I forgot every one of these horrific hazards and remembered only the romance of city life, the lure of journalism, the mystique of the two men dancing attendance, and Beverly's robust determination to make her own way. I will return to this issue of forgetting below, but first I want to take a sober look at what did not go entirely away.

If my filtering of the positive lessons from these silly books were "the end of the story," it would be a pretty metaphor for ways in which a child can extract what she needs from the most lurid and nonsensical raw material. Yet when I came to look more closely at the *Beverly Gray* novels, I discovered a depressing subtext lingering for decades in the basement of my own mind.

"Seeing" the World

Author Clair Blank wrote the first four books in the *Beverly Gray* series while still in high school and had them published within a year of graduation. Her own life reads much more like a pre-feminist stereotype than does that of her heroine:

> *Unlike Beverly Gray, Clair Blank did not lead the exciting life of a newspaper reporter and traveling writer. Clair never traveled to any of the exotic places that she describes in the* Beverly Gray *books. Clair graduated from college, worked as a typist and secretary, and during World War II worked as a volunteer for a group that drove visiting Army officers around locally. Clair quit her secretarial job after she married, choosing to write and take care of her two sons. (White, n.d., n.p.)*

Blank, it would seem, was open to operating from stereotypes of "abroad" every bit as much as any of her readers.

At the core of the series lies the yacht *Susabella*, owned by one of Beverly's rich friends. Beverly and her chums (plus a chaperone, since the pals include men as well as women) take a round-the-world cruise that lasts over several books and leads to many utterly implausible adventures. Three main titles dealing with this particular cruise are *Beverly Gray on a World Cruise* (1936), *Beverly Gray in the Orient* (1937), and *Beverly Gray on a Treasure Hunt* (1938); I read all of them.

Rereading these books many years later was a troubling experience. Beverly's high-minded determination to run her own life survived in a sunlit (if largely unvisited) corner of my mind. Beverly's melodramatic encounters and escapes seem to have discharged harmlessly, leaving no traces. But as I read these three novels, I found myself uneasily recognizing old, sinister stereotypes about the rest of the world that seem to have lingered somewhere in the basement of my mind, offering dismayingly familiar resonances as I met them again.

In many ways, I was not a curious reader. I took all my books on face value and pretty much assumed that any of them would necessarily include details that made no sense to me. I had no interest in pursuing these confusions any further and forgot plot details almost as readily. I assembled as much as I could of what the book supplied me in the way of tools for reading it and simply ploughed forward. Where I had relevant life experience, I imported it. Where I had intertextual reinforcement, I acknowledged it. Where I had almost nothing in the way of extra-novel support, I simply subscribed to the book's assertions on their own terms. I do not for a moment think I was unique in this attitude, though I know that other readers (among them, some of my brothers) would have assumed a more curious stance and, at a minimum, dug up a map to follow the friends' journey. I did nothing of the kind and simply took Blank's descriptions of the world "as read."

In the course of her world cruise and assorted side outings, Beverly visits many places, some clean and inviting. Take Switzerland:

Beverly stepped out onto the balcony overlooking the front of the hotel and stretched luxuriously. Early risers were already skating on the great sheet of ice that fronted the hotel. This was her first morning view and she marveled

at the serene calmness over everything. The fir trees and rooftops glistened
with snow. Behind the valley rose high snow-tipped mountains, one behind
the other. (Blank, 1936, p. 144)

This world made sense to me as a reader of *Heidi*. Other scenes are more exotic, and I had less potential for running intertextual checks. Here is Cairo, for example:

In all she saw the wonder of the East, the slow, leisurely world of which she
knew so little. A world which modern civilization was surely and relentlessly
smothering beneath modern machines and methods. And yet the Pyramids
would stand. The desert would remain even when these ancient shops were
gone. She thought as she strolled on of the saying she had heard: "All things
fear Time, but Time fears the Pyramids." (Blank, 1936, p. 191)

Since adventures are part of the package, it is not long before Egypt presents a more sinister and superstitious face. Beverly's friend Lenora insists on buying a scarab, engraved with the words, "Destruction to those who take from Egypt the things which are Egypt's" (p. 241). Complications inevitably ensue.

India is also a cliché. Still ruled by the British, it offers scenes of native crowds, the white magnificence of the Taj Mahal, elephants and polo matches, and big-game potential (for the men). The comforts offered by the Raj are matched by native squalor:

Benares, the sacred city, was literally the melting pot of all India. The sick
came to visit the ghats and bathe in the holy water of Mother Ganges.
It was the hiding and breeding place of criminals, the hatching place of
conspiracies.

What impressed Lenora were the fakirs, ragged, unkempt, ash-smeared
objects that seemed hardly human. Their attitudes and positions which they
chose to "acquire merit" were sometimes ludicrous, such as the prize fakir
of them all who had all his bones painted in white outline on his brown skin.
As Lenora remarked, it was like looking at a group of circus freaks. (Blank,
1937, pp. 88–89)

Naturally, when the gang of chums reaches China, their surroundings become even more mysterious:

It seemed incredulous [sic] that anything of this sort should happen in such modern times. Many people had told her that the Orient is strange. Many things happen there that cannot rationally be explained or corrected. Places such as this, built in the times of the ancient East, still exist behind the veneer of civilization. Modern education, modern science, modern manners—all these cannot reach to every corner of the Orient. (Blank, 1937, p. 238)

And so forth. The adventurers alternate between the bright, up-to-date glamour of the British and American sectors of various colonized countries and the native quarters of crowded shops and interchangeable and unknowable people.

There is nothing exceptional in these orientalist descriptions or the racist indifference to any points of individuality among the native populations. What surprised me as I read these pages again was the access they provided to a long-ignored matrix of stereotypical assumptions underlying my own mental sketch-map of the world.

As it happens, I was unlucky with my geography lessons. The exoticizing pages of Atwood and Thomas's *Visits in Other Lands* were followed by the geography of Newfoundland, then of Canada. In Grade 8 and Grade 9, as a consequence of moving, I studied Latin America twice. By Grade 10 I had moved on to Social Studies and its reduced geography quotient with a largely North American orientation.

My ignorance of world geography was an intellectual Achilles heel for a long time. I have always vaguely assumed that I really know very little about the eastern hemisphere. Instead of a reassuringly neutral empty set, however, I discover, when I look at these books, that the stereotypes of Beverly's world trip still resonate. When I summon "enough to be going on with" about many places of the world, some residual base "knowledge" supplied by Clair Blank still lurks below my level of conscious attention. Carolyn Haywood gave me a working schema of American Thanksgiving, one that I regularly revisited (and, of course, one that is exceedingly racist by omission). It seems that Clair Blank gave me a working schema of, say, the Taj Mahal. I am not sure I gave the Taj Mahal one single thought between the time of reading *Beverly Gray in the Orient* sometime in the late 1950s and the occasion of Princess Diana's visit in 1992, at which point I wondered vaguely how I knew about this famous site. Now I know: from the *Beverly Gray* books. My ignorance is not defensible, but it was real and made me vulnerable to some very suspect working theories about the world.

My notion of American Thanksgiving served as a *working* schema, available near the surface of my mind to be challenged by more complicated versions as I grew older. On the other hand, my inchoate ideas of Egypt, India, China, and several other significant countries, developed through my encounters with Beverly's world cruise, seem to have operated almost on the basis of *nonworking*, dormant schemas, which are probably even more insidious since they remain unchallenged.

I wonder if such idle and unthinking ignorance is even possible in the era of television and the Internet—but I suspect the main ingredient, a geographically incurious mind, is still all that is really needed. A diet of Disney and commercially protected websites for Barbie and the like would probably provide equally limiting fodder for basic schemas of the world. It is disquieting to observe my cherished childhood literacy fostering such an inadequate worldview—and even more disturbing to realize the longevity of some of these residual stereotypes latent in my mind to this day.

It is not that I don't now know better. Of course I do. My current mental globe is relatively accurate. I have equipped myself as well as I can to read *against* the kind of racist claptrap that dominates many of Blank's plots. I have travelled reasonably widely. My point is that even though these demeaning stereotypes have been replaced in my mind by a more robust and respectful sense of other cultures, they have not entirely erased themselves. Early reading does count. We know this, which is one reason why we encourage it. But, in part because of its very potency, early reading is not essentially innocent. I stepped into a world of ugly and unjust power relationships with these trivial stories, and their nasty traces remain buried deep.

Transient Stereotypes

Yet not everything lingers. Some information gleaned through my pell-mell rush through series books simply lasted only as long as it was necessary to fuel the reading itself, then disappeared without trace. I have referred earlier to my amazement at how completely I forgot the nature of Beverly Gray's stupid adventures. In some cases I dismissed even the working stereotypes that let me get to the end of a particular story.

One example that interests me is *Beverly Gray's Quest* (1942), which I mentioned in the first chapter of this book. I was quite sure I had read this novel, even remembered sitting on the window seat in my bedroom. A vivid start to my rereading experience with this title—but I was soon lost in confusion. In this book, Beverly's new fiancé Larry sets off on a

South American adventure, in pursuit of a giant emerald. Hollywood has purchased film rights for Beverly's novel, and she and her girlfriends decide to drive from New York to Los Angeles, passing many famous American landmarks along the way. They have not been long on the west coast, however, when they learn that Larry and his colleague have disappeared without trace in the Amazon jungle. Beverly talks a Hollywood colleague into lending her a plane and sets out to find Larry in the jungle. Superstitious natives, frightened of the emerald's bad name, refuse to take the search party all the way. Nevertheless, the group locates first Larry's crashed plane, next his colleague, and finally Larry himself in the depths of the jungle. Furthermore, while they are thus in pursuit, they run across Beverly's first boyfriend, Jim, who had headed to South America when it became obvious to him that Beverly loved another.

You would think it would be impossible to forget *all* of this, but the book seemed so unfamiliar that I thought I must have been mistaken about ever having read it. After all, even though I was skilful at forgetting silly adventures with head-shrinking natives (who duly appear in the last stages of this book), I normally retained information of potential utility for reading further books; and some skeletal notion of the American national parks, Old Faithful, Hollywood, and the like, might be sufficiently useful elsewhere that I would stow some of it away. Even if I only remembered essential links in the network of relationships, there was that astonishing reappearance of Jim after many books' absence; that surprise surely should stand out as memorable.

As I have described, a silly line of a misquoted poem was viscerally familiar to me, and it convinced me that I did indeed read the book at least once during my childhood. So not only the plot but also the working stereotypes that enabled me to finish the book in the first place have all vanished from my mind, leaving only an accidental trace of a line of jingle. Perhaps my understanding of geysers and Old Faithful was so tenuous that the mention of these phenomena in the book did not even upgrade to being a working stereotype in the short term, and so departed along with the head-shrinking natives, leaving no residue to offer any sense of identification. Or perhaps I read the book only once or twice and paid the price for my normal heedless dash through its pages.

In any case, the absence of almost any remote recognition of the different ingredients of the book is chastening. How much of what I read simply vanished? If nothing remains at all, are these hours of reading simply wasted? I may be self-justifying a childhood marked by exceptional futility, but it seems to me that even if there is no residue, that experience of "coming across" as a reader, of learning the power of the deictic shift *in the moment*, retains some value, not critical but deeply invested.

By contrast, the British stereotypes of children's lives that I encountered, most frequently in the various Enid Blyton books, were equally transient but in a different way. They confirmed that St. John's truly was a North American city, despite its strong ties to Britain and Ireland. I did develop some awareness, for example, that the "hols" of the British children in my stories were equivalent to our own summer vacations. But these holidays were especially significant because brothers and sisters attended separate boarding schools and did not see each other for months at a time. I learned that these conditions applied—but they held no resonance for me. I knew this information and I applied it appropriately as I read, but I could not imagine it or bring it to mental life. My brothers were so interwoven into my daily existence that I simply could not come up with an emotionally effective scenario in which they and I were routinely sent away from home in separate directions for months at a time. My engagement with the Blyton books, though I enjoyed the adventures, slid across the surface of the pages; the experience was simply not penetrable or porous to my own life experience.

The Live Power of Stereotypes

Stereotypes enable reading and they also constrain it. As building blocks they offer the possibility of developing steps and ladders and also the potential to create barriers. Pursuing this line of questioning through my childhood reading has been at different times exhilarating and sobering. To what extent did my early capacity to recognize and feel the appeal of a heroine's dress bind me to the whole idea of reading with ever greater loyalty? Or reinforce an uncritical sense of the material pleasures of femininity, to a degree that undercut my potential for analytical assessment? To what extent did my calculating importation of unfamiliar stereotypes into my daily reading lead me toward an intellectual life, in which I relished the delights of reading beyond what I could automatically understand? Alternatively, to what degree did such an approach foster an unquestioning acceptance of what I was told, even if it made little local sense to me? To what extent did (and do) those unrefreshed and unexamined stereotypes of foreign countries lie dormant in my mind like landmines? And how irrevo-cably lost is a huge amount of my life of reading because of my apparently unlimited capacity for forgetting?

Regardless of all these questions, I do not doubt that reading huge numbers of series books gave me the opportunity to develop fluency as a reader, provided me with a number of working understandings of the world (productive or pernicious), and introduced me to a form of pleasure that was paradoxically both deep and very shallow. If I had read only these books, however, shallowness would have prevailed.

If the vague and empty characters that Nodelman describes help us to gather speed and automaticity as we learn to process print, they serve a useful function. But the reader who stops at such colouring-book personali-ties misses out on confronting the individuality of more complex characters and runs the risk of reading only mirrors of her own perceptions. Even Judy Bolton, the most individual of the characters cited here (with the exception of Anne Shirley, visiting this chapter from the one that follows, so to speak), provided me with only general insights. Despite the generic and highly prej-udicial "otherness" ascribed to foreigners in many of these books, it was to the more challenging books that I would have to turn for knowledge that the world is made up of people actually (and in individual detail) very different from myself.

6
The Invitation
of Literature
Growing

As for Joe, he had finished the whistle he

for Rufus and had started making one for hims

the kitchen fire going, the ashes sifted, and the

from freezing. He tried to become more in

Catherine-the-cat, but her cold, aloof nature w

aking

kept

pipes

with

to be

ALTHOUGH I RACED THROUGH all my books in equally pell-mell fashion, both on first reading and again on later encounters, I was aware that not all books were created equal. As I reread my favourites over and over again, it was clear to me that some of them offered better possibilities for layering up a complex response than others did. In this chapter, I will explore this more challenging category of books, the ones we are more likely to mean when we talk about "children's literature."

A child is making sense of the world at all times. A book that successfully addresses a child often invites its readers to reflect on that sense-making activity itself, both explicitly and implicitly. Some of the best books offer a metacognitive hall of mirrors, and part of the delight of reading them lies in the acute recognition of *thinking at work*.

I will consider some of the implications of this form of metacognitive recognition by way of a detour into a very specific category of my adult reading that may offer some helpful vocabulary.

Reading of Validation

In my late twenties, living in the United Kingdom, I read *The Fire-Dwellers* by Margaret Laurence (1969), which my mother had sent as a present. I was still a momentum reader, but I found myself paralyzed on page twelve, unable to move on. The source of my fixation was laughably insignificant, a single sentence fragment: "On the train, a Newfoundland woman with six kids, going to join her husband in an army camp in Chilliwack" (Laurence, 1969, p. 12). I stared, hypnotized, at the page for a long time and turned it reluctantly.

Although this was my first reading of *The Fire-Dwellers*, I knew from experience with other Laurence novels that the author was speaking to me as a Canadian reader. That woman and her six children therefore acquired ontological status by osmosis. They were in a novel speaking to me; by implication, therefore, they had what can only be paradoxically described as a true fictional reality. I was moved to meet them, even though I never saw them again.

Perhaps a dozen years later, just after I moved back to Canada, I picked up *january, february, june or july* by Helen Fogwill Porter (1988), which is set in St. John's. This time the paralysis seemed to affect my lungs; I found it difficult to breathe as I encountered a written version of the St. John's dialect in a fiction for the first time in my life. I think I was donating my breath to the vivification of the words on the page: "I was wondering where you were to" (Porter, 1988, p. 8); "But you can't believe half what you reads in that thing" (p. 9); "I notice you don't mind reading 'em when I brings 'em home" (p. 9); "I was over to Lorraine's" (p. 9). The fictional voices rang in my ears in a way entirely alien to my normal reading experience. I could hear a complete environment of local and familiar voices suddenly represented on the page. If I were to sum up my response to this story, it would always be the same: grateful astonishment at the vividness of recognition that it offers me, and a complete inability to reach judgement on its literary qualities.

Over many years, I have spoken with other readers who describe books that affect them in similarly paralyzing ways. Often the cadence of the voices, whether authorial or character-related, is a factor in how these readers describe the encounter. Sometimes it is the intricate network of social and artifactual relations that appears in the story. Sometimes it is simple geography. In any case, readers have described to me the same reaction: a form of reading standstill and an incapacity to evaluate because the force of recognition is so overwhelming. Astonishment is frequently part of the scenario, because these are often readers who are underrepresented in the standard canon. Even as our literature becomes more broadly based and multicultural, a lot of readers are still left out, ready to be struck dumb or immobile when they finally encounter themselves in a fiction.

I call this kind of experience a *reading of validation*. It occupies a category separate from all other kinds of reading experience. It supplies a form of compulsion that overrides normal reading habits or learned responses. It may eviscerate judgement, but it is a highly significant experience for the reader.

Recognizing the Child Thinker

The category of reading of validation took on a new life for me when I began to contemplate just what it was that I loved so profoundly in Eleanor Estes's trilogy about the Moffat family: *The Moffats* in 1941, *The Middle Moffat* in 1942, and *Rufus M* in 1943. (*The Moffat Museum* did not appear until 1983.)

In the chapters featuring Jane, Rufus, and Joe (Sylvie is to all intents and purposes an adult), we gain a sense of "a child speaking to children," to kidnap Wordsworth's famous phrase. The Moffats mature slowly over the course of the books; the sale of their home in *The Moffats* moves Jane to reflect on the passage of time (Estes, 1959/1941, pp. 246–247), and Joe shows some signs of moving into adolescence in *Rufus M.* (1943, p. 107). Their lives and thoughts are generally childish, however. Estes makes lavish use of free, indirect discourse to take us inside the heads of Jane and Rufus especially.

This interior perspective of children learning to make sense of the world, developing scripts and schemas for themselves out of repeated exposure to experience, offers the potential for a form of reading of validation. It was not the external setting of Cranbury or the Moffat household with which I, as a child reader, identified so intimately, though many of the conditions of both were familiar to me. It was the experience of the internal settings of Jane's or Rufus's minds that struck me so powerfully. "I know this," I thought frequently as I read and reread these books, but it was not only the events or the characters, it was also the child's way of making sense (perceiving, extrapolating, and aligning with other already mastered information) that I recognized so acutely.

Many definitions of children's literature mention that the books are written by adults *for* children, and conclude that didacticism is inevitable in such an arrangement. My experience of the *Moffat* books was that didacticism was very low down the priority list; it was one of the things I liked best about them. As a reader of these books, I have always felt, however inarticulately, that the priority for Estes was to write herself into the minds of these children, and that the address to other children, the readers, from an adult perspective was secondary. Few books achieve this kind of balance—all the more reason to cherish the Moffat family.

Scripts and Schemas

We animate our reading with understanding from our own lives. "The text interacts with the reader's mental faculties, memories, emotions and beliefs to produce a sum that is richer than the parts: the text is actualized, the reader is vivified, by a good book" (Stockwell, 2002, p. 75).

Child readers participate in this kind of actualization but, even as they read, they are also learning about how this phenomenon occurs. Their stock of schemas and scripts is relatively small and fluid, still in development, so the book that presents schema development in action will resonate in particular ways.

Peter Stockwell's (2002) account of cognitive (or schema) poetics, of how we can understand the mental work of reading, suggests that the real questions

> are not whether context is important but how is it important and how is it used. Given the vast amount of historical context that is potentially available, and the hugeness of the imagined experience of the author and the contemporary society, and given the massive encyclopedic knowledge carried around in the heads of readers, how can we decide which bits of context are used and which are not, in a principled way? That is the ground of schema poetics. (p. 76)

Compared to the spare outlines of the world contained in even the most elaborated text, even children's modest sets of scripts and schemas are prodigiously rich and detailed. But the process of developing schemas is still relatively fresh to children, so they are perhaps more open than adult readers to the pleasures of contemplating that process itself, as well as considering the knowledge of the world thus incorporated.

Validating the Child Thinker

The three 1940s books about the Moffat children frequently offer readers access to the thoughts of Jane or Rufus as they puzzle out what they reliably know already, and what and how they need to extrapolate from previously established schemas in order to advance new understanding of a phenomenon. As a child, I spent a lot of time figuring things out in this way, and I identified such cognitive effort when I encountered it in the minds of the Moffat kids. Estes gives us clear examples of the children rehearsing schemas they have already internalized.

Here is Jane, for example, thinking what are obviously well-worn thoughts about being one of four children:

> *It was lucky there were four of them, she thought. Everything divided so beautifully into four parts. Sylvie, Joe, Jane, and Rufus could not imagine how it would feel if there were just three of them, or five of them, or any other number of them. Imagine having to divide into three parts like the Pudges. Or seven like the Cadwaladers! "I suppose they are used to it, though," she thought. But this way, having four in the family, everything was so easy. Cut a piece of chocolate into four parts. No difficulty at all. Or there was one apiece of four-for-a-penny caramels; or a half apiece of two-for-a-penny peppermints. Yes, it was very convenient having four in the family. "When we grow up we shall each have four children," said Jane to herself, "so things will always be easy to divide." Share and share alike was the rule of the Moffat household, and no one ever thought to dispute it. (Estes, 1959/1941, p. 197)*

Estes uses quotation marks to specify reflections that Jane is conscious of thinking. The rest of the observations run in the background on autopilot, a form of background chatter that is too familiar to need rehearsing in any direct way.

Jane, in fact, is rerunning this well-known schema in her head because she has been given a nickel and is contemplating not sharing, buying an ice-cream cone all for herself instead. Once she succumbs to this temptation, she is consumed with remorse because the rubric of dividing things up is so engrained.

Estes also provides clear-cut examples of children trying to incorporate new information into schemas that are already tentatively established. One of the most extended examples lies in the story of Rufus and the player-piano. I recall clearly that, as a reader, I also had no idea what a player-piano might be, and Estes had to provide a very plain description indeed for me to be able to make my own sense of this chapter. Rufus has no immediate explanation for how the piano can be played without a human performer, so he resorts to the ontology of some of his storybooks to make sense of it. He is delivering a piece of sewing for Mama to Mrs. Saybolt. When he rings the doorbell, no one answers but he hears the piano playing and assumes someone is home.

> [T]he music began again, so Rufus stepped into the parlor expecting to see Mrs. Saybolt playing. Then he stood transfixed in the doorway. There was music coming from the piano. The keys were hopping up and down, playing a lively tune. But, nobody was sitting at the piano playing it.
>
> Rufus recognized in a flash what it was—an invisible piano player!
>
> Rufus stood there watching. He knew about invisible people. Certain people who wore certain cloaks were invisible. Jane had read him a story only this morning about one of these fellows. That one happened to be a prince, an invisible prince. (Estes, 1943, pp. 59–60)

Every time Rufus passes the Saybolts' home after this experience, he ponders the daily realities of being invisible.

> He wondered many things about the man. He wondered if you could feel an invisible man or if touching him would be like touching air. He asked Jane.
>
> Jane thought a long time. Then she said she thought you could feel an invisible man. The only thing you couldn't do was see him. If he sneezed or coughed, she thought you could hear him. Hear him and feel him, that's what she thought. (pp. 61–62)

Rufus sneaks into the Saybolt house, determined to find out whether he can feel the invisible person when he touches where his hands should be.

> Rufus reached out his chubby fist. The keys kept hopping up and down very fast and Rufus swooped his hand up and down the keyboard but he did not feel anybody's hand there. It was a very scary thing to do, feeling for an invisible piano player's hands....
>
> Rufus began to feel bolder. He tapped where he supposed a shoulder would be if a man were sitting there. He felt nothing. He quickly touched

the stool, ran his chubby hand all over it. He still felt nothing. Rufus's spine tingled with excitement. He retreated across the room and stood under a big rubber plant. He had put his hand right through an invisible man! That was proof all right. An invisible man cannot be felt! He cannot be seen and he cannot be felt! He is like thin air and you can walk right through him or hundreds like him and never even know it.

Wait till he told Jane that! All the time she was going around thinking an invisible person can be felt. "That's not so. What would be the advantage anyway of being invisible if people bumped into you all the time?" Rufus thought in disgust. (pp. 65–66)

Eventually, Rufus learns that the player-piano is simply a machine; Mrs. Saybolt invites him and Joey in to listen to the music.

Mrs. Saybolt stood beside the piano and watched Rufus with an amiable smile.

"Plays nice, doesn't it?"

It! thought Rufus.

"Sure does," agreed Joey.

"Now I'll play a march," she said. She pushed a button, opened a little hole over the piano, took out a roll, put another in, and pushed another valve. The music began again. Rat-ta-tat! Boom! Boom!

Rufus looked at this proceeding with unbelieving eyes. The invisible piano player had been very real to him. And now instead of there being an invisible piano player the thing worked by machinery. Rufus felt cheated. (p. 76)

My lengthy quotes give only a partial account of Rufus's ruminations on the schematic details of being invisible; he works out an intricate framework in order to incorporate what seem to be new facts about the world into his previous understanding. As the truth about the player-piano's mechanical nature is revealed, Estes delicately withdraws us from his mind ("The invisible piano player had been very real to him"), but we have spent a number of pages inhabiting his hypotheses. Perhaps because I shared Rufus's lack of appropriate repertoire, I followed his line of thinking with deep recognition. The idea of a piano that played itself mechanically was, if anything, more alien to me that the idea of being invisible; like Rufus I had encountered this desirable state of affairs in many stories.

Vivifying the Moffats

The opening page of the first book, *The Moffats*, offers instant information about how these books will be told. "The way Mama could peel apples!" the book begins (Estes, 1959/1941, p. 7). We are immediately seeing with Jane's eyes. I always settled into the spaces inside the Moffats' heads with a sense of homecoming that I have never before analyzed to my own satisfaction. Now I understand it as validation.

Although I have not come across a full-fledged analysis of this kind of recognition, other people clearly share it. Sondra Gordon Langford (1991) expresses my own feelings very succinctly: "Eleanor Estes understood children and their deepest thoughts" (n.p.). Terri Schmitz (2001) points out, "Many of the situations could never happen to contemporary children—sliding down coal chutes, getting trapped in the bread box on the porch of the general store, hiding in a boxcar that suddenly starts moving—but the thought processes that propel the Moffats into these predicaments are recognizable to children everywhere" (p. 558). Kristi Beavin (2003) makes a similar point more indirectly when she observes, "The Moffats of New Dollar Street may not be as famous as the Quimbys over on Klickitat, but both families surely live in the same literary neighbourhood" (p. 1094).

The three Moffat stories from the 1940s are also blessed with dynamic, individual, and active illustrations. Jane Moffat is always entirely recognizable; whatever is going on in the illustration, it is always *Jane* who is there. At the same time as Louis Slobodkin creates this entirely identifiable personality, his pictures also always evoke a verb. Jane is always in some kind of motion. It seems a bit ridiculous to describe pictures in terms of linguistic grammar, but the illustrations do give us a clear image of a particular noun engaged in the actions of a specific verb. The solidity of this form of representation adds to the ease with which readers can become *familiar* with Jane, in the most significant sense of that word.

Developing Chronotopes

Other forms of mental activity also lead to the delight of recognition when a child encounters them in a book. Arthur Ransome is a master of chronotopes—the artistic thickening of relationships between time and space in order to create a fictional "reality" in a story (Bakhtin, 1981, p. 84). Ransome's *Swallows and Amazons* (1962/1930) *takes place* (the very phrase is a chronotopal metaphor) in a highly specified world in which the relationship between time and space is a major component of the story.

How long does it take to get to Wild Cat Island from Holly Howe or Dixons' Farm by sailing fair? by tacking against the wind? by rowing in calm water? Where shall the fire be built and how briskly must it blaze to heat a kettle to what degree of closeness to boiling? In order for this boiling to occur, how many people must collect firewood, for how long, and where should they go to find it? Ransome "thickens" his world to a very dense texture indeed, and readers often feel themselves moving in step with the characters.

My mother loved *Swallows and Amazons*, probably more than any other children's book. Her youth in Halifax included a certain amount of messing about in sailboats so she brought a better repertoire of relevant life experience to bear on the book than I could. I knew what it felt like to row a dinghy, but that was my limit.

The Swallows' experience of sailing, however, is inclusive rather than exclusive of nonsailing readers. I might not know what the specialist terms all meant, but I could savour the children's relish in their own expertise and share their qualms when they overstepped the limits of their competence (as John does, for example, in the night raid on the *Amazon* that does not go according to plan).

One major function of the detailed vocabulary is to move the children through time and space. Here is a short example (selected at random) from the occasion when the children set out to camp on the island. After acquiring much information about what was packed where in the boat, readers set sail with the *Swallow* and her crew.

The *Swallow* *slipped slowly out towards the mouth of the bay. She made at first no noise and hardly any wake. Then, as she came clear of the northerly side of the bay, she found a little more wind, and the cheerful lapping noise began under her forefoot, while her wake lengthened out and bubbled astern of her.*

Darien, the promontory on the southern side of the Holly Howe bay, was longer than the promontory on the northern side. Also Captain John was taking no risks. At the end of Darien there might be rocks. He held on straight out of the bay until he could see the bay on the other side of the point. Far away down the lake the island showed. It seemed further than it had from the top of Darien. At last John let out the mainsheet, and put the helm up. The boom swung out, the Swallow *swung round and, with the wind aft, John steered straight for the island....*

[I]n a moment they could see into the bay no longer. The bay was hidden behind Darien. Above them was the Peak from which they had first seen the island. The Peak itself seemed lower than it had. Everything had grown smaller except the lake, and that had never seemed so large before. (Ransome, 1962/1930, pp. 34–35)

According to Patrick Colm Hogan (2003), "We structure place around agency, most often human agency" (p. 126). Certainly this idea describes much of the plot of *Swallows and Amazons*. The four Walker children acquire new forms of agency in their relationship to the environment where they find themselves; they alternate between asserting the power to rename significant points in the landscape and actually moving through them and taking charge of them. The chronotope is not an accident of time and space happening to coexist; the children take actions to place themselves within both dimensions.

Ransome does more than articulate highly specific chronotopes, however. One element of the genius of *Swallows and Amazons* is the ease with which he doubles them. Titty is often the engineer of the plural chronotope, regularly moving between one fictional world (created out of quotidian detail by Ransome) and a second (created out of her vast imaginative repertoire developed from reading about explorers, colonizers, adventurers, pirates, natives, and savages). Titty frequently multiplies her landscape in explicit ways. For example, when she is left alone on Wild Cat Island to light the lamps for *Swallow* to navigate home in the dark, after the night raid, she moves between alternative scenarios very readily. The others have just sailed off, leaving her on her own:

She looked round the camp, and felt at once that there was something wrong. There were two tents, and a shipwrecked mariner on a desert island ought only to have one. For a moment she thought of taking down the captain's tent, but then she remembered that for part of the time she would not be a shipwrecked mariner, but would be in charge of an explorers' camp, while the main body had sailed away on a desperate expedition. During that part of the time the more tents there were the better. So she decided not to take down the captain's tent. "It's Man Friday's tent," she said to herself. "Of course I haven't discovered him yet. But it's ready for him when the time comes."

Then she went into the tent that belonged to her and to the mate. It was still a very Susanish tent. Susan had taken her blankets but she had left her

∧ Image from Swallows
and Amazons (Ransome,
1962/1930, p. 10).
[Artwork © Clifford Webb,
published by arrangement with
The Random House Group
Limited]

haybag. It was quite clear that it was a tent belonging to two people and not
a tent belonging to a lonely shipwrecked sailor. So the able-seaman took
Susan's haybag and put it on the top of her own, and spread her blankets
over the two of them. At once the tent became hers and hers alone, and it
would be easy enough to put the mate's haybag back in its place when it was
time to be on guard over a whole camp. (Ransome, 1962/1930, p. 192)

Titty is clearly a great reader when she is offstage, so to speak; she even
does some diegetic reading of Robinson Crusoe as she minds the island.
She is also an enabler of those real-life children learning to read this book
and others. This short passage contains four imaginary worlds, layered
over that thickly articulated chronotope of Wild Cat Island. For a moment
or two, we get a glimpse of the girls, Titty and Susan (Titty is not a fiction
to herself, but she is to us, and even young readers acknowledge this
divide). Even more briefly, we see them as the able-seaman and the mate,
and we are, of course, very familiar by now with these roles and the story
they imply (even if I never did really understand what an able-seaman

does). Then we have Titty's two fictions: the shipwrecked mariner and the guardian of the explorers' camp, the latter invention bearing a closer relationship than the former to her actual function and duties on this occasion.

Because the chronotope of Wild Cat Island and its child inhabitants is so richly specified, young readers are able to import their own embodied understanding of the relation between time and space. Such understanding helps equip them with what Fiona Maine and Alison Waller (2011) describe as a necessary "resilience" (p. 367) that equips them to persevere even when they do not understand everything that is going on in the story. Maine and Waller are clear that different readers draw on different strategies and priorities in their struggle with recalcitrant passages: "the ability to persist through difficult sections not only demonstrates the importance of reading resilience but also has its own rewards in moving readers on to more satisfying parts of the novel" (p. 367).

By setting the time and place of the events of his story so clearly and plainly, Ransome anchors readers (in more ways than one) and allows them to address how to deal with the elements of the story that may be more confusing to them. Maine and Waller, talking with both child readers and adult rereaders of *Swallows and Amazons* propose that their response "suggests that meaning can be made through problem-solving while being immersed in the text" (p. 365).

I was not the only reader who took Titty's gift and flipped it, mapping Wild Cat Island and particularly Swallowdale over my own daily universe. It was not the boating adventures of the Swallows and the Amazons that I lusted after; it was their camps. I made endless maps of my own secret valley and even more secret cave (I do not propose to explore the symbolic freight that must have been attached to such imagery as I moved into the prelimary stages prior to puberty, but I have no doubt that much was going on in the most profound depths of my psyche even as my child body organized for change). I planned virtual tents and provisions, and gave orders to my imaginary crew. Maine and Waller draw on the work of Eve Bearne (2009) who points out the following dynamics: "reading is a transformative act, having power not only to transform the here-and-now to what-might-be, but also transforming us as we develop as readers" (p. 219). In these terms, I brought my own embodied awareness of time and space to bear on Ransome; in return he gave me the power to look at my own universe as mappable.

Some of Maine and Waller's readers spoke of playing *Swallows and Amazons* in their own environment. Nicholas Thomas (1987) explores how Ransome creates adventure and meta-adventure in ways that children may model (as I certainly did): "These stories imply that ordinary people (and specifically children) can move from fantasies about adventure to real adventures....A crucial element of adventure is the reconstitution of the landscape, some things, and some social relations in new, imaginative terms....The substance of narrative in these stories is a transformation of *play* at adventure, which models experience on narrative, into actualized adventure which happens rather than being contrived" (pp. 9–10). The charm of this transmogrification is potent:

> [W]hat is "real" is paradoxically located not in ordinary behaviour but in the special action of stories. The object of desire is the transformation of one's own practice into something that has the same resonance as narrated adventure. Stories are models for play at adventure, which then acquires its own dynamic and may be transformed into lived adventure. The message is that the gap between desire and its object can be suppressed.
>
> The movement is, of course, not in reality but in Ransome's depiction. However, there is the strong implication that it can and should extend to readers, who might draw the adventures into their own activity, just as the children in the stories draw on other stories and fantasies. (p. 11)

Children perform their stories in ways that are embodied, yet that disrupt the relationship between those bodies and the actual surroundings in which they are set. In the print-dominated circumstances of his time, Ransome translated his cognitive and embodied understanding of sailing into words that his readers would have to re-embody. I, like many other children, played them out in that hybrid space that included my body on Pennywell Road and my mind on Wild Cat Island, in that hybrid time that included the gap between breakfast and dinner at my house and the length of time it would take explorers to map out their island in careful detail. Our vocabulary for this exercise is inadequate, but if it were possible I would say that my fictions were being embodied and enminded at the same time.

What If?

My tastes in fiction were then, and remain now, largely realistic and oriented toward relationships. I was much more interested in reading about Titty making sense of her adventure stories than I was in reading the adventure stories themselves, even though I could have filled a respectable bookshelf with her library, and Ransome provides plenty of bibliographic information about them. I did not very often make fantasy my first choice, though I did like the few fantasy books that I read. Most of the fantasies I enjoyed occupied the border of a world that was clearly perceived as normal by its regular inhabitants, even if some of the details were exotic to me, magic realism such as *Mary Poppins* and *The Borrowers*.

Mary Poppins

Mary Poppins taught me a kind of mental double declutching, so to speak. I loved the books for the charm of P.L. Travers's inventiveness. In many ways, the magic episodes made more sense to me than the daily life. Who could not appreciate the pure delight of having tea on the ceiling, or stepping into a chalk drawing on the sidewalk? On the other hand, it was harder to sort out a passage such as the one that appears in the early paragraphs of the first book in the sequence.

> *If you are looking for Number Seventeen—and it is more than likely that you will be, for this book is all about that particular house—you will very soon find it. To begin with, it is the smallest house in the Lane. And besides that, it is the only one that is rather dilapidated and needs a coat of paint. But Mr. Banks, who owns it, said to Mrs. Banks that she could have either a nice, clean, comfortable house or four children. But not both, for he couldn't afford it.*
>
> *And after Mrs. Banks had given the matter some consideration she came to the conclusion that she would rather have Jane, who was the eldest, and Michael, who came next, and John and Barbara, who were Twins and came last of all. So it was settled, and that was how the Banks family came to live at Number Seventeen, with Mrs. Brill to cook for them, and Ellen to lay the tables, and Robertson Ay to cut the lawn and clean the knives and polish the shoes and, as Mr. Banks always said, "to waste his time and my money."*
>
> *And of course, besides these there was Katie Nanna, who doesn't really deserve to come into the book at all because, at the time I am speaking of, she had just left Number Seventeen. (Travers, 1965/1934, pp. 11-12)*

There they were, all together, up in the air

The narrator of this story was clearly taking me by the hand to walk along
Cherry Tree Lane and into the door of Number Seventeen—so much was
readily established. But the poverty that drives Mr. and Mrs. Banks to such
"considered" choices concerning paint and children still allows for a staff of
four to look after a family of six.

The jokes in *Mary Poppins* assume a worldly understanding that I
could not always achieve. Mr. Banks went to work to make money: "All
day long he worked, cutting out pennies and shillings and half-crowns
and threepenny-bits" (p. 14). Mary Poppins, when questioned about references, says she makes it a rule never to give them (p. 18). There are many

of these sly comments, and I found them challenging. But the delights of Mary Poppins's "empty" carpet bag from which she takes a large number of necessities, the bottle of bedtime medicine that tastes different to each consumer, and other incidents of like nature in the first chapter soon made me aware, just like Jane and Michael, "that something strange and wonderful had happened at Number Seventeen, Cherry Tree Lane" (p. 23). And the *magic* always made sense.

One of the pleasures of the *Mary Poppins* books is their magic realism, the way that uncanny possibilities coexist with ordinary daily reality (even if it was a daily reality strange to me, there was no question about its quotidian status for the people inside the story). And the character of Mary herself (especially in those pre-Julie Andrews/Disney days) was appealing in its tart, no-nonsense, self-satisfied flatness, qualities reinforced by Mary Shepard's expressive drawings (another example of indissoluble linking of nouns and verbs: Mary Poppins is always very much in action in these illustrations). Mary Poppins herself never changes. The pedestrian realities of Jane and Michael's daily life never change (unlike the sentimental improvements in their parents' care and attention that are brought about in the movie version). But the wild possibilities of the magical outings are ceaselessly delightful. I could not feel validated in any way by the realistic elements, but I definitely loved the fun.

The Borrowers

Our copy of *The Borrowers* (Norton, 1953) was memorable for its physical form, but I was very taken with the content as well. My aunt lovingly assembled *The Borrowers* from a four-part serialization in *Woman's Day*, starting in June 1953; she taped the pages onto heavy green paper that she tied together with a ribbon. The result strangely suited the story itself: where the words ran on the front and back of a single page, she taped down the side and readers had to turn over to find the story. She cut out around the shape of the columns, which meant that some two-sided sections contained fragments of advertisements on the "wrong" side. A reader thus "uncovered" this story in ways that aligned well with its subject matter; and I read it again and again. This format had the extra advantage of slowing down my normal breakneck reading speed, so I savoured *The Borrowers* in unusual depth and detail. Not surprisingly, any ordinary book version of *The Borrowers* has always seemed tame to me.

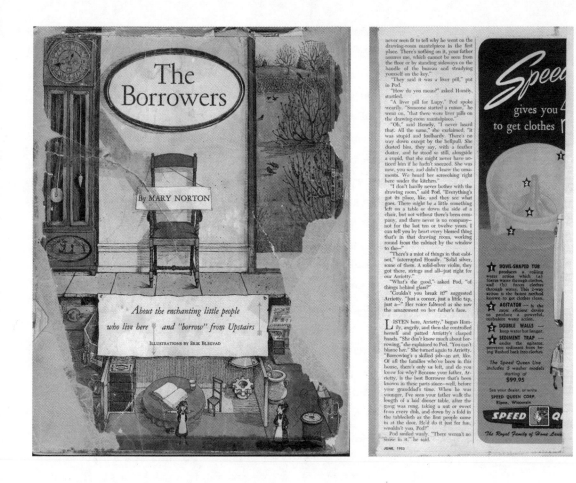

The plot of *The Borrowers* is both adventurous and highly domestic. The Borrowers are tiny people who live in the wainscotting and scrounge all those small domestic appurtenances that are always missing when needed by the humans in the house. The fantasy component in all senses lives *alongside* the ordinary realities of domestic life; the fact that little things do indeed inexplicably disappear in our own reality is used to reinforce the believability of the story.

For a lover of miniature domestic scenes such as myself, this book held a tremendous allure. (Note that for citation purposes, I quote passages and page numbers from the Puffin version [1986/1952], though for reading purposes I have returned to the old green scrapbook.)

Arrietty had wandered through the open door into the sitting room—the fire had been lighted and the room looked bright and cozy. Homily was proud of her sitting room: the walls had been papered with scraps of old letters out of

∧ *The cover of our copy of* The Borrowers, *assembled into a scrapbook from a magazine serialization, and a page from this scrapbook version of* The Borrowers; *the text on the verso is double-columned so it is necessary to include part of the advertisement on the facing side.*

[*Courtesy Peter Blegvad and Houghton Mifflin Harcourt Publishing Company*]

*waste-paper baskets, and Homily had arranged the handwriting sideways
in vertical stripes, which ran from floor to ceiling. On the walls, repeated
in various colours, hung several portraits of Queen Victoria as a girl; these
were postage stamps, borrowed by Pod some years ago from the stamp box
on the desk in the morning room. There was a lacquer trinket box, padded
inside and with the lid open, which they used as a settle; and that useful
stand-by—a chest of drawers made of match boxes. There was a round
table with a red velvet cloth, which Pod had made from the wooden bottom
of a pillbox supported on the carved pedestal of a knight from the chess-set....
The knight itself—its bust, so to speak—was standing on a column in the
corner, where it looked very fine, and lent that air to the room which only
statuary can give. (Norton, 1986/1952, pp. 17–18)*

I was a bit hazy on morning rooms, but I certainly grasped the nature of
"that useful stand-by—a chest of drawers made of match boxes." My own
shoebox creations always included chests of drawers, even when other
furniture was in short supply. Reading *The Borrowers*, I engaged my own
hand-knowledge all the way through, with a repertoire well-suited to the
demands of the story. That the eccentric configuration of the scrapbook
also occupied my hands in interesting ways was a bonus.

Unlike the world of *Mary Poppins*, this world was accessible to my own
private interests. I knew that safety pins and darning needles were likely
to disappear, so I could subscribe to the basic premise of the plot. As ever,
I liked the domestic parts better than the adventures after the Borrowers
are driven out of their comfortable home, but the charm of the miniature
sustained the logic of the action, which helped; and the universals of items
like stamps and chess pieces compensated for the foreignness of other
details.

The complexity of the frame story confused me a bit, but I soon learned
that you could gallop through the introduction without worrying too much
about it, so I dismissed my uncertainties with a cavalier insouciance that I
would very much like to recover today, and simply ploughed into the main
story. For all the magic in the plot engine and the foreign qualities of the
daily details, and despite the fact that my regular predilection always led to
realistic fiction, this was a book that came very close to inscribing me as the
implied reader, and I relished the ways it burnished both the logic and the
appeal of the miniature.

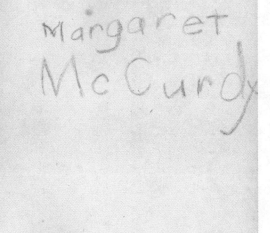

Beneath the Surface

The closest I came to complete indwelling in a story of true high fantasy was with George MacDonald's *The Princess and the Goblin* (1949/1872). To adapt the old Heineken beer ad, this book "reached parts that other books could not reach," introducing me to a subterranean and subversive world that was also, in the fullest possible literal meaning of the term, "subliminal"— even that most liminal space of the threshold itself, the doorway to Princess Irene's safe haven, is undermined by the mysterious digging of the goblins.

The book was one of the small number I owned outright, and I printed my name carefully in green crayon on the half-title page, becoming scragglier as I got further into the second word. To the best of my recollection we started to learn cursive writing in Grade 3, so the odds are very great that I was seven or just barely turned eight when I was given this book. It might have been a seventh- or eighth-birthday present.

I celebrated my ownership of this much-loved volume by abusing it in almost every way known to children. Most blatantly I tore strips off the wide margins and chewed on them. I scribbled a pencil border on the back

THE PRINCESS
AND THE GOBLIN

BY GEORGE MACDONALD

*Illustrated with line drawings
and 8 colour plates by*
CHARLES FOLKARD

LONDON: J. M. DENT & SONS LTD
NEW YORK: E. P. DUTTON & CO. INC.

To face page 10
'Come in, my dear, I am glad to see you,' said the old lady

∧ *The frontispiece and
title page of my copy of*
The Princess and the
Goblin *demonstrate
the contrast between
the black-and-white
drawings and the full-
page paintings that
appear in my copy in
colour (thus paying
complete homage to
the princess's golden
ringlets!).*
[Courtesy Penguin
Random House]

of one of the tipped-in colour illustrations. I connected all the dots in the table of contents.

I owe an enormous debt to Charles Folkard, the creator of the line drawings and eight colour plates of this book; I loved those pictures with a passion, especially the colour plates. As much as anything in the written story, they brought me back to read and reread this book. The line drawings were more vigorous and lively than the set pieces of the coloured pictures, but my attitude to grotesqueries was ambivalent, and I preferred the dainty princess (with her golden ringlets) to the goblins every time. And it wasn't as if she was a passive heroine, after all.

This book is about unseen depths. I will never be a psychoanalytical critic of children's literature, but it is impossible to read it as an adult without discovering that it is a book about subterranean mutability and danger, a very disturbing universe. The risks of mining are real and palpable; the peril presented by the goblins wanting to seize the princess to marry her to the terrible Prince Harelip were suggestively nasty, even to a small reader. The undercutting of the mountain is a hazard to everyone.

MacDonald published the book in 1872. It was thus written in the context of public reaction to Darwin's *On the Origin of Species* (1859). MacDonald took on board the eerie potential of maladaptation in his description of the goblins' animal companions:

> *The supernatural or rather subnatural ugliness of their faces, the length of legs and necks in some, the apparent absence of both or either in others, made the spectators, although in one consent as to what they saw, yet doubtful, as I have said, of the evidence of their own eyes—and ears as well; for the noises they made, although not loud, were as uncouth and varied as their forms, and could be described neither as grunts nor squeaks nor roars nor howls nor barks nor yells nor screams nor croaks nor hisses nor mews nor shrieks, but only as something like all of them mingled in one horrible dissonance. (pp. 87–88)*

Not content with this unnerving description, MacDonald supplies the evolutionary backstory of how this mutant army came to be:

> *They were, of course, household animals belonging to the goblins, whose ancestors had taken their ancestors many centuries before from the upper regions of light into the lower regions of darkness....[I]n the course of time all had undergone even greater changes than had passed upon their owners. They had altered—that is, their descendants had altered—into such creatures as I have not attempted to describe except in the vaguest manner—the various parts of their bodies assuming, in an apparently arbitrary and self-willed manner, the most abnormal developments....But what increased the gruesomeness tenfold, was that, from constant domestic, or indeed rather family association with the goblins, their countenances had grown in grotesque resemblance to the human. (pp. 88–89)*

In daytime, these evil-looking creatures lurk underground with their owners, in a network of caves and seams that the goblins are expanding with a view to flooding the safe haven of Princess Irene and her retinue. At night they come above ground and haunt the countryside.

I simply do not know enough about psychosexual development in childhood, and most certainly I do not remember enough, to be clear in my own mind whether as a young child I instinctively knew that surfaces were not to be trusted, or whether that dawning awareness was part of what this book taught me. It was probably the first book I read that addressed such insecurities in a literary way, and that breakthrough was itself important to me in a variety of ways that I cannot satisfactorily articulate, even now.

But this is a children's book, and MacDonald provides an antidote to the horrors that I could believe; the power of mothers and grandmothers in this story is something I understood at a very deep level. Irene discovers her great-great-grandmother in a room at the top of her home, and learns that this aged woman can conquer the threats of the dark and the underground. At one point, having been chased down the mountainside by unimaginable terrors, Irene retreats to her grandmother's room:

> Irene sat down in the low chair, and her grandmother left her, shutting the door behind her. The child sat gazing, now at the rose fire, now at the silvery light; and a great quietness grew in her heart. If all the long-legged cats in the world had come rushing at her then she would not have been afraid of them for a moment. How this was she could not tell—she only knew there was no fear in her, and everything was so right and safe that it could not get in. (p. 101)

Her grandmother supplies Irene with a ring to which is attached a magic thread that will always lead her home; she has only to reach out her fore-finger to feel it before her. How much greater security could exist? The princess need not cower at home waiting for trouble to reach her; she can set out confidently into the world, knowing that her connection to ultimate safety is always steadfast.

I find the role of girls and women in this book appealing. The miners and the king's guardsmen take on a great deal of the necessary fighting with the goblins, but Curdie's mother is also important. And the grandmother! Her light offers safety to anyone who sees it, and she creates the thread for Irene by that most feminized profession of spinning. Irene herself is an admirable heroine, fair and honest and brave. She and Curdie each rescue the other at different points in the story.

Fiona McCulloch (2006) suggests that the grandmother is a storymaker:

> Metaphorically, the grandmother's spinning of various "spiders webs"...
> forms part of the complex narrative structure, where tracing each thread

to its source results in an entangled spirally mass that constantly weaves back upon itself, enmeshed in a cyclical maze that disrupts the linearity of transparent realism associated with children's fiction. The house and cave settings enhance this labyrinthian untraceability, just as the novel's thread incorporates multiple voices and stories, self-consciously acknowledging the weaving of a multidirectional narrative. (pp. 58–59)

The story is indeed multidirectional, and the quotes I offer above suggest that it is not easy reading in terms of vocabulary and sentence structure. Yet I "read up" because I loved it. The princess did not have any more confidence in her grandmother's thread than I had in MacDonald's narrative voice. Even though my edition was slightly abridged and did not include the metafictional introduction ("But, Mr. Author, why do you always write about princesses?" "Because every little girl is a princess."), it took me only to paragraph two to arrive at MacDonald's direct address to me, the reader. "The princess was a sweet little creature, and at the time my story begins was about eight years old, I think, but she got older very fast....But I doubt if ever she saw the real sky with the stars in it, for a reason which I had better mention at once" (MacDonald, 1949/1872, p. 1). I reached out my forefinger and followed the clue with a sublime sense of readerly trust.

The ending of the book is actually rather indeterminate; MacDonald was clearly setting up a sequel. As an adult, I once bought a paperback version of *The Princess and Curdie*, but I could never make myself want to read it. As a reader, I am fully satisfied.

An Essential Didacticism?

Children's literature is famously construed as a mingling of instruction and delight. Theorists suggest that didacticism is inherent in children's literature because the adults who create it also create the child reader inscribed in their words. That adult construction of childhood is culturally bound, of course, but many critics seem to think that it must be culturally bound to be didactic. I wonder. I as an adult can certainly read didacticism *into* many of these books I loved so much. The books I have selected here for particular attention represent a subset of my reading that avoided the undeniably improving discourses of other books I loved equally well and read equally often: the Alcott and Montgomery stories, *What Katy Did*, and many more of that ilk.

In this chapter, I explore books in which didacticsm is a lesser feature. In these books, as child or adult reader, I do not have a feeling of being "got at." Certainly, even while I succumbed to dreams of excruciating virtue as I read *What Katy Did*, for example, I knew that I was being manipulated, and that the first half of the book was the better part, before Katy languished into insipid but virtuous invalidism. With *The Moffats*, *Swallows and Amazons*, *The Borrowers*, and *The Princess and the Goblin*, I think something else is happening. Estes, Ransome, Norton, and MacDonald have set themselves a different challenge, intellectual and aesthetic rather than educational. Rather than reforming children, they want to explore childhood complexities and limitations as truthfully as they can.

Krips (2000) makes the following comment, and Nodelman (2008) cites it with approval: "Perhaps few adults would want to return to childhood as it was actually lived, with all its unremembered difficulties, humilations, and problems" (Krips, 200, p. 16). This observation is probably true in terms of not really wanting to relive the past, but there is no reason to assume in consequence that every children's author makes such a refusal, blinded by nostalgia and/or fired by didacticism. "Returning to childhood as it was actually lived" is an honorable and difficult *artistic* ambition, and more than sufficient as an intellectual and affective challenge to fuel a children's book. No doubt the authors are fooling themselves to a certain degree that such an end is ever achievable, but the attempt to get there is to their credit, and certainly some books succeed better than others. Instruction and delight can be part of the package, but there is no reason why a children's book cannot also or instead take Wordsworth's (1960/1802) famous aim of "emotion recollected in tranquility" (p. 740) as a focus for the author's ambition. The authors I cite here do seem to me to have achieved a lesser-explored ambition that Wordsworth also expressed in the preface to the *Lyrical Ballads*: "I have at all times endeavoured to look steadily at my subject" (p. 736). As a child reader, although of course I never could have articulated it in these terms, I seriously appreciated that steady look at what it is like to be a child. I recognized it, I was validated by it, and it seems to me now, looking back, that I appreciated it as (at a minimum) didacticism-lite.

Maybe, like Wordsworth, I am simply opting for a romantic perspective. Maybe I am distracted by the instincts that guide this project, the wish to develop a perspective on childhood that operates, as far as I can possibly manage, from the inside of childhood looking out. Of course, neither I nor the authors I am quoting here can ever be free of the remorseless accretions that adulthood adds to the child's view on the world, nor am I suggesting that successfully recovering childish perspectives is ever possible. I do suggest, however, that such a focus leads to a different end product from what is created through didactic intentions. I know I noticed this difference as a child reader. I still see it as valid. Nostalgia and instruction may be indissolubly linked with children's literature (though I do not think the case has been made incontrovertibly, and most scholars making this argument are also very selective in their choice of specimen titles). At the least there is a continuum; the books I highlight in this chapter address direct cognitive, affective, and embodied concerns of childhood in ways that strike me as genuinely challenging.

Elizabeth Bowen (1986) describes a different kind of instruction and delight in the reading of the omnivorous child with an insatiable desire for fiction:

> Yes, one stripped bare the books of one's childhood to make oneself....
>
> What do I mean by those books making myself? In the first place, they were power-testing athletics for my imagination—cross-country runs into strange country, sprints, long and high jumps. It was exhilarating to discover what one could feel: the discovery itself was an advance. Then, by successively "being" a character in every book I read, I doubled the meaning of everything that happened in my otherwise constricted life. Books introduced me to, and magnified, desire and danger. They represented life, with a conclusiveness I had no reason to challenge, as an affair of mysteries and attractions, in which each object or place or face was in itself a volume of promises and deceptions, and in which nothing was impossible. (pp. 50–51)

Although I have here explored some of the books I loved best through the filter of developing narrative cognition, my experience of them involved much more than simple cognitive effort. Reading these stories allowed me also to "double the meaning of everything that happened in my otherwise constricted life."

Growing

So far I have investigated the worlds of some very satisfying heroines (Jane, Titty, the Borrower Arietty, the Princess Irene), and have admired them for how they represent the interior world of children learning to understand the universe around them. I have perhaps given short shrift to other fictional characters who played enormous roles in how I came to understand the "doubling" of the world permitted by fiction. Anne Shirley and Jo March, rather more than the girls listed above, do inhabit fictional universes where didacticism can find a sympathetic home, and I was always aware that both girls grew radically less interesting as they become older and inexorably more ladylike. But they did grow. They changed. And in that vital sense, they characterized a key element of childhood experience: its transience. Furthermore, we readers experience their growth from a very privileged point of view; we are more often than not inside their heads as they embrace, resist, and/or resign themselves to change.

I quite liked being a child. I appreciated many elements of my daily life. But I had to notice (especially as my younger brothers moved into spaces that I had barely vacated) that childhood is always on the move. Vital and lively characters who are aware of their own growth and change, therefore, offered me a different route into the experience of fiction. Montgomery and Alcott offered many exemplars of such insight.

Anne's zest for life in general embraced change, though she could occasionally be wistful about the past. Jo resisted change, both explicitly and tacitly, but had to acknowledge that she could not hold back the tide. Another Montgomery character, Pat of Silver Bush, hated change and clung to the status quo so vigorously that Montgomery was forced to impose change upon her in quite violent ways, though fire, death, and emotional betrayal (Sid's marriage). But these characters grow, and we learn to understand them from the inside out, even as they change. They have dynamic interior lives, and they invite their readers into an internal world of flux and development.

I first read *Anne of Green Gables* in a single sitting; I was sick in bed and my father recommended it on his way to work. I had finished it (through blinding tears over Matthew's death) by the time he came home. I remember quite explicitly thinking to myself at that moment that Thornton W. Burgess would never be quite the same again. Reading about change in Anne had changed me as a reader.

Roberta Trites (2014) suggests that our understanding of the concept of growth is "sometimes entailed by the way we map embodiment onto the concept of growth" (p. 20). While titles like *Anne of Green Gables* and *What Katy Did* might not qualify as full-throated young-adult literature today, they certainly move into that territory of what Trites calls "a genre saturated with conceptualizations of growth that imply growth is inevitable, necessary, sometimes painful, and must lead to adulthood" (p. 20). With these girls' books (the label conveys some of the ambiguity of the territory), I moved into ways of conceptualizing the fact that I was not simply growing *out* of my clothes every season, I was also growing *up*, and needed to find ways to start thinking about it.

So my life experiences and my fictions wove in and out of each other. I changed and developed in ways that seem coherent as I describe them here. But at the same time, my reading life was also more random than I have portrayed to date.

7

A Household Ecology

Sampling

[T]he family library, understood as the ordinary small- to medium-sized book collection, acquired and used by several family members, usually over two or three generations, has been oddly invisible to historians of reading. And yet it would not be especially reckless to say that most adults living in the developed world today either live with, or once lived with, a family library of this kind. They are simply "the books in the house"—those things that are inherited, exhibited, packed away, added to, sold, lent, borrowed, picked up, put down, read, written in, given away, and used to tilt the slide projector to the right angle—and their apparent invisibility is no doubt largely a function of their inseparability from the ordinary business of living.

The family library, in this sense, constitutes a real and distinct social deployment of books. (Buckridge, 2006, pp. 389–390)

PATRICK BUCKRIDGE may be overestimating the ubiquity of family libraries in the developed world, but without a doubt I grew up surrounded by exactly just such a motley collection as he describes. In this chapter, I explore some particularities and provenances of this assortment of literary materials. Accidental survival is a key component to membership of the perhaps not-so-select company that Buckridge describes; its impact on the development of tacit literacy understanding is difficult to overstate.

Brandt (1995) says families "accumulate" literacies over the generations, both in terms of "the rising levels of formal schooling that begin to accumulate (albeit inequitably) in families," and also "in a residual sense, as materials and practices from earlier times often linger at the scenes of contemporary literacy learning" (p. 652). In my own family, Mum's archival diligence ensured that such residual lingering featured importantly in our literacy diet.

Adult Miscellany

What kinds of literary assets lay around me as I learned to read? Our house was not exceptionally full of books and other reading fodder; we all, parents and children alike, acquired the majority of our books from the public library. If I had to come up with a single adjective to describe our family collection, that word would be *miscellaneous*. The sources of these materials were similarly random and various.

Dad, with an MA in history courtesy of legislation to fund the schooling of war veterans, was education-rich and cash-poor, a fact that affected our book collection among many other aspects of our daily lives. Mum could not afford university and took a Commercial course after high school (a program aimed at training secretaries; she learned typing, shorthand, and bookkeeping). She spent her life yearning for a better education than she had received and making spasmodic efforts to take courses, efforts that were frequently frustrated by family events. Both my parents were inveterate and reasonably promiscuous readers, and both were magpies at picking up reading material from any available source.

My daily life floated on a sea of reading materials, both owned and borrowed. Two daily papers, morning and evening, came to the house; and once a week the *Evening Telegram* included the *Weekend Magazine*, with its pullout section of colour comics. Mum read at least three women's magazines: the *Ladies' Home Journal*, *McCall's*, and *Better Homes and*

Gardens, and there was a long-standing family subscription to the *United Church Observer*.

My parents occasionally joined the *Reader's Digest* Condensed Books Club, or the Book-of-the-Month Club, selecting the initial free or 99-cent offer, carefully monitoring their purchases until they reached the minimum requirement, and then cancelling their membership. By these means and others, they sometimes acquired a current bestseller (always hardback) such as *The Man in the Gray Flannel Suit* (Wilson, 1955) or a lightweight comedy such as *Cheaper by the Dozen* (Gilbreth & Carey, 1948). At the same time, they read and reread a few classics: their single-volume copy of *Barchester Towers* and *The Warden* (Trollope, 1950) is well-worn. They regularly reread all the works of Jane Austen, and more occasionally Dickens.

Mum was a committed library patron. Dad certainly read library books, but I don't remember him ever having the time to go there, so Mum must have made choices for him. I never saw either of them pass any length of time without a book on the go.

The Children's Library

Our domestic children's collection was also circumscribed. A small number of picture books and assorted works of A.A. Milne and Thornton W. Burgess dominated the shelves. For a while there were a few books about Honey Bunch and the Bobbsey Twins kicking around; I have no idea where they came from or what became of them.

The children's bookshelf was expanded by some titles from my mother's childhood and a couple of books dating all the way back to my grandmother's youth. Mum (born in 1922) owned some British children's annuals and story collections. *The Oxford Annual for Girls* (1935) and *Ripping Stories for Girls* (n.d.) survive on my shelves today; others are lost.

The Bumper Book for Children (n.d.), still in my possession today, offered thick pulp paper, illustrations neatly coloured by a child, and stories that were both insipid and bafflingly English.

"The Captain and Jeremy," for example, tells a tale full of details and turns of expression that were utterly strange to me. As this story opens, Jeremy accidentally encounters the school cricket captain, Leslie Lawson, who discovers that Jeremy has seen a stray cat.

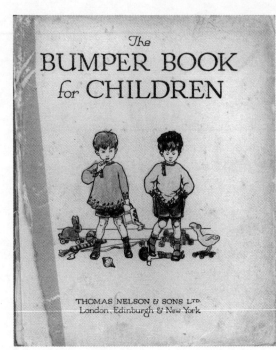

THE CAPTAIN AND JEREMY

JEREMY DACRE dashed out of his house shouting as loud as he could shout. And that was very loud indeed. Even Leslie Lawson, the captain of the school cricket team, who was strolling by, asked Jeremy what he was shouting about.

" It's that cat," burst out the excited Jeremy.

" A cat ? I thought the house was on fire. What cat ? "

" Can't you see him sprinting up the road ? "

" No, I can't—he's gone. What about him ? "

" He sneaks into our kitchen," blazed Jeremy, " and steals our food—when he can get any."

" Of course you feed him."

" Of course not."

Lawson whistled softly and looked surprised. Jeremy fidgeted uneasily. It was the dream of his young life to stand well with the captain.

" We had a cat once," remarked the latter, " not now, though. Have you twopence ? "

14

∧ The Bumper Book for Children, *title page* (*coloured by Mum or a sibling*) *and page 14.* [*Courtesy Thomas Nelson & Sons*]

Jeremy fidgeted uneasily. It was the dream of his young life to stand well with the captain.

"We had a cat once," remarked the latter, "not now, though. Have you twopence?"

Jeremy had, for a wonder. He brought out four sticky halfpennies.

"Those will do," Lawson graciously approved. "Perhaps you would just come down the road with me."

Wouldn't he just? To be seen walking with a Fourth Form fellow a head taller than himself and a cricket captain—crumbs!

Stiff and erect Jeremy marched beside him. To his amazement the captain turned into a butcher's shop. (Chandler, n.d., pp. 14–15)

The cat I could account for; we had cats. But the cricket, the Fourth Form, the halfpennies, and the butcher's shop were all alien, and I had to muster together some sense simply by applying first principles (a strong word to use in relation to this banal saga, I do appreciate!). And a phrase like "crumbs!" was obviously self-explanatory in terms of expressing awed enthusiasm—but represented a register I never encountered on human lips. Jeremy's stiffness and erectness did not concern me as a child, though I cannot read the phrase now without wondering about the mind that composed it.

All of these mysterious building blocks, consisting of life experiences I could not recognize, were assembled to create a story barely worth the telling; even as a keen reader with a shortage of reading materials I could never muster much enthusiasm for most of the narratives in this book. And yet I learned a lot about the processes of interpretation from this meagre little story and its counterparts: how to read past the details to the emotional core (which in the case of Jeremy's awe of the cricket captain was also alien to me but at least I could understand it). I learned that, in a way, it was up to me to make the story worth reading—and I also learned the very important lesson that, actually, sometimes it would never repay the trouble.

Only one story in this book gave me any pleasure to revisit for this project: "A Short Cut to Australia" by Mrs. J.T. Brown. Blanche is concerned that her beloved Uncle Wilfred will be shipwrecked on his coming trip to Australia, so she tries to dig a hole through the earth to provide him with a shortcut (forgetting that big fire at the core—a fact about the world that was certainly news to me when I read about it! In fact, I think there is every chance that it was from this story that I learned that the world is round). Uncle Wilfred trips in the hole in the dark and breaks his leg, so he cannot sail as booked, and the ship he would have boarded *is* shipwrecked, and so Blanche has saved the day. This story was also full of alien ingredients (gardeners, and nurses and maids) but something about Blanche's unspoken panic over her uncle's departure, and perhaps also that exciting intellectual discovery about the fire at the earth's core, stuck with me for many, many years. The rhyme and reason of what gives one story and not another some kind of emotional hook into your memory is a subject so complex that I suspect we will never truly understand it.

The Bumper Book for Children offered pretty dismal fare, but other titles at home were more promising. Some stories, of course, come pre-tested for memorableness. One example among the books I retrieved from my parents' shelves is *Grimms' Fairy Tales* (1945). I remembered the book perfectly clearly, but I had forgotten where it came from. On the first pages of this book is written (no fewer than three times but clearly in vain) the name and address of one of the girls living in the downstairs flat, 108 Pennywell Road. We had this book in our possession for many years; I recall reading and rereading these stories. Luckily for my literary education, the family downstairs had purchased a relatively unexpurgated version of the German folktales. This volume thus represents an important category in the development of many domestic collections: that of books borrowed and never returned, a set that increases the motley provenance of the household library still further. (And of course there is the impact of the corresponding empty set of books loaned out and never seen again.)

The role of private lending in a reader's life is even more difficult to track than other kinds of reading. Owned books linger on the domestic shelves; borrowed library books leave a trace in the lending records of the institution. A book that is borrowed from a friend and then returned simply disappears. I do dimly recall being a bit wary of books I acquired in this way—not that I was not delighted to get hold of them, but I knew it would be more difficult to reread them; friends were likely to think me peculiar if I returned to them incessantly to reborrow books they knew I had already read. The librarians didn't care, so a library book functioned every bit as well as an owned book for rereading purposes. Nevertheless, the books of other people oxygenated my access, and some stayed, with or without the owner's approval, and enriched my collection.

The Library Factor

The fall I turned eight, I joined Brownies. Every Saturday, I went to my Brownie meeting at school, then carried on down a short hill to the library before going home for lunch. The library collection was much larger than anything available to me elsewhere, but it was finite, especially for such a gendered selector as I was. After the first year, I reborrowed as much as I found new materials. Unfortunately, I have not been able to locate either the catalogue or the acquisitions list for the children's collection in the 1950s. This absence throws me back on my memories rather more completely than I had hoped, but even so, I can assemble a very long list of books I met in the library, many already mentioned in these pages.

The library filled numerous gaps in our domestic collection. I cannot remember whether the library offered Stratemeyer books such as *Nancy Drew* or the *Bobbsey Twins*; my best recollection is that they were not available there and that for these books I relied on those two indispensable cartons of the hand-me-down books and on loans from friends. Similarly, I simply do not recall whether or not I topped up my supplies of other series titles at the library. I think Cherry Ames (Wells) and Sue Barton (Boylston) were on offer, being vaguely more improving than some of the other series heroines, I suppose. A couple of hours with that lost 1950s catalogue of the Gosling Memorial Library would supplement this project very usefully.

Even reading as voraciously as I did, I missed a lot. I read *Farmer Boy* but didn't realize that Laura Ingalls Wilder had written many more titles, the rest all about girls (I would have eaten up the *Little House* series). I did not meet Ramona, though the first books about her were available. My father brought home some Kipling books from the library and tried to persuade me to read them, but I resisted; I found them hard to get into, a combination of unfamiliar register in the text itself and the book's dark, crowded pages of print. One title that my memory simply cannot disentangle is *The Secret Garden*; I do not remember reading it as a child, but when I encountered it as an adult, it seemed enormously familiar (not conclusive evidence, given its ubiquity in our culture). The librarians were certainly benevolent, but I do not recall them supplying much in the way of readers' advisory services, and I was a child who would have greatly benefited from some external assistance, all the more as I balked at so many of my parents' suggestions.

I read an enormous amount, probably more than I would ever read again in my life. The absences are haunting: no E. Nesbitt, no C.S. Lewis, no *Wizard of Oz* or *Just-So Stories* or *Peter Pan*. Nevertheless, I did read more broadly than this account so far indicates, and much of my cultural repertoire came from one now very obscure source.

The Keystone Book

As with my childhood access to books, the ecology of this study has its own terrifying element of randomness; my current collection of materials, inherited or reacquired, that I am carefully accumulating is dependent on many factors, not all of which I can control. This issue is highlighted by one mysterious volume that survived from my mother's childhood into my own, and that I fortunately still possess today. When I came to inspect it, I was astonished to see how many questions about my childhood reading it answered for me, vague but important questions that I had barely worked my way to formulating, for all my years of reflecting on my reading past.

For almost the entire duration of this project, I was unable to name this book. The spine and the title page are missing, and there is no internal publishing information to pin down what it might be called. Only excellent detective work by a diligent public librarian, right at the very end of my project as I prepared the final edits of the manuscript, gave me the title: *The Children's Wonder Book* (Crossland & Parrish, Eds., 1933). To have a title

CONTENTS

B.F.

11

for this compendium after so many years of thinking of it as an anonymous contributor to the literary compost heap in my brain is a very strange (but welcome) feeling. It was published by both Odhams and Collins, and I am still not sure which edition I own.

The book is big and navy blue, with an embossed image on the front cover of a rabbit herald, wearing an Alice-in-Wonderland tabard covered in hearts, holding a scroll and blowing a trumpet. Inside, I count 134 entries in the table of contents. As a superior children's treasury, it contains many stories that I met only in this volume: legends of Robin Hood; a complete *Alice in Wonderland*; "The Pied Piper of Hamelin"; tales from Grimm and Andersen and *The Arabian Nights*; and a complete *King of the Golden River* by Ruskin. In addition it features abridgements or adaptations of *The Water Babies*, *Robinson Crusoe*, *Gulliver's Travels*, and *A Christmas Carol*; a selection from *Aesop's Fables*; an assortment of legends from the British Isles and another of European fairy tales; a sampling of Edward Lear, Mrs. Ewing, Jules Verne, Nathaniel Hawthorne, Mark Twain, Thomas Hughes, Washington Irving, Oscar Wilde, and Kenneth Grahame. There are a couple of Lamb's *Tales from Shakespeare*, an extract from *Aucassin and Nicolette*, some Greek myths, and two stories from *The Mabinogion*. There is even a Chinese story, retold by Charles Lamb. In addition there are many poems, and the whole thing is richly illustrated in both colour and black and white.

If I did not still own this book, I would certainly be hard pressed to name half the titles I have listed above (and even if I had known or remembered the title, *The Children's Wonder Book* does not offer useful search terms). This anthology gave me countless hours of absorbed pleasure and also, even for the few stories I did not complete, provided me with a repertoire for reading other materials, a rich intertextual resource. I don't know that I have ever realized until now that I read bits of *The Mabinogion* in my youth. The *Arabian Nights* stories—Ali Baba, Sindbad, Aladdin—acquainted me with a set of exotically alluring stories that I never encountered anywhere else and provided me with a sufficient frame of reference that I could at least honour allusions when they were mentioned in other stories. And so with many of the entries; in addition to being a treasury of reading materials in its own right, it served as a source book, a companion, a handbook, informing my encounters with other children's books later in my life. It supplied me with a broader range of cultural literacy than I would have been able to invoke without it. As the series books provided me with a set of functioning stereotypes to aid my development into a fluent reader, so this treasury gave me a grander repertoire, many nuggets of which lurk in my memory to this day. It also supplied the great bulk of my fantasy reading. That enigmatic blue volume stretched the parameters of my reading tastes with its broad variety of imaginary universes.

Simultaneously, of course, I was being exposed to a broad swathe of the Western canon of literature for children. John Stephens and Robyn

McCallum (2013/1998) observe that one function of a canon is "to construct, preserve, and perpetuate particular forms of cultural knowledge....The effect of a canon is to mediate the ways ideas are transformed as they pass from one historical-ideological situation to another, in a myriad number of transformations" (p. 21). The collection presented in the book provides what Stephens and McCallum label as significant social functions: "Under the guise of offering children access to strange and exciting worlds removed from everyday experiences, they serve to initiate children into aspects of a social heritage, transmitting many of a culture's central values and assumptions and a body of shared allusions and experiences" (p. 3). It is undoubtedly true, as they argue, that much of the impact of retelling (or even reassembling, as in this example) is "overwhelmingly subject to a limited number of conservative metanarratives—that is, the implicit and usually invisible ideologies, systems, and assumptions which operate globally in a society to order knowledge and experience" (p. 3). What is moved from other cultures into this anthology is reframed as part of the great Western tradition, probably even more strongly because of the way it is presented in one single volume. At the end of my reading, in Walt Whitman's (1892) terms, "I [was] large, I contain[ed] multitudes" (n.p.), multitudes that I had certainly never imagined before. Yet, it would be possible to make a strong case that the "I" who featured in this expansion exercise was paradoxically more Western at its conclusion than at the start.

When I started this project, I knew that I had read many of these stories and poems at some point in my youth; I had no idea, until I looked at this book again, how many of them had been crammed into one 766-page compendium. Its very size and scale rendered all the stories in some ways similar to each other, presented as they were on identical pages. This phenomenon explains a kind of vagueness of provenance that I have long associated with some of the assembled titles. Once again I am reassured that my memory is trustworthy; that the amorphousness of what I recall in relation to these examples (Where on earth did I run into *Aladdin*? How do I know "The Pied Piper"? Surely I read at least some of *The Water Babies* at some point? And so forth.) is accounted for by the relative sameness in the page presentation of so many very different stories.

My own children read many, though certainly not all of these titles, but in freestanding, attractively illustrated, and distinctive books. They may have thus found some of the tales more accessible and more memorable in their separate presentations; what they may have lost is the sense of the collective riches of the world's story-trove that I gleaned from this tightly packed anthology—and then half-forgot until I began to look at it in some depth for the purposes of writing this chapter.

Clearly many of the stories in the big blue book were at least as exotic to me as the little tales in *The Bumper Book for Children*, but they provided considerably more return for the hermeneutic energy it took to comprehend them. They were baffling but in an alluring way. No reader could be desperate enough for print matter ever to care very much about Jeremy and his snobby yearnings over the captain, but Ali Baba and Gulliver and the Pied Piper and Alice had some meat on their bones; if they called for leaps of the mind just to establish some basic form of comprehension, they offered in return a sense of echoing mysteries beyond what could ever be established on the page. I suppose Jeremy and his ilk did at least give me some practice in recognizing the difference.

I am surprised at how many gaps are closed by this crowded volume. It is a reminder of the importance of the book as object; if I had met these stories separately presented, I am sure I would remember them more distinctly (I wonder if e-readers will find their recollected titles merging in similar ways because of the absence of distinctive pages). I am thankful that the book survived, even untitled, to remind me that my quotidian book reading was augmented with such literary richness. I know now that it opened doors to fantasy worlds, fertilized my cultural repertoire, and gave me at least an acquaintance with much of the world's heritage of children's classics. This most forgotten book of all the ones that I once read and have been able to retrieve again turns out to have offered the most lavish reading diet of everything in the house. It is a testimonial to the intellectual-compost-creating nature of the domestic library, I suppose, that for the longest time I could not even name it.

My respectful thanks go to Sarah Zakordonski of Strathcona County Library for sleuthing work that would do Nancy Drew proud; her main clue was a discrepant initial in an illustrator's name. I pursued her suggested title on a variety of sites and am 99 per cent convinced she is correct, even though some of the surviving copies have red covers. Every other detail matches, and the pictures of the red covers show the same embossed rabbit herald; the entries for the title record the same number of pages and list many of the authors and titles.

At one level, the name of this anthology is unimportant; the work it accomplished for at least one young reader offers the substance of the story. And yet to tidy up a loose end in this satisfying way adds an appealing note to the final laborious stages of this project. A children's novel would be proud of such a dramatic, last-minute flourish.

Jack and Jill

For a while in the late 1950s and perhaps into the early 1960s, we had a subscription to the American children's magazine *Jack and Jill*. The arrival of new reading material every month was a great luxury, and these magazines combined with several television programs to teach me many facets of American patriotism. To be fair to the editors, the contents of those issues I have been able to inspect for this project are far more international than I recall (and I do know that my only acquaintance with the alluring and repellant Baba Yaga and her mysterious house on chicken legs came through these pages; I have always been grateful that I met this strange being as a child young enough to be haunted by her).

My parents' monthly 35 cents was money well spent. The magazine refreshed the domestic reading supply. Nobody would call the stories literary, but it regularly introduced some revitalizing novelty into my reading life. It suggested crafts, and although my efforts were almost always more modest than theirs, it did open up the idea that children could make things out of very restricted supplies. The miscellaneousness of the contents was sometimes scattershot but did often hit a bull's eye. Finally, it introduced a few child voices to our reading mix, although it never would have occurred to me to *contribute* to the reader-driven columns, *At My Desk* and *North, South, East, West*. (Taking part in the world of literature was for children in other countries; I felt equally alienated from the Famous Five Club, advertised in the back of the Enid Blyton books and demanding a shilling to join. I did not even know what a shilling was, so I was obviously not welcome.)

The main ideological import of *Jack and Jill* (as I noticed even at the time; being an outsider can sharpen your perceptions) was nationalistic. The repertoires of child readers were taken for granted. Among the variety of puzzles, join-the-dots, crafts, and so forth is a colouring page: the state flag to colour for December 1959, for example, comes from Massachusetts, and we are given a list of factoids about that state as well as a bit of potted history. I wish I could remember when "not-American" became a clear part of my own sense of myself, but all I know is that I was very young and that this kind of exercise would have sharpened my awareness of the distinctions between American children and me. I did not have to care about Massachusetts while they apparently did, and no collection of little facts would ever make me do so.

The Women's Magazines

Money was tight in our household but some always went on magazines. Mum had a subscription to the *Ladies' Home Journal* (LHJ) and she intermittently acquired *Better Homes and Gardens* and *McCall's*, as well as the occasional *Good Housekeeping* and *Redbook*. I don't remember the Canadian magazine *Chatelaine* until years later.

"The Year without a Santa Claus" (McGinley, 1956) and "The Story of Holly and Ivy" (Godden, 1957) offered early opportunities for child reading in an adult venue (the latter probably gave me my first experience of learning to find the rest of the story, "continued on page 156"). I will return to these texts in a later chapter. The paper doll page of Betsy McCall (*McCall's*, ongoing) also suggested that there was a small space for children in a grown-up world. By restricted degrees, I began to read more of Mum's magazines. They were there, they offered the crucial temptation of novelty, and sometimes they pointed to a more exotic and mature life-world than ever appeared in my own novels. I attempted many of my first forays into adult reading with these magazines. Revisiting them was an exceptionally poignant experience, perhaps because my initial encounters were always in a context of very ephemeral contact. Lost specifics of my own life during a particular, labelled month and year brush the edges of these pages in suggestive ways. I ordered a small collection off the Internet and found them so appealing and informative that I went back and picked up a few more. Even in a study like this one that regularly calls up the flavours of the 1950s, these materials stand out as particularly evocative of daily life.

It is striking to the contemporary eye that the 1950s LHJ is extremely wordy, abounding in grey pages with multiple columns of print. The quality of the colour reproductions in the issues I now own is both garish and blurry. There are many stretches of pages, especially in the earlier issues, where the only colour comes in an advertisement.

I think I expected the columns to reiterate the dire sexism that the 1950s are famous for, but the texts are a bit subtler than that. There are references to a variety of options for women. What is never questioned is that the expert always knows best. The expert—doctor, psychologist, scientist—is usually male, and in that sense the magazine closed rather than opened doors for me. But in its reflections of contemporary life for women in North America, I found the LHJ a bit more plural than I had anticipated.

Take the monthly feature, How America Lives. Its contents varied widely. Some stories were cloying; some were cute. One entry contained a blow-by-blow account of a home birth (Younger, 1960); I have no memory of reading that article, and I strongly suspect that my mother hid it away.

In May 1959, the LHJ featured a woman bravely raising her four children solely on the 100-dollar monthly alimony she received from her ex-husband. One of her observations about saving money shocked me profoundly at the time: "Do you know that the more inexpensive your brand of toilet tissue, the coarser it will be, and the less the children—and I—will use?" (Hayes, 1959, p. 168). Our lives on Pennywell Road were not lavish, but we did not have to be *that* careful. It was an image of extreme penny-pinching that lingered for decades in my mind. No doubt even the mention of toilet paper in any but an advertising context caught me by surprise and made the image more memorable, but it was more than simple titillation. Buried in that sentence, so startling to me at the age of ten, was an image of adult desperation that opened new doors in my mind. It seems like something trivial, but it was never trivial to me. The burdens of adulthood still hover round that sentence as I read it today—and its evocation of an embodied reaction is hard to dispute.

Not all life in the pages of the LHJ was so bleak. I was an inveterate reader of Can This Marriage Be Saved?—a column that was still running, though in a seriously curtailed format, when the LHJ finally bowed out of the monthly magazine market in 2014, and that almost never presented a problem without a solution. Here, too, I learned about Life, though I was surprised in 2012 to discover that Life as represented in that column involved much more about sexual satisfaction than I recall reading at the time! It must have passed directly over my head; I am certain I did not know enough to make sense of the relatively explicit observations (explicit at least in 1959 terms) that regularly appear. As a rule, the marriage was indeed saved, once the expert started laying down advice, though there was one column in October 1959 that featured a marriage that could not be saved (Disney, 1959). As a rule, however, the happy ending was guaranteed (as indeed it is today). The column provides a mixture of pop psychology and common sense, and offers an interesting window on the times.

Patricia Meyer Spacks (2011), in a book on rereading that concentrates rather more on adult reading experience than my own project does, talks about her early encounters with the *Ladies' Home Journal* as a kind of guilty pleasure:

> *That was probably my first literary vice—and it persisted, I blush to say, for many years. My mother subscribed to the* Journal *so I started reading it when I was young, and I loved it all: stories, recipes, and especially the monthly feature called "Can This Marriage Be Saved?" The answer to that question was invariably yes, and I enjoyed speculating about and then discovering how the happy ending could be effected. I felt that by reading the monthly revelations about marital difficulties and their resolutions I was storing up useful information for my future. I still remember my dismay when, just before I went to college, the title changed one month to "This Marriage Could Not Be Saved." (pp. 218–219)*

For me, the *Ladies' Home Journal* seemed not a vice but a portal into a wider world whose constraints and limits were not apparent to me. As series books offered me useful stereotypes for reading about children's lives, the LHJ offered me the opportunity to try on some stereotypes of adult life. But an inspection of the December 1957 LHJ shows that stereotypes had to share space with more thought-provoking material.

The issue contains the lengthy story about Holly and Ivy by Rumer Godden, the concluding chapter of a serialized novel by Norah Lofts, and a complete condensed novel by Elizabeth Cadell. A surprising number of the many grey, three-columned pages are filled with fiction. The non-fiction runs a broad gamut, from an article entitled, "Do We Give the Mentally Ill a Chance?" to an article about a Moroccan princess whom the LHJ credits for battling the obligatory use of the veil in her country, to a description of Christmas in Saudi Arabia. At the same time, four of the rare colour-filled pages are devoted to an exotic fashion feature starring Mrs. John F. Kennedy and her sister, Mrs. Michael T. Canfield (later Lee Radziwill), in a range of very elegant clothing.

The instalment of Can This Marriage Be Saved? in this issue provides a clear example of how my retrospective project occasionally strikes a time warp. The couple's problems include the fact that the husband hits the wife from time to time, particularly after drinking. When the children object to this behaviour, he spanks them and sends them to bed without supper.

>How to Dress Well on Practically Nothing! Originally published in the May 1959 Ladies' Home Journal® *Magazine.*

[*Courtesy Meredith Corporation*]

The counsellor who gets things back on an even keel for this pair never mentions any of this violence in his lengthy summing up. I cannot read my twenty-first century sensibility "out" of this article. I find myself angry both on behalf of the wife and children in the piece and also on behalf of my nine-year-old self, reading this account as an acceptable resolution of real-life adult concerns. This article reminds me that any kind of historic recreation of my initial reading experience is impossible.

Hitting was commonplace in the 1950s. Nobody chastised Roy Rogers for his fisticuffs (and indeed that December issue of LHJ contain two full-page coloured advertisements for genuine Roy Rogers toys and commodities, a reminder of the enormous marketing campaign that fuelled his popularity). Similarly, nobody thought to mention that the husband in this article perhaps did not deserve the goodwill of his family when he treated them so brutally. Nobody objected to corporal punishment in the schools or took it amiss when teachers made fun of the poorest or stupidest children. This article highlights the kind of change in thinking over the decades in between that it is impossible to unthink. I cannot put myself back into a place where an early resort to domestic violence is the normal and unmarked behaviour, even though I know I lived through this era and was indeed spanked myself on occasion (though not so unjustly!).

My parents were very fortunate in their marriage as far as I was aware at the time, or indeed since. In view of my limited experience, Can This Marriage Be Saved? offered me a rather more complex texture of adult life. The polyvocal form of the column—first the wife, then the husband, then the counsellor, addresses readers directly—made room for me to be a spectator of their troubles, even if my understanding became a little blurry at the bedroom door. The format certainly enhanced my awareness that there was more than one perspective on any given set of events, and it gave me conceptual practice with a different kind of figure-and-ground exercise. My fiction reading, for the most part, was very much more monolithic in terms of point of view, and I learned valuable reading lessons from this column, however pat its conclusions and undesirable its social lessons.

Both these features were must-reads for me, certainly before my tenth birthday, but both paled in comparison to my favourite section of the LHJ: a little column, occupying about two-thirds of a single page and beguilingly entitled, How to Dress Well on Practically Nothing! This column more or less amounted to paper dolls for grown-ups, and knocked Betsy McCall out

TELL ME DOCTOR

CONTINUED FROM PAGE 38

helped Mrs. Weller regain the control she had come close to losing.

"Well, yes, Doctor, if it comes to that. But first—I did get a wild, fantastic hope. The other day I read a paragraph in a health magazine in my dentist's office. It said there is an operation now to repair tubes in women who have been sterilized. If there is any chance in the world that I could have a baby that would be my own and Phil's, that is what I want. But of course I wouldn't want to have another tubal pregnancy. And above all, I wouldn't want to bring some poor little blighted creature into the world. That is why I thought you ought to know the whole story. I warned you that my problem is complicated!"

"These cases are seldom simple, Mrs. Weller. Doctor Colt would not have sterilized you unless he had sincerely believed there were urgent reasons for doing so. I can see that you have taken some mighty tough blows with a wonderful spirit. Nothing would please me more than to be able to help you solve your problem. Let's break it down. Maybe it won't seem so complicated then.

"To your first question, the answer is that for some time now we have indeed been able to make a number of sterilized women fertile again through surgery. Under certain circumstances, that is.

"Let's leave that for the time being, and go on to the possibility of another tubal pregnancy and another blighted embryo. I agree that almost any doctor might very well have considered, a few years ago, that this combination called for prevention of further pregnancies. We know now, however, that a large percentage of women who become pregnant again after a tubal pregnancy have a normal experience in every way. If they have previously had normal pregnancies, their chances for further normal ones are increased materially.

"Another thing we have learned is that a blighted embryo doesn't necessarily mean that the ovum was defective at the start of the pregnancy. That was what bothered you particularly, wasn't it?" Mrs. Weller nodded, her eyes very bright. "Too, a normal embryo may be blighted accidentally—by something like an infectious disease suffered by the mother in very early months of pregnancy. When the mother is generally healthy, and there has been no family history of abnormal births, the chance of a recurrence is very small indeed. What I am principally wondering about is the reason for the tubal pregnancy. It might account for the blighted embryo too. Why, I mean, the fertilized ovum remained in the Fallopian tube, instead of passing on down to the uterus and growing there. Have you ever had infected tubes? Any trouble with your first two childbirths? Or afterward?"

"As I told you, I had irregular bleeding and felt pretty awful with my third pregnancy. And I remember now that I had a pelvic infection following the birth of my little girl. There was a bad pain, rather low down on the left side, with chills and fever. They kept me in the hospital for three weeks. Could some of the infection have remained?"

"It's possible that your left tube was damaged by the infection. That in turn could have caused the tubal pregnancy. Tell me something more. How long did it take you to get pregnant the first time?"

Mrs. Weller smiled. "Well, since we figured on a rather long string of pregnancies once we started, we took some time to adjust to marriage and to get our home ready for a family. But once we decided the time had come, I never menstruated again until after my first baby was born."

The doctor nodded. "Excellent! Mrs. Weller, I am going to say very frankly that under all these circumstances, today the abnormal embryo would not be considered a legitimate indication for sterilization. Especially when it occurred in a tubal pregnancy. So I am very glad that there is a possibility of restoring your reproductive powers. That will depend, it is my duty to warn you, upon the present condition of your reproductive organs. And also upon the method Doctor Colt used to

sterilize you. But if some of one normal tube remains, we often can patch things up."

"It's a pity I didn't learn more from Doctor Colt before he died. Can anything be done about that?"

"I am sure Doctor Colt's office records will be available. I will find out. And I can get your operative record from the hospital, unquestionably, if you will give them your permission to release it. Then you will have to come in again so that I can examine you thoroughly

and test your remaining tube. Get an appointment from Mary Anne, will you, please?"

Two weeks later Mrs. Weller was back in the doctor's consulting room, accompanied this time by her husband, at the doctor's suggestion. The doctor motioned toward a file of papers on his desk. "I have here Doctor Colt's complete records with regard to Mrs. Weller. I have made as thorough an analysis as is necessary of Mrs. Weller's status in regard to having babies. I think that now we are ready to get down to cases.

"I find that, according to Doctor Colt's report, the left tube was damaged by the tubal pregnancy," the doctor told them. "He re-

moved it in toto, which automatically rendered you sterile on the left side, Mrs. Weller, as I think you both know already. After getting Mr. Weller's consent"—Mr. Weller cast an apologetic glance at his wife—"Doctor Colt then removed about half an inch of the right tube, which appeared normal. The section he removed was pretty close to the outer end of the tube—that is to say, the end nearest the ovary. He crushed both of the cut ends and tied them with heavy sutures. This rendered it impossible for the ovum to enter the tube to be fertilized, completing the sterilization process. But it left Mrs. Weller with two good functional ovaries. And what is quite as important,

How to Dress Well on Practically Nothing!

Background for Summer...

Right now Barbara J. looks forward to warm days ahead, fashion-wise looks forward to the perfect solution for what to wear. She wants a dress to enter into her spring wardrobe now, and most of all to be her one important dress for all summer long. The prerequisite? A pretty look for daytime or evening, for office efficiency or weekends away . . . one dress to take on many moods. Barbara doesn't think this borders on the miraculous at all, and her solution is very simple. She buys a turquoise dress and with several additions the difference between night and day, one mood and another is very evident.   By BET HART

Barbara makes another, and an important, addition—an aqua rayon-linen coat. This one from Vogue's "Easy to Make" Design No. 4001 has a high pocket detail. Barbara might have the fabric waterproofed by her cleaner— would make a costume for all rainy days as well. Coat to make, $5.50.

© VOGUE

Barbara wears her new dress. To and from the office likes the added cover-up in a turquoise-and-blue hop-sacking print. Barbara makes this one from a pattern she already has, Vogue "Easy to Make" Design No. 9531 (she bought last August). Dress to buy, $10.98 Blouse to make, $1.71*

THE DRESS:

+ *A polka-dot scarf at the waistline. This addition costs $1.00 and is one of Barbara's favorites.*

+ *A white piqué bolero. A working day, a luncheon date and Barbara likes a short cover-up. $2.00*

+ *A romantic skirt in a sheer plaid— three yards of fabric, two yards of turquoise ribbon.*

DRESS BY MOD-GOLD

*For back views, sizes and prices, see page 172

of the ballpark. Part of its appeal lay in its cumulative nature; Barbara J., the model, was always busy assembling a capsule wardrobe for one season or another. Sometimes she mixed and matched with items she had acquired in previous columns, with cunning little thumbnail images of earlier purchases. For a while I cut the columns out and saved them. Seeing them again in 2011 and 2012 gave me a deep jolt of familiarity.

In one column from May 1959, some items are bought and some are sewn by Barbara. The dress costs $10.98 to buy, the coat she sews for $5.50. Other prices are just as remarkable. What I especially liked, I think, was not so much the economies or the resourcefulness that Barbara J. invariably manifested—rather more I was captured by the idea of being so calmly in control of life. Of course, the notion of having new clothes every month was also very appealing.

Sometimes I read the magazine stories; sometimes I didn't. Even if I didn't, I began to take in some of the names of the authors. LHJ authors Daphne du Maurier (May 1959) Norah Lofts (December 1957), Elizabeth Cadell (December 1957), and many others were names I would meet else-where, such as in the Book-of-the-Month Club. A complete list of authors whose names I first encountered in the pages of these magazines would represent a solid cross section of the popular reading of the time. The word "middlebrow" is almost entirely pejorative today, but these writers were often accessible to me, and they often wrote novels as well; their role in inducting me at least into the shallows of adult reading was very considerable.

But the magazines also contained mind traps. It has surprised me, returning to the pages of the LHJ, to discover how dull much of the material seems to me today. Like many contemporary readers, I am no longer comfortable with the leisurely style of much of this writing. I am even more uncomfortable with the way many authors cozily co-opt their readers in a kind of knowing conspiracy ("of course we all know this is the right way to think—don't we?"). At the age of eleven or twelve, I was flattered to be incorporated by this grown-up voice; now I find it infuriating, and very, very claustrophobic.

Take the work of Phyllis McGinley, much-loved author of "The Year without a Santa Claus." Her status and credibility were impeccably estab-lished for me, and I was pleased to recognize her name when she started writing for LHJ in the late 1950s. But McGinley's adult voice speaks to co-conspirators in the creation of a Correct View of the World, one that involved a strident (and dishonest) "back to the hearth" ideology. "We women," according to McGinley, were essential to the domestic well-being of our families—but as with many other female authors, including my mother's beloved Mary Quayle Innis (of whom, more later), the construction of womanhood developed in her writing deliberately excluded the kind of intellectual attainments that so manifestly marked the author's own life. At a time when I could have benefited greatly by exploring a variety of alternative life possibilities, I was shepherded again and again to the crossroads where I would have to choose between being feminine or being a person who was adventurous with ideas, and correspondingly *not* feminine. This false dichotomy became more and more restrictive as I approached adolescence and offers a clear-cut example of literacy as confinement rather than emancipation.

Of course, these authors were entitled to write as they chose, and they may well have been expressing conflicts that raged in their own lives—but, whatever they were working out for themselves, they missed an opportunity to open horizons for the girls who might follow in their paths.

Moving On

Gradually, selectively, and very tentatively, I moved into the world of adult reading. In some cases, I responded to a kind of "bait and switch" address, a text that invited me in on one set of terms and then changed the nature of my relationship with the fictional world. A very good example of this phenomenon is contained in the saga of my *Dick Tracy* experience in the early stages of my reading life.

I started reading *Dick Tracy* in the daily comics in 1956, initially seduced by the fabulous car owned by villain Flattop Jr. Credited by some with inspiring early James Bond vehicles, it was a miracle car that contained every convenience a person could want: a stove, a fridge, a record player, and many more home comforts. I was fascinated by this car, and when the story took a more sinister turn I followed right along.

Wikipedia, in a list of recurring *Dick Tracy* characters, supplies this profile:

Flattop Jones Jr. (1956)....was a talented artist and mechanical genius. A borderline juvenile delinquent, he lived in his "hot rod" car, which he modified by installing various electrical devices (including a stove) connected

to the dashboard's cigarette lighter. Driven insane by [the] ghost of [a] girl-
friend whom he had killed. ("List of Dick Tracy characters," n.d.)

The Wikipedia entry does not emphasize the nature of Flattop Jr.'s haunting by the murdered girl. Drawn as a transparent outline form, she clings to his neck and is present in every single picture. I find it hard to imagine how a writer could convey the relentlessness of that haunting. Saying, "Flattop, with the girl clinging to his neck" every time he is mentioned would soon become tiresome. Flattop's inability to shed his albatross for even a single moment is indelibly conveyed by the images, and the term "haunted" takes on a new and frightening connotation of permanence and inexorability.

One day, the longer weekend colour instalment recorded Flattop's undoing. I ran screaming to my friend's house, shrieking all the way, "They've got Flattop! They've got Flattop!" My mother was appalled at this wanton public display and decreed that I was not mature enough for such exciting reading fodder. She vetoed *Dick Tracy*, but I continued to read it anyway, of course; to abandon that thrilling narrative partway through was out of the question.

In 1956 I was seven years old; it is not hard to see my mother's point that this content might perhaps be a bit lurid for my tender eyes. In fact, it was one of the few occasions on which I even remotely approached the outermost gateways to the sensational; my reading of adult materials was largely harmless, with all the positives and negatives that such a label implies. At the same time, with the assistance of its illustrations as supplementary "handholds," so to speak, *Dick Tracy* taught me to follow interwoven sequences of events in surprisingly sophisticated ways. Television was slow, books were largely monofocal, but this comic strip ran several narratives at once and planted seeds for a new episode even before the previous one was finished, while also maintaining a backstory. Today's children encounter many different kinds of text with these qualities, but for me *Dick Tracy* was probably as advanced as it got. I would have been surprised to have this fact pointed out to me at the time; I internalized my mother's prejudice that comics were low-life. Fortunately I read them anyway, and at least one of them taught me some major reading lessons.

All the bright comics in the *Weekend Magazine* invited childish readers, and with my contemporary eyes, I now find their rampant and endemic sexism far more damaging than *Dick Tracy*'s melodramatic escapades (in fact, rookie detective Lizz is actually a bit of a model for girls). Nobody objected to the eponymous heroine's vacuous life with Dagwood in *Blondie* or the belittling exchanges between Maggie and Jiggs in *Bringing Up Father*; both women and men were demeaned in these theoretically funny strips. But far from being banned, they entered our daily vocabulary via the Dagwood sandwich and the Jiggs dinner.

The comics section was large and varied during those days; in one microfilmed edition of the *Weekend Magazine*, dated January 21, 1957, I counted twenty-six titles of individual strips. Many of them were graphic soap operas; only a few were directed particularly at children. It was an early introduction to the experience of a miscellany for me. Many of the comics were boring; I don't think I ever read *Rex Morgan, MD* or *Mary Worth*. I followed others such as *Joe Palooka* in very desultory ways. But *Dick Tracy* was a must-read, a threat to the steady pulse, and a challenge to my social and moral understanding as well as my reading acumen.

The newspaper comics addressed a wide age range and came officially into the house each weekend, but, as I moved through the later stages of childhood, I picked up much adult reading in more random and happenstance ways. Like most inveterate readers, I had to be reading something at all times, and if I ran out of kids' material, I might well grab something else if it looked halfway approachable.

"Approachable," of course, is in the eye of the beholder. At eleven and twelve I began to sample some of the more accessible adult novels lying around the house. A variety of scaffolds led me into this somewhat more ambitious reading territory. Comedy was one main portal to my earliest adult reading; I devoured *Cheaper by the Dozen* and *Belles on their Toes* (Gilbreth & Carey, 2002/1948, 1950). I gobbled up *Our Hearts Were Young and Gay* (Skinner & Kimbrough, 1944). I demolished all four volumes of *The Diary of a Provincial Lady* (Delafield, 1993/1947). Through these prisms, I developed some very frivolous and superficial notions of adult life. I began to acquire a new set of stereotypes.

Like very many pre-adolescent readers, I also cut my adult reading teeth on murder mysteries. By the age of thirteen, I was certainly consuming Agatha Christie, and I raced through the works of Mary Roberts Rinehart. For some time, as a result of the latter's powers of persuasion, I innocently believed that the main victims of the 1929 crash were wealthy bankers who metamorphosed from a life of luxury to one of penury, trapped in large and unsellable (and often sinister) mansions. When I finally got to *The Grapes of Wrath*, well into in my teens, my notions of the Great Depression required much mental "rewinding." But even when their political assumptions are delusional, murder mysteries, especially the conventional whodunnits, provide excellent scaffolding for a developing readers (see Mackey, 1991). The author lays out events, the reader peruses them, and at the end of the story the detective reprises them and points out how they *should* have been read.

My parents also read the titles I mention here, and we began to share a repertoire beyond the bedtime story list of A.A. Milne and Thornton W. Burgess.

The *Reader's Digest* Condensed Books were guaranteed to be less intimidating because of being so short and snappy, but I was choosy about subject matter. The books I selected can perhaps be best described in the cutting phrase of a friend of mine: "No young person would be seriously harmed by reading this book." They were sentimental but pretty toothless. *I Capture the Castle* (Smith, 1948) is also sentimental but in vivid and original ways—it takes the trope of sentimentality and pushes it to the limits. I first encountered it framed as an adult book, but its essentially adolescent strengths appealed to me greatly and, unlike much of the other adult pap I encountered, it stretched me.

I read one book just because my mother was so attached to it that I wanted to see what the appeal was all about. *Stand on a Rainbow* (Innis, 1943) was still on her bookshelf in 2007. By then Mum had already had the stroke that effectively destroyed her capacity to speak coherently, but when I asked her if I might borrow it, she managed a short sentence: "I love that book." The source of that appeal in this quiet story of a year in the life of an unremarkable housewife was not clear to me in my childhood and is not entirely transparent today, but the book was undeniably very important to my mother. Its significance to me altered when I discovered that Mary Quayle Innis was the wife of communications theorist Harold Innis and a formidable academic in her own right. Her sense of domestic oppression and (to be fair) domestic delight animates the book; the capacity to do independent scholarly work, a power that shaped her own life, is completely missing from the story. The housewife heroine Leslie is intellectually feckless, and she certainly offered me no sense that I could be a mother, a housewife, *and* (for example) a scholar (see Mackey, 2015, for further discussion of this title).

"The MAD Horror Primer" (Issue #49) received such a GREAT response from our readers (i.e. *"A GREAT disappointment!"*—B.F., Phila., Pa.; *"It would be GREAT if you discontinued this type feature!"*—L.D., Dallas, Tex.; *"Articles like that GRATE on my nerves!"*—F.H., Fresno, Calif.) that we've decided to present another primer. This one is for the benefit of any children under seven (in other words, ALL of our readers) who may possibly be interested in working in the advertising field when they grow up.

THE MAD MADISON AVENUE PRIMER

ARTIST: WALLACE WOOD   WRITER: LARRY SIEGEL

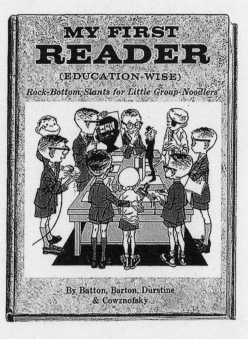

MY FIRST READER
(EDUCATION-WISE)
Rock-Bottom Slants for Little Group-Noodlers

By Batton, Barton, Durstine & Cowznofsky

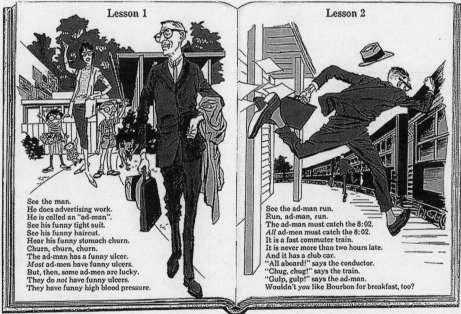

Lesson 1

See the man.
He does advertising work.
He is called an "ad-man".
See his funny tight suit.
See his funny haircut.
Hear his funny stomach churn.
Churn, churn, churn.
The ad-man has a funny ulcer.
Most ad-men have funny ulcers.
But, then, some ad-men are lucky.
They do *not* have funny ulcers.
They have funny high blood pressure.

Lesson 2

See the ad-man run.
Run, ad-man, run.
The ad-man must catch the 8:02.
All ad-men must catch the 8:02.
It is a fast commuter train.
It is never more than two hours late.
And it has a club car.
"All aboard!" says the conductor.
"Chug, chug!" says the train.
"Gulp, gulp!" says the ad-man.
Wouldn't *you* like Bourbon for breakfast, too?

∧ *A* MAD *parody from 1960, featured in* Totally MAD *(2012, p. 38).*

[From MAD #55 © E.C. Publications, Inc.]

There was little in any of these titles to trouble my orderly, middle-class, United Church, Canadian assumptions about adult life. My most icono-clastic reading was probably MAD *Magazine*, brought into the house by my brothers, and another exemplar of open address to a broad age range of readership. It was impossible even for the primmest of "good-girl" readers (and I was not quite that far gone) to resist its joyous irreverence. Parody was relatively rare in our ordered lives, and subversiveness was even more unusual. The political importance of MAD *Magazine* to me and to many other readers in the conformist 1950s and early 1960s was significant. The example from the magazine I include here, just to take one instance, offers MAD's familiar trademark blend of mocking both form and content: in this case both the early reader and the mindlessness of suburban conformity come under the microscope. I would certainly have been fully equipped as a reader to get the joke—though my repertoire would have been established largely through intertextuality since advertising men and commuter trains were alike alien to St. John's. On the other hand, I did know everything necessary about early readers.

Reading Up

Not long before my thirteenth birthday, toward the end of the timespan covered by this study, I was promoted upstairs to the adult library. It was good news at one level because I had truly exhausted the potential of the boys' and girls' collection, but I was utterly adrift among the monochrome bookshelves in the adult library. Dark-coloured spines and enigmatic titles gave me little to go on; at a single stroke I lost much of my expertise as a book selector. I recall very clearly my sense of desolation as I looked at these unfamiliar shelves and realized I had suddenly lost the value and utility of my familiar toolkit of loved authors, series knowledge, and general capacity to size up a book with a glance over its pages. It was a bleak time for me as a reader, and my parents seized the opportunity to "improve" my reading with adult recommendations. I rejected Dickens as entirely too wordy and strange, but I did take to Jane Austen (with a *frisson* of snobbish glee that I was reading something so distinguished at the age of twelve).

As I grew a little older, I began to delve into the melodramas that beset Jalna, the eponymous home centring Mazo de la Roche's epic series. The *Jalna* books were marginally less safe than my normal repertoire and the saga was as close to endless as made no difference to a rereader like myself.

I know I plunged deep into the series over a period of some years, but my recollection of the events and characters (save only for some vague memories of the virago-matriarch Adeline) was close to zero before I began to reread them for this project. Along with L.M. Montgomery, they were my only sustained Canadian reading, but the impact was considerably less permanent. And yet, I do recall the relief of having a place to head toward in the fiction section; the *Jalna* shelf provided at least one corner where I might begin to behave a bit more like an expert again.

Jalna, the first book de la Roche wrote, though not the chronological start of the saga, is racy stuff, compared to my usual fodder. Jalna is the name of the Ontario home of the Whiteoak family of five brothers and a sister (and that autocratic grandmother), and it is to Jalna that Eden Whiteoak brings his bride, Alayne. Before long, Alayne and Eden's brother Renny are hopelessly (but mostly honourably) in love with each other, and Eden himself has a brief affair with the wife of a different brother, Piers. Piers forgives his wayward wife, and they sort out an ongoing life together, but by the end of the book Eden, Renny, and Alayne are locked in a tragic triangle. As with *Dick Tracy* some years earlier, I was in way over my level of emotional comprehension with this stirring material, but I was gripped by the elemental forces of the story even when I didn't entirely understand them.

Other forms of adult reading introduced variations on concepts of femininity, though the restrictions of the dainty life always looked familiar. I tried a few historical romances by the likes of Georgette Heyer but they did not suit me. I simply read enough to reinforce a pernicious repertoire of the desirability of swishing skirts and lowered glances. I read a novelization or two about the various romantic Tudors. It was all predictable stuff and probably did more to alienate me from my own surroundings than any other kind of reading material.

It was not a happy time in my reading life. I missed the security of knowing how to assess a collection. Some of my new reading was bewildering, but I could not go backward. There was a limit to the number of times even I could reread my comfort titles. I scored an occasional bull's eye, but more often I wound up reading books I only sort of liked. I had more guidance at home than many young people, but I still felt adrift.

Between comedies, mysteries, the soap opera of *Jalna*, and the proprieties of a couple of Jane Austen titles, plus my sampling of LHJ fiction, I developed a motley and not overly distinguished "reading ladder" and began to clamber toward at least the popular forms of adult tastes. I learned many things about reading from this random potpourri, and a number of these reading lessons have had to be unlearned to enable me to take real adult nuances on board. It wasn't graceful and it certainly wasn't constant forward progress—but I floundered toward more mature reading nevertheless.

The Unmemorable

This project skews toward materials that offer at least a glimmer of memorability; for the most part, if I don't recall at least a single thread leading back to a text, it is not represented here. Fortunately for the comprehensiveness of my sample, however, I am able to produce one example of a book that was not worth remembering at all. More or less by definition, it must stand in for an unknown number of other such books.

On January 18, 1962, I recorded this line in my diary: "I am reading the most gorgeus [*sic*] book called 'Melora.'" I was thirteen and regularly dipping into adult reading at that point. But though I was impressed with *Melora* at the time, it was a title that meant absolutely nothing to me when I came across this diary entry more than fifty years later.

I located *Melora* through the miracle of online second-hand book sales, but I reread it without the slightest recollection of any single ingredient. *Melora* (Eberhart, 1959) is a page-turner with a certain easy-come, easy-go quality to its riveting suspense. The book amalgamates the more inane aspects of Mary Roberts Rinehart's mysteries and many Doris Day movies, with a strong dose of Daphne du Maurier. Anne, the heroine, is the second wife of a wealthy lawyer. Like the second Mrs. de Winter, she is haunted by the belief that her husband really yearns after his first wife, the eponymous Melora, an apprehension fuelled by insinuating comments from her widowed sister-in-law Cassie. Add a snowstorm that brings New York to a standstill and isolates Anne at home, and a strange knife-bearing man possessed of a sinister ability to get into that house even when the doors are locked, and you get the general idea.

A nameless contributor to girl-detective.net offers some further suggestions about why Mignon Eberhart might not linger in a reader's mind:

> *You have to be in the right mood to read Eberhart. Though plucky and*
> *well-bred, her heroines are some of the silliest in the mystery genre. The*

Melora

A novel of mystery and suspense
by the author of POSTMARK MURDER

MIGNON G. EBERHART

anonymous phone call bidding her hightail it down to the boathouse where murder has struck once before? She always answers on the first ring. Strange sounds in the attic of a house where murder walks the shadowy corridors? Sure, she's got five minutes to—er—kill; she'll just powder her nose and be right up. The smoking gun or bloody knife beside the still warm body? Never does the Eberhart heroine fail to pick it up and press her dainty little fingerprints all over it. Forget about the HIBK (Had I But Known) school, these chicks are at the top of the Why The Hell Would She class. They never have a decent alibi and they always have motive galore. (Girl Detective, n.p.)

Eberhart wrote dozens of these books; I am not sure if I ever read another. But this book holds the distinction of being the only title in my entire project that I recorded *at the time of reading*. It would have been a bit of a waste if the title had been one I remembered.

The class of books perhaps best designated as here today, totally forgotten tomorrow, actually represents a category that is sobering both in scale and in general cognitive insignificance. My memory for at least the titles of what I read in my youth is not bad, and it is augmented by numerous associations this project has unearthed. Nevertheless, I am sure there are many *Melora*s that I read, enjoyed, maybe even talked about (Mum would have read *Melora*, too), but then lost completely from all retrievable corners of my mind. Rereading the novel today, I cannot even credit it with adding much "compost" to my general reading repertoire. It is simply silly.

The Good, the Bad, and the Ugly

A certain kind of reading memoir would focus on the classic titles in *The Children's Wonder Book* (with a side reference to Jane Austen), allowing me to present myself as a refined reader with a taste for self-improvement. I certainly recognized at the time that much of the material in that treasury of children's classics was indeed mind enhancing, but it defined only one element in my reading identity, and I could be a much less discerning reader on other occasions. That anthology provided me with a great deal of cultural capital, but I read much, much more—more junk, more contemporary ephemera, more North American works. The focused selection of the "cream of the crop" in that compendium was only part of the input I tapped into. If children need roughage as well as nutrients in their reading diet, I was in good shape.

One feature of the domestic library is its time-capsule qualities. Much of what I read was mediocre, but, if I had read it when published, it might at least have offered contemporary reference points. Stored on our household shelves for as long as two generations, it lost even the virtue of topicality. Yet, in unquestioning, unintended ways, operating by default of long gestation on the shelves, some of these books introduced me to notions of change. I learned that basic assumptions could alter, and this lesson was more important than the sources from which it came.

Time capsules work in positive ways as well. Miss Effie Horwood, a revered and dedicated teacher in the PWC system, died in 1957 and left

Dad a few books. They occupied a place of honour on his bedroom mantel-piece, and I admired them greatly: the works of Milton (1912), bound in purple plush, and the works of Tennyson (undated but inscribed by Miss Horwood in Christmas 1908), in thick, padded brown leather. I considered that these sumptuous objects gave status and tone to our whole collection. My enthusiasm for their handsome covers did not, alas, lead me to any serious sampling of their contents, though I did glance through them in search of something easy to read. When I came to look at them again for this project, I was intrigued to find an obituary of Miss Horwood folded into the pages of the Milton book; it informed me that Miss Horwood had been a student in the old Methodist College that later turned into Holloway School and indeed had been a student of the highly respected headmaster, Robert Holloway, for whom the school was later named. Standing in my basement with this book in my hands, I was profoundly struck by the sense of the past reaching tangibly out to me; the vividness of being linked back so directly to Robert Holloway was at least temporarily more potent than anything Milton or Tennyson could offer me. Books are more likely than many household objects to preserve material connections with the past that are actually inscribed in the objects themselves; it is one of their more compelling powers that electronic materials cannot replicate.

The randomness of the material I encountered in my childhood was one of its important qualities. I learned a great deal about being a selectively omnivorous reader—just because I was desperate never meant I would read just anything; I would reread something else rather than persevere with material I found boring. Yet checking out the home shelves broadened my reading experience in unpredictable ways.

Many years ago, the respected children's author Peter Dickinson wrote a robust "Defence of Rubbish" (1970). Does the importance of rubbish increase at times of transition from one reading stage to another? I would make no case for the literary or social merit of the *Honey Bunch* books, but they gave me the skills to read chapter books. Agatha Christie, Mary Roberts Rinehart, and Mazo de la Roche moved me into forms of adult reading that shared many qualities with my early series reading, especially the colouring-book characters, whose skimpy outlines could be infilled by whatever details of adult life I was capable of processing. I did realize that *Alice in Wonderland* was a more stimulating and surprising book than many other more predictable titles, but I often wanted predictability anyway. Like my book supply, my reading choices were motley and often undistinguished. But my path, though often circular, was slowly heading toward adult-reader territory. By the time I was thirteen and a half, as this study concludes, I had begun to redefine myself as a cautiously aspirant reader, moving toward adulthood more rapidly in my books than in my daily life.

LANDMARKS

"THE ESSENTIAL CHARACTERISTIC of a viable land-mark...is its singularity, its contrast with its context or background" (Lynch, 1960, pp. 100–101).

Much literacy practice is remembered generally and repetitively, some-what along the lines of: "I read a lot of *Nancy Drew* books in my middle childhood." Sometimes, however, a literacy event stands out from the blur of dailiness in some kind of special way. In this section, I describe three landmarks in my literate life: two were unique and the third was repeated once every year.

My birth represented a one-off literacy event of significant proportions. Among the family documents, two baby books recording my arrival were folded into a box that also contained a loose set of the cards sent on the occa-sion of my youngest brother's birth. His cards were never compiled into a book because the realities of raising four children had taken over by then.

What is striking to me, in sorting through my baby books and a few other associated documents, is how my own ordinary birth, like that of millions of other Western babies, gave rise to a vast range of literate expres-sions. I was awash in written and pictorial messages, almost from my first breath. The range of discourses is largely limited to the genre of congratu-latory welcome-to-baby conventions, but there are official government and church documents as well, and some poignant life-management jottings by my mother that have survived by accident.

The first chapter in this section reflects on these literate reactions to the landmark of my birth. The second chapter describes a singular occasion a decade later. The summer I was ten I made a solo visit to my grandparents in Nova Scotia. This was the only time in my childhood I undertook any major adventure without the support of my parents and my brothers. I read books from my grandparents' shelves, and to this day I find these titles saturated with the uniqueness of that experience. This chapter looks at the role of reading context as it played out with four particular titles.

The final chapter in this section explores the complex and repeating literacies of Christmas—not singular but very definitely marked with ritual purpose and confined to one particular time of the year. Our family celebrated the season with gusto, and literacy played a performative role in many ways. Not only the reading of the Gospel stories in church but also our own domestic reading of the Christmas picture books made it *be* Christmas in very real ways. The carols on the record player and in the school assembly were also part of how Christmas was brought into active life. Our rituals enfolded a huge range of literate expressions, many of which I explore in this chapter.

Compared to the Paths section, the mapping metaphor works differently in this part of the study. Rather than maintaining the moving perspective of the sketch map, this section lingers to focus on particular viewpoints along the path. The process is perhaps analogous to the creation of a tourist map that features little inset photos of noteworthy attractions. The sense of brisk forward progress is correspondingly reduced, and readers may need to adjust to a change of tempo.

8
A Multimodal Literacy Event

Arriving

MY HALIFAX BIRTH in late 1948, like that of many other Western babies, sparked an explosion of literate events. The record of a set of highly specialized literacies has been preserved for more than six and a half decades. Markers of my arrival are coded in highly conventional and ritualistic discourses.

The documents I present here were largely preserved within two (inevitably pink) commercial baby books that I found crammed into a little box among my parents' papers. I vaguely knew that these books existed, but until I began to analyze the contents I had no idea of the wealth of discourses and registers they contained.

Three categories of document were stored separately. My birth certificate lived first in my parents' and subsequently in my own working files; its performative powers have served me throughout my life. A certificate of baptism was stored loose in the drawer; because of its size and stiffness it could not be displayed in the baby book. Photographs were mounted in a family album, a whole separate organizational apparatus.

An exploration of the vagaries of domestic document preservation would be a significant study; I suspect it would uncover many examples of the same kind of combination of some careful organization and some sheer, random serendipity that I discovered among these papers. In the future, the arbitrary nature of such collections will be augmented by haphazard decisions about what is born digital, what gets converted into digital status, what remains analogue but organized, and what is simply lost. I think it very unlikely that the fact of digitization on its own will suffice to whip family records into coherent order; arbitrariness retains its power in the digital domain.

My presentation of these documents will be roughly chronological, but many other frameworks would also work. In some cases, I will not present the actual materials for reasons of identity security, but the genres and formats will be familiar; the rituals of literate response to a baby's birth are highly conventional.

Announcements

The newspaper announcements of my birth appeared in my birth city, and in Truro, near my father's family home. In such announcements, babies are positioned in the literate world by a number of indicators: gender, name, weight, date of birth. The wording is formal and conventional: "Born to Mr. and Mrs. Sherburne McCurdy (née Elizabeth Jefferson)." The parents' names would probably not appear as "Mr. and Mrs. Man's Name" today; the custom has faded away and the use of *née* for the wife's maiden name is also now much rarer. The identification of the relevant maternity hospital was information of real utility in the context of 1948, giving an address for visits, and for sending cards, flowers, and baby gifts. Mother and baby would reliably have stayed in the hospital for a week or more. Today the new family heads for home almost at once.

The baby's name is an important literacy marker. That name will very often be the first word a child learns to read. The starting initial will affect many elements of organization in a child's life. My name was in some ways very traditional: one for each grandmother. Bearing ancestral names adds weight to any nomenclature.

The decision to place a birth announcement in the newspaper may be a class marker, though I suspect that in different eras, different class

∧ My birth announcement card from the baby book.

[Collection of the author]

statements would be made by the appearance of such a note. The newspaper, as the organ of record, still plays a role in public announcements today, but of course there are now many alternative vehicles; and contemporary babies are announced via text message, Facebook status alteration, tweet, blog, and many other routes.

Births then and now are also announced via specialist, dedicated cards, which today may be electronic rather than paper and may offer a home-designed montage of photographs of the announced infant. My parents preserved a copy of the notice they sent. It is less neutral than the newspaper item; the cultural statement it makes includes the commercial image and wording. The inside left-hand page is filled out with birth details in my mother's handwriting. The verse reads:

> *We admit she's pretty clever,*
> *And she's something to be seen!*
> *She knows her place already,*
> *And she's taken it as Queen!*

First Visitors
Daddy first and every day!
Grandmother + Grandfather Jefferson, Stephen - Maggie,
Miss Craigie, Fran Coolen, Phyllis Stott, Phil - Estelle,
Millie Hovey, Polly Griffin, Jenny Brenton, Betty Walker,
Vivien Roy, Jean Faulkner, Dot Davison, Sheila McCoubrey,
Pearl Amirault, Archie, Aunt Esther, Betty Routledge,
Rev. Frank Lawson,
Greetings and Gifts Olive Mosher, Gerald McCarthy,
Pat Hutchinson, Eva LeBlanc,
Jean Sewell,

From Margaret's first nosegay- sent by her Grandmother Jefferson

∧ *The record of visitors from the baby book.*

[Collection of the author]

∧ > *Posy wrapper and ribbons, plus florist's card from the baby book.*

[Collection of the author]

The pinkness was probably inevitable; I do not know if my parents picked the message as appropriate to my infant personality, but I am pleased that the word "clever" appears and the word "pretty" does not, except as a qualifier.

Records

My arrival was also officially recorded in my birth certificate. Bearing the imprimatur of the Registrar General of Nova Scotia, it establishes me as a citizen, a literacy event of performative significance. I have used it for material advantage on many occasions. It has allowed me to take part in other state-sanctioned performances: to get married, to acquire a passport, to pass on Canadian citizenship to my children born abroad.

Perhaps because I was their first child, my parents documented my arrival relatively formally. One of the baby books records, in intermittent fashion, my developments of weight and height, along with a few notes filling in the blanks supplied by the book manufacturers for the purpose of recording my first smile and so forth. My father completed the first page, but the running records are in my mother's hand. Some information seems to have been more important to her; she kept diligent record of those who visited the hospital, for example, but did not fill in the "Gifts" column at all.

Greetings

The second baby book is crammed with cards and other souvenirs, including a cellophane nosegay holder sent by my grandmother to her little namesake. The card reads simply, "Grandmother," and a second small florist's card saying, "Mother," also preserved, suggests that two bouquets came to the hospital from my grandmother that day. The literate investment is small—simply two words—but it is not difficult to evoke my grandmother's delight in being able to send these messages along with her posies. The words in my mother's handwriting at the top at the page ("From Margaret's first nosegay—sent by her Grandmother Jefferson") may represent the first time I was described in writing as a person with her own name and life events.

The commercial cards from friends and relatives present a variety of cultural images of babyhood and parenthood. Some are cute and perky, some are cute and funny (especially about fathers), some are cute and saccharine. Gender identity, of course, is a predominant indicator. Some senders clearly felt that the commercial card was not sufficiently unambiguous about gender. There are several copies of an identical card; it shows a pink bootee turned into a dwelling place. The intertextual references to the old woman in the shoe and to the idea of little boots as indicators of babyhood adhere to this simple image. The original card features a little cut-out window, with the flaps turned back to become blue shutters. The intrusion of even a bit of blueness in a pink world seems to have unnerved two senders; one turned the blue shutters to the inside of the card and the second cut them right off.

Although it is easy to imagine the world of baby cards as permanent and unchanging, in fact many of the images are evocative of their time. The kinds of pertness on offer in the funny cards, for example, look dated today. The notion that any connection between daddies and diapers is intrinsically funny is a motif in this little collection. And that microphone for Station B-A-B-Y is certainly redolent of its era.

Not all greetings came through commercial cards. Two telegrams swiftly appeared, via Canadian Pacific and Canadian National. The connotations of "special event" that still adhere to these documents is something we have lost in our age of instantaneous communication; with ubiquitous connection to each other, we no longer make use of any form as ceremonial as the telegraph. While discussing this work with a young colleague, I was struck

∧ *Cards taped into*
the baby book.

[*Collection of the author*]

> *A baby card from the*
baby book, unaltered.

[*Collection of the author*]

RAA403 14

     FD TORONTO ONT 20 742P

MR AND MRS S G MCCURDY

149 WALNUT ST HALIFAX NS

CONGRATULATIONS AND BEST WISHES TO THE THREE OF YOU FROM THE THREE

OF US

     THE MEGGSES

SCLTNA392 19 NL=FD TORONTO ONT 22

MR AND MRS SHERBURNE MCCURDY=

  GRACE MATERNITY HOSPITAL HFX=

DEAR SHERBURNE AND BETTY CONGRATULATIONS AT LAST SHE

ARRIVED MAY GOD BLESS ALL THREE OF YOU LOTS OF LOVE=

    DOT•

to see her pore over the image of the two telegrams; she had never seen one before. I did not see many in my childhood, but I certainly knew that their very arrival was a marker of solemnity, a literacy event unlike any other.

A few people wrote letters, which were stored separately in the box. One letter from an uncle starts conventionally enough: "Well, congratulations to both of you. I am sure that you both must be very pleased and we are certainly very pleased for you." He moves rapidly into family news. Soon he enlarges his scope to include local gossip: "Needless to say our reaction to Jack Yuill getting Grandpa's place was something the same as yours. I think Doug must be crazy unless he had gotten into financial difficulties which I would hardly imagine although he has spent a lot of money on the place since he bought it." He concludes with a sweep across the global scene: "The international scene certainly doesn't seem to be any better does it, what with disunited Nations, disunited Berlin, North Atlantic alliances, etc." For all the ritual emphasis that many items place on the date of birth, this note is the only item in the box that makes any reference to the contemporary world of late 1948 outside the lyrical cocoon of the new family.

Recording the New Life

A different letter serves as the jotting place for a few notes of my mother's. To me they read poignantly, but perhaps they represent relief as well as disappointment. My mother tried to nurse me but swiftly developed major problems and had to switch quickly to bottle feeding. Surprisingly, there is a written record of that sudden adjustment: notes written on the blank back of a congratulatory letter sort out intricate ratios of milk to water for my formula. Unlike the ceremonial uses of literacy that mark most of the contents of the box, these notes offer a vivid example of literacy as a life tool.

Finally, the baby book contains an entry from yet another organizational universe. At the top of the last page of the book, in a space eventually covered by taped-in cards, my father wrote the family allowance number. Presumably the baby book offered a handy piece of paper and also supplied potential mnemonic utility for finding the number again when needed, by simply lifting the covering card. In any case, it provides a startling shift of register into a world of practical necessity, money, government decisions, and participation in bureaucratic structures, all equally part of taking the new baby home. It provides a striking contrast to the preponderance of pink and frilly that otherwise dominates the book.

The Photograph Album

Another form of acknowledging and recording a baby's arrival, of course, involves photographs. There are very, very few pictures of my earliest days; the clearest come from March 24, 1949. I was around four months old.

As I peruse all these documents, I am immersed and sometimes moved, particularly with the documents that engage with the stuff of family life. My mother's formula jottings, for example, allow access into a passing moment of what I know was a very intense time in her life. Only the photograph, however, stirs any sensory response in me. I was a thumb-sucker for many years, and this photo agitates a reminiscent yearning in my hands to this day.

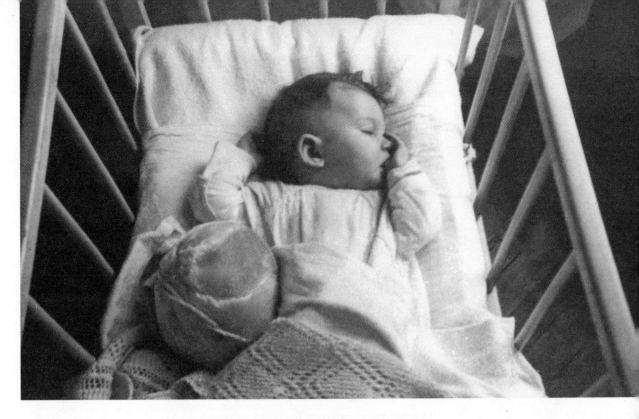

∧ *Margaret, aged four months, from the photograph album.*

[Collection of the author]

> *Formula jottings on the back of a letter of congratulation.*

[Collection of the author]

I have no audio or film record of my early existence, though other babies are well-documented in such media. My entire babyhood record is fixed and silent, a fact with significant mnemonic implications. I very much regret, for example, that I have no record of my childhood accent; despite my heavily documented youth, that essential element of my identity is lost forever. But the photographs do capture a moment and record some of the artifacts of my infancy—the shawl, the plush ball.

Joining Communities

I was officially recognized in another venue shortly after the photograph was taken. In May 1949, I was baptized in the Presbyterian Church of St. David in Halifax, one of three infants that day.

The bulletin informs us that the church service including my baptism was broadcast over the radio station CBNS as a public service. The fund-raising plea that accompanies this notice frames the broadcast as part of the church's "Home Mission." This cheaply reproduced church bulletin places me in the literate record of a particular community, with its Friendship Groups and lobster suppers.

The official baptismal certificate is an interesting artifact in its own right, with images of stained-glass windows, gothic lettering, a Latin scroll in the lower part of the certificate (not appearing in this image). My name is doubly inscribed, red shadowing black. The effect of pomp and ritual is strong, though the impact is slightly mitigated by the fact that the certificate is printed on stiff cardboard rather than the vellum or parchment whose conventions it appropriates. But it also contains the incantatory and performative religious language that establishes me as a member of this institution. My baptismal certificate is very much grander than my birth certificate and actually contains rather more in the way of useful information, but its function is not legally binding in the same way.

Mixed Reality Information Spaces

Bonnie Nardi (2008) discusses "mixed reality information spaces," defined as a fusion of "the physical and the digital" (n.p.). I like the term very much but will broaden its meaning to include any spatial arrangement that allows for differing ontological specifications to coexist. The box of baby documents is a repository of mixed reality information, which I shall explore by way of some large assertions about being human.

> *Church calendar for St. David's Presbyterian Church, Halifax, May 1949, from the baby book.*
[Reprinted by permission of St. David's Presbyterian Church]

∨ *Part of my baptismal certificate.*
[Reprinted by permission of St. David's Presbyterian Church]

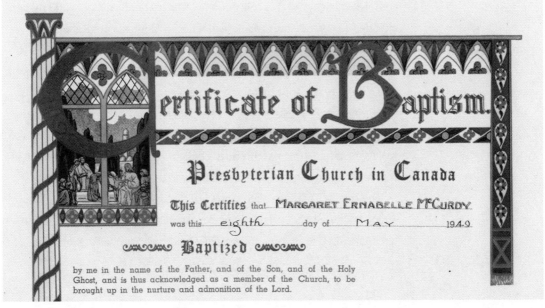

"To be human and to live in a meaningful way within a culture requires that we live in and through a sophisticated, abstract system that is largely imaginary," says Brian Vandenberg (1998, p. 297). An elaborated system sustains these baby documents and makes them legible today, though some of the surrounding assumptions have changed. The various documents participate in conventions and ways of understanding the world, expressed through a variety of literate formats. Vandenberg comments on the complexity of the challenge facing baby Margaret, who would grow up into a person able to make sense of this array.

> Development is not simply the acquisition of information about a given world. Rather, it involves becoming grounded in an uncertain world that is beyond understanding....This is achieved through enculturation into the meanings, myths, rituals, social practices, and assumptions that order, orient, and organize individuals in common ways and provide a sense of reality that allows for confident action in the world. What is real and what is illusory is not an obvious, directly perceived dichotomy but is based upon discerning conventional markers of communication. (p. 299)

What is real in this set of papers? My mother's anxiety about bottle feeding? My uncle's concern about the "disunited Nations," or the disadvantageous sale of the farm to Jack Yuill? The importance of a card for a baby girl being rendered maximally pink through the elimination of the blue shutters? The significance of the family allowance number, or the baptismal record? The need to "discern conventional markers of communication" is a complex challenge in this collection of ordinary family delights and responsibilities. Many indicators do indeed reflect a "sophisticated, abstract system that is largely imaginary"; the potency of pink, for example, is a complete invention, and at one point in time the gender significance of pink and blue were the opposite of today's convention. What is left out is also very selective. The deluge of cards proclaims the joy of a new baby, makes fun of the hard work, and ignores the terror and astonishment that are as real to most first-time parents as the delight. Yet the goodwill expressed in the cards for my parents and me is surely as real as it is ineffable.

The "reality" of these documents is altered again by scanning and reproducing materials that originally present variable tactile experiences. In the images in this chapter, the nosegay holder of crumpled cellophane resembles the telegrams with their pasted strips of words and also resembles the stiff cardboard baptismal certificate. For purposes of legibility and manageability, I have also adjusted scale. Furthermore, as José van Dijck (2007) reminds us, materials from an earlier era "beget a new illocutionary force when integrated in digital productions" (p. 140). These documents, in this new context, no longer say what they said originally, nor do they speak to the original interlocutors.

Indeed, the technology of baby book plus roll of scotch tape had already transmuted these documents long before I ever laid conscious eyes on them. To take one very simple but real example, the disappearance of all the envelopes alters the literate and tactile experience of reading cards or telegrams. The organization of documents and annotations creates a narrative that I have rearranged to write this chapter. My mother's creation of order out of a motley collection of the materials attending the arrival of her first-born contrasts with the "shoebox" assemblage of cards marking the birth of her fourth child, my youngest brother. These loose cards fill the remainder of the box into which the two baby books were wedged, but there has been no order imposed on them even though they are equally interesting. The absence of cards for my remaining three siblings from this box (though they were certainly saved at the time and may well survive elsewhere) raises further questions about accidents of preservation and the arbitrariness of what winds up being considered historically significant.

However random the lottery of preservation, what is not in dispute is the scale of literate investment that attended this unremarkable birth. The number and range of discourses and registers that have been preserved in this modest box are surprising to me, even though I expected a variety of riches. From the very beginning, my infant body and infant mind inhabited a mixed reality information space. Learning to manage this space would lead me to literacy.

Indeed, it is difficult to see how I could have avoided literacy, given the environment into which I arrived. Before I was six months old, a panoply of literacy signifiers marked many components of my existence. I took such indicators of a literate existence completely for granted long before I learned to recognize what they meant. From earliest infancy I was submerged in a profoundly textual world, shaped by literacy from my first moments of life.

9

How I Spent My Summer Holiday, 1959

Travelling

EVERY SINGLE READING EXPERIENCE of my life occurred in a specific place at a specific time. Occasionally a vestige of local memory clings to individual books, but for the most part the particular situation fades away, and what I recall is some trace of the book itself, set against the generic background of a home setting on Pennywell or LeMarchant Road. But a few occasions were unique, and the texts forever carry with them a much more specific imprint of the time and place of my encounter with them.

So it is with four titles I read in the summer of 1959, during a visit to my grandparents in Nova Scotia. It was the first time I ever left home on my own, a profoundly memorable event that permeated every page of the books I found on my grandparents' shelves. When I look now at *Emily's Quest* (Montgomery, 1980/1927), *Joan at Halfway* (Rogers, 1919), *The Wind in the Willows* (Grahame, 1961/1908), and "The Little Match Girl" by

Hans Christian Andersen (1845), all of which I read for the first time in the rectory of Granville Ferry, I can still feel something of the uncanniness of my situation there—at home but not at home, relaxed and cheerful in the company of my adored grandparents, fully rooted in the ancestral claims of Nova Scotia—and yet estranged, away from my immediate family, and aware, below everything else, that the agenda for the late summer of 1959 included moving house, away from the Pennywell Road flat to an actual house with a real front door and its own verandah. This impending change rendered every other event of that summer even stranger.

If a complete reading experience includes the warp of the reader's local situation and the weft of the text, then an exploration of my experience with these titles may prove illuminating. Although, like any reader, I can supply overall accounts of the life situation brought to bear on any given book, my memories are generalized, a smoothed-out average of weeks and years of roughly similar days. With these 1959 titles, I can explore the singularity of four readings in unusual depth and detail. Specifics of these texts are readily retrieved; it is easy to find quotes to support an argument. The weft is therefore relatively constant. In this case, I can also supply much more specific information than usual about the warp of my own locatedness at the time of reading. My sense of how the warp and weft of these childhood readings are woven together is thus more than normally balanced between the two.

Investing in Life Change

Even in children's short lives, turning points may be a long time coming. My Nova Scotian trip took more than three years to develop, with its roots in a noteworthy local outing.

The Christmas I was seven, by special invitation, Dad took my oldest brother and me downtown to the Royal Stores. On the top floor, the company's director, our family friend and benefactor Harold Macpherson, had accumulated a terrific collection of exotic piggybanks. He gave us each a pile of pennies and set us free to try them out. One cent disappeared into the maw of a bank when you balanced it on a little see-saw; another penny, via some elaborate clockwork mechanism, was deposited after you placed it on the tongue of a frog. There were many more marvels of this order, but I don't remember them all. What I do remember—vividly—is that after we had spent an hour or so scampering from bank to bank, Mr. Macpherson lined us up together. "How old are you?" he asked me. Seven, I told him, and to my utter and speechless astonishment, he counted out seven silver dollars and gave them to me. Family legend recounts the next two lines of dialogue. He asked my brother the same question and after a calculating look at my wealth, this mathematically adroit little boy answered, truthfully: "Six next week!" He got his six dollars.

I had never seen a silver dollar before (nor ever owned one since). I had never possessed a whole dollar of my own. I can feel the weight in my hands to this day. They were almost as big as my palm; I could barely close my fingers around seven of them.

Mum and Dad were as flabbergasted by this largesse as we were, but they wasted little time marching us off to the bank to deposit our surprise windfall. About nine months later, at the start of Grade 3, I joined the school savings system. Every Tuesday afternoon, I took 20 cents to school and put in it my account. I was saving rather less than a dollar a month, but it was found money. I knew well that my parents would never dream of giving me an extra 20 cents a week to spend, so after I handed it over, I gave it little further thought.

My parents had talked about me visiting my grandparents in Nova Scotia on my own, and by the summer of 1959, thanks to Mr. Macpherson's kick-start, my finances were in good enough shape to make such a trip a real possibility. Dad was active in the Canadian Teachers' Federation at that time, and the 1959 annual conference was in Halifax. A couple of weeks after my departure, he and Mum would attend this conference, and collect me when it was over.

A half-fare for an accompanied minor was $36. My parents found a couple of acquaintances, not known to me, who agreed to provide the notional "accompaniment" I required for the duration of the flight. My grandparents would collect me from Halifax and take me down the Annapolis Valley. Mum and Dad would later take me to Old Barns to see my other grandparents.

Heading off onto the plane with strangers took every bit of nerve I possessed, though we had all flown to Nova Scotia the previous summer and I knew the flight itself would be delectably fascinating (at the low altitude this flight then took, an entrancing miniature world below was constantly visible). But all did not go entirely to plan. To this day, I own a little scrap of newspaper that recounts the next chapter in this saga. Cut

> **Rev. and Mrs. W. E. Jefferson motored to Halifax on Friday to meet their grand-daughter, who was arriving from Newfoundland. Owing to fog the plane she was arriving on could not land in Halifax and so landed at Greenwood Airport.**

tightly around the words, it gives no information about provenance, but I imagine it came from the Granville Ferry report in the Annapolis Royal newspaper. It was sent to me by my grandmother. In its entirety, it reads:

> *Rev. and Mrs. W.E. Jefferson motored to Halifax on Friday to meet their grand-daughter, who was arriving from Newfoundland. Owing to fog the plane she was arriving on could not land in Halifax and so landed at Greenwood Airport.*

My apprehensiveness when the pilot announced the diversion can be imagined, and I expect it was paralleled in the hearts of the couple who had agreed to look out for me. But my grandparents had been informed in time and came racing into the Greenwood military airport just as I deplaned. This glitch heightened my sense of strangeness; the drive home to Granville Ferry was fatiguing. We came in the back door; the kitchen light in the rectory was fluorescent rather than our own more homely incandescent. I never step into a room containing that shade of lighting without experiencing a *frisson* compounded of exhaustion, desperate homesickness, and excitement—and, in every subsequent exposure to such a light, an acute longing for Granville Ferry and my much-loved grandparents.

Metaphorically, it is fair to say that over the next couple of weeks, my reading was all illuminated by the strange glamour of that unfamiliar light.

The interaction between the narratives and my own displacement remains vivid and distinct in my mind more than fifty years later. By chance, the books and story each featured complex considerations of the many resonances of "home"—a topic that I was able to bring to cognitive and affective life in the context of my own temporary absence from home and the coming upheaval of the move. If I had read these books in other circumstances, this theme might not have resonated in the same way.

Not Quite Home

My literate attention was constantly tweaked in Granville Ferry; home literacies did not quite work. To take one small example, the mail was not delivered to our door; I walked importantly with my grandfather to the post office to collect it. My grandparents subscribed to different magazines than my parents, and I read the comics in the Halifax *Chronicle Herald* instead of the *Evening Telegram*. Church services operated out of the Book of Common Prayer rather than the Bible and *The Hymnary of the United Church of Canada*, and my grandmother had to help me find my place over and over, while my grandfather served as the expert in the pulpit. The skill of moving knowledgeably around the different sections of the Prayer Book held its own allure, even though I never mastered it.

The books were titles I might have read at home—though getting three new books in a row was a luxury. Racing through them, I found they all addressed aspects of the slightly peculiar conditions of my current daily life as a visitor. They expressed conditions of longing and explored aspects of home.

Emily's Quest (Montgomery)

The sight of *Emily's Quest* on Grandmother's bookcase was a joyful one, and I know it was the first title I chose to read. Today's bookish children would find it difficult to comprehend just how long it took me to locate and read even a small sequence of three novels such as the *Emily* trilogy.

I had read *Emily of New Moon* and some of the *Anne* books at the time of my arrival in Granville Ferry. I had also read every Montgomery book in the Boys' and Girls' Library, so I was familiar with *The Story Girl* and other lesser-known titles. But neither *Emily Climbs* nor *Emily's Quest* had ever been available, so I pounced.

I had advanced reading skills in the specialized area of bridging *lacunae* in a sequence of narrative events. *Emily's Quest* was particularly annoying because it actually contains footnotes referencing the other two titles, only one of which I knew. But at least this book would give me the end of Emily's story. I don't think I could ever have written fan fiction. I could guess perfectly well that Emily would end up with Teddy Kent, but I needed to know the authorized version to be fully satisfied.

On the surface, *Emily's Quest*, like its sisters in the trilogy, is a *Künstlerroman*, a novel about an artist's growth to maturity. The act of writing and the quest to become famous for one's writing are certainly major elements of plot and theme in this book. But on rereading the story, I am surprised at the importance of a secondary theme: what compromises are acceptable in the cause of finding a true home? Emily's misbegotten engagement to Dean Priest, a man more than twenty years her elder, is transfigured by his purchase of the home known to her as the Disappointed House. I recognized this building from *Emily of New Moon*; it was one of the first things Emily found when she went exploring around New Moon upon her arrival, after her father died:

> *Off to the right, on the crest of a steep little hill...was a house that puzzled and intrigued Emily. It was grey and weather-worn, but it didn't look old. It had never been finished; the roof was shingled but the sides were not, and the windows were boarded over. Why had it never been finished? And it was meant to be such a pretty little house—a house you could love—a house where there would be nice chairs and cozy fires and bookcases and lovely, fat, purry cats and unexpected corners; then and there she named it the Disappointed House. (Montgomery, 1985/1925, p. 65)*

Montgomery is a self-indulgent writer when it comes to liberal use of dashes and run-on sentences. Her descriptions often overextend themselves, as if she is writing herself into a scene and cannot have enough of it. Sometimes (as here) she gets away with it: her own longing creates an invitation for the reader to join in. Sometimes she is simply prolix. When Dean buys the Disappointed House for Emily, their delighted conversation veers into the ludicrous. The following is only a short extract from one speech by Dean; we must accept that a man of forty-two would speak to his nineteen-year-old fiancée in such terms:

> *I want you to notice especially that little gate over yonder. It isn't really needed. It opens only into that froggy marsh beyond the wood. But isn't it*

a gate? I love a gate like that—a reasonless gate. It's full of promise. There may be something wonderful beyond. A gate is always a mystery, anyhow—it lures—it is a symbol. And listen to that bell ringing somewhere in the twilight across the harbour. A bell in twilight always has a magic sound—as if it came from somewhere "far, far in fairyland." (Montgomery, 1980/1927, p. 83)

Such a speech would not have particularly troubled me at the age of ten for the very good reason that I would not have read it with any close attention. With extended and predictable rhapsodies of this kind, Montgomery was one of the authors who trained me to skim, made of me even more of a pell-mell reader than I was already inclined to be.

Emily's raptures are equally florid, though conveyed through the more convincing frame of indirect discourse (and she has adolescence as an excuse):

She looked at the Disappointed House adoringly. Such a dear thoughtful house. Not an old house—she liked it for that—an old house knew too much—was haunted by too many feet that had walked over its threshold—too many anguished or impassioned eyes that had looked out of its windows. This house was ignorant and innocent like herself. Longing for happiness. It should have it. She and Dean would drive out the ghosts of things that never happend [sic]. How sweet it would be to have a home of her very own. (Montgomery, 1980/1927, p. 84)

Yearning for place is a dominant theme in much of Montgomery's work. Even her book titles are declarations of home: *Anne of Green Gables, of Avonlea, of the Island, of Ingleside; Jane of Lantern Hill; Pat of Silver Bush; Emily of New Moon.* Of these heroines, only Pat is secure in belonging to her home territory at the outset of the story; every other heroine must earn her place.

In a different exercise, I could make a critical argument about the role of yearning for home in the Montgomery books. I could certainly find abundant evidence in Montgomery's biographical circumstances to support such an interpretation, and no doubt her journals contain many similar passages, wallowing in dashes in a very familiar way. It would be a relatively simple argument, and I am not sure it would do much credit to my reputation for acumen.

In any case, such an argument is not the point of this project. Here I am interested in pointing out how this endemic motif in Montgomery's work spoke to one ten-year-old reader, who met this book for the first time in circumstances that heightened the import of that theme. Rereading this book as an adult well aware of Montgomery's unhappy life in Ontario, I can pick up some of the implications of her longing for Prince Edward Island in much of her writing. But the circumstances of my own autobiography also attend any rereading of this book. I am always the reader who first met this title as a homesick ten-year-old, and any theme of yearning is always going to be more plangent for me as a result.

In the particular circumstances of that summer, I was also open to relishing the potential of an unknown new house. Unnerved as I was by the coming departure from Pennywell Road, I was also excited. The house on LeMarchant Road bore this fleeting conceptual similarity to the Disappointed House: for a brief period of time, it was *all potential*. I am not sure I had even seen the interior at this stage. I know when we did move in I was myself "disappointed" at just how orthodox it was; I attempted mightily to discover "unexpected corners," but the house was ruthlessly rectangular. But that let down was ahead of me as I galloped through *Emily's Quest* in the Granville Ferry rectory.

Reading in a Nova Scotia house offered a more fitting context for Montgomery's home discourses than the austerities of St. John's. It was not often that my reading fitted so harmoniously into my own life circumstances; I luxuriated in the sensation and recall being conscious of it, with an edge of dismay that I could not feel this way more often. It was an occasion when I actively resented Newfoundland for being so idiosyncratic.

Joan at Halfway (Rogers)

Once I had roared through *Emily's Quest* at high speed, it was necessary to find me something else to read. My grandmother turned up a Nova Scotia novel published in 1919: *Joan at Halfway* by Grace McLeod Rogers.

I commenced *Emily's Quest* in the secure knowledge that I knew how to read this novel, save perhaps for a few missing local details lost through not reading the middle volume of the trilogy. *Joan at Halfway* was an entirely different kind of project. Its plain brown cover gave no hint of its contents or of what repertoire might facilitate its reading.

Yet it did not take many pages before I realized that at least some of the plot's founding conditions were well-known to me. Joan is an orphan, brought into her great-uncle's home, ostensibly to help her Aunt Hetty look after Uncle Garret (but halfway down the first page of the book, we learn that there is another, secret reason why Uncle Garret invited her to make her home at Halfway).

Joan is in a new home, yet there is an uncanny feeling of familiarity about the place. According to Robin Sutherland, introducing a reprint of this novel published in 2007, the story is actually set in the Annapolis Valley, exactly where I was staying when I read it. Although I did not register this final geographical detail, I was certainly very aware that I was reading a Nova Scotia novel while in Nova Scotia; I remember registering the anomaly of this alignment of book and reader as something (to use a paradoxical word) completely foreign to my experience.

There was more to this alignment than confluence of setting, however. Joan is quite sure that she recognizes the local village from the first moment of arrival:

> *And what was it that had made her feel* as if she had been there before, *on that road through the village!...[S]uddenly an oak clump, in cluster of three, great spreading trees, stood out plain, and strangely familiar, as if she had sometime played under their leafy roof and searched out their brown cup treasures.*
>
> *On, and a bend in the road showed a river, winding, and clear over a gravelly bed, with a ripple sweet as music, and as they rumbled across its spanning bridge she felt as if her own feet had once been upon it....*
>
> *And there was a brown, weather-beaten old chapel, with a towered belfry—and further on a big square one with double tier of windows, and tapering spire, and she seemed to be* expecting to see them. *As they slipped from her view they were like a bit of a dream, those familiar recurrent ones, that persist, in our brains, over and over, making us conscious only when waking from out them that we* have been to that place again—*just the brief fleeting tantalizing familiar impression, and it is gone—perhaps not to come again for months, sometimes years.* (Rogers, 1919, p. 15)

Even at the age of ten, I was familiar with that idea of the recurrent dream, but this passage struck even closer to home (so to speak). I felt its power when I read it, and I felt its echo when I drove with my father to Old Barns a few weeks later. I had been going to Old Barns intermittently ever since my birth; the area around my other grandparents' farm outside Truro almost certainly comprised the known-but-not-known landscape that informed my very engaged and sympathetic reading of this passage from *Joan at Halfway*. That this resonance arose from a Nova Scotia setting was even more satisfying. I could not have articulated how apposite this congruence was for me, but I felt its uncanny familiarity very acutely.

This early mystery of Joan's troubling sense of recognition was the main element of the book that I remembered over the years; I was surprised when I reread it to discover that, after a few more enigmatic references, everything is resolved by page 38 (the local postmaster recalls a visit by Joan at the age of five). I truly thought the whole book was shadowed by this haunting question of the uncanny; that everything so quickly reverted to matter-of-fact actually irritated me on the occasion of my reacquaintance with the story. That spooky sense of the just-barely-familiar had lingered in my mind over many years.

Perhaps it is not surprising that I read the next book my grandmother found me as a story about home.

The Wind in the Willows (Grahame)

Many people remember *The Wind in the Willows* for the adventures of Mr. Toad. For me, this annoying character simply interfered with the simple pleasures of the rest of the story: messing about in boats, enjoying Mr. Badger's hearth after the storm, and, most of all, joining Mole in his homecoming. Given my passion for domestic interiors and the traces of homesickness that underpinned even cheerful moments in the rectory, I was surely the ultimate implied reader for "Dulce Domum," the chapter in which Mole returns to the home he abandoned for the enchantments of the riverbank. I read this chapter with absorbed delight. I thrilled to the call alerting Mole to the nearness of home:

> *Home! That was what they meant, those caressing appeals, those soft touches wafted through the air, those invisible little hands pulling and tugging, all one way! Why, it must be quite close by him at that moment, his old home that he had hurriedly forsaken and never sought again, that day when he first found the river! And now it was sending out its scouts and its messengers to capture him and bring him in.* (Grahame, 1961/1908, p. 86)

I relished with Rat the inspection of the domestic quarters:

The Rat....was running here and there, opening doors, inspecting rooms
and cupboards, and lighting lamps and candles and sticking them, up every-
where. 'What a capital little house this is!' he called out cheerily. 'So compact!
So well planned! Everything here and everything in its place!...So this is the
parlour? Splendid! Your own idea, those little sleeping-bunks in the wall?
Capital!' (pp. 93–94)

Mr. Toad briefly had me fooled at the beginning of the book when his
gypsy caravan also offered cozy and compact interiors, but it was soon
evident that he was a tiresome character who only wanted to cause trouble,
and I had no interest in him thereafter. Nor was I impressed by the mystical
chapter, "The Piper at the Gates of Dawn." Well-provisioned picnics were
about as wild as I wanted to go with this book, and I returned to its pages
selectively over the years (I regularly borrowed it from the library until it
arrived in the house as a Christmas present for my youngest brother in
1962). I never skipped a section completely (that behaviour just seemed
wrong to me), but I certainly skimmed, and I skimmed through Mr. Toad's
sections with considerable disdain. Since his adventures dominate much of
the book, I ought to have disliked it altogether. Instead, I loved the domestic
chapters devotedly and always returned to them with enthusiasm.

"The Little Match Girl" (Andersen)

To this beguiling mix of yearning, uncanniness, and snug domesticity,
I added the wretchedness of possessing "none of the above" when
Grandmother found a magazine containing Hans Christian Andersen's
story, "The Little Match Girl." I read it on a sunny afternoon, reclining on
the rectory verandah. Clearly my situation epitomized the luxury side of
the wall in the story, but my heart switched sides at once, and I sobbed
inconsolably as the little girl lit that last bundle of matches. No amount of
eternal glory with her grandmother reconciled me to the grimness of her
freezing feet, or the pathos of her shivering by the wall, afraid to go home
because she had made no sales.

I had some experience of Victorian-era pathos by this time, but the
brutality of this story was something new to me, and I did not care for it
at all. Solace in heaven did not constitute a happy ending, and my unease
was oddly compounded by the random but very unsettling detail that I
had never seen anyone strike a match against a wall. Thus a small point

expanded the unnerving effect of the whole and added a bitter edge to my deracinated condition as a visitor away from home. The effect was deeply disturbing.

Embedded and Situational Reading

We cannot account for the circumstances of every reader in every encounter with a text. Just to make the attempt for oneself would be laborious and tedious. Nevertheless, the singularity of the occasion on which I read these fictions allows us to consider the significance of how reading is inevitably nested in local life. It reminds us that a more detached and critical approach to a text is an abstraction. One meaning of detached is "free from emotional involvement." In order to reach that abstract virtue, we must find a way to "un-attach" our reading experience from its initial situation. Professional readers perform this kind of surgery routinely and often do not consider any loss (see Mackey, 1993, for further consideration of the contrast between situated and abstracted reading).

If I did not recall that holiday in Nova Scotia so vividly, I might well pursue the notion of "home" as it manifests itself in any or all of these narratives and consider my observations to be neutral and disinterested. With this example, I can see clearly the degree of special pleading that would be involved in making any such case for detachment. I have no problem, however, in imagining circumstances in which the condition of my first reading of a book would be equally potent but much more invisible. Just because I was a reader "attached" to a particular element in these books does not render my observations wrong—but if I claim that they are objective, then I am being at best partial. My own local events shaped my perspectives.

I believe it is possible to develop layers of expertise, to develop ways of reading with and against the text with more insight and more theoretical understanding. I also know some readings are less "interested" than my own were on this occasion. But I do believe there is a cost to eliminating all shades of the embedded individual response; such an intellectual sleight-of-hand impoverishes our view of reading processes themselves.

My reading of "home" stories in the heightened setting of the two main events in my life during the summer of 1959 is perhaps an unusually clear-cut case. But the context of reception is always important. Whether reading for the first time or repeating an encounter with a text, we necessarily embed the textual experience inside the events and understandings of our own local life at the time. It is not an optional extra; it is woven into the experience itself. Even when our education leads us to endeavour toward more detached readings, its residue lingers. It is often our local life that enables us to see connections that would otherwise be invisible to us; it is our local readings that illuminate our discussions with each other, whether or not we actively acknowledge that sense of situation. We read our own worlds into the words of our books, and these worlds will not be subtracted from the understanding we develop from the texts.

10
Literacies
of the Season
Celebrating

THE EVENT OF READING ALWAYS TAKES TIME;
rereading is one way to recapture that time spent, though necessarily in a
new context. To explore the ritual texts associated with Christmas in our
ceremonially inclined family is to re-enter short passages of time, to evoke
past moments reiterated annually in circumstances prelabelled as special.

Because of the special conditions of storage and repetition, I have access
to a more complete textual ecology for our December literacies than for
more miscellaneous times of the year. In December, much of our literate
activity was unusually focused.

The Impact of Ritual on Reading

When a set of texts is packed away for eleven months of the year, all reading
associated with that twelfth month is ritualized to a greater or lesser extent.
Some of it even becomes a way of performing Christmas. We certainly

encountered the religious texts of Christmas; the cadences of the King James Gospel stories of the birth of Christ are deeply engrained in my being. But it is not just the heightened performance of the Gospel that is steeped in a sense of occasion. Every Christmas text of my childhood bears its own aura for me, no matter how mass-produced, no matter how superficial, trivial, or even cheesy. Some readings were necessary for it to feel like Christmas at all: Dad read *The Night before Christmas* to us on Christmas Eve, and there were also many readings of "The Year without a Santa Claus," a Phyllis McGinley poem cut out from the December 1956 issue of *Good Housekeeping* and stored carefully with the Christmas books and ornaments. Such materials made an essential contribution to the building tension and excitement of December.

A list of Christmas texts will almost certainly be partial, but for my childhood it included music (sacred and secular), Bible readings, Christmas cards, picture books, Christmas chapters in novels and the occasional complete Christmas novel, magazines (children's and adults') and their special Christmas features (which were sometimes saved for subsequent years), recipes, the occasional Christmas colouring book, letters to Santa, labels on presents, and many, many lists. Even the Sears catalogue took on new resonance in the context of Christmas coming. Learning to write your own tags for the Christmas parcels was a rite of passage. Last year's cards were saved to be cut up and glued into Christmas lanterns and chains.

Writing Christmas cards was an annual literacy event of some significance. Mum and Dad set up a card table in the living room, and for the best part of a week they spent every evening writing cards and letters. Unlike today, there were no shortcuts in the 1950s, and every word my parents communicated was written by hand. The sense of a weighty achievement was manifest when the last card went into the mail; one of the major literacy challenges of the season had been successfully addressed (so to speak).

Christmas Texts

Christmas comes with powerful music. Dad broke out the Christmas records at home on my birthday in November. At school we started singing carols on December 1. This music was also performative; it created the opening of the Christmas season and combatted the December dreariness (in St. John's, that month is more likely to be marked by sleet and fog than by anything as pretty as a decent snowfall).

"Christmas is coming," said the music, and for a small child that promise introduces schemas of time present and time passing. I do not remember a time when I did not lead a mental double life in December, raring to get to Christmas itself and yet knowing to savour the preparatory period.

By November we were saving our allowance to buy presents and entering into advanced calculations of what was desirable and what was affordable. I remember buying Dad a collapsible plastic travel cup one year; it was exceptionally cheap (the figure of 7 cents comes to mind) for the very good reason that it leaked like mad; but I was charmed by its ingenuity. Even within the terms of our humble budgets, Christmas incorporated a commercial intertext—though it was not as overwhelming as it is now—and we certainly perceived it as an entirely essential and desirable component of the season.

We owned a book that expressed my sense of the power of this anticipatory time, as expressed in its title, *Waiting for Santa Claus* (Martin & Cummings, 1952). It was a Wonder Book, a cheap hardback picture book sold in spinners in drugstores and supermarkets. Finding a copy in 2010 allowed me to look at a book in the conscious knowledge that it had been almost sixty years since I first saw it. At once utterly familiar, yet made strange over the gap of so many decades, it offered an uncanny and moving experience.

So what did I see? An early and very anodyne opening took my breath away simply because I knew it so well and had not given it a thought for so long. That image of rows of identical cookies, unnervingly flat and neat compared to our own more haphazard efforts at Christmas icing, had clearly been stored securely, somewhere in the back of my mind, for six decades. A vivid thrill of nostalgia is essentially built into this experience.

Even this reproduction gives some indication of the poor quality of the paper. Author Marcia Martin and illustrator Alison Cummings seem to be aiming for a story of a completely conventional Christmas. I recognized almost every scene in the book. The family even matched ours for a while; in early 1953 my second brother was born, so, for a couple of years, we had the elder sister and two younger brothers of this family.

The book's narration in the present continuous tense (probably my first encounter with this technique) successfully expresses the sense of limbo before Christmas when everything is special but *suspended*. Bobby and Sally say more than once that they can hardly wait till Christmas. The book

Mother makes Christmas cookies. Bobby and Sally help put on the icing. There is green icing for the Christmas-tree cookies, and white icing for the gingerbread-house cookies.

Baby sits in the high chair and watches. Then Mother gives him a cookie. Bobby and Sally each take a cookie, too. "But we must save the rest," says Bobby. "Oh, I can hardly wait till Christmas!"

∧ *Images from* Waiting for Santa Claus (*Martin & Cummings, 1952*).

[*Courtesy Penguin Group (USA)*]

concludes on Christmas night; my brother and I were greatly struck by the neat ending: "And as Mother and Daddy turn out the light, both children call: 'Oh, we can hardly wait till next Christmas!'" (Martin, 1952, n.p.).

Shirley Hughes, in *Lucy and Tom's Christmas* (1981), proves that it is possible to tell the story of two children's very ordinary Christmas experiences with much more artistry than appears in this nondescript little publication. But I, at least, invested this book with all my own excitement and treasured its annual appearance. It is impossible for me now to shake off my affection for it; for all its banality, it taps deep into my own emotional past and borrows the luminosity of my own anticipation to brighten its tepid pages. In its annual reappearance, it even offered a small gleam back into the Murk itself, as I refreshed my memory of early childhood via its pages every December.

Even insipid childhood books entwine themselves into our existence in ways that borrow power from our own lived and felt lives. An equally bland title, another Wonder Book, supplied an emotional charge that let me begin to think with greater clarity about my brother's death at an early age (that baby born in 1953 died in a car crash in 1975, just before his twenty-second birthday). This anecdote definitely moves beyond my self-declared

"Tomorrow is Christmas," said Billy. "I hope Santa Claus brings me a sled, a ball, a bike and a puppy."

"Me too," said little Davey. "Me too!"

"I want a doll that looks like a princess, a handbag, a dress and a doll carriage to wheel. Oh, I wish it was Christmas right now!" said Mary.

"Me too!" cried Billy.

"Me too!" cried little Davey. "Me too!"

They laughed and ran around and around the yard, and their cheeks were bright with the cold. And all the time the snowflakes were still falling.

∧ *From* Merry Christmas Mr. Snowman (*Wilde, 1976/1951*).

[*Courtesy Penguin Group (USA)*]

boundaries of the *particular* deep into the zone of the *personal*, but it conveys some of the importance of these books in the lives of their owners. We owned a copy of *Merry Christmas Mr. Snowman* (Wilde, 1976/1951). Its chief attraction for us older kids was that it featured a repeated line that drove our middle brother crazy: "'Me too!' cried little Davey. 'Me too!'" (1976/1951, n.p.). Our brother David, who considered himself radically equal to his elders at all times, did not react well to being taunted about being little Davey, the copycat baby always eager to emulate his betters.

Visiting St. John's for Christmas in 1976, twenty months after David's death, I came across a new reprint of this title in a drugstore. If it is possible to feel malicious sorrow, that sentiment pierced me as I realized I could never put this book in my brother's stocking to annoy him all over again. Initially, I left the book on the spinner and turned away. Poor David is dead; I can't tease him, I thought. But a stronger instinct made me turn back and purchase the book for my own shelf, as a reminder that my relationship with my lost brother still contained ingredients of disrespect and aggravation as well as nobler emotions, that the gulf between the living and the dead was not the only definer of what we meant to each other. It is hard for me to describe, but in the moment of purchasing that book, which would have infuriated him still, I restored some of the depth and complexity of our relationship, at least inside my own head and heart.

I tell this very private story to offer some sense of the significance of even mediocre children's literature as it feeds into and feeds out of children's own lives. These are aspects of reading that we understand only from the inside. There may well be no one else in the world to whom *Merry Christmas Mr. Snowman* is a profoundly important text—but it is to me. And one reason I can tell this story is that when this book was reprinted in 1976, it was identical to the artifact we owned in the 1950s. I could buy something that felt like a piece of my own childhood and revisit interactions with my brother that were woven into this text in lively and unkind ways. These connections remained vivid to me, even in the face of the overwhelming fact of his early death. It is hard to imagine a stronger challenge but this insignificant little book, priced at only 59 cents, even in 1976, still represents my own life as it was woven into the story in the 1950s, utterly free of the knowledge that David would die young—and of course, it now also represents that moment when I chose to purchase it in December 1976, in Churchill Square in St. John's, with fat snowflakes smacking the drugstore window. The startling power of literacy lies at least partially in this option to revisit both the textual world of the fiction and *also* the lived world of the time of previous readings, the life experiences that inflected the narrated world and brought it to life in the mind of the reader. The role of the object in the hand compounds the role of the text in the mind, and vice versa. This effect may be magnified when reiterated qualities of ritual are part of the package.

The original book and the purchased 1976 reissue were both printed and therefore preserved on paper. Will electronic words and pictures have the same power? Or will we maintain our attachment to paper in part because we recognize its totemic qualities and affordances?

On a more lighthearted note, "The Year without a Santa Claus" (McGinley, 1956) travelled through our family history as technology made new permutations possible. For a long time, we saved the original pages from the magazine, more dog-eared by the year. One year, after most of us had left home, at a point when public access to photocopiers opened up, Mum made each of us our own black-and-white copy as a Christmas present, carefully hand-colouring the illustrations.

At a later stage again, my own children made use of this copy to record an audiotaped reading for their grandparents, an artifact that subsequently

THE YEAR WITHOUT A SANTA CLAUS

by Phyllis McGinley

Have you been told?
Did you ever hear
Of the
Curious
Furious
Fidgety year
When Santa Claus
Unhitched his sleigh
And vowed he was taking a holiday?

How did it happen?
This way:

It was long ago,
Before you were living---
Not yet Christmas but past Thanksgiving,
Though I can't remember the very date.

Santa got up one morning,
Late,
Pulled on one boot,
Then its twin,
Ruffled the whiskers on his chin,
And sat back down on the side of the bed.
"Great North Star, but I'm tired!"
He said.
"Painting wagons
Red and bright,
Sharpening ice skates half the night,
Wrapping presents in tissue and gauze,
Has worn me weary,"
Said Santa Claus.

"Crick in my back,
Cold in my nose,
Aches in my fingers and all ten toes,
And a sort of a kind of a kink
Inside,
Whenever I think
Of that Christmas ride."

Into his workroom limped the Saint.
He sniffed the varnish,
He smelled the paint.
And a reeling
Feeling
Came over him stealing,
To see things crammed from floor to ceiling.
Rocking horses with shaggy manes,
Balls,

94

reappeared as another Christmas gift years later, when our daughters remastered the tape onto a CD and gave it back to my husband and me. In 2010 one of those daughters found a new picture-book version, and it became a Christmas present once more, this time for everyone. On each occasion that McGinley's flawless cadences spring to new life, the experience of her poem entwines itself into another iteration of Christmas in our family.

> *Have you ever been told?*
> *Did you ever hear*
> *Of the*
> *Curious*
> *Furious*
> *Fidgety year*
> *When Santa Claus*
> *Unhitched his sleigh*
> *And vowed he was taking a holiday?*
>
> *How did it happen?*
> *This way. (McGinley, 1956, p. 94)*

A punning description of the conditions of such Christmas texts might be that they are annually stored and annually restored; the seasonal books take their place in the domestic ecology on the basis of rhythms and rituals very different from those of most other reading materials, and this special treatment makes it possible for them to survive for longer periods of time. Nostalgia protects them, and the retrospective cast of Christmas itself helps to preserve them in live ways long after they would normally be outgrown. And, for me at least, the intensity of those early childhood Christmases floods even anodyne texts with an abundance of remembered meaning and excitement.

Books can preserve not simply past moments but also past sequences of moments. Tia DeNora (2000) speaks of music, but her words can also refer to texts that are designed to be read; both "may be seen to serve as a container for the temporal structure of past circumstances" (p. 67). Written texts like musical structures "may provide a grid or grammar for the temporal structure of emotional and embodied patterns as they were originally experienced" (p. 68).

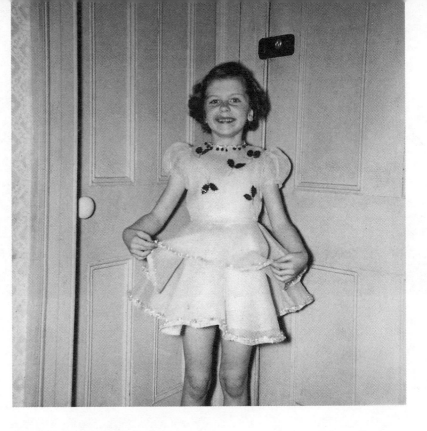

Records of Christmas Past

The significance of this preservation of a time structure is thrown into relief by comparison with a couple of snapshots. The Christmas concert was one of those important Christmas occasions that we were all *waiting* for. No doubt there was a script for the concert the year I was six and in Grade 1, but, while I remember practicing for it, I do not remember any of the substance of the event. My joy at the time and my entire recollection since centred on my dress as a Holly Fairy. I was desperate to have a nylon party dress with a crinoline and puffed sleeves, but my mother's tastes were more austere. The Holly Fairy dress, however, met all requirements, at least temporarily; when the concert was over, Mum handed it over for the school costume box, perhaps not caring to know that I would have happily worn its tinsel-bedecked ruffles throughout the entire winter.

Two records exist of me in what was possibly the most satisfying finery I ever donned in my life. The traditional entry in the family album comprises two photographs linked by a label written in white pencil: "Holly Fairy, Grade One Concert, 1954." Even a broken night's sleep on the very uncomfortable curlers that were require to torture my fine hair into glory could not dim my radiance at the allure of my outfit. The plastic holly leaves

and red berries sewn to the bodice of the dress and the tinsel edging on the skirt gave me profound satisfaction. I strongly suspect today that my mother's emotions as she took these pictures were a little more ambivalent than mine: pleasure in her child's manifest delight along with a shadow of concern about the threats of inculcated vanity, plus a certain logistical uneasiness about managing a child so thrilled, along with two little brothers equally wired, out the door on time for concert deadlines.

The second record of this momentous event comes in the form of the official stage shot. I am the Holly Fairy standing on the chair to the far left, and my posture perhaps gives some inkling of my extreme satisfaction.

There are forty-one of us in this photograph; to the best of my knowledge we comprised a single Grade 1 class. Apart from the few with narrative roles in the middle row, most of us were crowd cast. The boys were largely elves, and you can see a sample of the toys they were presumably working on, distributed across the front of the stage. The Holly Fairies and Snow Fairies had no known narrative role in the standard Christmas plots, but I did not care. In the Kindergarten concert I had been relegated to the Rhythm Band, wearing a sharp blue cape with a red lining and an uncomfortable pillbox hat, an outfit with no glamour at all. This time, a year later, I was sated in desire fulfilled, and to this day, an unexpected glimpse of tinsel gives me a shiver of remembered deep excitement.

Christmas trees, in the front corners of the stage contributed their inimitable fragrance to augment our thrills. Every effort was made to heighten our involvement in the importance of the occasion. That single night supplied me with a deep repertoire of distilled Christmas anticipation that

fuelled my engagement with holiday rituals for many decades, and it also gave me scripts to infuse into my reading about other children's Christmas concerts. Yet the snapshots record only a single instant, which must be fleshed out by memory. The "temporal structure of past circumstances" (DeNora, 2000, p. 68) must be inferred, because it cannot be captured in a still image.

Carols and Songs

My father's passion for Christmas music was restricted only by his sense of ritual and his strong capacity to obey rules even if those rules were invented by himself. The veto on listening to the Christmas records until my birthday in late November meant an orgy of anticipation for me from Hallowe'en onward.

At home we listened to a much wider variety of carols than we actually sang in school and church. Our carol repertoire was older, and more international overall, than our set of ordinary daily hymns. Given the parochial nature of so very much of our regular life and reading material, the carols offered a window onto the ancient and the exotic. Their motleyness was part of the appeal.

One of my gateways to this highly coloured past came through an extremely sentimental image. When I was very young, my Great-Aunt Flo gave me a book of Christmas carols and music, each carol illustrated with a full-page, black-and-white picture. This book was clearly popular; it was published first in 1938 and republished in 1942 and 1952 (my copy). I immediately lost my heart, not to the religious illustrations or to the sheet music, but to the saccharine full-colour picture opposite the title page, in which the carols' polyglot pedigrees are conspicuously not represented. I can rise to some detachment now in noting the wealth and whiteness of the assembled children in that sappy picture; I can comment on the idealized sentimentality of its presentation of an ideology of Christmas; but, for me, its aura is redolant of my own past, and about that I find it much more difficult to be objective.

The history of this carol book provides an example of the casual way in which materials in domestic collections drift in and out of the owner's possession. I always thought of this book as mine, but I lost track of it for decades, assuming it was somewhere in my parents' house. When they moved and it didn't turn up, I checked with my sister. It turned out to have spent many years living inside her trusty piano bench; she had always presumed it belonged to her. Fortunately for my case, it was doubly inscribed on the inside front cover. "Margaret from Aunt Flo" is written firmly on the top of the page, and alongside is a collection of "M"s, asserting my own sense of ownership.

The Great Story

Christmas music is not all about home and sentimentality. Sometimes we chose to listen to music after lights-out as an alternative to the bedtime story. I would, from a very young age, indeed, request the carol about the "little tiny child." This line features in the "Coventry Carol," one of the oldest carols extant in English and perhaps the one that tells the most terrible story. Taken from a medieval mystery play, it is sung by the mothers of Bethlehem, trying to hush their children so Herod's men will not find them and slaughter them. The carol fails to do its lullaby work, and the babies are killed later in the play. I did not work through the implications of the carol's first-person voice and second-person address to the baby until well into adulthood. But, from early childhood, I certainly knew the full Christmas story well enough to register at least the surface meaning of

"Herod the King / In his raging" and the carol is explicit about his appalling command, "All young children to slay." Nobody could call this story saccharine or safe. But I loved the minor key of the lullaby lines, and something about the opening lines, "Lully, lulla, thou little tiny child" made me feel as if I were being included and spoken to in this world.

I was less clear about other aspects of the Christmas story. Nobody explained what was meant by a "virgin undefiled" or "unspotted"; even "being great with child" meant little more to me than a collection of sonorous rhythms. And while I did know about the slaughter of the innocents, my narrative focus always centred on the hero baby who escaped rather than the unfortunates who were trapped. Nevertheless, the harsh edges of the Biblical story established shadows even in my coziest Christmas schemas.

Of course we knew secular Christmas music as well, but it did not resonate for me in the same way, then or ever since. What survive are the power of the great carols and the potency of the story that fuels them.

For the Record

Our Christmas music was both recorded and live. I actually own a snatch of audio recording of a Christmas music event: Carols by Candlelight in Gower Street Church on December 22, 1957. Dad sang in the choir, so we were at church early that evening, and I remember clearly that two events happened simultaneously before the service began: the tallest bass lit the candles around the choir loft and one of the tenors bustled around setting up a huge reel-to-reel audio-recording apparatus in front of the pulpit. Many decades later, through a series of accidents and coincidences, I acquired an audiocassette, perhaps edited down from a single reel: it begins and ends in the middle of the service but is not continuous.

There is a print record of the evening: the church calendar. The impact of colour printing on this weekly item all by itself marked the service as a special occasion; normally the calendar, a single sheet of folded paper, was entirely black and white. The red and green images and lettering of this document would have struck us as magnificently festive. Colour printing carried more semiotic charge when it was rare.

Here is an example of recorded texts where the print version offers the equivalent of a snapshot, the table of contents so to speak of a temporal event, with almost no durational qualities of its own. The specific

*> Church bulletin
presenting the program
for* Carols by Candlelight,
December 22, 1957.

[*Reprinted by permission of
Gower Street United Church*]

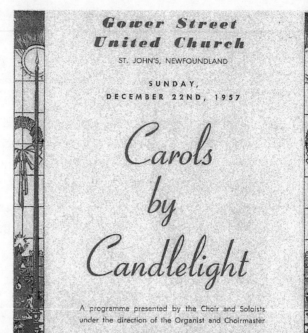

**Gower Street
United Church**

ST. JOHN'S, NEWFOUNDLAND

SUNDAY,
DECEMBER 22ND, 1957

*Carols
by
Candlelight*

A programme presented by the Choir and Soloists
under the direction of the Organist and Choirmaster

DOUGLAS OSMOND, L.R.A.M.

NOTE: All the items will be sung unannounced. The congregation are
invited to join in the singing of the Hymns.

Carols by Candlelight

ORGAN PRELUDE—"Puer Natus in Bethlehem". Dietrich Buxtehude

CALL TO WORSHIP

INVOCATION

THE LORD'S PRAYER

HYMN —"The First Noel."

CAROLS—

"What Tongue Can Tell Thy Greatness, Lord."

"Now Let Every Tongue Adore Thee."
.... Johann Sebastian Bach

SOLO —"Nazareth" .... Charles Gounod
Gordon Campbell

SCRIPTURE — Luke 2 : 1 - 20.

CAROLS — Ladies' Choir

"Ding-dong! Merrily on High" ...... Arr. E. Harold Geer

"While by Our Sleeping Flock We Lay". Arr. Homer Whitford

PRAYER

HYMN — "Hark! the Herald Angels Sing."

OFFERTORY AND OFFERING (in aid of Choir Fund)

SCRIPTURE — Philippians 2 : 1 - 11

SOLO — "A Slumber Song of the Madonna"........ Michael Head
Mrs. James Hough

CAROLS —

"Nativity Cradle Song" .... Sir Hugh Roberton

"The Echo Carol" .... Arr. Alfred Whitehead

DUET — "Sweet Marie and Her Baby" .... John Jacob Niles
Edna Mitchell, Claudia LeDrew

CAROL — Male Choir

"Go Tell It On The Mountain" .... Christmas Spiritual
Arr. John W. Work

SOLO — "Gesu Bambino" .... Pietro A. Yon
Claudia LeDrew

CAROLS — Male Choir

"In the Bleak Midwinter" .... Gustav Holst

"When de Stars Begin to Fall" ...... Arr. Sir Hugh Roberton

SOLO —

"Good Will to Men" .... Geoffrey O'Hara
Dorothy Templeman

HYMN —"O Come, All Ye Faithful"

CAROL —

"All Hail the Pow'r of Jesu's Name"........ Tune —"Diadem"

BENEDICTION

ORGAN POSTLUDE —"In Quiet Joy" .... Dietrich Buxtehude

The cover of the RCA Victor album, Christmas Hymns and Carols.

[*Courtesy of Sony Music Entertainment*]

performance over time is partially captured instead in the recording of the event. Its omissions mean it is not an aural transcript of the whole evening (and it is, of course, the print record that identifies the gaps), but what is available provides an acoustic replica of what I heard in 1957. My recording includes the congregation singing "The First Noel"; it is thus the only recording I own that includes my own voice, raised—indistinguishably, alas—with the congregation.

I have also acquired digital remasterings of two commercial recordings we used to own: *Christmas Hymns and Carols* and *Christmas Hymns and Carols Volume I* by the Robert Shaw Chorale. The former was a set of four shellac records, featuring three tracks per side; we manoeuvred the records into place so that one dropped on top of another to permit a form of continuous play. *Volume I* was an early LP, much simpler to manage.

I located the album art on the Internet, the same image for both sets. The visuals are not as evocative as the vocals, but this image is still very potent for me. The RCA Victor dog listening to His Master's Voice on the gramophone was one of the first brand images I learned to recognize. Although, of course, I had no idea in the 1950s how many different forms of audio equipment I would use in my lifetime, this image of the horn did make me aware that technological change was part of the recording industry, a fact that also helped me to understand some books set in earlier times. This insinuation of half-understood repertoire back and forth between media was important even in my day, and is probably a much bigger factor for children today as they learn to understand the world.

I thus own three recordings that tap directly into my aural experience of Christmas through the 1950s, and their affordances, similarities, and differences offer considerable illumination on the possibilities and parameters of an audio text. All three recordings share the attribute that they enable me to repeat a series of consecutive moments from my childhood. The Robert Shaw recordings were reiterated on many occasions in my youth; the Carols by Candlelight occurred just once, and I did not hear that exact music again until I was in my forties and discovered that my parents had a copy of this tape. Perhaps one result of the multiple replayings of the Robert Shaw music is that these American accents are what now sound unmarked to me; the St. John's cadences in the Gower Street recording, the accent in which I spoke myself in my childhood, now strike my ear strongly as distinctive and unusual. "The First Noel" is a well-known Christmas carol, likely to be familiar in thousands and thousands of locations, yet with our comfortable vernacular pronunciation, we made it ours, made it a local text.

I am, of course, because of my date of birth, very much a child of the album. Even our shellac 45s of the Robert Shaw Chorale could be stacked so twelve tracks played at a time. The song order of the LP was even more sacrosanct. There was no such thing as a mix tape then, and we did not often shuffle the running order of the 45s.

When Daniel Leviton describes the reward structure of music in the brain, it seems to me that his theory must also account for a sequence of different music in invariant order. There is nothing in his analysis that rules out such an assemblage:

> *Music appears to mimic some of the features of language and to convey some of the same emotions that vocal communication does, but in a nonreferential and nonspecific way. It also involves some of the same neural regions that language does, but far more than language, music taps into primitive brain structures involved with motivation, reward and emotion....*

Music breathes, speeds up, and slows down just as the real world does,
and our cerebellum finds pleasure in adjusting itself to stay synchronized.
(Levitin, 2006, p. 187)

When I found the Robert Shaw Chorale CDs, remastered from remembered recordings, even the breathing, the speeding up, and the slowing down were *just* as I remembered. In some ways, this is a more exact rerendering of childhood moments than any abstract printed text could offer. With reading, breathing and speeding and slowing are supplied by the reader and may alter; with recorded music, the rhythms and pauses are invariant. All recorded audio material, verbal, musical, or mixed, carries this inviolate temporality, a fixed incarnation of extended time. Its potency is often underestimated.

Music generally may be nonreferential and nonspecific, but the custom of associating it with a single celebratory season does align it with other specific elements that are also pleasing: darkness and coloured lights, good smells and tastes, and, indeed, the tactile, visual, and anticipatory pleasures of green nylon frills edged with sparkles of bright silver. When primitive brain structures can be attached to seasonal specifications in such ways, it is perhaps not surprising that emotions run deep.

The Ephemeral Texts

I have acquired four December magazines: *Good Housekeeping* for 1956, the *Ladies' Home Journal* for 1957 and 1958, and *Jack and Jill* for 1959.

"The Story of Holly and Ivy" by Rumer Godden (*Ladies' Home Journal*, December 1957) delighted me from the moment I first sighted the beguiling illustration, included here. Almost all my reading of Godden occurred with magazine publications, yet I knew right from my first encounter that here was a writer of mettle. The surface plot is as sentimental as the red and green outfits of little girl and doll in the picture, but Godden's astringency is marked enough that even just turned nine, I recognized and appreciated its qualities. Godden fills in the details of her story with acerbity and real menace. Abracadabra, the nasty toy owl, bossing and tormenting the toys left in the toyshop on Christmas Eve, taunts the new doll, Holly, with the spectre of being unwanted for Christmas. All the toys still in the store share the same yearning, expressed by Mallow and Wallow, the velvet hippopotamuses: "We have never felt a child's hands" (Godden, 1957, p. 42). At

> Illustration by Reg Harris for "The Story of Holly and Ivy," originally published in the December 1957 Ladies' Home Journal® Magazine.

[Courtesy Meredith Corporation]

the same time, not every child is secure: "The toys thought that all children have homes, but not all children have" (p. 42). Ivy is the only orphan in St. Agnes's children's home not to be taken home for three days over Christmas by a kind family. She is sent to the infants' home in the country because there is nowhere else for her to go. But Ivy insists she has a grandmother who wants her, and, once safely alone on the train, she tears off the label on her coat giving directions. For much of this story, Ivy, aged six, is entirely on her own, while Holly waits to be wanted.

> Holly held out her arms and smiled her china smile.
> "I am here. I am Holly," she said and she wished, "Ask for me. Lift me down. Ask!" but nobody asked.
> "Hoo! Hoo!" said Abracadabra. (p. 156)

Even at age nine I sensed that Godden was capable of the utmost ruthlessness. This story was risky reading. And yet those red and green clothes in the picture held out such promise of a secure and happy Christmas at the end of the story. And indeed, Godden sheathes her claws and develops an enormous string of coincidences that lead to exactly such a finale. She stresses, however, the great unlikelihood of this happy ending, and concludes, "I told you at the beginning that it was a story about wishing" (p. 160). The implication ought to be that longing is enough to make good things happen—but Godden creates the opposite effect even as she makes it all work out. I was happy to accept the safe ending, but the experience of getting there was uncomfortable in a highly pleasurable way, and I developed a lifelong taste for Godden's children's stories.

Other Christmas magazines offered different delights. The December 1959 issue of *Jack and Jill* marks a culture in transition. Although the front cover is a conventional drawing of Santa's face inside a wreath, the story flagged above the magazine title is a behind-the-scenes account of a television program.

The first story in this issue is a very traditional piece about a boy stuck in a snowstorm in a bus on the turnpike overnight on Christmas Eve (he and his fellow passengers manage to create Christmas spirit against all odds).

The second feature, however, is "A *Jack and Jill* TV Prevue" that provides a combination of nursery rhymes and line drawings together with photographs of scenes from *Shirley Temple's Storybook* featuring Mother Goose. In an early example of a magazine feature that supplies children with insider information about a TV show, we learn that Shirley Temple's son Charles has a single important speaking line in the show. The final photograph is a family shot of Shirley and her three children, all in costume and encircled by a wreath, reading *Mother Goose* together (1959, p. 13).

The exigencies of the Newfoundland time zone, combined with the strict bedtime regimen in our house, meant we would not be able to watch the program. This feature, therefore, was of limited interest to me, though I was familiar with Shirley Temple in both child and adult incarnations. Today, it intrigues me as a harbinger of endless TV programs, websites, and magazine articles, all providing background information of this nature.

This issue of *Jack and Jill* had a clear Christmas focus. My copy is missing the four-page centre pullout on heavier paper, which almost certainly featured Christmas images for children to cut out and glue together. Counting these four pages, and counting the Mother Goose feature as seasonal (it is decorated with a wreath and some evergreen trim), Christmas dominates forty of the seventy pages. Hanukah is mentioned once or twice, mainly in the writings by child contributors. The Nativity story is given four pages.

Ritual and Ossification

Other period pieces carry a double freight. They offer a condensation of that mystery known as the Christmas spirit, preserved from one year to another in text form, annually brought to life in waves of new emotional commitment. Simultaneously, these texts also carry ideological expectations, wrapped up—though not camouflaged—in Christmas joie de vivre (or, as in *The Birds' Christmas Carol*, even joie de *mourir*).

While the Angels Sing by Gladys Hasty Carroll was published in 1947, one of many novels by this prolific author. The narrator, a widowed grandmother newly moved into her daughter's house, tells "the story of an American Christmas" (Carroll, 1947, n.p.). She is highly directive about how readers should respond to events such as the children's Christmas play. One special argument, however, Carroll puts in the mouth of the daughter's middle-aged friend who says categorically, "No girl is really a person until someone else thinks she is" (p. 71). It is clear that the same restrictions apply to adult women.

> *Because it is far more likely that a man of middle age will find a woman who knows he is a person, than that a middle-aged woman will be found by such a man. And, even if he doesn't—I feel quite sure that no man is as dependent on being valued highly by a woman or by any single human being as a woman is. Things can make a man into an integrated person. Experiences can. His own understanding of himself can. I don't believe any woman can understand herself until some man has understood her. (p. 72)*

I read many versions of this crippling theology of femininity; such attitudes blighted my adolescence severely. Its appearance in the domestic Christmas canon, preserved in a story that was ritually reread every year, gave this particular version of the handicap of being female the potency of reiteration. It was an arena of my life in which my literacies helped to limit me, to domesticate me, to confine me for many years within an artificial sense of the things that were not possible for me because I was a girl.

And yet I still respond to the seasonal and emotional appeal of other aspects of this story. Like many readers, I am skilled at bracketing out what I do not want to consider as I move through my recreational fiction. When I look at *While the Angels Sing*, I am horrified at its belittlement of women's agency, but I can also never forget how my mother would put it out on my bed when I arrived for a Christmas visit as an adult. The description of the Christmas concert comes close to capturing the felt experience of my own history with such events (both as a Holly Fairy and also as a parent). In this case, the book is as much a vehicle for preserving charged moments of my own life story as it is a purveyor of events in the lives of its characters. The relationship between two real women, my mother and myself, completely trumps any connections between the paper characters in its pages.

At the same time, however, the message of female passivity and woman's essential dependence on man was reinforced in many explicit and implicit ways throughout the 1950s and early 1960s. I ran into the same strictures in many different guises and barely noticed the implications of this lecture on womanhood because it was so familiar. I have no doubt that for a long time I believed that this argument described the true state of the world.

An older book that lurked in the house, probably once owned by a grandparent, had much less impact. *The Birds' Christmas Carol* by Kate Douglas Wiggin (1886) took up an equally well-worn motif, that of the saintly dying child. Little Carol, suffering from a terminal illness, on the very eve of her death brings Christmas joy to the Ruggles children who live in poverty outside her back lane. Christian noblesse oblige was familiar to me from many stories but did not deeply impinge on my sense of myself, though Wiggin does her best to lay it down as a model for all children to follow. Reinforcement in the culture was no longer salient, and I was able to ignore the moral as well as the pathos of this oversweetened story. The scenario itself lacked an incentive scheme. I could feel some inexplicable thrill in the idea of being profoundly *understood* by a man; the cause of dying beautifully offered no recompense to the child who dies. I was certainly aware that this flaw in the story was fatal in more ways than one. The ideological freight of this book had lost its support system by the 1950s; simply being literate and reading this book among others was not sufficient to make me susceptible to its sanctimonious message.

So even in the conservative cyclical rituals of Christmas, cultural fashions made their mark. The season's self-aware emphasis on preserving past ceremonies and material objects created a perceptible drag on changing times. But inexorably, the Christian pathos of little Carol's saintly death was replaced in popular focus by behind-the-scenes information about Shirley Temple's television Christmas special. Even in the backward-looking literacies of the season, forward movement could not be denied.

NODES

THIS SECTION STRETCHES Kevin Lynch's vocabulary some-
what, but the concept of intersecting paths is robust and interesting enough
for my organization that I think it is worth pursuing the metaphor regardless. While my childhood literacy was always in development, always
in movement along the paths I have described earlier, there were many
areas of my life where significant crossovers took effect. The three topics
described in this section meet this criterion in different ways, but they all
represent significant intellectual, affective, cultural, and social intersections.

In the first chapter of this section, I look at applied literacies relating to
many different aspects of my everyday life. I am sure I have inadvertently
omitted many quotidian examples, but the range is startling all the same.
Very few activities of my life were literacy-free, but the scale and scope of
such daily reading is often invisible to us, both as we engage with these
unassuming materials and later when we look back. I have tried to fill in
this blank, at least in a preliminary way.

The issue of watching connects very firmly to the time and space in
which I found myself as a child. Unlike many children of my era, I did not
have a movie-going youth. There were very few cinemas in St. John's, and
my parents did not organize movie outings for children. To the best of my
knowledge, I saw my first moving images on a television set at the age of
seven. I also viewed a small and extremely random assortment of films,
a set mostly comprised of what was showing at the Paramount Theatre
during the week of my friend's July birthday through the late 1950s. But I
was unlucky in the titles I now remember, and, for the most part, I simply
didn't understand them.

Nevertheless, developing awareness of how to interpret moving images
was a crossover feature of my youth, and I explore this topic further in the
final chapter in this section on "claiming." In this chapter, I attempt to explore
the ways in which different stories told in different media but bearing a

similar ideological message wove in and out of each other in ways manifest in my daily life and experience, and how they became important to my imaginative identity.

Nodes such as these could be said to have "thickened" my singular path through a literate childhood. No doubt many further examples would be possible—and no doubt some chapters placed elsewhere in this study could also feature here. What I hope to do with these three examples is argue that any singular sense of literate development is actually misleading, and that crossovers, intertextual and intermedial, actually complicate any reasonably full picture of a reading life.

With Nodes, we begin revisiting territory already delineated in the earlier chapters. As with the zoom function on a Google map, when we look more closely at complicated junctions, we find them charted in denser detail. The network of information provided on the map becomes more complicated, inviting a pause for further consideration.

This section, and those that follow, set up a more meandering approach to the landscape of my childhood literacy, exploring the territory on the basis of different perspectives and priorities.

11
Miscellaneous and Utility Literacies

Doing

THE VAST BULK OF MY READING was fictional but, like any literate child, I applied my skills in a broad range of fields, many of which are partially recapturable today through the retrieval of the materials involved. Participating in household literacies meant using texts that were purposeful in real-world terms. Some texts allowed me to make measurable changes, however short-lived, in the world around me. Others offered different ways of thinking about the universe. I consciously applied myself to some; others I absorbed through osmosis. But these different forms of applied literacies operated in my life on a daily basis, although I don't recall particularly thinking of them as examples of reading.

Practical Reading

I still own Mum's battered copy of *The Boston Cooking School Cookbook*, created by Fanny Farmer (a 1945 Christmas present from my father to my

GERMAN CHOCOLATE COOKIES

2 eggs, lightly beaten
1 cup brown sugar
2 ounces sweet chocolate, grated
¼ teaspoon cinnamon
½ teaspoon salt

Grated rind ½ lemon
1⅛ cups almonds, blanched
    and chopped
1 cup flour
1 teaspoon baking powder

Add sugar gradually to eggs and continue beating. Add remaining ingredients. Drop from tip of spoon on buttered cooky sheet and bake in moderately slow oven (325° F.). *Makes 36.*

CHOCOLATE FRUIT COOKIES

¼ cup butter
½ cup sugar
2 tablespoons grated chocolate
1 tablespoon sugar
1 tablespoon boiling water

1 egg
½ cup nut meats, finely chopped
½ cup seeded raisins, finely chopped
1 cup flour
1 teaspoon baking powder

Cream butter and add ½ cup sugar, gradually. Melt chocolate, add remaining sugar and water, and cook 1 minute. Combine mixtures and add remaining ingredients. Chill, roll, and bake. (See Sugar Cookies, p. 666.) *Makes 36.*

CHOCOLATE WALNUT WAFERS

½ cup butter
1 cup sugar
2 eggs, well beaten
2 squares chocolate, melted

1 cup chopped walnut meats
¼ teaspoon salt
¼ teaspoon vanilla
⅔ cup flour

Cream butter and add sugar gradually; add other ingredients in order given. Drop from tip of spoon on a buttered cooky sheet 1 inch apart and bake in moderate oven (350° F.). *Makes 36.*

BUTTERSCOTCH BROWNIES

⅛ cup butter
1 cup dark brown sugar
1 egg, unbeaten
¼ teaspoon salt

¾ cup cake flour
1 teaspoon baking powder
½ teaspoon vanilla
½ cup nut meats, broken in pieces

Melt butter, add other ingredients, and spread in buttered pan, 8 × 8 inches. Bake 25 minutes in moderate oven (350° F.). Cut in squares or strips. *Makes 16 or more.*

mother, it was published in 1941, a "new and completely revised" edition of the 1896 original). At age seven or eight, I made my first foray into baking, a tin of squares. Fanny Farmer called them Butterscotch Brownies, but in our household, for reasons now lost in history, we named them Chewy-Dewies. (My brother Earle's explanation is simply that Chewy-Dewy is an excellent name for a square, a point that is difficult to argue.) The specialist reading of the recipe took some interpreting, and it was one occasion when I was humbly prepared to follow my mother's guidance. A pencilled note in the margin in my own handwriting says, "Double this," presumably a nod to the rapacious capacities of the square-eating population in our household. The page on which the recipe is printed is a good example of the book's overall grubbiness; it was one of the hardest-working texts in the whole house.

Reading to bake is a literacy endeavour that leads to direct feedback. With three brothers ready to applaud my achievement in very practical ways (not to mention my personal enthusiasm for Chewy-Dewies), my commitment to cooking was instantly reinforced.

At age eleven, I was recruited for serious routine baking; for five years, until I got too busy with homework, I made oatmeal bread every Saturday morning. The words of the recipe translated into tactile experience that, for years, shaped my sense of Saturday morning time (the oatmeal sits for an hour; the yeast rises for ten minutes; the bread is kneaded, then proves for two hours, and so forth). My mother cooked baked beans while I made bread, and we ate both for dinner every Saturday night for many years.

Another form of applied reading came in Grade 4, the spring I was nine. We spent months of that school year sewing a chintz bag with French seams, about a foot square, all hemmed by hand. My chintz was flowered blue, and I stitched it relentlessly, from September to April. When I finally inserted the drawstring into its handsewn channel, I still had class needle-work time to fill. Miss Bradbury taught me to knit.

I have been a knitter ever since. This accomplishment is one occasion where the role of a particular text in the achievement can be pinned down with exactitude. Mum had a Paton and Baldwin pattern book full of doll's clothes, and she supplied a ball of leftover pale-blue wool. The pattern was ideally suited to a novice knitter, being all knit and purl. Mum helped with casting on and off, but I did the rest. Then I knit a pink doll's dress for my friend's birthday from the same pattern. By the time both dresses were done, I was adept enough to tackle the rest, and my friend's present was a complete layette. I was launched.

The Internet is a wonderful place for trivia, and "Paton" combined with "doll's clothes" made a sufficient search term. In 2012, by recognizing a picture of a doll's outfit I knew I had knit, I turned up a version of the pattern book in Australia and acquired it on eBay. The photograph of the dolls is deeply evocative to me, and my first knitting pattern reads exactly as I recalled it.

[Continued on page 17]

∧ *Image from* Patons
Craft Book No. C.5, 2.
*This secondhand copy
was not mine originally,
but I recognize the
marks of wear on it.*
[Used by permission of
Yarnspirations]

Cast on *52 stitches.*

1st row.—Knit plain.

Rep. 1st row eight times.

10th row.—K.1, purl to last st., K.1. (Patons Craft Book No. C.5, p. 3)

I liked the sense of interpreting a very specialist code. I certainly liked the doll's clothes. Since they could be made out of scraps of Mum's wool, there was usually no problem with the raw materials (always a consideration in my frugal childhood).

The sense of being knowledgeable in such applied fields as cooking and knitting was very appealing to me. My sense of expertise was probably overblown, but certainly I was adept on the lower slopes with both these activities. The distinctive physical rhythms of kneading and knitting became very familiar to me, and the obscure lines of the coded instructions opened up to actionable meaning.

Fiction and Practicalities: A Permeable Border

Some cookbooks are entirely "efferent" (Rosenblatt, 1978, p. 24) and practice oriented. You read for the take-away value of the instructions. Many, however, occupy a border territory between reality and wishful thinking. In Grade 7, against all the odds of my actual practice in class (spotty at best), I won a Home Economics prize: *Betty Crocker's Guide to Easy Entertaining* (1959). This little period piece was illustrated by Peter Spier, later a picture-book artist; and his jaunty drawings do liven up some very starchy content. Betty Crocker, that imaginary merger of cook, hostess, and brand image (the title page asserts "Betty Crocker is the trade name of General Mills"), had very firm ideas about etiquette that dominate this coil-bound volume at least as importantly as the recipes. For example, in her twelve-page chapter on "Invitations, Acceptances, and Regrets," she includes a list of what were not then called Frequently Asked Questions. Among them is this passage, utterly confident in its statement of an immovable world:

> *Does the wife always give the invitation to a party?*
>
> *Except when a bachelor is host, invitations always are given by the hostess, or in her name, and are addressed to the other women involved, even if they have not met....*
>
> *If it is complicated for the hostess to reach a guest by telephone, and there is not time for a note, the invitation can be given by the host quite properly. He gives it in his wife's name, however, such as, "Betty has not been able to reach Jane, so she told me to ask you to save Friday night for us." In this case, the answer might be, "Jane is hard to reach. I'll ask her to call Betty in the morning." (pp. 18–19)*

Spier, who would later produce the multi-ethnic picture book *People* (1981), saw fit in this case to illustrate this idiotic roundabout of formal-speak with a picture of a very ladylike First Nations woman sending smoke signals. Smoke signals could hardly have been more opaque to me than this tara-diddle of silly rules and regulations, but I read the book more than once. Did I revisit this foolish book because I was perennially short of reading material? because the lively illustrations drew me in? because this insight into being a particular kind of grown-up held its own allure? because the mix of real life (the cooking) and fantasy (the husband and suburban lifestyle) was potent, especially as I gathered speed toward adolescence? All of the above

∧ *Peter Spier's*
illustration in Betty
Crocker's *Guide to Easy*
Entertaining *(1959, p. 19).*
[*Used by permission of*
Peter Spier]

are undoubtedly part of the mix. Had I first read this book as the "bride" who is so frequently invoked in its pages, I might have felt more anxiety about the near certainty of getting it "wrong" at least some of the time; but no such qualms troubled my twelve-year-old self.

As I learned to become a child cook, I developed a small-scale form of tacit literacy, highly unimportant at one level but very deeply evocative. Its potency became explicit to me only when I returned to Canada after an absence of nearly twenty years. On my first grocery shop, stocking the cupboards of our new Canadian kitchen in 1989, I found myself transfixed in the aisles of the supermarket. The baking powder tub was brown and yellow! The baking soda had a cow on the box! The flour bore a profile of Robin Hood! A hiatus of nearly twenty years made brand recognition feel very significant somehow. I stood riveted in the aisle with tears springing to my eyes. It was an example of literacy as homecoming, even though that particular form of literacy is both specialist and highly manipulated by the marketers of the products I suddenly recognized so profoundly.

Piano Lessons

One other applied literacy that dominated many hours of my life for seven years between the ages of six and thirteen was the reading and performance of piano music. I was astounded to discover in 2012 that my first primer was available for sale online, though when I acquired my contemporary copy of *Teaching Little Fingers to Play* (Thompson, 1994) it was a much livelier and more heavily illustrated document than the austere booklet of my youth. The tunes are the same, however, and come in the same order, presumably because they still build the skill set in some rational fashion. I normally write with music playing on my computer, but I found I needed to silence it in order to be able to describe this modest pamphlet. The little ditties with their three- or four-note tunes and simple words are hardwired in my head and would not permit any mental competition from other melodies. I look at the first one ("Birthday Party," played on the notes of C, D, and E, and containing these words, "Here we go, / Up a row / To a birthday party"), and my fingers remember it at least as well as my ears and eyes do. Furthermore, the subsequent tunes follow in my head as remorselessly in the correct order as any recollection of an album of recorded music. "Sandman's Near," "Baseball Days," "The Postman," "Rain on the Roof," "Song of the Volga Boatman," and so on. All my brothers toiled through this book in their turn, so it is not only my own efforts that I now recall so seamlessly.

Not even the knitting patterns call out muscle memory like these music scores. For two or three years, my teacher decreed that I should learn music by Bach and music by Bartók. Relocating that specific book of Bach music for young pianists has proved almost impossible, but I did track down the Bartók volume, *Little Pieces for Children: Book 1, for Solo Piano*. I detested those pieces from start to finish, but now when I look at the pages they are deeply familiar; my eyes, my ears, and my hands and arms all recognize them profoundly. Even my sitting posture is captured in these pages of notation. Hearing a professional play them is a very strange, out-of-body experience; these notes known by my whole body are transfigured into something much more melodic than I ever mustered.

Presumably athletes watch televised sporting events with this physical knowledge as part of their experience; I was never athletic enough to develop such a physiological viewing repertoire. But Bartók's piano notes are inviolable; I, toiling resentfully through my half-hour daily practice, and the world's greatest concert pianist play them in the same order and most probably with the same juxtaposition of fingering. My capacity to listen to these little songs, as a result, is infused with vivid physical, emotional, and contextual associations that have been preserved in my mind and body for fifty years and more.

The Performance of Hymns

This topic could fill a whole chapter, but I will be terse. Collectively and individually, we engaged in many kinds of singing (intergenerational popular songs in the car, campfire songs at Brownies, playground ditties in the schoolyard, and much more).

A great deal of the emotional content of the songs on the hit parade, with their relentless emphasis on love and pining, was opaque to me as a child. Sometimes, however, a song would be more accessible. On our long walks to school, my friend and I were occasionally moved to belt out a parody of such a tune at the top of our lungs. "Splish-splash I was taking a bath," we hollered, for example. "And then I slipped on a cake of soap!" We thought we were devastatingly witty.

We also danced—square dancing in gym class, with some preliminary efforts at jiving during the final period of my time frame. The excruciating experience of ballroom dancing with the boys in gym class lay ahead of me, a Grade 10 horror.

Without a doubt, however, the dominant form of musical performance in my young life, to a degree that will seem strange to many people today, was the singing of hymns. I am no longer a church-goer, but the hymns live on in my head.

Most families went regularly to church in St. John's in the 1950s, and we were no exception. As heirs to the Methodist tradition, we participated in a vigorous culture of hymn singing. The role of the hymnbooks (the *Canadian Youth Hymnal* [1939] in school, the *Hymnary of the United Church of Canada* [1930] at church) was potent.

Alisa Clapp-Itnyre (2010), writing about nineteenth-century children's hymns, testifies to the "great empowerment of children through music's physical agency" (p. 144). She also highlights the "'adult' approaches to hymn writing, and the intellect required to negotiate through theologically disparate texts" (p. 144). Hymnbooks, she points out, are "compilations of many writers' hymns; in becoming multivoiced, hymnbooks took on a fluidity of authorship that presented quite an ideological banquet for the discerning child" (p. 146). I endorse all her points and suggest there is a further bonus of an aesthetic banquet as well, in that hymns (at least in my hymnbooks, and I suspect in most others) are equally variable in their artistic qualities, and a child can develop some judgement.

With morning assembly in school, weekly church services, and Sunday school for all but the summer months, I calculate I sang between six hundred and 650 hymns a year, not counting any practices. Unlike most other situations in which I sang, I read the shaped lines as I performed them and gained a strong repertoire of many formal elements of literary language use: rhyme, metre, stress, and scansion; vocabulary; grammar; archaisms; rhythm and melody; variant translations; and performance. I also acquired a large and reliable (though highly specific) intertextual repertoire. More implicitly, I picked up what I can best describe as a kind of "musical mouth test" for the organization of words in a phrase or a sentence. My hymn singing affected my actions as a reader, but it much more profoundly shaped my behaviour as a writer. Performing the shape of organized sets of words, over and over, develops sensibilities of ear, mouth, and breathing; these then pass through to and are enacted by the hands in writing or typing or keyboarding.

Through all these literary elements shines the content, and of course I acquired theological and liturgical information from these hymns as well. But it was the shaping of words and lines in musical ways that spilled most strongly into the rest of my life.

My hymns were international but collected in Canadian editions, and John Beckwith (1988) suggests that this fact is significant. "The hymn tune remains a grass roots cultural symbol and aural image. As with the secular popular song, many examples are retained in memory from early childhood through adolescence by large segments of the cultural community. This account has tried, therefore, to recall what was once, and perhaps still dimly is, a part of the aural memory of many members of Canadian society" (p 231). As a child I took my immersion in this culture completely for granted, and I knew no other way of growing up. I enjoyed singing my favourites, disliked many others, and seamlessly folded the ideological impact of this experience into my daily life.

I value what I learned from these hymns, even if I wish they occupied a bit less real estate in my brain today. The true physical, psychological, cultural, and ideological pleasure of the act of singing together supplied me with a rich experience and a continuous literate thread throughout my childhood.

Then there was the content. There were life lessons in the hymnbook, and I contemplated specific lines. Often these included references to death rather than life: "Frail as summer's flowers we flourish; / Blows the wind and it is gone" (Lyte); "We blossom and flourish as leaves on the tree, / And wither and perish" (Smith); "Frail children of dust, / And feeble as frail" (Grant). The glories of an eternal God were presented in stark contrast with the sin, suffering, and mortality of the little humans in His care. Ever one for the minor key, I liked these mordant reminders, even though I understood them only in vague and sentimental ways. They provided a reality check for my normally cheerful fictions and supplied resonance for the occasional death in my stories.

The hymns often supplied a transcendent note of grandeur in my humdrum life. The King James Bible was also sonorous, but I had much less to do with its performance. With the hymns, I was an agent who sang majestic lines:

> O tell of His might,
> O sing of His grace,
> Whose robe is the light,
> Whose canopy space;
> His chariots of wrath
> The deep thunder-clouds form,
> And dark is His path
> On the wings of the storm. (Grant)

Finally, and not trivially, the hymns equipped me to read many of my recreational materials. The culture of church, Bible, and hymnbook permeated many of the novels I read, even when their direct intention was not religious instruction. I was able to align myself effortlessly with the role demanded of the implied reader in these cases, with a full repertoire of embodied understanding.

Thus, I was acculturated into a long-standing literature, one that is itself becoming more archaic and specialist. The original Wesleyans and other English-speaking Christians shared the kind of cultural knowledge I am describing here across all levels of society. As the importance of the church in society changes, the received wisdom and the received grammar and linguistic knowledge I assembled from these hymns place me in a minority, even compared to the situation in my own childhood. But they certainly represent knowledge I cannot and do not want to erase, even though I no longer share the guiding energy that gave it life in the first place.

The Book of Knowledge

When we moved from Pennywell Road to LeMarchant Road in 1959, Dad built bookcases in the alcoves alongside the living room fireplace. The lower left-hand shelves housed *The Book of Knowledge* in many brown leather-ette volumes (McLoughlin, 1955).

I was never very enthusiastic about non-fiction reading, but I did dip into *The Book of Knowledge* from time to time. Mostly I read the sections on stories, poetry, and myths and legends, with occasional forays into history and some accidental reading of science on the side if I got going and simply didn't want to stop.

I have had trouble locating the exact edition we acquired in 1959, possibly as a second-hand purchase. The title, of course, is useless as a search term because it is so general. I thank Perry Nodelman, who scanned the title pages of his own volumes to give me at least an editorial name to work with: E.V. McLoughlin. With this essential addition, I acquired two samples: Volumes 9 and 11 of the January 1955 printing of the 1954 version. They look more or less right. Their general impact is exactly as I recall it, and this is one case in this project where "good enough" will have to suffice. The visuals of my copies are certainly correct: glossy paper, with double columns of print interrupted by dark diagrams or the occasional murky photograph. The contents also ring true: a very random assortment of topics with a certain "lucky dip" component to their juxtaposition.

Take for example the section "Things to Make—and—Things to Do" in Volume 11 (pp. 4013–4018; these enormous page numbers were part of the exotic charm). It kicks off with an article on semaphore (and I find, looking at the drawings, that I actually do remember the body motions from my Brownie days). "Fun with Your Typewriter" follows, with some illustrations of shapes you can make with creative use of keystrokes. Next comes "Preparing a Picnic Lunch Basket" with some suggestions for portable meals. After that, we move effortlessly to a short section on "The Greek

Alphabet," and hence to "How to Make a Useful Workbench" ("This useful workbench may be made by any boy who is able to use simple woodworking tools and who can secure the necessary lumber" [p. 4017].) Finally a set of rules for "The Game of Egg Hat." This game can be played by anywhere between five and ten boys, with the proviso that each must have a cap (p. 4018).

More substantial information is provided in the nine-page Science section on "Current Electricity" (pp. 4033–4041). Refreshingly, all the peopled illustrations include girls as well as boys. The science itself is fairly hardcore, by the anemic standards of information literacy that I brought to bear on it.

> If we immerse the two electrodes of a battery in certain kinds of liquids, and so make electric current flow through the currents, some remarkable things may happen. In water (made more conducting by mixing into it a few drops of an acid) we shall soon see bubbles of gas rising from the electrodes. The passage of current through the water (H_2O) helps to tear apart the hydrogen (H) and Oxygen (O) which make up water molecules; and both gases rise separately, one at the negative electrode, the other at the positive one. This process is called Electrolysis, and it is often used to get pure gases conveniently. (p. 4037)

I wish now that I had read these books in more dedicated ways. My life would have been richer if I had been better informed about the world. Even so, these volumes provided what sense I did get that the universe was full of intricate and interesting wonders; they comprised my earliest introduction to any real science beyond the basic nature study that made up our school experience before junior high.

Being a Brownie

I joined Brownies during the fall I turned eight and passed the recruitment test in February 1957. I was a Pixie and gradually moved from the rank and file to the higher status of being a Seconder and then a Sixer. Few records remain from this chapter in my life, but my Brownie test card somehow survived and makes interesting reading.

Tests for the Golden Bar and Golden Hand divided into four categories: Intelligence, Handcraft, Health, and Service. The Recruit Test involved the arcane insiderness of being a Brownie: "A Brownie must know:—The

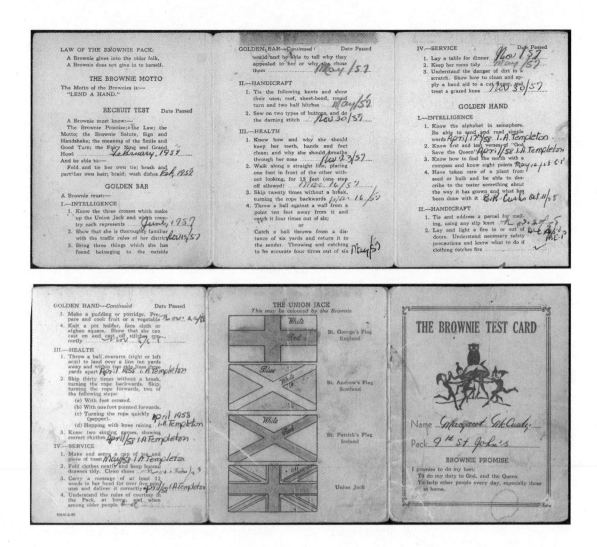

∧ *Brownie Test Card*
for Margaret McCurdy
of the 9th St. John's
Brownie Pack.

[Collection of the author]

Brownie Promise; the Law; the Motto; the Brownie Salute, Sign and Handshake; the meaning of the Smile and Good Turn; the Fairy Ring and Grand Howl." There were also requirements of personal hygiene; a Brownie must also "be able to:—Fold and tie her own tie; brush and part her own hair; braid; wash dishes." Subsequent tests were patriotic (though knowing the three crosses that make up the Union Jack or two verses of "God Save the Queen" indicated a removed form of patriotism); or domestic (with inbuilt assumptions about the Brownie's home life where it would be a meaningful activity to "lay a table for dinner" or "fold clothes neatly and keep bureau drawers tidy. Clean shoes").

There are references to an adventurous outdoor life, with the Brownie learning knots, and the alphabet in semaphore, and the points of a compass.

We did not camp as Brownies, and I missed my first Guide camp by moving to Alberta, so I never got to apply this esoteric knowledge, but I liked knowing it; it also served a useful role in the compost heap of general knowledge that helped me read *Swallows and Amazons*.

The various symbols of the uniform were also pleasing: the Pixie emblem, the achievement badges, the Sixer stripes. I had some slender experience of "reading" clothing from the elements of my school uniform, including the crest on the tunic; but the Brownie uniform offered a much more engaging challenge. I could never embellish my school uniform with any emblems of progress. But I could actually enhance my Brownie uniform with added insignia through my own endeavours, so there was considerable satisfaction in observing the increasing elaborateness of its semiotic freight.

The Literacies of Sports

Domestic Impact

In our family, you simply knew a lot about sports, and the only choice was whether your knowledge was explicit or tacit. I had plenty of exposure to explicit sports literacies, both in the daily newspapers and in the many forms of documentation my brothers assembled. They drew numerous pictures of hockey players, both mug shots and action scenes, recreating the conventions of the genre very faithfully. They collected tables of statistics for both baseball and hockey.

Everyone except Mum supported big-league teams, but I was the family nonconformist. Dad and the boys cheered for the Toronto Maple Leafs in hockey and the St. Louis Cardinals in baseball; I preferred the New York Rangers and the Chicago White Sox. (Mum was a conscientious objector who detested all spectator sports.) A picture of New York's captain, Andy Bathgate, cut from *Weekend Magazine*, adorned my bedroom wall for some years.

I didn't play hockey, but I did play many scratch games of baseball in the Green Gate, and so I have always understood the game differently through that physical experience. The boys played hockey endlessly, either floor hockey, with sticks and a tennis ball, or else table hockey. A family photo shows that Bruce, barely turned two, knew at least the posture and the general idea of how to play the table game. Initially we owned the basic game that the little boys are playing in this photograph, but not too long

> *Bruce, aged two,*
and David, nearly five,
play table hockey.

[Collection of the author]

∨ *A complete set of*
hockey coins mounted
on the display shields,
and a single hockey coin
featuring Andy Bathgate.

[Photo courtesy of Dennis Kane]

afterward, we acquired a more sophisticated version that allowed the tin players to move up and down their fixed slots as well as spin on the spot. This gadget called for more spatial awareness than I was ever able to muster, and I was a flat failure at playing with it. Whether this lack of talent caused me to dislike it, or whether I was simply playing gender resistance games is now not clear to me.

The boys also collected hockey coins (plastic discs about the size of a loonie); we spent a number of winters eating Sherriff's Luscious Jelly (which I never liked and still don't) and Sherriff's Lemon Pudding (which I enjoyed), in order to acquire the coins inserted in the boxes. There were twenty coins for each of the six National Hockey League teams, and the names of the players remain exceedingly familiar to me. The act of collecting entailed many trades and much hoarding and gloating, and I was at least tacitly aware of which players were scarce. The hockey coins also played protracted games against each other, using a chewed-up wad of paper as a puck and being manipulated by as many as four hands at a time. But it was ownership that was the prime focus, and my brothers sent off for a collecting rack and display shields.

Both table game and hockey coins provide classic instances of "scriptive things" (Bernstein, 2011, p. 8). Bernstein's analytical questions lead to some interesting answers. "The operative questions are, 'What historically located behaviors did this artifact invite? And what practices did it discourage?' The goal is not to determine what any individual did with an artifact but rather to understand how a nonagential artifact, in its historical context, prompted or invited—scripted—actions of humans who were agential and not infrequently resistant" (p. 8). Resistance to the table-top game was just about impossible; you played by the terms scripted by the handles that controlled the tin players, or you refused. The hockey coins scripted acquisition and display, but these plastic chips had a broader repertoire. I was cavalierly in favour of using them for completely other purposes, such as representing money in a game of shop, but my brothers were very uneasy about interfering with the script to such an extent. Their game playing with the wadded-up puck involved a homemade script; although my hands do remember the experience of negotiating a chewed-up puck with a plastic chip, it was not a game I joined on more than a couple of occasions.

In the relative ease or difficulty with which they could be acquired, the hockey coins were never equal. The two names of Bronco Horvath and

Chico Maki come to mind; the former, as I recall, showed up over and over again to the collectors' great frustration. Maki, by contrast, was rare. As a reminder of how specialist and situated a literacy can be (and how germane details can linger), here is my oldest brother's 2013 account of acquiring the Maki coin sometime in the early 1960s:

> *Chico Maki was a tough one. My recollection is that no one at Holloway School had him. I found out, probably by reading the small print on the package, that you could in fact peel the picture off a coin, and there was a number embossed on the plastic. You could then send that coin and purchase up to that number of coins (with the photos still in place). You could specify the ones you wanted; they'd accommodate the request if they could, but no guarantee. It cost a very small fee—a nickel each or something and probably a couple of box tops.*
>
> *Anyway, that's how I got Chico Maki, and a couple of other hard-to-gets. I don't recall what the drill was on Bronco Horvath. Think he was probably an easy one. The two guys I remember being particularly easy to get were Aut Erickson, an otherwise obscure defenceman, and Bruce Gamble, a goalie then with Boston who went to play with the Leafs for several years. If you really want fine detail, Erickson was #112 in the series, and Gamble was #119. (Earle McCurdy, personal communication, June 20, 2013)*

The names of Erickson and Gamble had completely slipped my mind, but, the minute I read my brother's e-mail, they bounced right back in, trailing a highly evocative redolence of the Pennywell Road kitchen where the jelly boxes were torn open as soon as they arrived with the other groceries.

I am sure the Maki coin, when it finally came in the mail, never did anything but take pride of place in its display slot; no reckless messing with the scriptive orders was permitted. Aura trumped action when scarcity value ruled.

Tacit Sports Literacies

My interest in professional sport was largely tacit. I liked the atmospherics of baseball, the cadences of the game on the radio or the TV set. We all explicitly enjoyed the antics of Dizzy Dean and Pee Wee Reese who called the TV baseball games (search "MLB NBC game of the week 1961" on YouTube for a fragment of one of their joint games). Mum tutted over Dizzy's awful grammar, but my brothers rejoiced in lines such as, "Folks, this here pitcher has just throwed up five straight curves." When the game got a bit slow (it's been known!), Dizzy would sing "The Wabash Cannonball," or be filmed throwing peanuts in the air and catching them in his mouth. We loved it.

Mostly, however, Diz and Pee Wee simply called the game. Marie-Laure Ryan (2006) writes vividly about the rhythms of live baseball commentary, which necessarily entails "a largely nonselective enumeration of events" (p. 81). The primary task of the announcer is to report on events as they transpire on the field, she observes, a need that may conflict with television and radio's stern requirement for continuous entertainment.

> *The necessity to fill up the entire time of the game with talk limits the simul-*
> *taneous report of events to less than half of the broadcast. The rhythm of*
> *the game is not a steady flow but an alternation of slow periods and sudden*
> *outbursts of action. It is only in fiction that time adjusts to the pace of the*
> *language. In the real-time narratives of the real world, language must play*
> *catch with time. The relation between the duration of the narrated and the*
> *duration of the narration is rarely comfortable; there is usually either too*
> *much or too little time for language to capture the action live. (pp. 81–82)*

The rhythms of that game of catch between language and time are specific to the sport being announced; I was homesick for baseball cadences during the nineteen summers I lived in Britain. Cricket rhythms were no substitute, though they were profoundly comfortable to my English friend. It was a surprise consolation of moving back to Canada at the age of forty to find myself "at home" with the baseball commentary rumbling in the background on the TV set, another case (like the familiar baking powder tub) of a known literacy fitting comfortably into corners of daily life.

The rhythms of a called hockey game are much more frenetic but equally unmistakable. They played a lesser role in my childhood because of one simple and intractable element of that "real time" of sport that Ryan alludes to. The game started at 8:00 P.M. Eastern Standard Time (EST) on Saturday's *Hockey Night in Canada*—it was already 9:30 P.M. in Newfoundland, and we were already in bed. The cure for that problem was the move to Edmonton, where, miraculously, 8:00 P.M. EST was 6:00 P.M. Mountain Standard Time, and everybody who wanted could watch the game.

My tacit sporting awareness was more attuned to elements of the experience like the cadences of the radio program than to details of wins, losses, standings, and statistics. I did absorb a good deal of knowledge (and was struck, when I moved to Britain, at how illiterate in the languages and texts of sport I instantly became, and how much small change of social interaction was therefore inaccessible to me). I knew the specialized codes; my father, to the end of his life, read current and historic box scores of the Cardinals' baseball games just for pleasure, and I certainly could have traced the meanings of the cryptic entries if it had ever occurred to me to bother to do so. For the most part, though, my sports knowledge was a kind of wallpaper; my engagement was peripheral and superficial.

Active Spectatorship

The one area where I was actively engaged with spectator sports was in the interschools hockey league in St. John's. In Grade 7, just before my twelfth birthday, I moved to the upper school in the Prince of Wales system. School rules decreed that you had to be in Grade 9 to go to school dances, but everybody at PWC was eligible to go to the hockey games.

The denominational breakdown of schooling in Newfoundland sharpened the rivalry between schools. The arch-enemy of the Collegians at that time was the team from St. Bon's, then the premier Catholic boys' high school. The whole school took the competition very seriously, and if our boys won the championship, we all got a half-holiday. In my desultory diary, school hockey games probably rate more entries than any other topic.

By Grade 7 I was living on LeMarchant Road, but the arena was on the school athletic grounds, so I revisited my old haunts on Pennywell Road every time I went to a game. The sense of knowing the lay of the land in huge detail offered an unexamined emotional undertow to the experience of the hockey games; at one level, it was completely irrelevant, but in another way it was part of how I belonged to the experience of the games. I belonged to the Prince of Wales side, I belonged to the spectator set following the ins and out of the game, I belonged to my father's family (Dad was famous as a principal highly invested in his teams' successes and failures), and I belonged to the local landscape in which the arena was set. Of such obscure and multiplying threads is knowledge assembled in its full complexity; my current (reasonably substantial) knowledge of hockey somewhere still includes the remnants of these factors that comprised my first detailed attention to the game.

Board Games and Card games: Numeracy and Cultural Capital

My brothers never met a competitive game they didn't like, and sometimes they roped me into playing with them. My parents both liked card games; only I disdained gametime. But I learned how to play checkers and chess, dominoes, cribbage, some lesser card games, Monopoly, and my favourite, crokinole.

To play any of these games required a certain quotient of numeracy, and all three of my brothers left me standing when it came to arithmetic. I liked the rhythmic and satisfying chant marking the progress of the cribbage pegs: "Fifteen two, fifteen four, fifteen six, and a pair is eight"—but it has to be earned, and I was usually not the winner in these contests. Naturally it was incumbent on me to cultivate indifference.

Cribbage and dominoes (both hard to alter) were almost the only items of cultural literacy in terms of gaming that I was able to maintain when I emigrated. I was horrified to discover that the British play Monopoly on a different board, and crokinole seems to be largely a Canadian game. The game we called Clue was Cluedo in the United Kingdom, and Parcheesi was named Ludo. Even though I was not a fan of any of these games, I found it all very unsettling and actually organized the acquisition of a North American edition of Monopoly so that my own children could learn the site names that resonated with me (but then their British friends found our game very strange).

Another invisible facet of cultural literacy, this national finessing of familiar games into something just different enough to be uncanny. We underestimate the security offered by these forms of low-level familiarity, these local game literacies that operate at a family or neighbourhood level but provide a form of important cultural glue.

Festive Literacies

Certain forms of literacy were reserved for annual extravaganzas. Valentine's Day, for example, was associated with a series of strictly regimented literate behaviours. At school a cardboard box was covered in white paper and red construction-paper hearts. We cut out our valentines, filling in the "To" slot with the names of our friends but scrupulously writing "Guess Who!" in the line for the giver. We enveloped them, addressed them, posted them in the classroom mailbox, and waited in great anticipation for the mass delivery on the afternoon of Valentine's Day. Of course the

> *Crokinole.*

[*Used by permission of Willard and Bruce Martin, "*WILLARD*" boards ™*]

> ∨ *Monopoly.*

[© *Judith Collins / Alamy Stock Photo*]

∨ *Cribbage.*

[*Used by permission of David Westnedge Ltd.*]

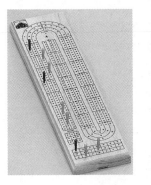

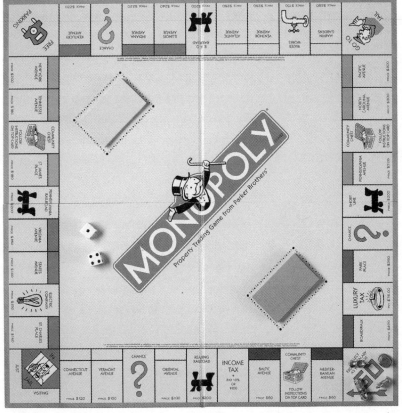

∧ *Vintage valentines*
with their envelopes.
[*Courtesy Penguin*
Random House]

popular children got the most, but the de rigueur anonymity camouflaged the social dynamics of this classroom literacy event to a certain extent; and I seem to recall that everyone got cookies. The cheap-and-cheerful cards relied on cheap-and-cheerful puns to make their point, but we were not interested in romance, so these stupid jokes suited us just fine.

For home use, we made valentines out of construction paper and, in a good year, paper doilies. Nobody was ever able to buy a useful Valentine's Day pad in which every sheet of construction paper was red, so we had to come up with some ingenious work-arounds after the red pages were all used up.

Our simple efforts supplied enough of a repertoire to enable me not simply to comprehend but also to covet the more elaborate arrangements of Marjorie and her friend Delight, two heroines of a series of books that came in that carton of treasures from Mum's friend. I lusted after Delight's craft supplies and also after her dexterity and refined imagination, as presented in the following luscious scene:

> *It was easy for Delight. Her deft little fingers pinched up bits of tissue paper*
> *into charming little rosebuds or forget-me-nots, and her dainty taste chose*

∧ Mrs. Duder's Grade 1
class, Prince of Wales
College, Hallowe'en, 1954.
[Courtesy Clarence Button
Collection, Archives and Special
Collections, Memorial University
of Newfoundland]

*lovely color combinations....Delight cut a heart-shaped piece of cardboard
and round the edge dabbled an irregular border of gold paint. The inside she
tinted pink all over and on it wrote a loving little verse in gold letters. (Wells;
1909, p. 141)*

How I would have loved to be able to create charming little rosebuds, or to
be possessed of deft fingers and dainty taste. As usual, my reach exceeded
my grasp, and my own homemade confections were seriously more
ordinary.

Hallowe'en was less associated with prescribed literate actions.
Nevertheless, I was pleased to locate the Hallowe'en class picture from
Grade 1, featuring me and my classmates in full costume (I am on the far
left of the front row and I recall my annoyance at having to cobble up a
costume from the dress-up box rather than buying a store outfit like, say, a

proper Nurse ensemble, or that Little Dutch Girl get-up you see in the back row).

What strikes me now, though, in looking at this picture, is the quantity of explicitly Hallowe'en-related literacies arrayed on the blackboard behind us. The calendar is full of themed images and what looks like weather reports. On the right-hand board are the words to a Hallowe'en song that I could still sing, if pressed. The artwork decorating the top frame of the blackboard is utterly seasonal. And of course the huge excitement of the dress-up party was a focus of our attention for weeks prior. The ceremony of the class photograph provided another ingredient in the sense of occasion.

Daily Life and Literacies

Thus were multiple skills and understandings woven through my daily life via a highly miscellaneous collection of texts, in domestic, school, and social settings alike. Applied literacies operate on an ontological basis that differs from that of the literacies of fiction, though sometimes the firmness of the border wavers or dissolves. Using literacy to function practically in a range of roles was simply a normal part of daily life. Only when I come to tease out the interwoven strands of various literate endeavours do I register the complexity of the interactions between life and a broad assortment of texts.

The performative quotient of many of these texts remains unchanged; that's what literacy does for us. I could today bake some Chewy-Dewies, knit a doll's dress, assemble a valentine envelope, tie a reef knot, or play one of Bartók's "little pieces," and the outcome would be the same as it was fifty years ago. What has changed, of course, is that all these texts are now layered with a patina of nostalgia impossible to eradicate. They are charming and evocative to me now, where they were once simply ordinary. But through that overlay, it is still possible for me to discern some of the affect that originally surrounded them: the sense of accumulating achievement and mastery (well, not with Bartók, but with most of the others). I look at these items and I remember the shift from explicit to tacit, from laboured to automatic. I remember the triumphs of achieving something useful and the pleasures of being knowledgeable about things.

Not much applied knowledge arrived in my life in any literacy-free way. When I search my memory for examples, almost the only semi-skilled activity not associated with reading that comes to mind is gardening with Dad, who grew a handsome border of flowers all along the edge of the

Green Gate and helped us kids grow nasturtiums, cosmos, and sweet peas. That experience is not quite text-free—one evocative memory entails going downtown with Dad to the Gaze Seed Company, breathing the warm fecundity exuded by a shop floor full of plants, and diligently reading seed packets to decide what flowers I would grow myself. But for the most part, in the garden I dug, planted, weeded, inspected, and waited in a lather of expectation, all without benefit of textual assistance.

I also learned physical skills without reading about them. I learned to somersault forward and backward, to rotate my body round the guard-rail of the soccer pitch and to hang upside-down from it, to climb trees, to toboggan and skate, and eventually to ride a bike, all without reading a word. I learned to play jacks and marbles ("alleys" to us) and skipping and hopscotch and various elaborate solo games of catch ("Eeny, clapsy, whirl-around, tapsy"); I learned playground games with elaborate rules. Reading and writing had no place in any of these activities, though the disciplines of oral culture marked the games.

In general, however, I learned with and through printed materials. I mastered a variety of codes and began to think about the world in different ways. Sometimes I took actions based on what I read. In some cases, the point of reading was to take those actions, and in others there was a modest overflow of pleasure from the text itself.

At school our dull and repetitive seatwork books were called our *Think and Do* books. For the most part, the kinds of literacies described in this chapter could well be described as *Read and Do*. Such a relationship with texts marked a substantial contrast with my fiction reading, which largely amounted to reading as an antidote to or escape from *Doing*. With these non-fiction materials, I began to get (as we say) a preliminary handle on the world.

12
Cowboys and Others
Watching

Four childr

Three horse t

One amazing a

I LEARNED TO READ, at least at a basic level, before I ever saw a television set. I viewed my first TV program in my friend's house the year I turned seven. We acquired our own television set the following year. It was a "new media" experience for everyone.

My brothers and I learned *how to watch* in cognitive terms—all the more because we had no prior experience of the moving image in the absence of a movie-going childhood. We also incorporated television into our daily lives in more social ways. Shaun Moores (2005) talks about times when "individuals make the transition into a new stage of life. Such shifts in daily time-space paths can involve modified relationships with media" (p. 22). In this case there was also a reverse effect: our modified relationships with media, as we learned to fold domestic viewing into our lives, led to shifts in our "daily time-space paths"—literally, as those paths often led straight to the TV set after school. Our parents had to come to terms with an element of daily life that was as new to them as to us.

Rules for television, at least initially, were strictly enforced in our house. After-school TV was fair game, and we watched *The Howdy Doody Show*, *Maggie Muggins*, *Lassie*, and a variety of cowboy series. In the evening we each selected one half-hour program for watching—but we could view only our own selection; we could not piggyback on a sibling's choice. I chose *Leave It to Beaver*, *Father Knows Best*, *I Love Lucy*, and musical variety shows such as *Don Messer's Jubilee* and *The Perry Como Show*.

We learned how to watch television by watching television. Up to this point, our young lives had included only print and audio. I wish I could remember everything about my first encounters with TV because they do represent a particular moment in history. I was a young child but not a baby or a toddler, for whom television would have been only one of many new things in the world. I had working notions of representation in other media but television offered a novel challenge.

To discuss the kinds of literacy involved in understanding television narratives, it is useful to invoke all the elements of Mark Reid's helpful list of twentieth and twenty-first century media languages. If we decide to adopt a definition of literacy that is broader than strictly comprehending the written word, he suggests, we can come up with a short list of language systems or modes that cover most of our media exposure. Here is his list: speech, writing, pictures and moving pictures, music, and the dramatic modes of performance, gesture, and *mise en scène* (Reid, 2009, p. 20).

Seeing at a Distance

The literal meaning of the word television is "seeing at a distance," and that phrase certainly describes my experience with early TV. To say I had never seen anything like it is the literal truth and also a vast understatement.

The Howdy Doody Show was one of the earliest programs for children, and the American edition combined a puppet with very visible strings, a silent slapstick clown, a host who combined his entertainment duties with sales pitches for Colgate toothpaste and other commodities— all performing to a live audience of children, known as the Peanut Gallery. CBC Television showed a Canadian *Howdy Doody*, starting November 15, 1954, but our first television in St. John's was through CJON, an independent channel; CBC was a latecomer. It seems more likely that we watched the American version, which may be as well, since the Wikipedia entry on the program says, "The Canadian show appeared more low-budget than its American counterpart and seemed watered-down, with less raucous plots and less villainous villains, as well as a more educational orientation" (*Howdy Doody*, n.d.). The concept of "more low-budget" than the American *Howdy Doody* is startling; nobody would call that program lavish. The interweaving of program and commercial content is extreme, even by the extremely lax standards of the time. The Peanut Gallery is invited to sing advertising songs, a degree of child complicity that would fail all tests today.

The Peanut Gallery did more than sell toothpaste, however; I believe it played an important role in training us newbies to watch television. Those lucky children on the scene were our assurance that the frenetic activity of the puppet Howdy Doody and the clown Clarabell was truly happening *somewhere*. This insight may well have been one of the important lessons we learned from *Howdy Doody*; otherwise, the elements that Reid outlines were coarse, indeed, in Howdy Doody Time.

The Peanut Gallery served us poorly as a form of *quality* assurance, but it was very helpful as a kind of *modality* assurance. According to Bob Hodge and David Tripp (1986), modality "concerns the reality attributed to a message" (p. 104). But, they continue, "Modality is not a fixed property of a message: it is a subjective, variable, relative and negotiable judgement.... It is not merely reproduced, it is individually constructed; and since there is so much to learn about so many modality cues, about communication and the world, it is very likely that the modality judgements of children will be systematically different from those of adults" (p. 106).

We needed all the help we could get. Early children's television was casual, indeed, when it came to modality. *Howdy Doody* was famous for its cheap production values (those visible strings!), and the child witnesses provided some testimony that there was some relationship between that frantic universe and our own world. It was certainly possible to learn that a television show was a construct from this combination of unlikely ingredients. Other programs offered less guidance about how to watch, and the interface between telling and selling was often very blurry.

The Roy Rogers Show provides an excellent example of the kinds of modality switch we had to learn to master. Those children who, like me, were too small or too sheltered to have explored the movies took on an elaborate challenge in watching a "simple" cowboy show. A detailed analysis of a single episode of *The Roy Rogers Show*, "Bad Neighbors" (1954), provides an instructive template of some of the lessons we needed to master (or to learn to ignore, always an alternative). It aired around the time of my sixth birthday, so I know I did not see it on its first appearance, but I watched many episodes like it. The DVD of this episode includes all the advertising, so it serves me as a convenience sample presenting an enormous variety of modalities and rhetorics.

"Bad Neighbors"

"Bad Neighbors" begins with Roy on his horse Trigger, firing his gun. A male voiceover tells us that Post Cereals and Jello Instant Puddings "bring you Roy Rogers, king of the cowboys, Trigger, his golden palamino, and Dale Evans, queen of the west, with Pat Brady, their comical sidekick, and Roy's wonder-dog, Bullet." Filmed images of each character soon became very well-known to us, as the introduction never varied. A lively musical soundtrack ramps up the excitement. In our house, we soon learned to chant that intro, word for word. We never questioned why Trigger was billed ahead of Dale Evans.

After the introduction fades to black, we see Roy sitting on a fence, ready to introduce us to a commercial for Jello Instant Pudding, featuring Dale as his wife and including their own real-life children in a mini-drama that constitutes the sales pitch.

The relationship between this Roy and Dale and the characters they portray in the dramatic program that follows is contradictory. Advertising Roy speaks directly to viewers and exhorts them to pester their mothers for this pudding. Dale supplies the back-up appeal to moms about the virtues of the "busy-day dessert." Roy and Dale's actual children meet them in the yard to sing an advertising jingle.

The subsequent program requires us to understand different connections between characters. For example, fictional Dale's relationship to character Roy is ambiguous. They are not married; she is an independent woman running a café in Mineral City. Raymond White (2005) describes their connection as follows:

> Her relationship with Rogers in the series appeared to be purely platonic.... Rogers certainly felt that his youthful audiences did not want him kissing anyone, except maybe Trigger. In the television series, Rogers and Evans were good friends who talked and worked together to solve local problems but never kissed or showed any overt affection. (p. 93)

Yet in this particular show, Dale takes a dim view of Pat's joke about the beauty Roy met in Kansas City until Pat reveals he is talking about a cow.

"Bad Neighbors" opens with news that the area is deeply divided between ranchers and farmers. We infer that one reason relationships have deteriorated so badly is that Roy has been out of town. Fistfights and gunfights ensue. Roy doesn't shoot much, but he is very quick to hit. Pat Brady supplies slapstick interludes from time to time.

At a key moment in midstory, the action stops (three animated bears assemble a sign saying "STOP") for a cartoon advertisement for Post Sugar Crisp. The three bears who appear on the box front are in peril; an animated Roy gallops to their rescue and sings a song with them about Sugar Crisp. As they ride past a billboard photo of Roy, it comes to life, and Roy says, "Yes sir, buckaroos, Sugar Crisp is my favourite too."

After the ad break, the story develops further. At the climax, violence between the antagonists is averted, thanks to Roy's intervention; they attend a meeting in the Town Hall instead, and a compromise is sorted out. Roy says, "There's always a peaceful way to resolve an argument." The story ends with another comic scene.

After a last advertisement, credits label this show a Roy Rogers production. Roy and Dale appear one last time, cantering on Trigger and Buttermilk in front of some fine mountain scenery. They sing their famous sign-off song and wave to the viewers:

> *Happy trails to you, until we meet again.*
> *Happy trails to you; keep smiling until then.*
> *Happy trails to you, till we meet again.*

Learning to View

After the opening credits, this program begins and ends with Roy speaking and waving directly to camera, and, for us as new child viewers, all our schemas of social interaction would have informed us that he was addressing us personally. His opening comments to us, within the frame of an advertisement, suggest that we are expected to understand his relationship with Dale outside of the story. The Rogers/Evans children do not feature inside the diegetic world of *The Roy Rogers Show*, so we must have some repertoire for making sense of them in the advertisement.

It is instructive to explore how I learned to master Reid's list of speech, writing, still and moving pictures, music, and the dramatic modes of performance, gesture, and *mise en scène*. When I first watched Roy Rogers and other early TV shows, I already knew about speech and was beginning to gain a handle on writing. I had a developing schema for what constitutes a plot. I had some understanding about how to interpret a still image, from my picture books, from the small number of paintings on the walls of our home, from the stained glass windows in church. I was familiar with music and, of course, I knew enough about gesture to recognize a fist or a wave. The three new components were the moving image itself, the element of performance (fictional or persuasive), and the role of *mise en scène*, which I recognized from still pictures.

The continuous moving image was relatively easy to process, with its strong relationship to the visual elements of day-to-day life. Learning to read the cuts took rather more in the way of active attention. *The Roy Rogers Show* was careful to provide redundancy when providing information through cuts. In one short scene in "Bad Neighbors," Pat's Jeep Nellybelle develops a flat tire. Fixing it, Pat carefully props a stone in front of the front wheel, so the car will not slide down the hill. Then he forgets about it, and, when the car won't move, he asks Dale and another woman to push. The scene cuts back and forth between long shots of the car with Pat at the wheel and the two women pushing, and close-ups of the rock in front of the wheel. Finally Dale discovers the stone and threatens to throw it at Pat. The scene adds little to the dramatic plot development and serves as comic relief. Viewers must develop some sense of continuity across cuts; must learn some awareness of the relationship between parts and whole, figure and ground; must deduce that the rock is present in both scenes; must discern that the close-up image of stone and wheel folds into the larger image of the long shot, even when Nellybelle's tires are not visible.

I know very well that I first encountered this effect of the pleasures of alternating between figure and ground, not in *The Roy Rogers Show* but in a set of still images in the picture book, *Prayer for a Child* (Field, 1944), shown on page 125. The televised scene of the rock would not offer the same detailed appeal as the reassuring room in the book, nor would the images hold still for me to relish checking back and forth between them; nevertheless, there was a connection. And since the function of cuts was new to me, I drew on all available conceptual resources.

The music in *Roy Rogers* largely duplicates and/or heightens the action on the screen. Occasionally it provides some relatively heavy-handed foreshadowing. It was most likely my first experience of soundtrack (i.e., narratively significant) music, so its obviousness had learning advantages for me.

The closing music of "Happy Trails," in contrast, involves a different function; it is part of Roy and Dale's friendly direct discourse, speaking or singing to viewers at home. The pragmatics of Roy and Dale singing straight to me were familiar from radio programs; CBC's *Kindergarten of the Air* certainly taught me about song as direct address from the media figure to the child listener or viewer.

With the images and the music, I did therefore have at least some relevant prior knowledge that I could apply to my interpretive efforts. Learning to interpret the dramatic language of performance, on the other hand, was completely new. I had not seen acting before, difficult as it is today to conceptualize a child entirely missing out on what we currently take as normal daily exposure to drama. And with the elision of characters and advertisers, I had to acquire some procedures for assessing the function of different performances in fairly short order.

Roy Rogers was a veteran of radio and film long before he hit our television screens, and many of his viewers would have known him through these media or through the comic books, audio recordings, and other artifacts purporting to tell some version of his story. We knew Roy exclusively through television, and we learned about television through Roy. What can "Bad Neighbors" tell us about what we might have learned?

The decade of the 1980s takes a very bad rap for the deregulation of children's television and the introduction of half-hour children's programs that were effectively little more than animated commercials for story-based commodities. The mercantile import of Roy's personal approach to these advertisements of the 1950s is at least as totalizing in how it incorporates child viewers into a cycle of consumption. In our house we ate porridge for breakfast, except in the summer holidays, and even then the number of very sugary cereals was substantially rationed. But we did occasionally get Sugar Crisp, and we did regularly eat Jello Instant Pudding; to that extent we might have been able to recognize one element of Roy's world. It is hard today, in the plethora of cross-marketing that surrounds all children, to sort out the significance of a singular point of connection for a child viewer such as myself. How small does an element have to be before it loses its importance as pivotal for recognition? "Something that's normal for me is normal in this world." This sentiment may never be articulated but it nevertheless provides a benchmark for assessing modality.

It is very possible that the advertisements on *Roy Rogers* were the first commercials I ever saw, and I am grateful that my DVD version preserves at least a few of them, when so many silently edit them out. The seamlessness of Roy Rogers's movement between story and sales pitch meant that the pragmatics of the program were actually quite complex. Most of the direct address to viewers in "Bad Neighbors" is commercially motivated (though the rendition of "Happy Trails" is mostly focused on inviting us back to another show, so it involves largely self-advertisement).

Unlike the commercials, which play complex representational games, the dramatic portions of the show are relatively consistent: Roy and Dale as characters interact with each other and with the other characters; the diegetic world is shaped through moving images, speech, music, and some fairly blunt instruments of the dramatic modes. Gesture is relatively primitive: much communication takes place via a fist or a gun. *Mise en scène* is repetitive. Performance is skilfully orchestrated; the acting is competent, and Roy and Dale even manage to sound relatively sincere with their moralizations at the end of the show. Their characters are limited and predictable, which in some ways was helpful to us.

The paratextual elements of "Bad Neighbors" add complexity to the simple diegesis. The Sugar Crisp advertisement in the middle of the show invites us to recognize the animated version of Roy Rogers (we are assisted, of course, by his fancy cowboy outfit and his horse. Those who had access to *Roy Rogers* comics would have recognized the drawn Roy faster than we did, but it was not a complicated transition). After identifying our hero, we must acknowledge the incongruity of animated Roy galloping past the billboard image of photographed Roy. Next, we have the surprise of the still image turning into a moving, speaking image, as Roy comes to life to address "buckaroos" about the virtues of Sugar Crisp. At the end of the show, a circular image of Roy's face makes a visual reference back to this billboard image. Children watching see Roy's face framed in different ways, and the frames themselves adjust and shift. The thematic unity of the program steers us through all these different versions of Roy (a kind of "fuzzy set" of the Roy Rogers variations) by means of the strong continuity of his character, a benevolent and infallible father figure; this persona varies very little between advertisements and story, even though his purpose changes. Such consistency would have provided some structural support for children learning to manoeuvre through the shifting address of *The Roy Rogers Show*.

The commercial impetus that drives Roy's mutating persona actually allows viewers to develop some sophistication in assessing shifts of register. The repetition of settings, stereotypes, and attitudes across a variety of cowboy programs also allowed us to develop a certain awareness of conventionality. From the beginning, even as new viewers, for example, we were able to appreciate George Burns's joke with the cowboys and Indians in *The Burns and Allen Show*: he would stand in front of a TV screen on which one party would gallop madly past the landmarks in the foreground, followed closely by a second group that would pause, perplexed. "They went thataway," George would tell them, helpfully pointing his cigar off-screen, and the pursuers would gallop off in a cloud of dust, following his extra-diegetic reference. We loved that joke from the first time we saw it and never tired of its many repetitions; yet there is no doubt it required a modest degree of narrative sophistication to comprehend and enjoy.

The Lone Ranger offered a different perspective on the constructed nature of TV programs. It was casual about continuity errors; the hero would take a ducking in a pond or a puddle, but his cowboy outfit would be clean and dry in the very next frame. I remember very scathing playground conversations on this discrepancy, though I am certain we were extremely vague about any explanation of our viewing problems. We had no conception of editing; as far as we knew, television came into being whole and complete.

Learning the Sitcom

Cowboys were exotic; the domestic tales of *Father Knows Best* and *Leave It to Beaver* were somewhat more recognizable. The mother is named Margaret in *Father Knows Best*, always a good start; and she was the character with whom I identified most strongly, realizing early on that the kids were ciphers in this program. The irony in the title is slim; *pater familias* Jim Anderson really does rule the roost. In one early program I watched, "The Mink Coat," which aired on February 13, 1955, Jim lectures the family about the need to trim expenses, and Margaret sits on the sofa with the kids and is chastised right alongside them. Such a scenario would simply never have occurred in my own family; the grown-ups were a team in our household. On the other hand, I had no trouble imbibing the show's generalizations about "men just wouldn't understand," and "if you were a woman, you'd know." That particular binary was reinforced on every side.

Some of my childhood texts interconnected, not always in a good way. The suburban sitcoms and the *Ladies' Home Journal* certainly worked as a tag team, and between them they provided a frame for the modest number of contemporary American family stories that I read (Haywood's *Betsy* stories, for example). As a result, I was entirely persuaded by the portrait of America that they collectively produced.

My notions of conventional, suburban, mainstream, white American life took on a substantial reality in my mind. So many sources in agreement must be describing the actual world. What was missing from this universe simply held no place in my mind, at least as long as I was involved in the story. Of course, to subscribe to this vision of the world, I had to erase many details of my own daily existence (including my own sense of appropriate relationships between girls and boys, men and women, which were more egalitarian, partly for the very simple reason that I did not choose to be on the inferior side). This exercise of ignoring my own felt life was remarkably easy to achieve, as long as the story held. Such action was simply part of engaging with an American narrative, and I was soon able to assume the mantle of the implied viewer with great ease.

Of course, many American viewers were also outside the charmed circle of this bland, WASP world, but I could not consider that fact because I simply didn't know it. Through middle childhood, white middle-class American mores dominated my mediated life.

Local Television

For the most part, television offered us the conventional "window on the world," augmenting the vague and restricted sense of "elsewhere" that we had already achieved through listening to the radio (especially Dad's daily news broadcasts). But from one early form, we also learned that television is *produced*, that it actually does have some modal connections to the real world.

Don Jamieson was a founder of CJON television in St. John's, and the presiding genius of their early news telecast, *News Cavalcade*. This program, which we watched nightly at suppertime, offered my first experience that television could connect with local life, that it was not merely a storytelling vehicle portraying fictional worlds (news included). Don Jamieson was accounting for a known territory.

My understanding of this connection became visceral (I still remember how strange it felt) when my youngest brother and his little friend, aged three and four, got lost one day. We older kids and our friends were recruited to check all the nearby backyards in case they had wandered there and become too preoccupied to come out. I don't think anyone harboured any huge fears about abduction in those days; the threat that turned my mother pale was the ever-present prospect of drowning (the friend lived near a stream).

When all our avails proved fruitless, the next, draconian step was to phone CJON. Don Jamieson reported the missing preschoolers along with all the other local items on *News Cavalcade*. A phone call to the station followed rapidly; a woman on Merrymeeting Road, not far away, reported that two little boys were sitting on her front doorstep; she would take them in and give them cookies while they awaited pick-up.

The drama was over, but the sense of strangeness lingered, not so much because my brother had been missing, though that experience was certainly upsetting, but more so because our local problem had been turned into news. The concomitant suggestion that all news was a local event for somebody took on a small flickering life in my mind; I think it had truly never occurred to me before.

Jamieson went on to become a federal cabinet minister, but at this time he played something of a "Walter Cronkite" role in St. John's; it wasn't really news if he didn't mention it. His children were at school with us, though in different grades; there was sometimes a Christmas family special where the TV cameras went into their home (glimpses of these Christmas specials can be seen on *Just Himself: The Story of Don Jamieson* [2011], and, for me, they are still disconcerting to see today). The experience of watching the Jamieson family specials was very different from viewing the home life of Roy Rogers and Dale Evans; in the truest sense of the term, these were amateur productions, and it felt odd to be seeing children whom we might encounter on an ordinary school day somehow transfigured onto the television screen. Again, it troubled my modality assumptions about the invented nature of television life.

The Big Story

Most of my viewing experience was televisual: segmented, sequential, cyclical, interspersed with advertisements. I had much less exposure to larger stories told in movie form, but I did see a few; they stand out in my mind for their rarity value. The titles indicate the random nature of my movie-going life; essentially, if it was showing at the Paramount Theatre around the time of my friend's July birthday, we saw it as a birthday treat; otherwise, we did not. Thus, I watched *Bernadine* with Pat Boone and *Raintree County* with Elizabeth Taylor, both movies of late 1957 that reached St. John's many months later.

Bernadine

I think I saw *Bernadine* first in the summer of 1958; I was nine. It took me a long time to acquire a DVD copy of this movie, so watching it again was one of the very last encounters with a text unseen for decades that this project allowed me. I certainly recognized the prosperous, white suburban background from many intertextual connections, but everything else about the film was alien and confusing. The plot, obscure and offensive, involves a group of lacklustre high-school boys who have developed an elaborate fantasy about the perfect girl, whom they name Bernadine. The following plot summary, given on lovingtheclassics.com, gives some idea of the focus of this insipid film:

> Ultra-pasteurized pop singer Pat Boone makes his feature film debut in this comical and tuneful look at adolescent life in the late 1950s. A group of teenage boys discuss the attributes of the perfect girl and proceed to create a mental image of their dreamboat. Later they find her in the form of Jean, the new telephone operator in town. One of the lads, Sanford Wilson, falls hard for the comely lass. They begin dating, but as final exams approach, Sanford must temporarily shift his attention to his school work. To keep her from the other less-honorable boys who want her, he has handsome Lieutenant Langley Beaumont squire her around. Unfortunately, she and Langley soon fall in love, causing the anguished Sanford to join the military and leave for a year and a half. (Geri, n.d.)

Jean's feelings are completely immaterial to these boys; such comedy as the movie aspires to convey arises completely out of their feeble competition with each other for the swaggering rights of conquest. Watching the film again was a dismal experience—though the opening moments did dimly bring to mind my awe at my first sight of the large screen and the expanse of colour in the credits. The only other positive association I brought to this 2013 experience was completely alien to the movie itself, and I introduce it only as one more peek into the strange ways that memory works in the mind. As I looked at the 1950s cars on plentiful display (these boys are rich), my hands felt some reminiscent pleasure. When I disentangled this unlikely reaction, I realized I was remembering a large set of inch-long plastic cars we owned for a long time. They were cheap and hollow; the exterior shell constituted their entire being. Tiny extruded plastic letters on the trunk gave each car's name. The physicality of handling their distinctive rounded contours evidently survived unvisited in my brain; it is safe to say these cars would never have made an appearance in this study if I had not seen *Bernadine* again. And yet they do offer a peculiar intertextual reference for this terrible movie, and supply a reminder of just how intricate are the connections that feed our literate reactions.

Raintree County

The following summer we went to *Raintree County*, which starred Elizabeth Taylor, Montgomery Clift, and Eva Marie Saint; see any trailer for this movie on YouTube to get an idea of its lurid contents. My explicit memories of this very long film were sparse: I recalled much emphasis on some truly sumptuous crinolines and the huge number of tears I shed at the end. Unlike probably every other viewer in the movie's reception history, I missed a great deal of heavy-handed foreshadowing and so the death of Taylor's character at the close of the movie was a tremendous shock to me.

Watching it again at the beginning of 2013 reminded me once more of my sense of wonder at the opening shots in Technicolor on the enormous screen, but it also filled me with pity for my earlier self. Three hours is a very long time to donate to a completely opaque plot. From *Little Women* I had some small understanding of the Civil War (though Alcott's references are mostly oblique and assume that readers already understand); but the Civil War comes very, very late in *Raintree County*'s story of misplaced lust, sexual deceit, potential and actual miscegenation, slavery, war, and madness. For all this long list of melodramatic plot ingredients I had no repertoire whatever. For much of the movie, I simply had no idea what was happening. Even watching it as an adult in 2013, I found the first hour to be hard work. The characters speak rapidly and their references to the mystical "raintree" that seems to offer some kind of secret of life do not make a lot of sense. Montgomery Clift, the romantic lead, doesn't even seem to look the same from one shot to another, the result of a car crash he sustained partway through the filming. As an adult viewer, I found these visual shifts in his facial appearance subliminally upsetting until I found out the cause of the problem; I am fairly sure that when I watched the movie the first time, this sad continuity discrepancy simply contributed to my constant feeling that my grasp of the characters was utterly insecure. The consequence of these cross-compounding problems was a very garbled and unsatisfying sense of the story as a whole. It is a wonder I ever went to another movie.

We pay little attention to the idea that some literate encounters simply fail. When we consider our own literate histories, the memories of such debacles often just do not occur to us. I knew I was baffled by *Raintree County*, but it was not until I went to the trouble of watching it again that I realized and/or remembered just how confused it made me. I would have discarded a book that was so alien, but because of the enormous ceremonial importance of this birthday outing to the cinema, I was bound to my seat for three hours, bewildered and eventually very upset. I felt both emotionally and intellectually vulnerable as a consequence; not only had I been made very sad but I was also made to feel like an idiot, an entirely inadequate viewer. If I had seen more films, the bad taste in the mouth might have lingered less long; but my experience with *Raintree County* ensured that for a long time I was cautious about movies.

I emphasize this pathetic story, partly because it was an important small chapter in my own life but also because that idea of literacy events that fail and discourage is an important one, to which we pay too little attention. How many children in school are left upset and humiliated by the fact that they have not been able to interpret a text in any satisfactory way but do understand enough to be affected by the emotional impact? Such a situation involves the worst of all worlds; I suspect it is more common than we realize.

The Hybrid World of Bush Christmas

Another movie, one that at least had the virtue of being made for children, was shown in school, on the last day of term with us all packed into the assembly hall; we certainly saw it on more than one occasion, but I do not remember how many times. It is very possible that it was actually the first film I ever saw. One of the most triumphant days of this project came in the summer of 2012 when I successfully located a copy. I remembered little about the movie beyond the fact of watching it: I knew it was Australian, I knew there was a lot of horse riding, and I knew there was a dramatic scene at the end of the film where the bad guys hang the intrepid children by their belts from some meat hooks in a barn. It should be possible to track down such a vivid detail, but without any kind of title information it was very difficult to make progress on locating it until my Australian colleague, Kerry Mallan, told me about the Australian Centre for the Moving Image. They supplied a possible title, *Bush Christmas*, and I ordered a second-hand DVD.

Bush Christmas (1947) was, in many ways, an imaginative choice for our teachers to load onto the clunky and seldom-used film projector. When I watched it in 2012, once I recovered from my reaction to the breathtaking racism of some of its guiding propositions, I found it an interesting hybrid of Enid Blyton and our beloved cowboy programs. The plot involves five children—three pure blond Australians, one Brit wearing glasses (and thus flagged, even to a naïve viewer like myself, as a second-order hero), and one Aboriginal—who set out to track the horse thieves who have stolen their father's herd.

I find it impossible to watch this film with 1950s eyes. Narrator John McCallum introduces the protagonists right at the beginning of the story. We see them riding their horses home for the Christmas holidays. "This is Helen," says the narrator, and a moment later, "This is John, her brother." John, however, is not the only boy on his horse; a dark-skinned child clings on behind. The narrator ignores him as the camera moves to the next horse: "And Snow, the baby of the family." The camera slides back to the two boys on the same horse. "Neza, the Darkfellow behind John here, is Neza, the son of one of the stockmen on Mr. Thompson's property." The British boy, Michael, wears spectacles and doesn't look quite so comfortable on a horse, so we immediately learn to watch him more superciliously as we learn that he was evacuated from Britain at the time of the story events but has now returned home.

The narrative voice-over does quite sophisticated work, especially for children who are not experienced film viewers. It sets up the story: the sleepy valley where nothing exciting ever happens, except for last Christmas when there was too much trouble. It introduces the protagonists with a nod to the fact that narrator and narratees share some deictic space on the screen in references to the images such as "John here." It provides a very conventional foreshadowing moment: "Now there would never have been any trouble if the children had gone straight home that afternoon." John proposes a detour down by the ridge. Neza slips off the horse and declines to come with them: "That bad place." "What's up with Neza?" asks Michael. "Goodness knows," replies Helen. "The blacks have their own ideas."

Neza's otherness is always emphasized in this story (it is a huge joke when the children black their faces for some night exploration and Neza does, too), but in fact, as the children divert a planned camping trip to track the horse thieves, Neza is the one who actually knows what he is doing in the bush. It is more than possible that the film was perceived as progressive in its time, and certainly the white British boy is also an outsider. Nevertheless, my 2012 viewing of this movie represented one of the moments in my project where it was most starkly clear that the *lacuna* at the heart of the study, the irrecoverability of my childhood eyes and ears, presents an insurmountable obstacle to retracing that innocent viewing experience in Pitts Memorial Hall.

Evocative of its own time and place—the patriarchal certainty of that Pathé-news style voice-over; the Aussie mockery of wimpy Michael, the British boy; the politeness of the Thompson children who knock nicely at each door in the deserted town before pushing it open; and the resourcefulness of Neza who emerges (at least to me in 2012) as the true hero of the story despite the condescension of his white chums—all the ingredients of this 1947 story make it a period piece. By 1958 the British Empire was history, but there was a certain empire solidarity about our viewing of this movie in Newfoundland. For very many years, indeed, it represented my sole window on Australian life, a sobering reminder of how singular were our opportunities in those days for learning about the world.

The alien accents, the hot and sunny Christmas holidays, the luxury of horses and wide-open spaces, all combined to fix this film in my mind as exotic to the last degree. It gave me a hint (misplaced but the best I could muster) of how all those Blyton children might sound when they uttered

their exotic sentences about "hols" and "lashings of ginger beer" and the like. It was a world outside my own, and never more so than in the startling scene with the meat hooks. I'm not sure my heart has ever thumped so hard again. Such peril was seriously outside my normal reading repertoire, where if something was scary you could just skim over it.

There was an absolute gap of more than fifty years between my first viewings as a child and my adult reception of this story; during that time I encountered no clip, no quote, no hint of any fragment from this film. The time-capsule effect was very intense when I finally viewed it, and although I can never look at this movie the same way, I do find some fossil traces in it of what a very new viewer I was when I watched it first. It reminds me very sharply of how fast I had to recognize the necessity and simultaneously take the step of actively tuning my ear to an alien accent. There was no time to lose as we scrambled to make the cognitive effort; crucial information was clearly being presented. I vaguely recall the difficulty in watching unfamiliar activities as opposed to reading about them, where you could slide over the confusions and just keep going—or turn back the pages and read again.

I saw no British films in my childhood; *Bush Christmas* was my only intimation that a film need not be set in America. That insight sounds too silly to be a true discovery, but it definitely was news to me in the 1950s. I thought watching TV or the movies meant assuming the role of implied viewer in an American way; I became quite glib in my ability to don this perspective. *Bush Christmas* surprised me by confounding those expectations.

The Pleasures of Adaptation: Heidi and Pollyanna

Unlike today's children who cut their baby teeth on different versions and adaptations of the same story, I inhabited a relatively monovocal narrative world. In my experience, a story belonged to the voice that told it—and for the most part, there was only ever one voice. Once or twice, however, I gained access to a fictional world that I already knew, recreated for a different medium: for example, with the movies of *Heidi* and *Pollyanna*.

At some point in my childhood, I saw bits and pieces of old Hollywood movies on television, maybe once or twice a complete film, though I do not remember any titles or details. I suspect the movies were aired during the afternoon, allowing me occasionally to come across a snippet or two despite my mother's best efforts at policing our viewing hours (maybe she was the one actually watching, for all I remember now).

I am fairly certain that it was in such a fashion that I saw at least some of Shirley Temple's rendition of *Heidi*. I saw *Pollyanna* more officially, at the movie theatre, as a treat in honour of my twelfth birthday in November 1960. In both cases, I was thoroughly familiar with the print version and able to perform as Linda Hutcheon's (2006) "knowing audience" (p. 120). Hutcheon expands on this idea in ways that certainly ring true for my experience as a novice coming to terms with what she labels "the adaptation's enriching, palimpsestic doubleness" (p. 120):

> *To experience [a work]* as an adaptation...*we need to recognize it as such and to know its adapted text, thus allowing the latter to oscillate in our memories with what we are experiencing. In the process we inevitably fill in any gaps in the adaptation with information from the adapted text. Indeed, adapters rely on this ability to fill in the gaps when moving from the discursive expansion of telling to the performative time and space limitations of showing. (pp. 120–121)*

This chapter is not the place to create a comparative critique of these two films, though the temptation is strong because they share many ingredients and tropes: an eponymous heroine played by a major child star (Shirley Temple had already received a special juvenile Oscar when she played Heidi; Hayley Mills was awarded a similar prize for her role in *Pollyanna*); a story involving an orphaned and unwanted little girl who warms all hearts around her and works a variety of social and emotional miracles; the plot engine of a child unable to walk; and a set-piece interruption to the plot showcasing the child actress in performance (the dream dance routine of "In Our Little Wooden Shoes" in *Heidi*; the heroine's singing of "America the Beautiful" in *Pollyanna*, which Disneyfies a production that had been relatively successful in flying beneath the Disney radar up to that point). Both movies take something foreign (setting, actress) and render it legible to American audiences—and, indirectly, to me.

I, of course, saw them separately, in different viewing conditions. I will therefore resist the comparative urge except where it may usefully contribute to the perspective of what I might have learned as a narrative interpreter from the experiences.

The knowing interpreter is not always at an advantage, especially if the film shortchanges the dramatic rhythms of the book. Unbelievably, the producers of *Heidi* did not show the sleepwalking scene, abandoning the opportunity to milk Shirley Temple's capacity for pathos to the utmost heights. Instead, the grandfather comes to Frankfurt, and he and Heidi make a getaway in a chase scene that must have already been banal in 1937.

As a reader of *Heidi*, I had an intertextual reference for sleepwalking, which was fortunate because it was a topic that otherwise would have meant nothing to me. Freddy Bobbsey's sleepwalking constitutes a major plot feature in *The Bobbsey Twins: Merry Days Indoors and Out* (Hope, 1950), the first book in that series and one of the first chapter books I ever

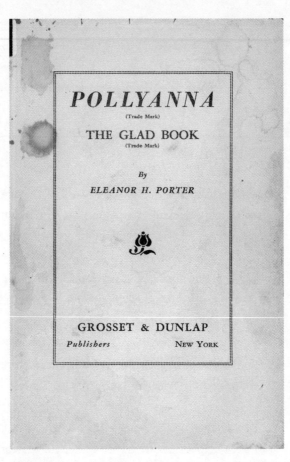

read. Heidi and Freddy are each taken to be a ghost, and the adults in both novels seem to take the ghost threat very seriously. Freddy's nocturnal wanderings turn out to be simply the result of too much strawberry short-cake, but Heidi walks in her sleep out of desperation to return to the Alps and her grandfather. It is a very memorable scene and creates a major plot turn.

The movie version abandons this affecting moment and correspondingly reduces the complexity of the story. Adaptation theorists are a bit inclined to mock those viewers whose only criterion for judging an adapted story is fidelity (see for example, Welchan 1999; Albrecht-Crane & Cutchins, 2010; and Hutcheon, 2006), but I think the case is more complicated than that. A film is radically shorter than a novel, even a children's novel, and deletions must be handled with care. The Shirley Temple *Heidi* omits one of the core emotional engines of the plot, and, as a result, it tells a lesser story.

The film version of *Pollyanna* offers rather more complex questions to consider. I still own the copy of Eleanor H. Porter's *Pollyanna* that I read as a child, published by the ubiquitous Grosset & Dunlap. Its front cover is

The following appears within the book title page image:

The POLLYANNA GLAD BOOKS
TRADE-MARK
Each, 12mo, Cloth, Illustrated — $2.25

*POLLYANNA
SIX STAR RANCH
By* ELEANOR H. PORTER

☆

POLLYANNA AT SIX STAR RANCH
By VIRGINIA MAY MOFFITT

☆

POLLYANNA GROWS UP
By ELEANOR H. PORTER

☆

POLLYANNA OF THE ORANGE BLOSSOMS
POLLYANNA'S JEWELS
POLLYANNA'S DEBT OF HONOR
POLLYANNA'S WESTERN ADVENTURE
By HARRIET LUMMIS SMITH

☆

POLLYANNA IN HOLLYWOOD
POLLYANNA'S CASTLE IN MEXICO
POLLYANNA'S DOOR TO HAPPINESS
POLLYANNA'S GOLDEN HORSESHOE
By ELIZABETH BORTON

☆

POLLYANNA'S PROTÉGÉE
By MARGARET PIPER CHALMERS

☆

* POLLYANNA OF MAGIC VALLEY
By VIRGINIA MAY MOFFITT
Price, $2.50
L. C. PAGE & COMPANY
53 Beacon Street • Boston, Mass.

Another GLAD BOOK

POLLYANNA
TRADE-MARK

OF THE

ORANGE BLOSSOMS

By
HARRIET LUMMIS SMITH

Grosset & Dunlap
Publishers
NEW YORK

∧ *The* Pollyanna
*sequels list in the
Grosset & Dunlap
edition of* Pollyanna of
the Orange Blossoms.

[*Courtesy Penguin Group (USA)*]

missing, but it is otherwise intact, and on the title page, to my surprise, it reads as follows: "*Pollyanna* (Trade Mark) The Glad Book (Trade Mark)." This 1940 "Popular Edition" was "published by arrangement with L.C. Page & Co.," the original publishers of the book version of *Pollyanna* in 1913.

The *Pollyanna* franchise was substantial. I also read at least two of the sequels, *Pollyanna Grows Up* (Porter, 1915) and *Pollyanna of the Orange Blossoms* (Smith, 1924). My second-hand copy of the latter title is an undated Grosset & Dunlap edition, containing a long list of other *Pollyanna* titles by a total of five different authors. I do not remember how many I actually read.

In short, *Pollyanna* was a thriving franchise at the time that I read it, and I brought knowledge of the characters and settings supplied by at least two authors to my viewing. Hutcheon does not address situations where the knowing viewer is actually at a disadvantage, but I think a case could be made to that effect with this example. A reader of *Pollyanna of the Orange Blossoms* would know that she needs to find a way to configure

Jimmy Bean as a romantic hero. Disney cast Kevin Corcoran in that role, and he plays a standard-issue Disney boy—yappy, pushy, always underfoot when not wanted and never there when needed, and exuding, with his whiny voice, a tiresomely clichéd aura of boyish innocence at all times. Jimmy's role is much more prominent in the movie than in the book, and his characterization is much less subtle than that of Pollyanna as played by Hayley Mills. He also seems very much younger than Pollyanna, and while they are of an age where such a discrepancy might be realistic, it does raise issues for that knowing viewer who is trying to metamorphose him into the bridegroom.

As with *Heidi*, the movie version of *Pollyanna* shrinks the story and creates a much more overdetermined plot. Instead of being hurt by a random passing car late in the story, Pollyanna is injured when she falls out of a tree that she is climbing because Aunt Polly has forbidden her to go to the fundraising fair. Aunt Polly is thus very much more to blame for Pollyanna's paralysis, and the story inches closer to melodrama.

The economies of viewing attention may necessitate this tightening up, this elimination of anything random or superfluous except when it plays an ideological role (Pollyanna singing "America the Beautiful" at the fair comes to mind). For a knowledgeable viewer, however, watching the film in light of awareness of the book(s), the result is restrictive, perhaps even claustrophobic. In the movie, every detail is owned by the plot. Shirley Temple could not rescue the movie of *Heidi* from sentimentality, but Hayley Mills does her best to salvage *Pollyanna*. Her acting of the artless child provides the main vehicle for the inconsequential in this film; all other ingredients are heavily fraught with consequence. But in the end, the "Disney-ness" of this movie overwhelms her delicate approach, and the story is reduced to essential ingredients only.

Making Sense

My film-viewing history is poverty stricken, compared either to my own reading life or to the viewing habits of most of my North American contemporaries. Newfoundland was clearly at the end of a very long distribution chain, and our three cinemas did not allow for much range of choice. My television watching, on the other hand, was not much more restricted than that of most of my generation—first one channel and then two. The only major limitation on our viewing came from the discrepancies of time zones.

I very seldom saw *The Ed Sullivan Show* or any of the Disney TV productions, for example, simply because they aired so late at night. But that was a domestic ruling; many of my friends had parents who were more lax about bedtime and so these shows were commonly discussed in the playground, and I learned to bluff.

As I have already mentioned, our move to Edmonton, though beyond the limits of this project, caused a revolution in my viewing habits. TV shows appeared early in the evening, and Jasper Avenue was lined with movie theatres; in my mid-teens I routinely went to one or two films every weekend, and I caught up with the appeal of the format in a big way. By the time we moved back to St. John's, the Avalon Mall featured a new cinema, and movies arrived in the city in a more timely fashion.

Throughout my early life, however, movies were almost completely alien. I liked the big screen, the darkness, the popcorn, all the ritual—but the films themselves did not necessarily entertain or engage me, and so the rest of it fell flat. I learned the schema for the event and ritual of movie-going, but the pleasure of the film itself often escaped me. I was probably a more uncritical viewer of *Pollyanna* because of my relief at simply being able to follow the story. My film-viewing history is a sad and depleted corner of my early literate life.

13
Settler Stories
Claiming

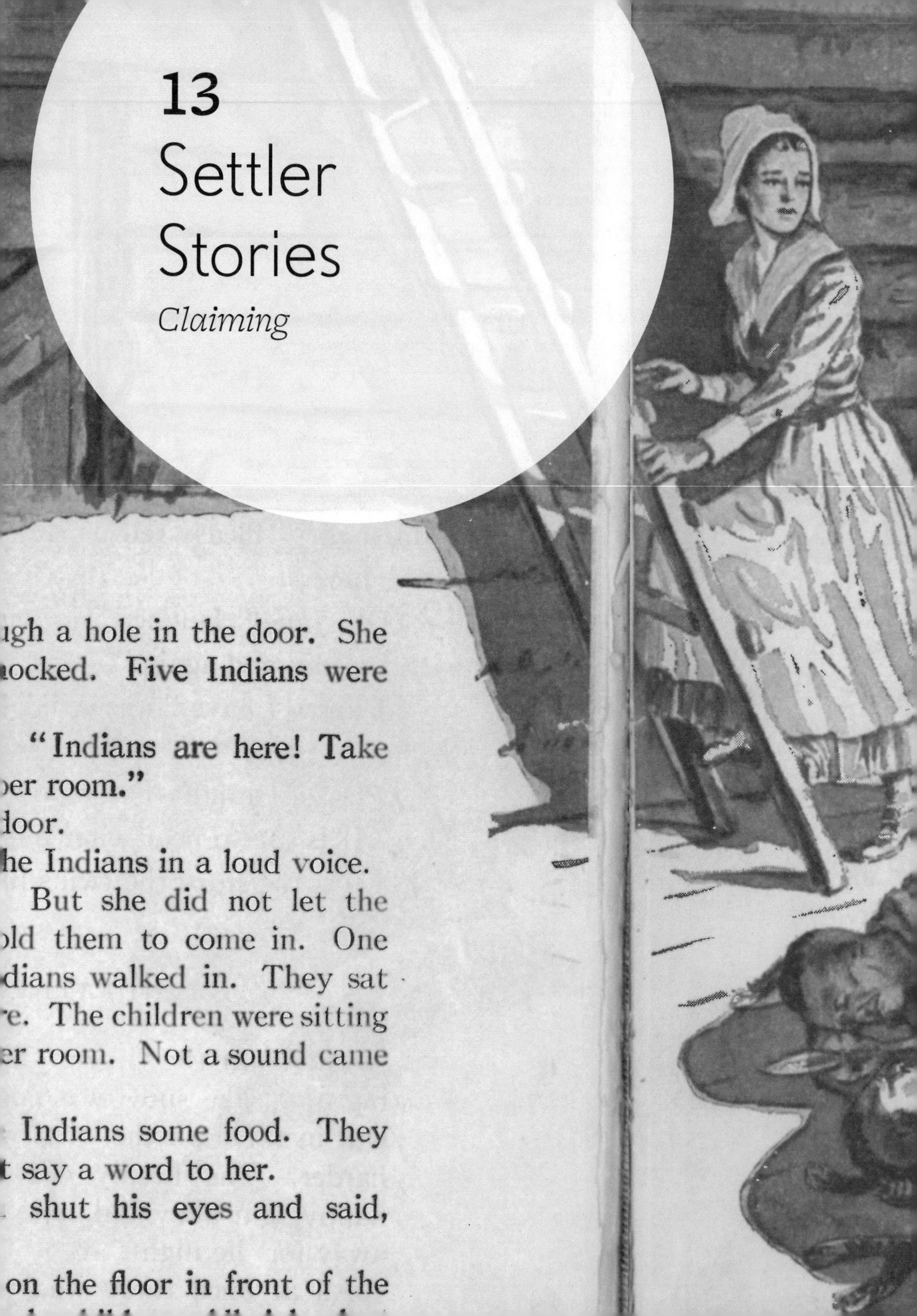

ugh a hole in the door. She
ocked. Five Indians were

"Indians are here! Take
er room."

oor.

he Indians in a loud voice.

But she did not let the
old them to come in. One
dians walked in. They sat
e. The children were sitting
er room. Not a sound came

Indians some food. They
say a word to her.

shut his eyes and said,

on the floor in front of the

GROWING UP INVOLVES DEVELOPING cognitive and affective awareness of complex questions, and increasing literacy contributes in appropriately complex ways. In this chapter I address some of the psycho-social issues surrounding the settler culture of North America, and Newfoundland in particular. As a North American child reader and citizen, I "sampled" this issue across a great variety of media, formats, and venues. I choose this topic to demonstrate the crossover impact of a "literacy in the round." I did not become literate in "books about settlers" or "TV shows about settlers"; rather, this important issue twined in and out of various literate encounters and contributed to my growing sense of myself and my place in the world.

Part of our education involves locating ourselves in space and time. For a culture of incomers, this project necessarily entails sorting out elements of the historical encounter with the peoples who inhabited the space before the settlers arrived. Stories of the relationships between white settlers and Indigenous inhabitants loomed large in many of the texts at my disposal then; it seems to have been a major cultural preoccupation of the 1950s. School textbooks, television programs, classic pioneer fiction for children, all strikingly enforced a particular kind of assertion, though not in completely monolithic ways. The generic discourse was also modified on occasion by the specifics of our local experience in Newfoundland, involving a history in which the first inhabitants were actually wiped out altogether.

For a long time, Newfoundland was not really a settler culture at all. The harshness of the winters, combined with the arbitrary management of the European fisheries, meant that fishermen visited for the season and headed back to Europe before winter came. The impact of these newcomers on the Aboriginal culture was harmful nonetheless. Newfoundland is one of two places in the British Empire where an Indigenous nation died out completely after the arrival of the Europeans (the other was Tasmania, where there is now some dispute about how completely they vanished). The Beothuk in Newfoundland officially became extinct with the death of Shanawdithit in St. John's in 1829.

The Grade 5 history book, *The Story of Newfoundland and Labrador* (Briffett, 1954) does not make light of this tragedy. It says that the English found Shanawdithit with her mother and sister; all three were starving and the other two were dying of tuberculosis. Shanawdithit, named Nancy by the English, was sent to St. John's to the home of William Cormack, where she drew pictures of Beothuk life that inform our understanding of that culture to this day (unfortunately the history book does not reproduce any images, though they did survive, and I have seen them since). Despite Cormack's efforts to save her, she did not last very long. Grade 5 children read these words: "Nancy was the last of her tribe and she died of tuberculosis although everything was done to help her. We have much to feel ashamed of in our treatment of these shy, brave people" (Briffett, 1954, p. 22).

I was most certainly incorporated into that guilty "we" by virtue of my skin colour, but I did not feel a complete part of the collective "we" of Newfoundland society. "The Ode to Newfoundland" that we sang every Monday in assembly, for example, actively excluded me: "As loved our fathers so we love, / Where once they stood we stand." I read about the calamity of the Beothuk with a reduced sense of responsibility as an established outsider to Newfoundland society and history, and it never crossed my mind to consider the potential complicity of my own ancestors elsewhere. In any case it was never made clear to me or my classmates how to address our own potential guilt or responsibility for the extermination of the Beothuk or the mistreatment of anyone else.

Questions about an extinct culture may be appropriately addressed by a museum. From Grade 3 onward, I regularly visited the Newfoundland Museum (now called the Provincial Museum of Newfoundland and Labrador), every two or three months. The museum was my main route to any kind of understanding of Newfoundland history before I hit the overarching narrative of the Grade 5 textbook. I gazed with curiosity but also with relative equanimity at Beothuk skeletons (which have since been removed for more respectful disposal). Beothuk means "people," and it is perhaps fitting (though undoubtedly presumptuous) that one of these first *people* gave me my earliest understanding of the "bone house" underlying every human body. Yet I saw myself as spectator rather than heir to the rich story of Newfoundland's past.

It is not surprising that the whole question of the First Nations and the relationship between them and the broader North American settler society to which I indubitably belonged was confusing to me. The discourses that explained these relationships were complex and contradictory. Even in the same Grade 5 chapter that described how "we" should be ashamed of "our" treatment of the Beothuk nation, it is possible to find a conventionally racist account of the Beothuks of Trinity Bay: "In many ways these people were like children. They loved to dress up. When the chief was given a towel, he put it on his head and then he and his friends joined hands and laughed and sang. Like children, too, the Indians were ready for a picnic on the beach" (Briffett, 1954, 19).

It did not remotely occur to me, at the age of ten, to question this assessment. Nor was it my first encounter with such officially sanctioned attitudes. The history book at least overtly dealt with political questions; in the Grade 3 language book, the racism simply slipped in as fictional local colour to sweeten the grammar lessons.

In *English: Grade 3* (Stoddard, Bailey, & Lewis, n.d.), the Marshall twins kick off the first chapter by asking Grandfather for one of their favourite stories. Grandfather obliges with the tale of the visiting Indians. It begins as follows: Father is away. A knock on the door reveals five Indians. Mother

The text within the illustration reads:

Mother looked through a hole in the door. She saw then who had knocked. Five Indians were standing in the snow.

"Sam!" she called. "Indians are here! Take the children to the upper room."

Mother opened the door.

"Eat," said one of the Indians in a loud voice.

Mother was afraid. But she did not let the Indians know. She told them to come in. One after the other the Indians walked in. They sat down in front of the fire. The children were sitting on the floor of the upper room. Not a sound came from them.

Mother brought the Indians some food. They ate it, but they did not say a word to her.

Then one of them shut his eyes and said, "Sleep."

They went to sleep on the floor in front of the fire. Mother went up to the children. All night they watched the Indians through a hole in the floor.

4

∧ *Some child has put a tick-mark at the beginning of every line in my secondhand copy of English: Grade 3, 2nd ed. (Stoddard, Bailey, & Lewis, pp. 4–5).*

[Collection of the author]

sends Sam upstairs with the other children before she opens the door. The story continues:

> "Eat," said one of the Indians in a loud voice.
>
> Mother was afraid. But she did not let the Indians know. She told them to come in….
>
> Mother brought the Indians some food. They ate it, but they did not say a word to her.
>
> Then one of them shut his eyes and said, "Sleep." (Stoddard, Bailey, & Lewis, n.d., p. 4)

The story is careful to point out that the Indians brought turkeys to the house a total of four times that winter as a thank-you gesture. But the subsequent discussion on the importance of complete sentences re-establishes the significance of being part of that non-Indian "we" that can afford to be condescending.

When the Indians came to the door, one of them said, "Eat." He had never been to school, or he might have said, "We want something to eat." When the Indian said, "Eat," did he say something you could understand?

What did he mean when he said, "Sleep"?

The Indians did not know many of our words. How did they show Mrs. Green what they wanted?

After the Indians had gone, the children came down into the room. All were talking at once.

"All gone," said Baby, who was just learning to talk.

"Yes, they have gone," said Mrs. Green.

"Father will be home before night," said Sam in a happy voice.

"Home," said Baby.

You and your friends do not talk like Baby. But once in a while boys and girls say things that are hard to understand. Most of the time this happens because they say only part of what they mean.

If we had heard only what Baby said, what would we have thought? We might have thought that Mr. Green was at home then. We understand Sam's whole thought, "Father will be home before night." Sam used a <u>sentence</u>. A sentence always tells a <u>whole thought</u>. It is something that we can understand.

What did Baby mean when he said, "All gone"? (pp. 6-7)

The book does acknowledge, once, that the Indians were speaking in a language foreign to them. For the most part, however, the default explanation is that they are ignorant, having never gone to school, and childish, in speaking like Baby. And yet these are clearly "good Indians" who honorably pay back their debt.

This story introduces almost thirty pages of work on complete sentences, capital letters, storytelling, playwriting, and so forth (one example of proper capitals includes this explicit judgement: "The Indians went to sleep by the fire. They were good Indians" [pp. 12–13]). When the chapter shifts focus, we stick with the Marshall twins but move on to an account of telephone manners and the etiquette of proper introductions, as the twins invite their teacher to dinner. The Indians with their peremptory demands could make another appearance here as a very bad example, but they do not, though brief mentions of them continue throughout the entire fifty pages of the chapter.

The mixture of middle-class gentility turned into a school language lesson on manners and etiquette, and the bland demeaning of the Indians' prowess in a language not their own, all combined in the same chapter, leads to uneasy and unpleasant reading for contemporary eyes. The exclusion of possible Aboriginal students from the address of this book is complete, a tacit omission that would have supplied me with some nasty notions to bring to my museum outings as they began during that same year. Assumptions of class and gender privilege are also important components of this package. The rules concerning how boys and girls should be introduced to ladies and gentlemen, for example, are not open to interrogation, and I certainly never questioned any of the ideology of this chapter.

The section on the teacher's visit for dinner in the Marshall home includes a section on subject-verb agreement that categorically excluded many of my own classmates and exposed them as outsiders also. Many of the local dialects in St. John's operate a variant version of subject-verb agreement—equally consistent but different from received English. "I goes, I says" and so forth are common; "he do" is not unknown. If it had ever occurred to our teachers to point out that dialects are equal and interesting (even if they had then still gone on to hammer home the mainstream version), we would all have learned much better. But there was no mercy for non-mainstream usage in our written classroom English. Not surprisingly, this constant drill had little actual impact on the outdoor vernacular of many of my young classmates, though I suspect the tacit impact on me was real enough: I learned to be smug about my own "superior" grasp of "good" grammar. This assumption did me no favours.

How the West Was Won

The mixed messages about settler cultures continued in the television cowboy stories that I loved and imitated in my play. *Roy Rogers*, *The Lone Ranger*, *Annie Oakley*, and *Hopalong Cassidy* occupied different ontological and ethical territory from the textbooks, and to some extent from each other. The mythical home of the cowboy shows, nevertheless, was always recognizably the same, and an *unquestionable* version of white supremacy—in the literal sense of making no room whatsoever for questions—was conveyed alike by all of them.

I recently watched a sample of each of the first three television titles listed above and found the treatment of the Indigenous issue contradictory and sometimes confusing. In the *Roy Rogers* instalments that I watched ("Bad Neighbors" [1954] and "Strangers" [1954]), there were no local Indians in Roy Rogers's neighbourhood—though this did not prevent comical sidekick Pat Brady making racist comments in each episode. I viewed the origin story of *The Lone Ranger*: "Enter the Lone Ranger" (n.d.); while the Indigenous Tonto is the saviour who protects and tends to the Lone Ranger after he is wounded and the rest of his Ranger buddies massacred, the slaughter of the Texas Ranger brigade is engineered by a treacherous "half-breed," who is respected by no one. And, of course, Tonto would find himself very much at home with the other monosyllabic Indians in the Grade 3 language book. *Annie Oakley* offers an approach that might be described as liberal for its time. In "Ambush Canyon" (1954), Annie meets an Indigenous woman, Priscilla Bishop, adopted daughter and heir of a local mine owner. Priscilla, misled by her father's partner, proposes to adopt a new mining technique that will flood the local farmland, laboriously cultivated by white farmers; she plans to use the profits to help her own people. Annie shows her the spread of fertile lands that will be destroyed, introduces her to the hardworking white farmers, and also points out to her that justice has already been established by the American government. "The US government realizes what a great injustice has been done," she assures Priscilla, "and they're doing everything that they can to help them with money, land, medical care, and food. They're doing much more than you could ever hope to do." All of Annie's statements can be proved, she says. "You can check with the Indian agents or even the tribes themselves." Finally she points out, "Two wrongs don't make a right." Priscilla changes her mind, reprieving the farms; it turns out that the partner's motives for wanting the flooding to go ahead were suspect, so justice is served and white interests addressed, all in the same magnanimous gesture.

Insofar as these programs inflected each other, the liberal apologetics of *Annie Oakley* seem to me now to have sanitized the more brutal politics of other shows. If everything is all right, really, then this whole cowboy universe becomes more enjoyable.

∧ *The Google Earth*
street scene of what
was once the yard of
106 Pennywell Road.
[© *Google Earth 2010*]

Cowboys as Heroes

In the early cowboy programs, certain stretches of scenery reappeared in different shows, and there was a generic resemblance of setting among all of them.

Acting out some of the cowboy scenarios in our own environment was an important part of my childhood. Looking back now, I see us particularly engaged with the dramatic modes of performance, gesture, and *mise en scène*. We engaged in some dialogue and we occasionally fired guns (usually our fingers) at invisible enemies, but mostly we galloped. Questions of plot were normally not significant to us in our games. It seems to me now that one element of our play involved acting out the settler role, over and over again. We were claiming the land beneath our galloping feet for ourselves.

It intrigues me today to consider why we should have played in this way. Shelby Wolf and Shirley Brice Heath (1992) say that children always rework their stories. "A text that is known to a child does not remain in its original state or even in a steady, stable form; instead, the child rewrites it. Texts become transformative stock to which young readers can return again and again as they figure out their own roles, words, actions, and critiques of their current situation" (pp. 109–110). At least part of our play was undoubtedly an engagement with this kind of "rewriting."

A Google Earth image shows the scene of our games, along the line where the taxis are now parked on the gravel patch. As we galloped "into" this picture with the hill on our right, we had the wild patch known (accurately) as the Thistle Yard to our left. It was almost useless for play because of its forbidding prickles, but it certainly provided atmospheric resonance for a Western setting with its persuasive stand-ins for cactus plants. If in this game we were setting ourselves up in relation to any distinctive part of the *Roy Rogers* world, it was surely to the *mise en scène*.

We usually played *Roy Rogers*, as it had a suitable cast of characters. (When Mum said we had to include our youngest brother, we kindly cast him as Bullet, "Roy's Wonder Dog." He got to gallop as much as the rest of us.) Occasionally I would put my foot down as the oldest, and we would play *Annie Oakley* so I could gallop in front. (I feel a strong sense of obligation to her even now for making this variation possible; it was hugely important to my sense of myself.)

We played cowboys regularly—never cowboys and Indians, just cowboys. We pursued invisible, imagined "baddies." Whether this reflected our local culture with its complete absence of Aboriginals, whether it was a factor of our shortage of personnel and our personal unwillingness ever to accept an enemy role, or whether it reflected our predilection for exploration over plot, or for a binary good/bad division, or just general pusillanimity, is all impossible for me to disentangle today. We were certainly very competitive with our board games, for example, and we would do our best to avoid being It in a game of tag or frozen tag, but our narrative games were largely non-combative.

Rewriting Roy

As it happens, I have a description of our cowboy games, written by myself at around the time I turned twelve. It survives in a book of stories I wrote for my parents' seventeenth wedding anniversary in December 1960.

"Looking back, rather scornfully," I wrote from the vantage point of age, "to those years when I played cowboys with my brothers, I recall one particular game which was, at the time, exciting and is now a humerous [*sic*] tale of young cowboys." My prose style was as flat as my sense of page layout. The story is utterly pedestrian, but it does provide a sense of how we overlaid our TV experience on our own landscape. The remarks in parentheses below come from the original text.

Roy Rogers and Dale Evans were returning from a friend's house (you see how closely we followed the action of the television program) heard shots. Stopping at the bank they learned where the killers had gone and with a "come on Pat" they galloped away.

Pat manfully did his best to catch up with his faithful friends but being considerably smaller his efforts were to no avail. Finally he sat down and cried until Mum took him under her wing and put him to bed.

Meanwhile Roy and Dale were fast catching up with the bandits. They got close enough to their enemies to crawl on hands and knees and then on stomachs through the wet grass when the "bads" disappeared.

"Come on," whispered Dale and with great cunning and carefulness and ingenuity we crept closer to our friends [sic].

Soon we were close enough to hear the wicked men planning. Unfortunately, lack of candidates made it necessary for Roy and Dale to speak for the bandits.

The "plot" of this little yarn invokes the complex layering of our pretend play (displayed through the shifting pronouns of this extract), our intertextual sources, and the physical location of our game. Defeating our imaginary enemies, we then fall into an actual fistfight with each other over who caught the most bandits. The fight is interrupted when a soccer ball soars over the fence and hits us. A thunderstorm adds the final indignity.

A roll of thunder brought us both to our feet. The football players glanced at the sky in consternation, but Roy and Dale, capturers of several thousand bandits heeded them not as they dashed blindly to the house amid the rain that followed. Frightened and trembling, we reeled into the house where we were scolded roundly for playing in the wet grass and sent to bed.

My "humerous" tale offers a small sense of how we placed our bodies in our own local environment to explore the implications of the dramas we watched on television. Performance, gesture, and *mise en scène* are all present in this plodding little story. The speech had to be doubled, as we played with a shortage of actors.

The artifact of the exercise book containing that story carries its own message of cultural location. I absconded with a school notebook to create my anniversary gift for my parents. That little book offers its own social,

> Unfortunate Cowboys
>
> Looking back, rather scornfully, to those years when I played cowboys with my brothers, I recall one particular game which was, at the time, exciting and is now a humerous tale of young cowboys.
>
> One evening, long ago, my brothers Carle and David and I decided to play cowboys. Carle was Roy Rogers, I was Dale Evens and David was the comical side-kick, Pat Brady.
>
> It was approximately seven o'clock when the curtain went up on this thrilling performance. The soccer game being played behind the house was noisy but we did not mind that.
>
> Roy Rogers and Dale Evans were returning from a friend's house (you see how closely we followed the action of the television program) heard shots. Stopping at the bank they learned where the killers had gone and with a "Come on Pat" they galloped away.
>
> Pat manfully did his best to catch up

cultural, and political record. The "Canpad" notebook makes a fleeting connection with Canada in its label and its "Made in Canada" tag, but the rest of the book is highly British. The picture of the Queen on the front is matched by columns of British arithmetical tables on the rear: the currency table is sterling; the avoirdupois weight table includes measures like the "stone" that are alien to North America; and the utility of some of the older measures can only be described as debatable. At no point in my life have I ever needed to know (or indeed met anyone who did know) that cloth is measured in the following way: 2 1/2 Inches = 1 Nail; 4 Nails = 1 Quarter of a Yard, and 4 Quarters = 1 Yard. The Apothecaries' Weight for mixing medicines involves useless but pretty labels; what hard heart could fail to be enchanted by knowing that 3 Scruples = 1 Dram? I associated such arcana

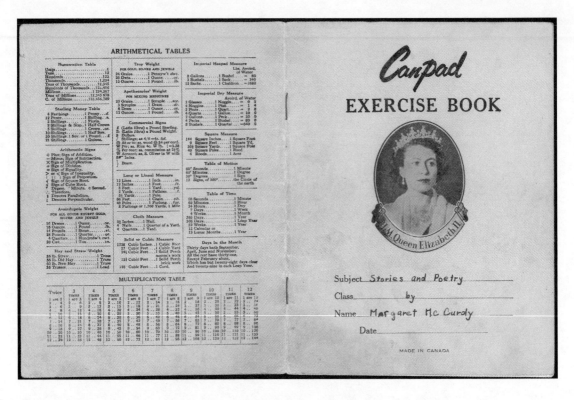

∧ *The 1960 anniversary notebook.*

[*Collection of the author*]

with the practice of writing throughout my entire childhood. The colonial overtones of the notebook provide a fittingly layered setting for the doubled life of the cowboy story inside.

Full Circle

A short story, "The Young Cowboy" (Stong, 1942) from *More Streets and Roads*, the Grade 3 reader, also explores some of the interactions between fiction, known territory, and real life. This story involves Sam, a boy who lives among real cowboys—not the kind who fight "bads" but the kind who rope and brand calves. Unlike us, as the picture in the story shows, Sam came equipped with an actual horse and an appropriate *mise en scène* of mountains and prairie; nevertheless, he, too, had to invoke his imagination and practice with a stump-post.

Just as Sam has the perks of horse and scenery, so he eventually gets to practice with a real calf, and when an emergency comes along as the cattle are being branded, it is Sam who saves the day. To my interpretation of this story, I would have brought expertise gained from watching television. *The Roy Rogers Show* with its passing attention to the actual work of cowboys would have given me just enough repertoire to bring this story—otherwise utterly alien to my east-coast existence—to life.

> *Image from* The New
More Streets and Roads,
(*Gray, Monroe, Artley, &
Arbuthnot, 1956, p. 236*).
[*Collection of the author*]

236

As Sam pulled his pony to a stop at the corral one day, Shorty smiled proudly.

"Fine!" he said. "You ride like a cowboy. But if you want to be a cowboy, I'll have to start teaching you to rope calves. First you'd better practice on fence posts. At least they'll stand still while you rope them. Calves won't."

With Shorty's help, Sam learned the trick of throwing a rope.

At the beginning Sam roped a post in the corral fence while Texas stood still. Then he tried it while Texas walked. That was harder to do, and Sam often missed the post. But he practiced patiently day after day.

Finally Sam learned to rope the post with Texas going at a full gallop.

Television viewing thus meshed with my playtime and with my school life. It also activated the imaginary existence I created to while away solitary walks to school when my friend was ill (any lengthy walk on my own always involved much galloping and a relationship with an imaginary horse and collie). To my viewing I applied experience gained from other activities, such as reading picture books and listening to the radio. In my play I worked out on the ground some of the details and even more of the general aura of the programs. Later I reworked these interpretive efforts into my own story, which pays considerable attention to the process of applying the television world to our own territory. And all of these efforts circled the notion of claiming the land.

The cowboy stories offer only one example of such interpretive efforts, but they provide a rich and complex specimen for exploring the multi-faceted nature of children's developing literacy. Today the complicated interaction between versions and reworkings is much more visible, but intricate cross-referencing was not invented with the Internet.

Marginalizing the Indigenous

The mirror role played by Indigenous peoples in my cultural stew was more complex. To assert the righteousness of claims on the land is a positive step. To undermine and/or efface the claims of others is an uneasier challenge that my texts addressed in a variety of ways.

Indians as Decorations

Our monthly copies of *Jack and Jill* supplied many features with "Indigenous" elements. Often the Indian motif offered to make the lives of suburban white children more "colourful," as in the cover image from August 1958 (Ruth and Charles Newton).

Or consider the address of this Things to Make column, written by Rita N. Oliver, undoubtedly to a white child:

> #### Indian Headdress and Wampum
> *Wearing these ornaments, you can really look like an Indian at the beach, with your tan and some water-color war paint on your face. Make a two-inch band from heavy paper to fit around your head. Overlap the ends two inches and paste together. In this extra thickness cut slits to hold one or two gull feathers. Add Indian designs to the band. For your wampum, find a shell with a hole, usually an oyster shell. String the shell on twine, tie the ends, and wear it as shown [suspended around the neck].* ("Things to Make," 1959, p. 11)

Indians as Plot

First Nations elements also supplied much in the way of plot and drama to many of our stories. The discourses were varying in their levels of

sympathy or hostility to the Aboriginal people involved, but, regardless, the white people always wound up looking heroic.

A small sample from a fairly typical *Jack and Jill* story highlights this tendency. This story calls itself "true." The Pilgrims, starving and without seed corn, find an Indian cache and plant it for themselves to avoid starvation. They are uneasy about their theft of this corn ("theft" is my word, not that of the author) and spend much of the story trying to ascertain from which tribe they have taken it; eventually, through identifying the creators of the distinctive storage baskets, they locate the right people.

> *The Pilgrim men then went to the common house and chose gifts for the Indians. From their sea chests they took colored cloth and knives and beads, and other goods. These they brought and placed before the Indians. "We give these gifts to you in exchange for your corn which we found and took on Cape Cod," the governor said. "Without your corn we could not have grown food to live. We are grateful for it, and we hope you will be our friends."*
>
> *And that was how those early American settlers paid their first debt to the Indians. (Hays, 1958, p. 14)*

This story does not explain how the Indians survived the winter without their seed corn. The word "stealing" never appears; Hays focuses completely on the scrupulous and sensitive consciences of the Pilgrims.

Pioneer novels offer a larger stage on which to explore the conundrum of how white people may take over Indigenous land while still remaining decent and honorable in the eyes of the readers. It is worth taking a closer look at one example that at least acknowledges a small taste of moral complexity.

By the standards of the era, *Caddie Woodlawn* (Brink, 1990/1935) offers a relatively layered account of relations between different claimants to the same land, though the author tamps down the seriousness of the terror by emphasizing the excitement. The character of Caddie is based on the author's grandmother, and the account of pioneer life arises from the grandmother's stories to her grandchild. The threat of "Indian attack" haunts the early stages of the book, and at midpoint suddenly looms much larger, as rumour of a planned massacre sends the settlers into a frenzy.

Chapter 11 is entitled "Massacree! [*sic*]" and starts off grimly, buttressed, of course, by its status as a largely "true" story, guaranteed by the great authority of a grandparent:

> *In those days the word massacre filled the white settlers with terror. Only two years before, the Indians of Minnesota had killed a thousand white people, burning their houses and destroying their crops...Other smaller uprisings throughout the Northwest flared up from time to time, and only a breath of rumour was needed to throw the settlers of Wisconsin into a panic of apprehension. (Brink, 1990/1935, p. 118)*

Brink provides a more nuanced approach than most of my television programs (not difficult) and offers greater complexity than the little stories of *Jack and Jill*:

> *The fear spread like a disease, nourished on rumors and race hatred. For many years now the whites had lived at peace with the Indians of western Wisconsin, but so great was this disease of fear that even a tavern rumor could spread it like an epidemic throughout the country. (p. 119)*

Rumour of massacre brings people flocking to the Woodlawn house as the best place to house large numbers. Mother bakes and organizes, and the children enjoy the "emergency" aura and ensuing school holiday. Inevitably the first high excitement wears off. When there is no attack, the settlers become restless, not sure whether to return home or not. Father is sure the Indians are being maligned, and Caddie trusts her friend Indian John. When she overhears men plotting to end the uncertainty by making a pre-emptive attack, she slips away to warn the Indians. Indian John believes her and arranges for his people to depart; then, at considerable risk to himself, he rides with Caddie back to the farm. They are intercepted by Father and the hired man, keeping watch, and the following scene suggests that good men can trust each other in all circumstances:

> *[Father] was silent for a moment, and Caddie stood beside him, shivering and oppressed by the weight of his disapproval. In the swaying lantern light she searched the faces of the three men—Robert's honest mouth open in astonishment, Father's brow knit in thought, John's dark face impassive and remote with no one knew what thoughts passing behind it.*
>
> *Caddie could bear the silence no longer. "Father, the Indians are our friends," she repeated.*
>
> *"Is this true, John?" asked Father.*
>
> *"Yes, true, Red Beard," answered John gravely.*
>
> *"My people fear yours, John. Many times I have told them that you are our friends. They do not always believe."*
>
> *"My people foolish sometimes, too," said John. "Not now. They no kill white. Red Beard my friend."*
>
> *"He brought me home, Father," said Caddie. "You must not let them kill him."*

"No, no, Caddie. There shall be no killing tonight, nor any more, I hope, forever."

Over her head the white man and the red man clasped hands.

"I keep the peace, John," said Father. "The white men shall be your brothers."

"Red Beard has spoken. John's people keep the peace."

For a moment they stood silent, their hands clasped in the clasp of friendship, their heads held high like two proud chieftains. Then John turned to his pony. He gathered the slack reins, sprang on the pony's back and rode away into the darkness. (pp. 141–142)

It is noteworthy that although these two men treat each other in relatively equitable terms in this sentimental scene, and, although it is considered admirable in this story for Father to be compared to a chieftain, it is the Indians who have to move away. Indian John is granted a certain (inscrutable!) agency in this story, but his people are still doomed.

As for Father, the road from Father leads directly to the Atticus Finch of *To Kill a Mockingbird*—another noble white man who does right and is heroically ineffectual. It is as if the presence of a good white man were enough to establish morality, in and of itself. It is easy today to sneer at the palliative nature of these stories, but as late as 2006, *To Kill a Mockingbird* was by far the most frequently taught novel in Grade 10 English classes in my home city (Mackey, Vermeer, Storie, and DeBlois, 2012). The white hero still creates his own moral geography in the twenty-first century.

"Placing" the Stories

I lived in the very white city of St. John's in a territory whose Indigenous population had been extinguished, their culture represented to me only through tools and ornaments (and those skeletons) in the museum. I could truly imagine only the white characters in all my fictions and textbooks. Post-hoc remorse in the history book gave me no inkling of the complicated relationships that persevered in other parts of the larger Canadian culture to which I also belonged. I vaguely acknowledged that a benevolent white person was a better human being than a racist when the question became a plot issue, but manifestations of bigotry largely escaped my notice if the text itself did not highlight them. Indian John was as close to a First Nations voice as I ever heard. Although the different discourses to which I was exposed were not in complete accord with regard to details and attitudes, they spoke with one implied voice when it came to asserting that the best outcome of any story had to entail what was best for the white characters. If it could be "good" for the Indigenous population—as determined by the white population—so much the better, but that cause was a secondary priority. In any case, so far as I knew, any "real" (i.e., fictional) "Indians" lived in the United States, which largely existed in my mind as a kind of vague setting, an indeterminate place where the story happened. The idea that "real" descendants of the figments created for my fictions might be living through real consequences of racial injustice in my own country simply never occurred to me, and there were no available triggers, either in my books or in the assumptions of my world, that might raise the question in my mind.

Claiming

One element of the settler stories, however, continued to resonate significantly with me, though in largely tacit ways: the idea of claiming the land. My need as an outsider to establish some sense of rightfully owning my territory was strong. Whatever else I was playing as I galloped along the base of our hill, night after night, I was establishing "foot rights" to our land. The cowboys were asserting their ownership of their territory, and at least part of the appeal of this game for me was the opportunity to play out that affirmation in my own space. The assertion of settler ownership was a continent-wide preoccupation in the 1950s; in my own way (and oblivious to any political implications of my white skin but aware of my local status as incomer), I made my personal and emotional claim on the land through the activities of my own feet.

In keeping with the random nature of many children's literate development, my notions of asserting ownership of the land were intertextually reinforced in an unlikely way. The idea of claiming the ground through walking it forms a major plot component in a book I read more than once as a child, a book that baffled me in its details but resonated in terms of its emotional elements. It is hard to imagine how a book could be further removed from cowboy stories, though I suppose there is a certain pioneering element in the genteel-family-on-hard-times plot. *The Islanders* was written by Theodora Wilson Wilson (the double surname is correct), a Westmorland pacifist who lived between 1865 and 1941, a feminist, a Quaker, and the author of children's and adult books. WorldCat dates the novel as published in 1910. This book came from my mother's childhood and maybe my grandmother's as well; and it still lurked about our family bookshelves in my time.

The characters in *The Islanders* must walk the boundaries of an aristocratic estate once a century in order to maintain title to the land. This imperative of walking the land to claim it is explicitly laid out by the nobly born Joan de Renegil, older sister of the rapscallion Sir Bobbie (home from Eton for the school holidays, a marker of bona fide aristocracy that was utterly lost on me until I reread the book as an adult):

> It is the Boundary Riding—the great event that happens every hundred years, to keep the de Renegil rights as Lords of the Manor. We are arranging it as a grand wind-up to Bobbie's holidays. We start at eight in the morning, and follow the old boundary, right up the face of the scar, down on the mosses, along by the river, and, in fact, wherever the boundary runs. Last time it was ridden the estate lost thirty acres, because a corner was missed! And there will be sports, of course, and tremendous feeding, and a whole roast ox, and fireworks. (Wilson Wilson, 1910, p. 36)

The boundary is in fact walked rather than ridden, and those who arduously complete its circumference are awarded a medal and permitted to sign the "Deed." This act of territorial assertion provides the climax of the book, and I am certain its romantic imperialism informed my own tramping of my territory.

The haphazard interaction of cowboy shows on the new medium of television and the medieval throwback of Wilson Wilson's romance for young people is probably meaningful only to me; I am very possibly the only person in the world whose personal and psychological needs as an incomer were so precisely met by these two particular categories of text, acted out, explicitly or tacitly, on a specific stretch of ground. But such motley meetings-up and random intertexts are exactly what makes the act of becoming literate so very local. Even my co-cowboy brothers did not read Mum's book; to them it was a girls' story. I would not say that *The Islanders* informed my games directly—but the background resonance was important.

The settler question is relatively easy to follow across media, in both official and unofficial literacies. Other large social questions undoubtedly manifested themselves in similar complexity. As school textbook reader, as museum-goer, as magazine subscriber, as TV viewer, as fiction devourer, I grew physically, mentally, and emotionally, both within my own personal world and simultaneously within a relatively motley assortment of textual worlds. It is difficult to disentangle my civic self and my literate self. We delude ourselves, I believe, if we think we can divorce the study of texts from the settings of their creation and also of their consumption. In the world of reception, they cross-inform each other in ways that sometimes reinforce and sometimes challenge. Child interpreters *place* them within the terms of their own local understanding, sometimes literally, as with our cowboy games, and sometimes more metaphorically. An unlikely, idiosyncratic, highly personal, and elaborately entwined intertextuality is overlaid on the known world of the child, in ways that support or contest the child's own priorities and imperatives. Sorting out the single strands is difficult and often reductive. This chapter only begins to address the kinds of messy complexity that comprise a developing literate life.

EDGES

EDGES, according to Lynch (1960), "are usually, but not quite always, the boundaries between two kinds of areas" (p. 62). The clarity of an edge contributes to the coherence with which an urban space can be imagined. In this section I examine the physical and discursive limits of my world, exploring ground rather than highlighting figure. This section is an analogue of the topographical map that represents the shape of the landscape rather than the road map designed for going places.

I learned to be literate in a place and time where the boundary between my lived experience and my reading life was very often sharply marked. At the same time as I was learning to function in a particular social setting with a distinctive geography and history, I was developing a conventional repertoire for dealing with my literary experiences. My readerly sense of threshold was acute. Like any reader, I abandoned normal daily rules in order to read fairy tales and fantasy; I developed similar cognitive tools for stepping into realistic contemporary fiction as well, since the boundary between the worlds described in these books and my own normality was also sharply etched.

In this section, I attempt to establish some of the social, historical, geographical, and cultural limits that made my experiences meaningful, and I explore some of the texts that shaped or warped how I perceived my world. Edges provide limits in more than physical ways, though Lynch's instances of rivers and railway lines emphasize real-world boundaries. His examples also remind us that edges are not always immutable; they can burst their banks. In the third chapter of this section, I take a brief look at how our discursive understanding of these limits has altered since the 1950s, affecting how we may perceive this world as open to further exploration and reassessment.

The word "citizen" has active and passive connotations; using the passive meaning of the word in the sense that everyone belongs to a particular place, time, and civic arrangement, we all learn about reading as citizens of *somewhere*. In my case, the boundaries of my known world, as I understood them at the time, were very clear-cut; the challenge of describing them in relatively terse terms is easier than it might be if I came from a society less marked by exceptionalism. But those boundaries have been challenged in numerous ways, as the final chapter in this section demonstrates. The contingency of limits is dramatized by multiple discursive shifts that have led to our contemporary—and very different—delineation of how perceived boundaries shape Newfoundland society. What we surely knew in the 1950s is no longer convincing; what is the impact of retrospective dismantling of the givens of our lives in Newfoundland?

One of the active connotations of citizenship is its sense of allegiance. In that sense, no matter how my name and family background marked me as an outsider, there was never any question in my mind of where I belonged: on Pennywell Road, in Holloway School, in St. John's, on the Avalon Peninsula. If anything, I was more articulate about these allegiances because they were occasionally shadowed by questions. More mindlessly, more passively, even helplessly, I was a citizen of the 1950s. In this section, I investigate some of the consequences for my literate life of these issues of placing and timing.

14

Now and Then, Here and There

Placing

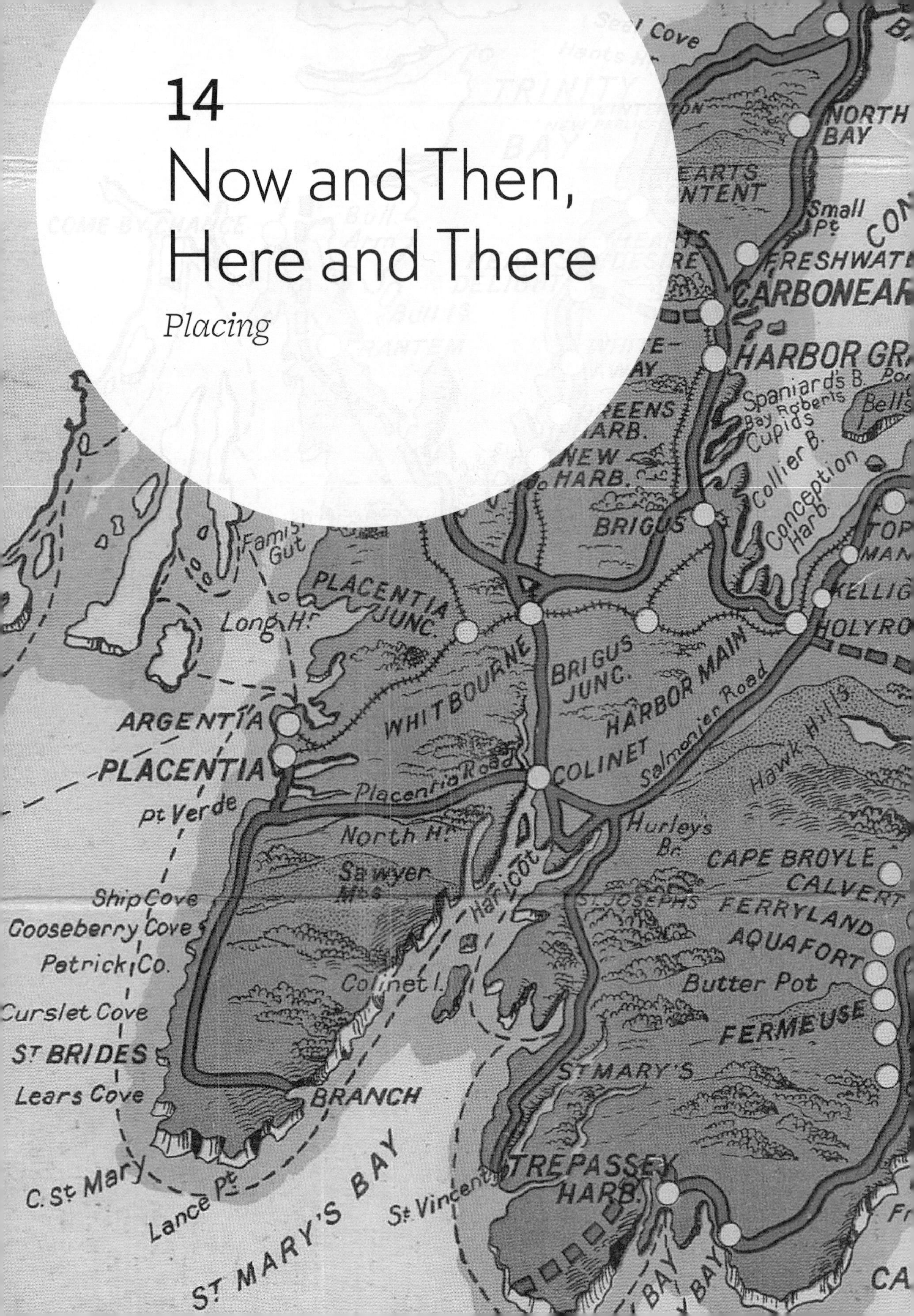

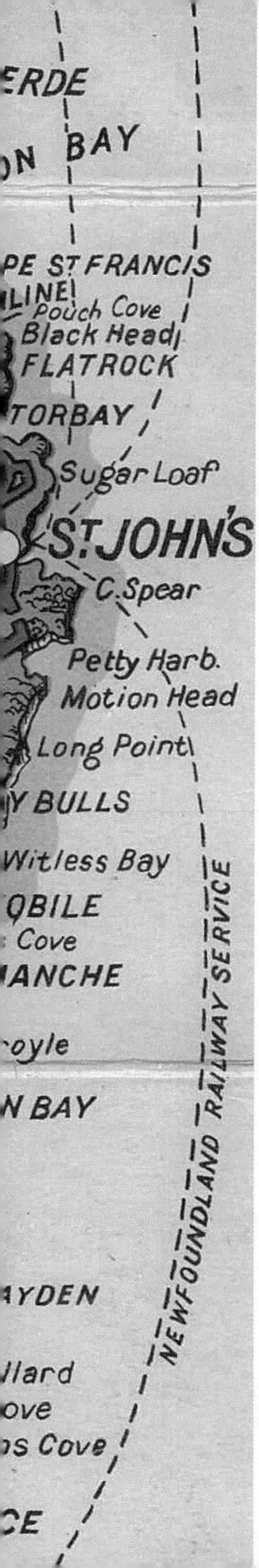

ERDE

N BAY

PE ST FRANCIS
LINE
Pouch Cove
Black Head
FLATROCK
TORBAY
Sugar Loaf
ST JOHN'S
C. Spear
Petty Harb.
Motion Head
Long Point
Y BULLS
Witless Bay
QBILE
Cove
ANCHE
oyle
N BAY
YDEN
lard
ove
s Cove
CE

NEWFOUNDLAND RAILWAY SERVICE

IT IS EASY TO CREATE an account of romantic exceptionalism to describe St. John's, the Avalon Peninsula, and the island of Newfoundland. The island occupies its own unique time zone, half an hour out of sync from the continent, providing a starting point for the kind of narrative that fuels the exotic and sentimental images purveyed by the current, burgeoning tourist industry.

That sense of being slightly askance to other places is common to many islands, and Newfoundland certainly featured its share of idiosyncrasies over the centuries. The currency shifted from pounds, shillings, and pence to dollars and cents in 1865, but the dollar was pegged to the pound in parallel to the West Indian currency, rather than aligned with Canada or the United States. Newfoundlanders continued to drive on the left-hand side of the road until 1947, when vehicles shifted to the right to match the rest of the continent. The railway tracks were narrow gauge rather than the

367

standard Canadian width (cargo had to be expensively transferred rather than simply shipping loaded railway carriages onto the ferry, an economic consideration that contributed to the demise of the Newfoundland railway in 1988). The island asserted its independence from its much larger neighbours and claimed a maritime allegiance that often looked east to Britain and south to the trading partners of the West Indies.

Newfoundland's tapestry of geology, geography, and history is indisputably rich and fascinating, though little of it was passed on to me in any effective or interesting way in my youth. I grew up appreciating the austere, even harsh beauty of the hills and the ocean, but I was oblivious to the deep background of Newfoundland that would have caught my imagination even as a very young child. Yet that background profoundly affected the surface I inhabited, so I present a brief account of it here, along with some reflections on the impoverished geographical and historical vocabulary that was available to me in my childhood.

The Avalon

The Avalon Peninsula is extremely old. It was created out of the clash of three continents. Tectonic upheaval caused moving land masses to collide together and be fixed in a stony matrix of many different rock formations. The experience of walking across an eastern Newfoundland field is entirely distinctive; you do not go very far before your feet encounter rock.

Parts of the geological mosaic of the Avalon Peninsula are more than 600 million years old. At Mistaken Point, at the southeastern tip of the peninsula, geologists have discovered

> the oldest deepwater fossils in the world. These 620-million-year-old traces of soft-bodied marine creatures are almost three times older than the oldest dinosaurs....This fossil bed and its matching site along the coast of North Africa offer up some of the most potent evidence for the theory of continental drift....In the eyes of many scientists Mistaken Point is central to the whole debate about the origins of life on this planet. They tell us that in these fossils lie the beginnings of animal life as we know it today. (Major, 2001, p. 4)

In terms of human scale, Newfoundland and the Avalon feature importantly in the history of the colonization of North America. The original inhabitants were the Beothuk, about whose origins little is known but whose extinction in 1829 is a calamitous landmark in Newfoundland history. To our knowledge today, the earliest European settlers were the Norse explorers who built a community at L'Anse aux Meadows in northern Newfoundland more than a thousand years ago. After John Cabot's landfall in 1497, other Europeans attempted to create early "New World" settlements on the island, though many failed to survive the harsh conditions. From the St. John's harbourside, Sir Humphrey Gilbert claimed Newfoundland for Queen Elizabeth in 1583.

A major colonizing figure gave the Avalon its romantic name. In 1620 Lord Baltimore (later of Maryland fame) purchased a plantation in Newfoundland that included the community now called Ferryland, not far south of St. John's. He named his new colony Avalonia, a name associated with Arthurian legends and Celtic mythology. There seems to be some doubt about whether Baltimore was himself an incurable romantic or perceived this notion of a colony in the "island to the west" as a marketing tool when he canvassed for funds to build his plantation. Bernard Fardy does credit him for being an idealist in envisaging his colony as a haven of religious tolerance. Although Baltimore himself did not last long there before heading for the more benevolent climate of Maryland, the colony he founded thrived over a more extended period of time. It is now an intriguing archeological site with public access to the dig and to a museum that displays what has been found there:

> *artifacts from the past 400 years which reflect the history of the area*
> *before the coming of the colonizers, and the everyday life of the settlers*
> *of the early 17th century: everything from Beothuck Indian stone arrow-*
> *heads to cannonballs from the days of conflict with the French and Dutch,*
> *and everyday items such as padlocks, gold rings, keys, clay pipes, pottery,*
> *ceramics and stoneware, glassware and glass beads, iron axe and tool*
> *heads, nails and other ironmongery, coins and official seals and medals,*
> *and even pieces of gravestones. (Fardy, 2005, pp. 192–193)*

The displays in the Ferryland museum strikingly manifest an artifactual luxury that contrasts strongly with the later hardscrabble lives of the fishing families. They also reflect a history of European conflicts in which coastal communities and fishing rights were fiercely contested.

Baltimore was not the only significant colonizer in Ferryland. He was succeeded by Sir David Kirke, whose wife Sara later took over the planta-tion. Lady Kirke was redoubtable. "[A]ccording to census figures from the

1660s and 1670s, Lady Kirke owned more stages, boats and train (cod liver oil) vats and employed more servants (fishermen and fish processors) than any other planter on the English shore, including her sons. If Lady Kirke was not the first Newfoundland proprietor to make the fishery profitable, she was almost certainly British North America's first woman entrepreneur" (Colony of Avalon Foundation, 2013/1999, n.p.).

Both pseudo-Arthurianism and swashbuckling entrepreneurial spirit escaped my childish attention and enthusiasm. The archaeological work that makes Ferryland a fascinating destination today had not begun. To me, Lord Baltimore was simply one more colonizing name to be memorized and nothing more.

When I look now at the Grade 5 textbook that was my main point of access to this history, it is easy to see why I was so uninterested. If the author and editors had set out to be selective of the facts in the cause of being dull, they would not have made very many different decisions. Here, for example, is the account of the naming of the Avalon: "Calvert called his colony Avalon after Avalon in the west of England and he made Ferryland his capital" (Briffett, 1954, p. 47). Lady Sara Kirke disappears altogether, subsumed into two nondescript references to Sir David Kirke's family: "In 1683 he came with one hundred men and his wife and family, and settled in Lord Baltimore's house in Ferryland....Kirke had been unfair to his partners. He was dismissed and a new governor, John Downing, was sent out to take over the colony. The Kirke family continued to live at Ferryland for many years" (p. 48).

In this history for ten-year-olds, the ideological framing of the settlement of Newfoundland is not very subtle:

> *Poets and noblemen were not able to colonize Newfoundland. The true colonists were those brave and sturdy fisher-folk who settled in tiny groups—often no more than the members of one family—in the little coves and on the islands along the coast. They went wherever codfish was plentiful and where they could build houses and boats. No weak or lazy person could stand the kind of life they lived in those lonely settlements. The children of these settlers grew up strong and self-reliant. We are proud to think of them as our ancestors, and we like to think, too, that we still possess some of their qualities of courage and independence.* (Briffett, 1954, p. 50)

I would certainly have registered the exclusionary definition of that "we" (it made no room for me), but it was not such an attractive or romantic past that I burned to be a part of it in any case.

Instead, I knew the road to Ferryland as something much more corporeal. On summer weekends especially, when there was no Sunday school to fill the afternoon, we would frequently go for a drive, and one of our many drives was down the Southern Shore toward Ferryland. We kids loved that road, naming it the Bumpety-Smooth Road as the surface was better graded in the built-up areas than in the rough and dusty stretches between communities.

In larger ways, similarly, either I was ignorant of any potential romance in Newfoundland's past or my daily realities simply won out. The exciting archaeological discoveries at L'Anse aux Meadows and elsewhere were far in the future; being briefly surprised by the bizarre name of Leif the Lucky was as close as I got to the fascination of the past.

The textbook's account of the history of St. John's tells of privation, battles, fire, and suffering. It is also an exceptionally male story. Stories of hunger abound in this book, no doubt accurately. Fire swept the city in 1846 and in 1892. It is not really the kind of past that you might want to pretend yourself into unless you have a taste (I did not) for imagining yourself triumphing over every kind of privation.

The lengthy history of Water Street might have stirred my imagination to a small degree, but I was only aware that Water Street still served the fishing port of St. John's in my youth. In such ports, the sense of smell is more potent than any sense of historical glamour. In the 1950s, there were still fish flakes—wooden frames on which the split and salted fish dried in the open air—in the Battery at the foot of Signal Hill, picturesque without a doubt, but I usually perceived them as too stinky to be completely appealing. Fishing boats came into the harbour for shelter or restocking, most noticeably the Portuguese White Fleet. We reserved our admiration, however, not for the skill and strength with which the Portuguese fishermen plied the North Atlantic but rather for their brilliance at playing soccer on the wharves in their bare feet. Romance was for other places and other times; daily life in Newfoundland was utilitarian rather than even faintly exotic. My knowledge of the city was pedestrian in many senses of that word; my discursive understanding of the past was slight and, rather than augmenting, it interfered with my chances of developing an intelligent understanding of my environment.

History, Romance, and the Other People

Something about Mary Quayle Innis's *Stand on a Rainbow* (1943), spoke profoundly to my mother. The source of that appeal has never been entirely clear to me. In all my readings of it at different points in my life, at no time has my heart or mind been captured as hers was, and I cannot say what spoke to her so acutely. Nevertheless, it is in that book that I find a strong statement of what I missed (and was even dimly aware that I missed) in St. John's in the 1950s.

Innis's housewife heroine Leslie has read an 1825 account of people who lived more or less on the same spot that is now occupied by her suburban Ontario home. These previous inhabitants haunt Leslie's awareness of her own neighbourhood. She thinks of them as "the other people."

> *The other people had no name. She had not thought of them for months till the loneliness of this immense cold brought them to her memory. For them the forest had stood dense as a wall between the tiny cup of the clearing and the long palisaded road. Such cold as this would creep through the closest chinking of log walls and gather itself in corners close to the open fire. The other people were quite as real to her and the children as many of their neighbours. (Innis, 1943, p. 177)*

Visiting our Nova Scotia grandparents in the Annapolis Valley, we always called in at the Port Royal Habitation, a recreation of Champlain's settlement of the early 1600s. The rebuilt fortifications scaffolded our thinking about how "the other people" once lived in the very same place. It was an embodied awareness to the extent that we were startled by the low doorframes and short beds, and realized we would have to imagine our predecessors on this spot as diminished in stature compared to contemporary adults. St. John's is full of stories about previous times that would have been perfectly accessible to a ten-year-old, especially one who was desperate to *think romantically* about her own place. But somehow, the interesting stories, the stories with the tiniest evocative capacity, all disappeared from the history book and instead we learned dates of treaties and which coastal fishing territories were ceded when to the French.

My sense of the other people of St. John's, my historical predecessors in this place, was almost an empty set. The history book implied that the Beothuk did not spend any time on the Avalon. Humphrey Gilbert, in 1583, "did not find [the natives] in Conception Bay for at that time they were not seen south of Trinity Bay" (Briffett, 1954, p. 18). And St. John's was barely recognizable as a town at all, for long after Gilbert's time:

> At the beginning of the nineteenth century, St. John's was only a small fishing town. Less than six thousand people lived there. The "Lower Path" or Water street was so narrow that two carts had trouble in passing. The citizens had to walk under flakes or along by-paths covered with piles of rubbish. Nobody had the legal right to build a house with a chimney, nor could he own land. Houses could not be built without the governor's permission. Gower Street was begun in 1804 by Governor Gower who opened a road thirty feet wide and allowed people to build facing the harbour— provided they gave five or ten pounds to the poor. But some of the officers of the garrison had very fine gardens even at that time.
> In 1811, the terrible laws against building were removed, and two years later people were allowed to own land. St. John's began to grow up. Wealthy people built beautiful houses, but the poor still lived in wretched slums.
> (p. 90)

Living as I did in a very cold and drafty house, I had no need to imagine being even colder in the past, and Governor Gower, however worthy, did not engage my attention for longer than it took to memorize his name and role for the ever-looming test. It is possible that I made some connection between Governor Gower and Gower Street United Church, but I don't recall being excited by it (in fairness to my earlier self, as a factoid it does lack a certain historical *jouissance*). And the church building itself, like almost all the cityscape that surrounded me, dated back only to the aftermath of the 1892 fire.

Most of my classmates would have had much better access than I did to the vivid oral culture that enriches Newfoundland society. As an immigrant, I had no local Nan or Pop to fill in the blanks left by the textbooks and to supply family stories of outport life; no extended Newfoundland clan to provide a personal sense of the geography of significant places in the province; no family access to the lively folk culture of legend and song.

The aridity of the history textbook was one problem; another major element of my ignorance was the poverty of discourse of historical *otherness* that my recreational books taught me as an alternative. My notion of a desirable and interesting past was shallow, feminine in the most pejorative sense of the word. If it did not involve swishing of petticoats, it wasn't my kind of history. I cut the teeth of my historical imagination on paragraphs such as this one, found in Irene Boyd's (n.d.) "A Day in the Forest":

> *My Lady Griselda sat sewing within her mother's bower, and rebellion was in her heart.*
>
> *The bower maidens chattered above their tapestry, the Countess yawned among her cushions, and through the mottled green glass of the casement streamed the spring sunshine of 1398. Somewhere out there in the blowy meads—thought Griselda—young Richard, a-horseback, would be riding beside his father in chase of the wild deer, while she, his twin, must sit within the castle and stitch the sunny hours away. (n.p.)*

We learn that Griselda was wearing a "long fur-bordered gown" (n.p.), but it did not satisfy her heart (though it would have warmed my own). Not entirely surprisingly, she borrows her twin brother's more liberating clothes and heads off into the forest for adventures. This story appeared in Mum's old anthology, *Ripping Stories for Girls*. Within its covers, much historical swashbuckling takes place, but I could not imagine such stories occurring in my world.

Even more influential on my sense of the past was the melodramatic *Tower or Throne?* (Comstock, 1933/1902), a wildly romanticized account of the childhood of Queen Elizabeth I. Although a child in considerable peril, she still managed to have it all as far as I was concerned: a will and an intellect that far surpassed that of any boy *and* those flowing skirts and petticoats.

Tower or Throne? had been presented to my mother for work in Mathematics at LeMarchant School in Halifax, the year she was in Grade 8, about 1936. I don't know what Mum made of it as a girl, but I can testify that its impact on my own historical imagination was almost entirely pernicious. It is full of pages such as the following:

> *"Look! Bess, who rides down from London way? Methinks I see horsemen." The Princess Mary shaded her near-sighted eyes with one thin hand, and gazed down the highway.*
>
> *Elizabeth, weaving a chaplet of leaves, dropped her work, and looked eagerly in the direction Mary mentioned.*

> *"Oh, 'tis many horsemen, sister Mary," cried the little maid delightedly. "I warrant you they are from our father's Court with some great news." She danced about in glee, clinging to Mary's hand.*
>
> *The two princesses, plainly clad, were allowed by Lady Bryan to walk abroad unattended. (p. 58)*

Plainly clad and unattended, the sisters are enabled to deceive the courtiers at Mary's suggestion.

> *"List you, Bess; let us bide here by the roadside 'neath this tree. Perchance they will take us for village maids. There is always some one ready to talk; we may learn much and so be prepared for whatever has happened. 'Tis long since Court news has sifted down to Hunsdon."*
>
> *"Oh yes!" laughed Elizabeth. "'Twill be great sport, sister Mary. See, let us go to this little spring; belike they may wish a drink of the cold water." (p. 59)*

Comstock diligently maintains this faux-historical discourse for more than 250 pages. My current distaste for it might be taken as anachronistic but, in fact, *The New York Times*, as long ago as 1906, chastised Comstock for her fast-and-loose approach to the facts:

> *Mrs. Harriet T. Comstock's "Tower or Throne"...clearly revealed her as one whose romantic admiration for England's Elizabeth is not to be cooled or checked by any new views of her character....There is so little actual history in the tale that it may be read without vexation of soul as to its precise place in the long procession of Elizabeth's years, and that is an advantage to one who reads for amusement.* ("Boston Notes," 1906, n.p.)

For an adult reading for amusement, this tosh may indeed pass the time pleasantly. As a child reader, I took it very seriously, indeed. For a royal princess, one even held prisoner at times, this Elizabeth has remarkable freedom of movement, as long as she takes pains to disguise herself. Inspired by the moments in which the apparent crone flings off the cloak and is revealed as the true princess (a scene that invariably ends with harrowing farewells, usually forever), I began to search out my best domestic substitutes for dungeons to visit in disguise. In both houses I inhabited as a child, there was a coal cellar that could serve the purpose adequately, and I spent (wasted?) hours tiptoeing down the back stairs, one hand gathering my imaginary skirts, the other holding a torch aloft, as I made my way to the deepest cellar available. It was one of my favourite solitary games, but it never really went anywhere; my plot reached its moment of climax as I arrived at the coal cellar door, flinging back my "hood" and hissing "'Tis I" through invisible bars.

While working on this section about St. John's, I have been reading Paul O'Neill's massive history of the city. A single line from this book, describing life on Water Street, would have gone straight to my frivolous ten-year-old heart: "Red-coated soldiers from the garrison helped housemaids carry their market baskets, as tightly corseted ladies in fancy bonnets nodded to dandies in close fitting trousers and high collars who tipped silk hats when they passed" (O'Neill, 2008, p. 622). I had no interest in imagining myself back into a life of poverty and squalor, still less to a life of "making fish," the backbreaking work of turning the cod to dry in the wind. But that single line would have had me walking Water Street with my imagination ablaze. Unfortunately, I did not read it, or anything remotely like it, until 2011 (at which point, I must confess, the essential appeal of this petticoated image has dissipated to the point of no return).

One pleasure of this project has involved the development of a more layered and nuanced awareness of St. John's and its past. I grieve over the scanty understanding that impoverished my historical imagination as a child, but it remains a fact of my early literacy and cannot be altered now, only remedied retrospectively. Decades after reading *Tower or Throne?*, I found a Newfoundland poet expressing some of my childish ambivalence about my home. It was surprisingly comforting to see an inevitable bitterness of colonial life expressed so eloquently:

> *That town was my first love, profound*
> *and partial and easy enough to betray*
> *with the suspicion important things lay*
> *elsewhere, a hunch kept under the mattress*
> *and thumbed through in my dreams, a compulsive tic.*
> *(Crummey, 2013, p. 62)*

Revisiting some of the foolish stories that burned themselves into my memory and imagination, I balk at the idea that literacy is inevitably emancipatory. Such reading alienated me from my own environment and gave me some very silly ideas about the world that I took as true for a long time indeed. Although there was certainly some volition in my resolutely sentimental approach to times past, the sense of history I developed from my books represented in many ways a case of literacy as intellectual betrayal. And in my turn, I betrayed my own place, as Michael Crummey describes, wished it always to be something else.

Time layers into our reading in complex ways. Let us return briefly to *Tower or Throne?* Tudor events of the sixteenth century, many of them cutthroat, have since taken on considerable romantic allure, courtesy (at least in part) of many fictional rewrites. In 1902, when Comstock was mingling swashbuckling with petticoats, the British Empire was at the peak of its glory and the hard questions raised by the First World War were still a decade in the future. Comstock's sentimental extravaganza found a natural home in imperial bombast.

The Statute of Westminster had already changed the nature of the British Empire by the time this shallow story was reprinted in 1933. My mother, in Grade 8, a few years later, was more directly affected by the Depression than by the glories of the Mother Country. The time of my own reading in the late 1950s represented the early stages of what was sometimes labelled the second Elizabethan era. Certainly I knew of Elizabeth II in a context much more domestic than swaggering, but I was easily persuaded by the rhetoric of the novel to prefer the heady glamour of conflict. By 2011, when I reread the book for this project, the post-colonial fallout from the empire was much more apparent than the assumptions of its one-time grandeur. More than a century after its first appearance, the pages of the book remain the same, but multiple shifts in reading repertoires have moved readers in many different directions.

But a reader's earlier occasions of reading do not evaporate because they have been rendered out-of-date. At the age of twenty-one, visiting London for the first time, I made a beeline for the Tower of London and stood overwhelmed at the Traitors' Gate, which features prominently in the Comstock book, as its title suggests. It was possibly the very first occasion in my life that I had a vivid sense of the overlay of text and history, present and past time layered in a single place. Multitudes of "other people" walked the land around me. Thus the delusional vapours of *Tower or Throne?* linger in my own autobiographical sense of myself; bad fiction cannot simply be effaced from a reader's history, no matter how much she might like to expunge it.

Geography and Setting

My historical sense of St. John's and the local vicinity was thin, to put it mildly; but my awareness of the geographical appeal of our surroundings was acute. The Avalon Peninsula is ruggedly beautiful, with miles and miles of forest, cliff, and shoreline. It is dotted with plentiful lakes and ponds, and rinsed through with innumerable brooks and streams.

In the summer of 1952, we acquired a car for the first time. My parents, in a family memoir, describe this event. Harold Macpherson (hero of the silver dollars) was a local businessman, active in the United Church community, and always very generous to us:

> It was that same summer that Mr. Harold Macpherson "lent" us a car "so we could see something of the countryside." We have never forgotten this act of great kindness; teachers' salaries, even principals' salaries, were not big in those days, and a car had seemed beyond our reach. When the summer was over, I tried to return the car, but no dice; Mr. Macpherson said there were lots of vehicles on his farm, and we should have a car of our own. It was a gesture we shall never forget, and it symbolizes for us the thoughtfulness and generosity of many Newfoundlanders. (McCurdy & McCurdy, 2010, p. 22)

We scoured the local vicinity in that grey Vanguard. At every opportunity, my parents revelled in the chance to organize a drive or a picnic. We had picnics even for breakfast. Most often we went to Leary's Brook, then on the outskirts of the city. The brook was diverted to a culvert in the early 1960s and the Avalon Mall built on our cherished picnic site. Before this catastrophe, the site was idyllic, with woodland, meadow, and stream, the closest fit to Thornton W. Burgess scenery in the whole area. A little rock dam created a shallow pool, and we played at swimming there. We hunted for violets in the wood as the last dispirited snowdrifts evaporated, even before the cold and the fog gave any sign of yielding to spring.

Another frequent picnic spot was Bowring Park, a beautiful landscaped site along the banks of the Waterford River. There were rustic log bridges (one over a small gorge of white, rushing water always gave me a shiver of utter terror, as it wobbled when you walked on it, no matter how careful you were). There were picnic tables, landscaped flowerbeds, flowering trees, stretches of meadowland. There was even a nifty set of cultivated beds spelling out "BOWRING PARK" in flowers. Above all, there was (and is) a sense of pervasive tranquillity; it is almost always possible to escape the crowds.

We did not picnic on Signal Hill, but it was a destination for many a short drive, and we were profoundly familiar with the view: the vast Atlantic to the east, the harbour entry of the Narrows to the south, and the relatively sheltered streets of the city to the west. Being able to see our space from above offered us great aesthetic pleasure, and I believe it was also an intellectual affordance; I am not sure that children in flat places would gain the same sense of perspective and relationship among known places that we relished on Signal Hill.

Once a year, with much planning and anticipation, we drove nearly all the way "round the bay" to Northern Bay Sands, the only large sandy beach on the peninsula. It was one of the highlights of the summer and constituted an all-day outing (for a distance of roughly 135 kilometres, or slightly less than 85 miles). It provided our one annual swim in the Atlantic, so it was scheduled for August when the water would be maximally warmed up (a highly abstract concept, as it was still bitterly cold). We wound past the little outports and drove through exciting stretches where the road had been blasted out with dynamite; the rock walls on either side of the car were stark and intimidating. Northern Bay offered a vista of sand, some relatively gentle breakers, a shallow stream running across the beach to the sea, and a (disappointingly insignificant) cave. You could almost be an Enid Blyton child in that setting.

A number of Dad's colleagues and friends had summer cabins on local lakes, at that time well beyond the city limits though today most of these locations host luxury suburban homes. We never had a summer place of our own, so we often packed a lunch (so as not to impose on our hosts) and visited one pond or another. When I locate them on a map, I can trace the roads; we made the trips often enough that I have a relatively accurate recollection of the order of left turn and right turn; I experienced the camber of the journey literally through the seat of my pants and in my inner ear. Partly because I got queasy if I tried to read in the car, my sense of where we were going was undocumented; I did not try to make any connection between the roads we travelled and the road map that outlined our route. My experience of the geography of my home region was considerably more unmediated than my sense of its history.

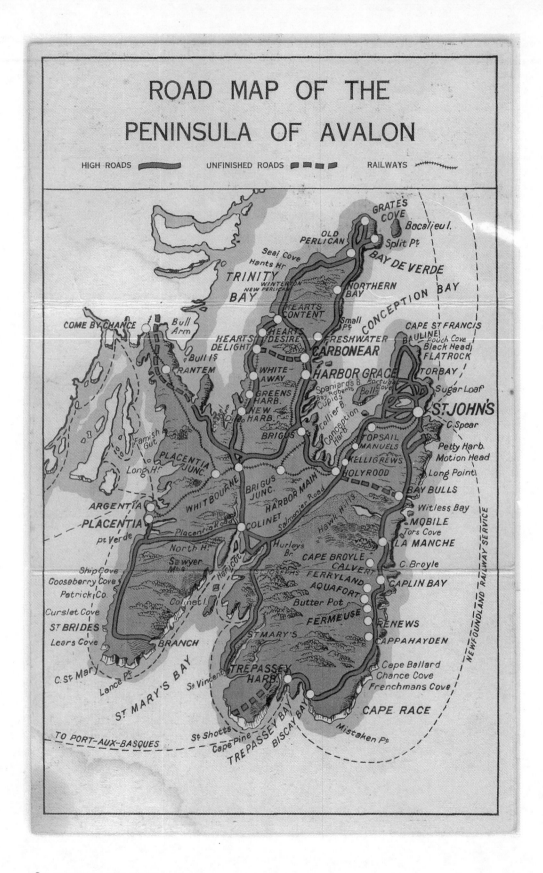

ROAD MAP OF THE
PENINSULA OF AVALON

HIGH ROADS ━━━━ UNFINISHED ROADS ▪ ▪ ▪ ▪ RAILWAYS ✕✕✕✕✕

In these summer cabins of the other teachers, I did most of my reading of American comics. Mum was opposed to comics, and we were not supposed to spend our allowance on them. Dad's teacher colleagues had no such qualms, or they relaxed them for the summer, and their children's bedrooms were crammed with *Donald Duck*, *Superman*, *Archie*, and other heritage titles. We read them greedily, even when the alternative attractions were swimming and boating. To this day if I hear "Scrooge McDuck," my immediate association is "Topsail Pond."

One favourite destination was Hughs Pond, where the Grade 1 teacher, Mrs. Duder, had a cabin. At school, she taught all four of us in turn (one of the few teachers we all shared), and everybody loved her. It was under her tutelage that I first took off as a reader, and I suspect all my brothers would say the same. At Hughs Pond, she took us out in her boat and taught us to row, another peerless gift to any child.

Mr. Deare, who delivered eggs to us, had a small farm in Topsail (not to be confused with Topsail Pond), and we learned much of what we understood about the origins of eggs and milk from visits to his smallholding. Mrs. Deare kept a great stack of old comics in her front room. Even in summer that room was icy, but I was occasionally permitted to go in and read the comics while my brothers rampaged around the acreage. I recall these comics as black and white, with no speech bubbles but a strip of narrative under each picture panel, the format most often seen in British comics, though there is a possibility they were American in origin. I have hunted diligently for a comic that resembles what I remember so clearly, but so far in vain. I read fragments of serialized, adapted classics in this format (*Lorna Doone* for certain, and I have a notion that the very implausible title of *Tess of the d'Urbervilles* was also on offer; unlikely as it seems, it also seems a strange thing to have invented). My experience of these classics was strongly informed not only by this novel format and radical abridgement but most of all by the fact that I read each one in fragments, out of order and never complete. Along with much of my series reading, this experience trained me to read as if I knew what was happening and to retain awareness of gaps in the story in hopes that they might be filled in by a later encounter with a prior episode.

Driving around the countryside suited me, and my literacy memories of specific destinations merge with a recollection of general contentment at simply enjoying the scenery. I frequently wandered off on my own, to meditate beside ocean or brook. Mum knew a great deal about wildflowers, and I took in a certain amount of information by osmosis, always resisting direct instruction but able to look in some detail at distinctions of petal and leaf and colour. My early awareness of the world included all these pleasures, and my feeling of geographical allegiance to Newfoundland was (and remains) wholehearted, not undermined by the frustration that marked my historical sense, though occasionally discouraged by fog and general dampness.

Reading the Landscape

I also encountered texts that taught me ways of looking at landscape. The gulf between my school reading and my recreational reading was not so damaging for my geographical sense as for my sense of history, partly because I could bring more of my own evidence to bear on my geographical awareness, and partly because the styles of writing were so divergent that there was no point in trying to unite them into any general sense of the world.

The chief architect of my landscape sensibilities was L.M. Montgomery, who was capable of making a sentimental fetish out of every flower, rock, or breeze. I loved all of Montgomery's characters with their vivid internal lives, but, as I've already suggested, there is no doubt that, as an author, she could be longwinded. Here is part of a single example out of very many lushly descriptive paragraphs about Silver Bush, the farm where Pat Gardiner grew up:

> It was so beautiful in the garden, in the late twilight, with a silvery hint of moonrise over the Hill of the Mist. The trees around it...old maples that Grandmother Gardiner had planted when she came as a bride to Silver Bush...were talking to each other as they always did at night. Three little birch trees that lived together in one corner were whispering secrets. The big crimson peonies were blots of darkness in the shadows. The blue-bells along the path trembled with fairy laughter. The late June lilies starred the grass at the foot of the garden: the columbines danced: the white lilac at the gate flung breaths of fragrance on the dewy air. (Montgomery, 1988/1933, pp. 17–18)

Pat of Silver Bush and *Mistress Pat* (1988/1935) may be fuelled by Montgomery's own sickness for home, but, for whatever reason, a gleaning of equivalent descriptions from the two books would fill a fair-sized volume all on its own. This very purple passage does succeed in presenting a distinctive climatic feature of eastern Canada: the late, very rushed spring that causes many flowers, elsewhere spread across a longer season, to blossom all at the same time. It did not occur to me that this seasonal extravaganza might be more diffused in other places; what I took in as I galloped through the pages (I never devoted much attention to these lengthy asides) was the claptrap about whispering secrets and fairy laughter. As with the historical toshery, it is not a literacy legacy that nourished me in any truly helpful way.

By contrast the Grade 6 geography book, *Newfoundland, Our Province* by Edith M. Manuel, provided me with perhaps the most sterile of all my school experiences. The book was dull, and my teacher's pedagogy was duller. Night after night, we memorized facts and figures, page by agonizing page. Day after day, she questioned us, up one row and down the next, always in the same order, two questions apiece every day. If we got the first question wrong, we stood up beside our desks for the remainder of the interrogation. If we also got the second question wrong, we were in detention. Frequent tests offered the only variation in this wretched and humiliating scenario.

It is perhaps not surprising that I hated this geography book with a passion I rarely mustered, good or bad, for any schoolbook. When I looked at it again in the Memorial archive, I found it hard to be dispassionate about it, even fifty years later. Certainly it does not seem to be a book designed to be memorized. To be fair to the author, her aim seems to be to pique children's curiosity about their province, and the book is substantially made up of questions. In our classroom, however, we had access to no other books that might help to answer the questions, so the approach simply increased my sense of futility about the whole enterprise.

Newfoundland, Our Province was published by A. Wheaton, educational publishers located in Exeter. Memorial's copy is listed as the fifteenth impression, dated 1960. No original publication date is provided. Here is an example of what we memorized so diligently. There is nothing harmful in this prose but nothing very catchy either.

> *Newfoundland has very few level stretches of land, some highlands ranging from 500 to about 2,670 feet above sea-level, much marshland and many river valleys. In fact, the surface of Newfoundland has been described as*

undulating or billowy like the waves of the sea. The longest range of hills
is on the west coast and is called the Long Range. It extends in three parts
from the south-west corner to within about fifty miles of Cape Norman.
From the relief map, try to find each of the three parts of the Long Range.
What bays or rivers separate each part?

  Other highlands, mostly under 1,500 feet, lie to the east of the Long Range.
Most of the land east of a line drawn from Notre Dame Bay to Fortune Bay
is below 1,000 feet in height. The general slope of the land is from north-west
to south-east, but there is also a slope towards the north-east. (Manuel,
1960, pp. 41–42)

The relief map in question, provided in black and white with a very inadequate key, served only to augment the frustration engendered by the incomprehensible final sentence in this quote. And Manuel herself would have been hard pressed to answer that question about the rivers from the information provided in her map.

My frustration turned to fury as the book embarked on a voyage around the island by coastal steamer. From page 53 to page 82, we imagined ourselves steaming from one outport to the next, memorizing not only the names of these hamlets but also their correct order. It was the kind of activity that led to the necessary invention of the term "soul destroying" to encompass the scale of pointlessness involved. I hated my teacher, I hated the book, and I came very close to hating Newfoundland in Grade 6.

But even as I struggled with this gradgrindery, we continued our drives, our picnics, our visits to friends in the country, and I lost none of my taste for the actual delights of the Avalon Peninsula. School simply became ever more compartmentalized; I never worked so hard to separate work and play as when I was actually learning about my own surroundings. The whole operation was a kind of intellectual and spiritual death that I still regard as probably the greatest shame of my entire educational experience.

As for the impact on my own discourses and ways of viewing the world, I can conclusively state that Montgomery won, at least in the short term. My evidence lies in an exercise book of poems I wrote in Grade 8 and Grade 9. This is what I wrote, for example, on February 21, 1962, halfway through Grade 8:

The Coming of Spring

When does the Spring come?
How can we tell?

A softly whispered word from a gentle south wind.
Spring is surely in the air.
A green shoot of crocus showing through the earth:
Soon there will be blossoms there.
A shrinking drift of snow and a puddle by its side;
Soon it will be grassy, where
'Tis now a wintry scene that is gloomy and grey,
Dingy from the winter wear.

How does the Spring come?
How can we tell?

Softly it steals in, softly thro' the dusk;
On a sunset path it treads,
With a faint air of flowers from the Springs long ago,
From the ancient flower beds.
Or it comes noisily in the gurgling of a brook
As it works free from the ice.
But no matter how or when the Spring comes
It never is the same Spring twice.

Subsequent titles include, "It's Spring," "August," "Spring Sunset," "Evening," "Autumn," "The Waterfall," "Advent of a Storm," "Summer Twilight," "Dawn," "June Twilight," and many more of this nature. A title that stands out from this pallid list is "The Forest Fire," written on May 1, 1962. I am sorry to say that the main plot point of the poem is that, while the fairies danced heedlessly, a small violet "tinted soft blue" is unnerved by the fact that a bank of smoke is obscuring the view. The final two verses serve up tragedy with a lachrymose flourish:

Not suspecting the fire the fairies danced.
Only the violet wondered, or guessed

> That death was near for these people entranced
>> These silver trees would burn with the rest
>> And the fire would ravage the sparrow's nest.

> It was much too late now to save them all.
>> Even then the crackling fire drew nigh.
> The fatal fire would end the fairies' ball.
>> The violet gave up with a sigh,
>> For all she had left to do was die.

The summer of 1961 had been a brutal year for forest fires, and it was a phenomenon of which I had some actual and close-up experience; walking through a burned-out wood, about a month after the conflagration ended, was (and remains) one of the eeriest events of my life. For a number of August days in 1961, the city streetlights came on in early afternoon because the smoke was so dense from fires many miles away. It may be cruel and unfair to say that this experience went through the Montgomery-filter before showing up as this poem, but certainly something of that kind occurred. A different child might have mapped out the acres of nearby destruction as reported in the local newspapers, but Miss Manuel succeeded in putting me off maps for a long time. My schema for storytelling and writing was that fairies were pretty essential. My genuine love for my surroundings was vivid and entirely fairy free, but it was inchoate and it would not have occurred to me to try to muster an original way of writing about my world.

Working through Limitations

Little in my early education taught me to look with an informed curiosity at my own environment. Instead, I learned to set up a watertight compartment marked "School," stowing all textbook information safely away, a skill it took a long time to unlearn. My recreational literacies served me no better in terms of educating me in an attempt to observe my own world without blinkers; whether the veils were historical toshery or scattered violet sunset clouds, the general effect was of obfuscation.

Fortunately, I had a wonderful art teacher from Grade 5 onward; she was very stern about the need to *look*. There was no textbook for nature study, and so I am limited in what I can revisit in terms of our early science classes, but I know that we were scaffolded in precise observation in that arena as well. Our social science education about our own space and society was less constructive. The province was poor, and the education budget was further fragmented by being divided among many denominations; it is perhaps not surprising that we had so little in the way of locally developed and locally focused textbooks. The good teachers did what they could with meagre materials; it was my bad luck to have unimaginative teachers in Grade 5 (for Newfoundland history) and Grade 6 (for Newfoundland geography). Other students fared better, but we were all constrained by lack of access to alternative sources.

As a consequence, along with many other Newfoundlanders I was electrified in 1974 when Peter Neary and Patrick O'Flaherty produced their seminal "Newfoundland and Labrador anthology," *By Great Waters*. In their preface, they describe their intention as offering readers "a selection of Newfoundland writing which would illuminate the unfolding of the province's history and culture, and at the same time merit attention as literature" (Neary & O'Flaherty, 1974, p. xi). It is hard for me to overestimate the impact of reading these primary accounts of Newfoundland experience. Had this book been available even fifteen years earlier, my education would have had a much better chance of firing my imagination.

It is very much a case of better late than never, however; and the flowering of Newfoundland writing since 1974 is testimony to the importance of engaging the whole mind in the study of the local world. Today I, along with other Newfoundlanders, can *look again* with new knowledge, deepening and enriching my understanding and delight.

15
Marking the Years

Timing

MASSEY'S (2005) IDEA OF SPACE as a site of multiple intersecting trajectories runs the risk of suggesting that time, however plurally configured, is a linear, arrow-shaped construct. But time is profoundly complex—even experiential time as lived by a young child. Much of my earliest conceptual understanding of time was cyclical. Day and night, summer and winter, old school year ending and new school year starting—these and other occurrences and recurrences shaped much of my first chronological understanding. *Kindergarten of the Air* taught me about days of the week in the time before school when really only Sunday had any distinctive identity—a conventional labelling experience without any meaningful content for me. Seasons, on the other hand, were existentially different from each other, and I knew them apart long before I knew their names.

The binding of space and time was formative. It was, for example, not simply a case of learning a generic schema for the seasons—it was winter and summer, fall and spring, *there*, in St. John's, Newfoundland, whose climate is often dismal. The city, perched on the edge of the North Atlantic, contends on a regular basis with the fogs that arise from the confluence nearby of the Labrador Current and the Gulf Stream.

The climate is forbidding enough that overwintering was unusual in the early days of the European fisheries. It is a maritime climate and temperatures are moderate, but Wikipedia describes well some of the daunting qualities of the St. John's weather:

> *Of major Canadian cities, St. John's is the foggiest (124 days), snowiest (359 cm (141 in)), wettest (1,514 mm (59.6 in)), windiest (24.3 km/h (15.1 mph) average speed), and most cloudy (1,497 hours of sunshine). Despite the high snowfall totals, St. John's experiences milder temperatures during the winter season in comparison to other Canadian cities and has the mildest winter for a city outside of British Columbia.* ("St. John's," n.d., n.p.)

A mild winter with lots of snow also entails much sleet and a great deal of thawing and freezing. And spring is worse. "Rain, drizzle, and fog" often comprise the reiterated weather forecast through that long, slow, cold, and late season that supposedly marks the advent of summer. Those picturesque icebergs that float down the east coast of the island dissolve into fog when they hit the Gulf Stream, and St. John's can go a long time without sight of the sun in a bad spring.

It is fair to say that a good Newfoundland summer is ravishing, and that fall can be utterly delightful. And I like winter (though I prefer the cold and sunny Edmonton version) and am as captivated by a snowy landscape as any Montgomery heroine. But in Newfoundland, and particularly in the exposed city of St. John's, the long, often very grey months between November and June make their imprint on the local character, and a grim stoicism is often necessary. A contemporary of mine in St. John's, Rosalind Gill (2013), explored the impact of that bleakness on a developing sensibility:

> *I'm made up of the "Itness" of the St. John's I grew up in. It's ontological. That's what's in me. Sleet and wet snow. Storm doors banging in the wind. Winter mornings when you crawled up the treacherously glittered-over hump of Leslie Street to get to the bus stop. The long sunless month of*

March, so raw, so elemental in its greyness, the dullness seeped right into
you. Staring up at the frozen South Side hills, I learned the meaning of philo-
sophical despair, figured out how totally absurd life is. Camus should have
come here to write his Mythe de Sisiphe. (*p. 34*)

A child growing up in this climate gains bleaker schemas of winter and
spring than the cheery versions found in much literature. Many areas of
Canada experience this gap. Paula Simons (2002), for example, writing in
the *Edmonton Journal*, expressed the seasonal dichotomy between life and
reading very clearly when she talked about television coverage of the death
of the Queen Mother, which occurred in the midst of a radiant British spring:

It was the perfect English storybook spring, like a scene out of The Secret
Garden *or* Watership Down. *It was the literary spring I always dreamed*
of, as a colonial prairie girl poring over the imperial children's classics.
No wonder an Edmonton spring, with its brown grass, its mud puddles, its
potholes, and its melting dog poop, always seemed like such a bleak disap-
pointment. No wonder it never seemed "real"—when all our books and
movies and TV *screens told us "spring" should look quite another way.* (B1)

The child learning about spring in much of Canada learns to measure
time via a long-term investment of endurance, and through small markers
of progress, often experienced in highly embodied ways as the heavy encum-
brances of winter clothing are gradually put off. While the final grimy
snowdrifts diminished, we often played our spring games under chill and
cloudy skies, but we still broke out the marbles ("alleys" to us) and the jacks
and hopscotch stones, and noted that things were getting slightly better.

A beautiful spring day is a triumphant event amid such low-grade expectations, and most springs would provide a sample of them—enough to
enable me to understand my Montgomery books and the lyric poems that
were my regular diet in school literature classes, and enough to encourage
me to contribute a few perfervid examples of my own. Even a young child
learned to appreciate such days all the more for their scarcity value. Overall,
however, my phenomenological experience of spring included a large dose
of those virtues celebrated by the lions at the New York Public Library:
patience and fortitude. I learned to hunker down, lower my expectations,
and wait rather than expect. It was not the kind of long-term attitude that I

ever saw reflected in my literature, where spring was a synonym for a glad, soft anticipation.

The first local representation of my own experience of winter and spring that I ever encountered came in visual rather than verbal form: a painting by well-known Newfoundland artist, Christopher Pratt. He attended Holloway School and Prince of Wales College, and was taught by my father, so it was not surprising that my parents acquired a book of his paintings (Silcox & Weiler, 1982). When I was in my mid-thirties, I found there an early watercolour that riveted my attention and my imagination. Called *Battery Road*, it depicts a street not far from Holloway School near Signal Hill. (The National Gallery of Canada provides a colour version online, and it is well worth a look.)

This painting shows the remnants of dirty snowbanks, the mix of ice and rain on the street, the pervasive fog. It conveys something even meaner, if that is possible: the utterly hostile feeling of a raw, dispiriting day in St. John's, inimical to the human body and the human spirit. Photographs of such weather—squalid rather than dramatically terrible—are rare, and a snapshot probably could not convey the same bleakness as this painting in any case.

The picture transfixed me. At last—my childhood life was *spoken* by somebody else. Someone *saw me* and understood my experience—and created a representation of it so I and others could stand back and contemplate it. Most of Pratt's work is highly stylized and does not include the level of explicit emotional content that I found here and that took me so by surprise when I opened the book. But I have lived with a (no doubt illegal) colour photocopy of that painting on my office wall ever since. It calls my childhood to full, vivid, phenomenological life every time I look at it. It is a space that holds many repeated traces of my daily combat with the elements that passed for spring, and in that way it sums up the qualities of duration that I learned through these recurring journeys.

Part of my deep understanding of time, from the heart of my first place, is that its lived durational qualities can be wildly variable. Two walks along the same route do not equal the same felt investment of time. The trudge and the dance mark the moments in different ways. The dance is more likely to be recorded; Pratt's painting is a tribute to the trudge.

Time was woven around me in rich, complicated, and protracted ways. It was often simpler in my reading materials, where authors, for example, frequently skipped over winter by the simple expedient of not mentioning it or slipping it by in a single paragraph ("That year the snows were heavy. It was not until April that…." or the like). Even as I learned the phenomenological force of real time, I was learning to come to terms with mediated time.

Gérard Genette has developed an extensive analytical toolkit to help us explore how writers manipulate time. For example, with regard to aspects of duration, he posits four possibilities for the author: ellipsis (in which the passing time of narrated events is simply omitted from the narration), pause (in which the narration lingers over considerations that involve no time passing within the narrated events), scene (in which there is some conventional form of match-up between narrated events and narration; a common example is dialogue), and summary ("a form with variable tempo") (Genette, 1980, p. 94).

Even as I learned to experience daily and seasonal time, I also had to learn to read mediated time. My own experience was not purely an asset. Genette's set of writerly tricks featured even in books for very young readers, as the following examples attest.

Building a Mediated Sense of Seasons

At the same time as I learned about narrative time, I was building up some sense of intertextual connections. The concept of intertextuality is contested, but in general terms it represents for readers some of the ways in which experience of one text may shape experience of another. In the case of a child learning to read from the kind of miscellaneous collection I have described in this project, some of those connections are necessarily very arbitrary in nature, and in the case of the kinds of mediocre fiction I often read, the connections may also be very limited, and limiting. I want to explore this idea in a small way in relation to two books I read and reread as a relatively new reader: *Honey Bunch: Her First Winter at Snowtop* (Thorndyke, 1946) and *The Children of Brookfield Hall* (Phillips, 1902). I will return to issues of narrative time after I have explored the glories of winter as offered in these two books.

The *Honey Bunch* series is a product of the Stratemeyer Syndicate, and my copy includes a list of thirty-two titles in the series. "Helen Louise Thorndyke" is a pseudonym. My edition of *The Children of Brookfield Hall* has unfortunately lost its title page, but WorldCat lists it as published by the Religious Tract Society in 1902. This book belonged to my grandmother, who was born in 1896, and my mother also read it as a child. I have been able to find little information about author Lydia Phillips.

Two Winter's Tales

Honey Bunch: Her First Winter at Snowtop (published late in the series in 1946) naturally includes many references to winter (a subject on which I was knowledgeable) and is relatively plot-based rather than featuring the episodic sentimentality of earlier books. Daddy Morton is called to help Mr. Vasa, whose distinctive items of jewellery are being copied in cheaper versions. Mr. Vasa has a little girl just Honey Bunch's age, and it is agreed that the Mortons will all go to the Snowtop Inn, near the Vasas' home.

The book is full of accounts of tobogganing, skating, snowman building, and the like. What particularly caught my attention, however (so distinctly that I remembered it more than fifty years later, which is remarkable given how much I have forgotten), was the account of how Mr. Vasa designed his jewellery:

One of the windows there [in Mr. Vasa's workshop] was open several inches. Every few seconds some snowflakes would blow inside, and the jeweler

*would catch a single flake on a small piece of ice-cold glass. Instantly he
would put it under his microscope and look at it.*

*A special kind of camera stood near by. If Mr. Vasa liked the design of the
snowflake, he would photograph it at once.* (Thorndyke, 1946, p. 136)

Mr. Vasa uses the snowflakes as models for his jewellery, so no two are alike.

This concept was clarified for me through my intertextual experience of
The Children of Brookfield Hall, which I read at about the same time. This
book tells the story of Winnie and Walter, their mother, and their Uncle
Charlie. At the start of the book, the children and their mother are just
arriving at Brookfield Hall from India, following the death of their father.
Uncle Charlie is an invalid whose life is brightened by the appearance of
his small niece and nephew. Their experiences in India have not prepared
them for the very different seasons of English life. Luckily Uncle Charlie
is a gifted naturalist and an instinctive teacher, very keen to show these
children the miracles of God's work on Earth as manifested in the English
countryside. Even more fortunately, he has the time and the budget to do
it thoroughly. When the children first see snow, he provides a large book of
snowflakes seen under a microscope to supplement what they take in with
their own eyes.

*The two gazed in wonder; for the page was covered with most beautiful
forms, some like stars, some like flowers—in short, every shape which could
be imagined, but very few alike.*

"But our snow doesn't look like this," said Walter.

*"Not to your eyes. That is a picture of snow as it is seen under a micro-
scope. We call these beautiful forms snow-crystals, and it takes many of
them to [make] a single snow-flake. But every one is perfect in its way, and
all are beautiful, though they are too small for our eyes to see without help."*
(Phillips, 1902, pp. 69–70)

Uncle Charlie is nearly as saccharine as Honey Bunch, and considerably
more didactic, but Winnie and Walter have a bit more spark to them, and
I found the book readable, although puzzling in places. This universe, so
clearly managed by God, did not resemble my own world in crucial ways.
For example, Chapter XI, "Snowdrops," begins irrefutably: "Winter was
really very long that year. For seven weeks after that first snowfall the frost
lasted" (p. 129). For us, winter was a minimum of four months in a good

year. God's role in this conundrum simply made the whole situation more cryptic.

Honey Bunch's winter was a bit more recognizable. We were familiar with the need to dress up warmly, a theme that recurs regularly in the *Snowtop* story; and we certainly had our share of winter sports. But there was little in this book of the primal physical realities of the winter I knew; everything was picturesque. The snow mounted in pretty drifts instead of stinging your cheeks in driving pellets. For a brief interval in the book, the snow falls so thickly that they can barely see where they are going, but the three family members are snuggled together in the cutter (whatever that was); there is none of that chill sense of being isolated from the entire world that regularly inflected my school walks on stormy days.

Even these simple stories manipulate time along Genettian lines. The summary line about the seven-week winter was probably more opaque to me than complete ellipsis would have been. The two scenes of the photographed snowflakes involve a double mediation, amounting to a pause in the story: the evanescent moment of a snowflake is rendered permanent by the mediation of the camera and the microscope inside the context of the story, and we readers linger further over the event of the snowflake's existence, an event that in our own lives would last only seconds. Such small details of the reading experience compound over time (the reader's own invested time), and young readers become more skilful in interpreting them.

These adjustments between narrative time, reading time, and experiential time are complex and constitute one element of what Wolfgang Iser (1978) labelled the gaps and blanks of a text: "Whenever the reader bridges the gaps, communication begins. The gaps function as a kind of pivot on which the whole text–reader relationship revolves. Hence the structured blanks of the text stimulate the process of ideation to be performed by the reader on terms set by the text" (p. 169).

I believe Iser is correct to the point that the terms are at least initially set by the text, though reader resistance may lead to more complex results than the obedient relationship he describes here. He makes no room, however, for the reader with discrepant information that cannot be rammed into the available gaps. The example of my surplus of knowledge about winter represents one such incongruity. While I was reading, I bowed to the supremacy of the text, but after I put the book down, I was often puzzled. Intertextuality allowed me to lend gap-filling information from one book to another, but perplexities remained.

Netsook is watching his father build the snow igloo which will be their winter house.

∧ *Netsook's igloo provided a more exotic answer to winter than anything we could supply in St. John's. (Atwood & Thomas, 1943, p. 36).*

[Collection of the author]

Real, Literary, and Ceremonial Moments of Winter

Winter featured in many texts of my early reading life. Section 2 of the geography book, *Visits in Other Lands*, featured Netsook and Klaya, Baffin Island siblings. Like us, Netsook and Klaya knew a lot about long winters, as the textbook pointed out:

> *"You mustn't think, though, that the end of the winter night means the end of winter. Each day the sun will stay above the horizon longer than it did the day before, but many weeks will pass before the days are longer than the nights. The weather will still be cold, and spring will be late in coming."* (Atwood & Thomas, 1943, p. 40)

But other aspects of Netsook and Klaya's lives were far more exotic than anything we could aspire to. The glamour of the igloo was indisputable; nothing about Pennywell Road was half so compelling.

Other school materials, such as stories in the school readers, domesticated winter, made it pretty, simple, romantic, and fun. We did, of course, have sunny days when we tobogganed in the picturesque clean snow behind our house like the children in the Grade 3 reader, but such actions represented only one facet of our winter experience.

In short, just to take the example of winter in our lives and in our books, we certainly brought a vast repertoire of life knowledge to bear on our reading, but we were actually burdened by an excess of winter experience.

> *From* The New More
Streets and Roads,
"Pictures in the Snow"
by Schoolland (Gray,
Monroe, Artley, &
Arbuthnot 1956, p. 6).
[*Collection of the author*]

Pictures in the Snow

One cold winter morning Northfield was
an all-white village. A cover of snow lay
over it. Snow lay on the streets, on the
trees, and on all the roofs.

The snow was fine for sliding. So the
village children had gone to North Hill
with their sleds—all except George and
Judy Bell. They were late. So they were
going a shorter way. They could save time
by going the back way through the woods.

6

The samples of text I offer here provide scientific, commercial, religious,
exotic, and domesticated stories of winter, but very little that describes the
nature of the endurance that even we as little children had to apply to our
own lives. The map of winter supplied by our books was simply not very
adequate to meet the fullness of our experience.

Of course there are children's books exploring just such questions of
endurance that I simply didn't read. *The Long Winter* by Laura Ingalls
Wilder, for example, answers many of my complaints about the over-pretty

nature of winter in books. Fortitude is required on almost every page, and the strength it takes for Laura to look winter full in the face is something I would have greatly appreciated.

Marking Time

Seasons were large-scale shifts in time, marked by major changes in weather and perhaps even more definitive changes in the kinds of games we could play (my friend and I always rejoiced when the clocks went back, for example, because we had a game called "Airplane" that could only—inexplicably—be played in the dark, before supper).

But our time was mediated by more than calendars, and our notions of time were not just large scale. A variety of news media marked the days and hours, with morning and evening newspapers, a morning news magazine on the radio, and Don Jamieson's television newscast at suppertime. Though not all are retrievable, these documents did mark time in a way more closely resembling that standard forward arrow, and they certainly inflected how we understood time.

Daily Life in the Media

Mum was groggy first thing in the morning, so Dad (who was not) was in charge of breakfast. He was a great believer in organization and a very energetic scheduler; and he never knew a routine moment that couldn't be improved by having the radio on. Our morning chores all were marked by the CBC's morning service. News, weather, advertisements, the news-magazine program called *The Musical Clock*, and numerous time checks—a time capsule recording of even a single morning's programming would be a very potent mnemonic for many moments now irretrievably past. My brother and I as adults once entertained ourselves (if not everyone else in the car) for a number of tedious driving hours by competing to see who could recite the largest number of radio advertisements from the 1950s; they were surprisingly adhesive.

The *Daily News* was also around every morning, and I'm sure Dad's schedule included time to give it a quick once-over. We kids vied for a read of the comics, and my brothers scanned the sports page. Otherwise, our capacity to be oblivious of the news content of both radio and newspaper was well-developed. The *Evening Telegram* arrived sometime after we got home from school, and at suppertime, we all watched Don Jamieson's *News Cavalcade*. This mix of international and local news, interspersed with local advertisements, was a major component of the day's rhythm, even if the actual content often meant nothing to us.

Mediated History

From the late 1950s onward, our Sunday evenings included Walter Cronkite's contemporary history program, *The Twentieth Century*, sponsored by the Prudential Insurance Company and branded with its image of the Rock of Gibraltar. As Wikipedia points out, this CBS program "presented filmed reports on news and cultural events that were important for the development of the 20th century. The show did not just present the events, but also interpreted them" (*The Twentieth Century*, n.d., n.p.).

Cronkite and his program were enormously important to my capacity to make any sense of my own time at all. My first school history book was entitled *The Stream of Time* (Ambler & Coatman, 1936), and it introduced me to the ancients. *The Twentieth Century* was my introduction to the stream of my own time (though, as I recall, it did not run to any kind of coherent sequence). It provided almost my only access to any kind of information about the Second World War; my father was one of those legendary veterans who almost never spoke of his overseas experience, and school history never dealt with anything so current. The program also gave a certain amount of international context to my somewhat more advanced understanding of the First World War, a conflict that was paradoxically more "present" in St. John's life, in the haunting aftermath of the slaughter of the Royal Newfoundland Regiment.

It is surprisingly difficult to find any traces of this television program; even YouTube has let me down. It ran for 121 thirty-minute episodes over nine years, from 1957 to 1966; I watched many episodes, and it no doubt contributed to my propensity (not entirely defeated even now) to think of the great world wars in black and white. Its framing perceptions were, of course, American, but I had little external experience to enable any kind of critique. I simply took the trustworthy Cronkite at his word.

Recording School Life

The rituals of daily life were also recorded in school documents that are inherently temporal. My report cards have vanished, but I do have a few copies of the school newspaper. *The Pow-Wow* (an acronym for "Prince of Wales Words of Wisdom") was laboriously typed and mimeographed.

In keeping with its title, it bears an image of an Indian chief in full regalia, a colonial stereotype no doubt regarded as witty in its day.

Clubs were for students Grade 9 and above, so, by leaving St. John's at the end of Grade 8, I missed all the action that *The Pow-Wow* reports:

> *The following clubs were formed: Biology Club, under Miss Hilliard; the Glee Club, formed by Mr. Osmond; the Science Club with Mr. Ivany as leader; the Debating Club, having the capable assistance of Mr. Russell; Mr. Andrew's [sic] Ping-Pong Club; the Chess Club with Mr. Hoyles; the Bowling Club; the Photography Club; the Maths Club; the Sewing Club; and the Theology Club under Rev. McKim.* (The Pow-Wow, 1961, n.p.)

Mr. McKim also ran a boys' band with seventy-two members, but *The Pow-Wow* was able to console the female students: "Don't fret girls, there's still a part for you to 'play' in this band. Mr. McKim is looking for majorettes....You will have to be trained, of course, but it will add to the band and take from your middle!" (n.p.). Remarkably, every issue in my possession concludes with two long and full pages of school gossip, along the lines of this sample from April 6, 1962: "George W. is going out with Linda. I saw Bill W. in the show with Kathy P. last weekend. Joan B. and Wayne M. are going out together. Bob Noseworthy and Gail are going steady. We also heard that Dean and Pam like each other, that's the story" (n.p.). The heteronormative pressure is palpable. No matter what you might feel about what was said about you, to be left out was even more humiliating. This is literacy as a form of social control with a vengeance (all seen as good, clean fun at the time, of course).

The yearbooks offered less prurient insights. They were printed and could contain photos—mostly formal shots of school teams and those clubs that *The Pow-Wow* enumerated, a head shot of each graduating student along with a few descriptive phrases, and some pictures of school events. There was a section for student writing; I published the occasional florid poem. We may have been living in an isolated city on the edge of the continent, but every school in North America would have recognized our yearbook.

Recording Home Life

As I learned to process mediated time in my fictions, I also set about preserving some of my own time for future reference, frequently remediating at second remove through curating media materials that were in some way relevant to my own life. I collected, I edited, I arranged. I cut and glued. I wrote accounts of my own, usually very short. A range of domestic documents still survives to testify to this instinct and to present snatches of saved time from my youth.

Highlights in the Scrapbook

For two different years, I kept my own scrapbook of "current events," mostly items of limited domestic interest but intriguing to read now. Unfortunately only the later one (1961–1962) survives; the 1958–1959 book has vanished.

The 1961–1962 volume would be recognizable to many people, with its cover featuring a deer and some wild fowl at the waterside. It cost 29 cents; I got my money's worth in terms of capturing significant moments of my life during that year.

Two major events of 1961 included celebrities far beyond our normal expectations or experience and dominated the early pages of my scrapbook. Lady Baden-Powell attended a Guide rally in St. John's that was also attended by me. Hard on the heels of this visit came the opening of the new campus of Memorial University, one of Joseph Smallwood's chief ambitions fulfilled. I marched in the enormous parade of schoolchildren that he decreed symbolically appropriate for the occasion; Eleanor Roosevelt cut the ribbon; and I filled many pages of my scrapbook with items from the newspapers' special supplements.

More routine items followed: concert programs, birthday cards, exam results, and hockey schedules. Gala red headline print was broken out on February 20, 1962, for John Glenn's space travels, and I duly clipped and glued. I saved newspaper reports of sports days and prize givings. One of the last entries in the book is a newspaper clipping (source and date not supplied) about my father winning a fellowship of $2,400 to help subsidize his studies at the University of Alberta. "Mr. McCurdy will leave July 1 for Alberta," says the article. "He will be accompanied by his family during his two-year leave of absence from Prince of Wales" (source unknown). In this timely way, my scrapbook marks our departure from St. John's on the date that closes this project.

Mundane Records in the Diary

On two occasions (birthday 1959 and Christmas 1961), I received lockable five-year diaries. Both survived and, in their limited way, they represent a successful enterprise of pinning down some daily details of time passing, one of the major accomplishments of literacy.

As is often the case, these volumes testify to initial good intentions and a woeful lack of follow-up. The entries are excruciatingly dull or painfully self-remonstrating on the subject of unkept resolutions. Occasionally a spark of real life slips through into the tiny entries in the first diary; for example, on November 7, 1960, I wrote: "Made deal with boys for Christmas presents. They supply wool; I make presents. 1¢ hr." Or a March 1960 entry: "Dad's birthday. Went up from music, bought tie and handkerchiefs but lost handkerchiefs. Dad liked tie." Many of the 1959–1960 entries, however, simply mention tests and exams, marks returned, skating sessions, school hockey games, and the occasional birthday party. Sometimes a picnic is recorded, but a picnic was a commonplace enough treat that it didn't necessarily warrant breaking out the diary.

With the later volume, I made an executive decision from the outset to use the entire page rather than the 1/5 slot allotted to each year. This choice makes room for a bit more of the texture of daily life, but the entries remained pedestrian; for example, January 12, 1962:

> *Mum and Bruce are sick today so I'll have a jolly weekend.*
> *We had singing this morning and we did festival pieces.*
> *After school this afternoon, we had House elections for captains. Pitts girls will know the results on Monday. The grade six girls and on up voted this year for the first time.*

The 1962 diary is a vivid reminder of why there will never be an adolescent sequel to this project. As a preteen, I was heavily into self-examination and recriminations about resolutions not kept, self-improvement not taken seriously enough. My resolutions for 1962 were solemn and sincere, but it is hard not to smile now at the mix of small- and large-scale virtues encapsulated in a short list:

> *New Year's Resolutions*
> 1. *I will not cry at every little thing.*
> 2. *I will not eat so much.*
> 3. *I will make my bed and tidy my room every morning.*
> 4. *I will be honest in the little things as well as in the big things.*

I am not sure how well I succeeded with resolution #4, but the diary testifies—and I can remember perfectly well—that I was a flat failure with the first three.

Pre-adolescent rites of passage gain the occasional mention. On January 5, 1962, I wrote, "Yesterday afternoon I went to the library and downtown. I got a lipstick—Tangee Natural. It seems queer for me to have lipstick and a compact. For years I played at having them and now I do."

I did record John Glenn's flight into space, and the diary includes one reason why I was so impressed by it: at school, our normal boring day was interrupted from time to time by news of the space flight, supplied by a radio pushed up next to the public address system. Children today might take such a media intervention in the day for granted, but for us it meant that something historic and auspicious was occurring.

So I preserved snippets of my daily realia. Alas, most pages are blank.

Reading even brief glimpses of my early adolescence flashing in the 1962 diary reminds me that the closure of this project represented by the end date of June 30, 1962, is an artificial conclusion. Time did not stop on that date. It is simply a "dipping-out" point in an ongoing story.

One of the last major diary entries in 1962 comprises three pages covered in dense pencil. The unusual length, reinforced by numerous exclamation points, clearly refers to an intense experience, but it also contains a reminder of the potency of literacy. To cut a long story short, it describes a surprise farewell party held for me and a classmate just before we both moved away to separate destinations. I started reading it with the utmost perplexity, wondering what on Earth this special entry could be describing. Even after reading the full description, I have only the slightest memory of the party itself. But toward the end of the long entry, I made this confident assertion: "Whew! It's been an exhausting day but one I'll always remember."

Well, I haven't remembered. Even when prompted, I didn't remember. But the little brown book has remembered for me, charged with the power of *writing down*.

The McCurdy News

We marked time in one other way, in what are perhaps the most beguiling of the family documents at my disposal. In the spring of 1961, my brother and I took up the idea of creating a family newspaper, to be named *The McCurdy News*. My recollection is that this publication took life because Dad was heading off to Alberta for the summer to work on his M.ED. Whether that fact was the originating spark or not, Dad reported that all his friends gathered when an edition of *The McCurdy News* arrived in the mail. And small wonder! Who could resist the news digest crammed onto page one of the first edition?

2¢   May 15, 1960   1st Edition

The McCurdy News

Main Section   Editors - Margaret & Earle McCurdy

STORM WINDOWS TAKEN DOWN
by Earle

On Saturday morning all our storm windows were taken down by David Parsons, Billy Dobbin, David and Bruce McC. and me. All helpers received 10¢ from Mr. McCurdy. Everyone bought a bottle of pop up at Jardine's

Bird's Nest
by Margt.

In the tree in front of 200 LeMarchant Rd. there is a bird's nest. It is not known whether the birds are still building or sitting on eggs. People are asked not to climb that tree

Guide Cookies
by M. Margt.

Girl Guide cookies are being sold by all the Guides in the city.

Church Parade
by Marg.

The guides of Prince of Wales College attended a church parade at the Kirk this morning.

Advertisments

For Sale	Wanted	Wanted
1 dozen packages of Guide cookies waiting to be sold at 200 LeMarchant Rd. Notify Margaret McCurdy at the above address	Ideas for game to make for Earle McCurdy's toymakers badge in cubs will be gratefully received	A maid so that we will not have to clear up our rooms and clear tables and do dishes

Sports

Football Game

Pat Dobbin Jr. Star In 4-1 Victory

WINNERS	G.A.	PTS.	LOSERS	G.A.	PTS.
Pat Dobbin	3 1	4	D. Parsons	1 0	1
Ebby McGraw	1 1	2	B. Dobbin	0 0	0
Earle McCurdy	0 0	0	J. Lush	" "	"
TOTAl		6	D. Sellars	" "	"
			TOTAl		1

The reproduction is not very clear, so I will quote the headline story (by Earle) in full.

STORM WINDOWS TAKEN DOWN
On Saturday morning all our storm windows were taken down by David
Parsons, Billy Dobbin, David And Bruce McC and me [*the last two words*
squeezed in belatedly above the line]. *All helpers received 10¢ from Mr.*
McCurdy. Everyone bought a bottle of pop up at Jardine's. (May 15, 1960)

My folder contains eight editions, spread over three summers with one Christmas issue. *The McCurdy News* was a reliable source of entertainment for many years—first when it was originally pencilled laboriously onto the page, second when Dad and his classmates passed the copies around in Edmonton, and then later, any time a few family members thought to haul out the file for a reminiscent laugh. As adults, we would occasionally turn out a new issue for a family get-together, but these later efforts were self-conscious pastiches and lack the earnest charm of the article about taking down the storm windows, in which the purchase of a bottle of pop is news.

Many issues carried very detailed sports reports with columns of statistics lovingly assembled according to all the conventions of the real sports page in the newspaper. There were advertisements, and at one point we ambitiously developed a McCurdy News Seal of Approval ("Garanteed [*sic*] Satisfaction"). In the issues sent to Dad in Alberta, Mum sometimes colonized a few inches to offer a Behaviour Report—not our favourite element of the operation.

Our parents, of course, had nothing to lose from this project. It kept us occupied for hours, supplied family talking points for much longer periods of time, amused Dad far from home, and gave us practice in reading and writing, though nobody would argue the exercise did anything for our penmanship. We internalized many ideas about the layout of the page and the complexity of making our columns of prose match up to each other. The inconsequentiality of the content is staggering, but these small items comprised important daily components of our world. Apart from the fact that we all desperately missed Dad (I remember the scalding tears I shed when he departed that first summer, to be away from home for six long weeks), *The McCurdy News* is perhaps the most joyful text in this whole collection. Our long-ago enthusiasm springs from its grubby pages. Its artless "news" items are redolent of the rather scruffy dynamics of family life, not dressed up for company but just the ordinary daily version. For all the elaborate conventionality of its page layouts, it bursts with careless energy.

Mum had a temporary job in the summer of 1961. *The McCurdy News* recorded its conclusion and added details far too mundane ever to be remembered by anybody:

> *Mrs. S.G. McCurdy has finised* [sic] *working and is spending her days entirely at home. Her children have also been earning money by doing the housework.*
>
> *Both David and Bruce McCurdy have bought Corgi Bentleys with opening trunks and a spare tire. Earle McCurdy has bought a baseball. Margaret McCurdy put $5.00 in the bank and has $1.00 left to spend.*
> *(August 6, 1961)*

I am very sorry that there is no report on how I spent my dollar, though I can't think what I could have bought to match the appeal of those Corgi Bentleys with their spare tires. Our literate endeavours preserved a glimpse of raw ordinariness beyond even the capacity of photographs to record; the scale of events under review is simply too small. In Genette's terms, we were creating summaries of our own local events, undeterred by the trivial nature of the details being marshalled. As participant-recorders, we glossed over weeks of housework, but the rhythm of our account slowed right down to savour the acquisition of our rewards (or to savour the anticipation of such rewards, in my own case) in a formula more closely approaching the pause of an appreciative stasis.

Thus "the times" were captured and displayed by my siblings and me in assorted ways. It is my good fortune (and a tribute to my mother's care in storing these treasures) that so many of them remain available to me today. It has been a strange experience to delve into them in sequence—the scrapbook, the diaries, the school publications, the family newspaper. Not even the picture books have so strongly drawn me back to an earlier stage in my life. The fact that all of these documents come with dates attached somehow makes them even more lively and intense.

Some of the elements of these documents are unlikely to be replicated by today's children. Contemporary families might well produce their own newspaper, but they would be much more likely to type it and the computer would set up the columns and the tables in much less haphazard form; the final result would be more polished but maybe less satisfying, and the sense of *touching* the past that comes through so strongly with my shabby originals of *The McCurdy News* would be considerably abated. Yet contemporary children may be able to produce multimodal records of family life that supply their own vivid slice-of-life appeal.

In any case, this time travelling has been a poignant experience, a testimonial to the strength and evocativeness of children's own literate powers, and a reminder that the passage of time is marked personally as well as locally and universally. Some of the collected trajectories of a given space are very small.

16

Shape-Shifting Discourses

Mutating

THE NORTH ATLANTIC PROVIDES a physical boundary to St. John's, but many of the limits of our world were discursively constructed and surprisingly contingent. I spent much of my childhood coming to terms with regularity, pattern, and singularity, but, like other children, I then had to find ways to process the ramifications of plurality. Newfoundland itself provides a paradigmatic and complex case study of unreliable discourses, many of which once seemed sacrosanct. The startling shifts in how Newfoundland has been understood and described over the past fifty years remind us that the world is radically and profoundly provisional and can be only provisionally described. In this brief chapter, I will outline the nature of these discursive changes as a modest case study of contingency.

During the early 1950s, when I was first figuring things out, a new civics was being instituted in Newfoundland as the dominion became a province. Since that time, almost every descriptor that I mastered in my childhood has been troubled or upturned or completely discredited. The complete-ness of the list is startling, and it serves as a telling reminder that, even as our reading lives are guided by the local and particular of our settings, as well as by the cognitive universals of our active minds, we must learn to shift our local as well as our global understanding.

I began to understand my world from my body and my bedroom outward. My initial awareness was of a domestic setting that, in all its essentials, probably greatly resembled many other domestic settings of its era (though it lacked the suburban aura of many of my fictions). The wider social world of St. John's was in many ways more specific and individual. The impact of this wider setting on my developing literacy was consider-able and important—and vice versa. My literacies did not all serve a better understanding of my home, nor did my home setting always help me to make sense of what I encountered in print and on TV.

I began my reflections about literacy in small and local ways. My reading development was rooted in a particular time and place. My ability to make sense of the world using St. John's as my model signifier led to a sense of location—but understanding dislocation is also part of becoming a contem-porary reader.

My childhood in Newfoundland occurred at a point of great social and political change, as I was partially aware at the time. The decades following my cut-off point of mid-1962 led to revolutionary rethinking of many discourses describing this island. In this chapter, I address these upheavals in local terms; I also consider more broadly the paradoxical importance of instability in the developing capacities of *any* reader.

Margaret Mahy, writing about being a New Zealand reader, directly addresses the idea of volatility as part of the life of a locally rooted reader. Mahy talks about fault lines in her existence: the geological fault lines that riddle New Zealand and the metaphorical fault lines that arise out of being a European reader in a Polynesian setting. She reiterates some of Malouf's points about the first place, in eerily similar terms; and she raises some very interesting questions about "What next, after the first place is clarified?"

I did indeed grow up with a fault line running through me, but that is a very New Zealand feature when you consider that it is a country of earthquakes and volcanoes....Dislocations can expose the secret nature of the land. They can make for an intensely interesting landscape, provided one does not come to feel that a landscape full of fault lines is the only legitimate kind. Dislocations made me a world reader rather than a local one: they made me contingent rather than categorical. (Mahy, 1991, pp. 11–12)

Mahy raises important questions about how a locally placed reader may move from "categorical" to "contingent." If my original "categories" were grounded in the history and geography of the Avalon Peninsula, how did I learn to move away in metaphorical as well as literal terms?

If we take Massey's plural definition of space as a baseline, part of the answer was there all along, and I had only to recognize it, in true fairy-tale fashion. The "categories" that I learned as a child were *themselves* contingent, and as I have kept in touch with them (as we say) through my adolescent and adult life, I have moved into contingency whether I planned to do so or not. The trajectories passing through my space in the 1950s have kept moving. The story of Newfoundland and how we understand it has also changed fundamentally in the fifty-plus years since 1962, and these developments dramatize the idea of discursive contingency in radical ways.

Contingent Discourses: "Send for Rewrite!"

I inhabited St. John's and the Avalon Peninsula in both spatial and chrono-logical terms, and as a child acquiring literacy, I also unavoidably acquired local discourses that shaped my interpretation of my home. Through a historical accident of timing, much of what I learned of the history and geography of Newfoundland in the 1950s and early 1960s became obsolete only a few years later. Some changes are concrete, others involve a mix of historical and scientific discoveries that altered our understanding of the nature of the physical and social make-up of our local world. Developments in the publishing world also affected what explanations and narratives have been made broadly available. Inevitably, perspectives on the physical and social make-up of Newfoundland have changed.

Perched on the easternmost coast of Newfoundland, the most easterly urban community in North America, the foggy city of St. John's offers a veritable case study of shifting discourses. Yet though the city has expanded hugely since my time, its physical geography feels implacable and unchangeable. Stone is never very far beneath your feet in St. John's. Signal Hill and the Southside Hills shelter the city from the Atlantic, and their large outcroppings of bedrock are visible from most parts of the city. These cliffs emanate a strong sense of solidity and reliability, and provide a constant orientation for the city's inhabitants: Signal Hill to the east, the Southside Hills roughly to the south.

But much about the city is nowhere near so permanent as its rocky hills connote. The list of narratives about my home that were rendered unreliable either as I learned them or very shortly thereafter is comprehensive and extremely disconcerting.

Physical Geography

City historian Paul O'Neill (2008), in a passage very unsettling to any St. John's inhabitant, points out that the streets that run up and down the harbourside hill (which today feel so permanent and definitive of the shape of the city) were once rivers: "Originally a line of beach cliffs ran close to what is now the north side of [Water Street], and there was a narrow foot path along this shore interspersed by many rivers and several marshes. The coves, which have since been covered by roads and buildings were the mouths of these rivers and marshes" (p. 621). The hills themselves would have been different, drained by such streams and waterfalls.

O'Neill's work would have spoken very strongly to me if it had been available in my youth. When I was sixteen, a school assignment led me to read some of Sir John A. Macdonald's personal letters; I was instantly fascinated by the vividness of the local details. Equivalent voices from the past of my own city would have mesmerized me, and I would have leapt to answer the invitation to imagine "this but different."

Geology

During the 1960s, just after my project's arbitrary closing date of 1962, geologists developed theories of tectonic plate movement that altered our view of how the world originated. Scientists on the Avalon Peninsula contributed significantly to this work, as the ancient Avalon is composed of conjoined fragments from three different continents.

As perhaps the ultimate metaphor for that contingency, Signal Hill is a plural composite of a variety of competing forces, as this lay account makes plain:

> The rocks of Signal Hill tell stories too—of the geological past, more than 550 million years ago. At that time the Avalon Peninsula was part of Gondwana [a supercontinent in deep geological history that fragmented to form parts of the Southern Hemisphere continents—and the Avalon Peninsula].

Tectonic forces wrenched the continent, uplifting large blocks of crust and creating basins between the higher regions.

    The St. John's area was in such a basin....[O]ver time an alluvial plain of river sediment formed as the basin filled in.

    Later events tilted the rock layers on edge, with the oldest in the west and the youngest in the east. The walk [on Signal Hill] from Outer Battery Road to North Head is literally a walk through time. (Hild, 2012, p. 210)

Today a geological museum on Signal Hill points out some of these contingencies and features a grand wall of living rock; but in my childhood a stone was something you simply took for granted as permanent.

History

In 1969 archaeologists uncovered the remains of the Viking settlement in northern Newfoundland, changing the historical record in irrevocable ways. Suddenly the attested timeline for a European presence in this area was doubled, from five hundred to a thousand years. I had to question the "facts" I had learned in the Grade 5 history book—a book that had not really supplied any kind of intellectual tools for questioning its own didactic certainties.

Architecture and Urban Planning

Not just riverbeds are impermanent. Over and over again through its history, St. John's was destroyed by fire. Water Street can plausibly claim to be the oldest commercial thoroughfare in North America, but most of the city buildings were built little more than a century ago. Architectural landmarks, where not destroyed by fire, were often obliterated through civic and corporate decisions, with an equal mix of casualness and ruthlessness. The harbour, the reason for the city's existence in the first place, has been dug out, filled in, broadened, narrowed, shortened, and otherwise altered over the centuries. The fisheries that, even in my lifetime, used to dominate the waterfront have largely disappeared from the city. The finger piers that zigzagged along the waterfront have been replaced by the straight line of Harbour Drive. Public access to the harbour is much reduced because of an anti-terrorist fence, built to protect the cruise ships that now contribute to the civic economy.

Politics

Protocols of governance have been equally transitory. The island of Newfoundland and the territory of Labrador experienced three very distinctive forms of governmental structures in the twentieth century alone: modified self-government as a separate dominion in the British Empire at the start of the century, direct rule from London in 1934, after the bankruptcy, and its current position as a province of Canada since 1949. St. John's served as capital city in all three arrangements, but its role kept changing. When I moved there in 1950, it was newly coming to terms with life as a provincial capital in Canada.

Climate

St. John's' well-earned reputation for a harsh climate would seem to be a fixture. But climate, as we all now appreciate, is in flux. The impact of the shrinking Arctic ice cap on the Labrador Current is open to question; what is not debatable is that the Labrador Current dominates the weather of St. John's, and any effects on its behaviour are highly salient. Even our discussion of the weather is more tentative than it used to be.

Economics

In 1962 I could not have imagined that a mere thirty years later the cod moratorium would shake the economics of the province to its very foundation. The pulp and paper industry has also collapsed, and some mines are exhausted. Hydroelectricity is a source of political disagreement and ferment. Oil and gas bring new money to the area, but there is concern about how long the boom can last. The tourist industry attempts to commodify the most romantic elements of the local culture I drew upon to leverage my own understanding of the world (Wyile, 2011). Such reification diminishes this culture and points to the limited and transitory nature of what I thought I knew in the 1950s.

In short, the economic foundations of this society have broadly and profoundly altered over a period of less than half a century. It is a story still in motion.

Civic Institutions

St. John's has a long, honorable history of activity in arts, letters, and science. In the nineteenth century, the city boasted libraries, reading rooms, theatre stages, and a museum. But the strictures of poverty and the different economic blows of the Great Fire and the Great War meant that civic life in the first part of the twentieth century was seriously impoverished. St. John's acquired its own public library only in 1936, and the Newfoundland Museum was closed between 1934 and 1957. The region's ability to sustain its own cultural records was in doubt for much of the twentieth century. The richness of the surviving materials today is a testimonial to decades of very devoted work, against heavy odds.

The Rooms, opened in 2005, transforms the urban skyline and also revolutionizes how the city and the province represent themselves—to themselves and to visitors. The architecture exudes self-confidence and a sense of assurance that the story of this place is interesting and important.

Education

In 1961 I participated in the parade of school students celebrating the new campus of an expanding Memorial University, the manifestation of a new social compact with a much greater focus on education. Memorial itself has contributed in many disciplines to our improved understanding of the province.

At the school level, the old denominational breakdowns have vanished (although not until 1997). There is now public education in Newfoundland as understood elsewhere. No longer do you participate in a religious sorting exercise simply by naming the high school you attended.

Social Geography

Already by 1962, the Smallwood government had begun its drive to relocate far-flung communities into more centralized locations. The resettlement program hit its peak in the 1960s, and the social geography of Newfoundland was altered irrevocably ("No Great Future," 2004). By the 1970s, that program was in abeyance, but the outflow of the population to the mainland of Canada and elsewhere in pursuit of opportunities to earn a living continued unabated. Those who returned as the oil boom took hold had a different perspective on Newfoundland's place in the world.

Civic Ethos

In my childhood, authority figures were authoritative, even if (as with the example of Premier Smallwood) their control was sometimes arbitrary and erratic. In Newfoundland today, as elsewhere, that master narrative of authority, that taken-for-granted stricture that "father knows best" is contested—in gender terms and also in many other ways. The culture of deference that I remember from my youth has been disrupted in thorough, sometimes cynical ways. Indeed, Newfoundland is now home to some of Canada's most significant political satirists and comedians.

Suffrage and the Role of Women

Although I was not aware of it in the 1950s, Western certainties about the place of women in society were already in a condition of pre-turmoil, so to speak. Not long after the conclusion of my time span for this project, my mother acquired a copy of *The Feminine Mystique* (Friedan, 1964/1963), and I read it as soon as she was done with it. I was fourteen or fifteen, and I could never feel the same way again about what I had taken to be eternal verities about how to be a good woman.

I did not know about the battles for female emancipation that had earlier occurred in St. John's. The first campaign for female suffrage in Newfoundland took place in the 1890s, led by the Woman's Christian Temperance Union (Morgan, 2014, p. 33). In 1908 an extended public debate about the vote for women led to the production of a suffrage manifesto by Amine Gosling (later famous as a driving force behind the establishment of the Gosling Memorial Library in St. John's and the donor of her husband's and her own book collections, which formed a core section of its early holdings). The First World War shook up many assumptions, and by 1921, female property owners were permitted to vote in the St. John's municipal election (Duley, 2014, p. 138). In 1925, as a result of broad social pressure across the island, a woman's suffrage bill passed unanimously in the House of Assembly: women had to be twenty-five in order to vote, while men could vote at twenty-one (Duley, 2014, p. 142).

Such a complete rethinking of women's place in the world was long under way when I began to pay attention to what it meant to be a girl in the 1950s. All I knew at that time was certainties. Like many women of my age and older, I owe a great debt to Betty Friedan for pointing out the restrictions of this received wisdom and, with many other engaged women, unleashing a force for change that resounds into our own day.

Definitions of Race

As I was moving toward the close of this project in 2014, another truism of Newfoundland history was thrown into upheaval. There is still agreement that the Beothuk died out in the nineteenth century, but there is now controversy over the survival of the Mi'kmaq (usually perceived as based in Nova Scotia) on the west coast of the island.

The 1949 Terms of Union of Confederation make no mention of Aboriginal peoples in Newfoundland, and, as a result, they are not subject to the Indian Act. The government, in 1949, believed there were 530 First Nations people on the island (though considerably more in Labrador), and they were "perceived to have assimilated, intermarried or chosen to hide their identity" (Friesen, 2014, A8). By the twenty-first century, however, in the face of changing attitudes about Aboriginal ancestry, there was sufficient demand from locals that the government set up a registry for a landless band named the Qalipu, open to people who could prove Mi'kmaq descent. To their consternation, they received more than 100,000 applications—about one-fifth of the population of the province. At last report, the government was moving to tighten the criteria for applying.

There is no indication that these Mi'kmaq people lived in the eastern part of the province, so I do not have to rethink many of my own observations of the very white population that surrounded me in St. John's. Nevertheless, given the foundational nature of that story of the extinction of the Beothuk, this new development is disconcerting, to put it mildly. My very strong suspicion is that, in the 1950s, many more people would have hesitated to identify themselves in this fashion. The idea that Newfoundland was bringing into Confederation an Indigenous population proportionately higher than that of Ontario or Alberta or British Columbia might well have changed the tone of the discussions in those overtly racist times. The whole controversy over who is entitled to claim what offers yet another spin to a discourse that I once thought was safely settled.

Linda Cullum and Marilyn Porter, who in 2014 published a book about the years 1900–1950 in St. John's, talk about "unspoken or elided categories" of ethnicity (p. 10), and observe,

> [T]he overwhelming "whiteness" of all classes in St. John's in the period rendered ethnic identity invisible to the participants. There were, of course, non-white people in the country: diverse Aboriginal populations, Mi'kmaq, Métis, Inuit, and Innu, lived on the island and especially in the geographically distant Labrador, the boundaries and ownership of which were finally settled in 1927. There were also small but significant groups of immigrants,

especially Chinese, Lebanese, and Jewish people who arrived during the late nineteenth and early twentieth centuries. Despite the presence of Aboriginal populations and ethnic immigrant groups, between 1900 and 1950 Newfoundland was still one of the most Caucasian parts of Canada. Those holding power were overwhelmingly white, and this white racialized positioning of the state and society, and its contribution to Newfoundland's sense of identity is implicit. (p. 10)

That implicit sense of whiteness certainly lingered into the 1950s and beyond. The ethnic groups often chose the United Church school system (as the least assertive in doctrinal matters, I believe), but there were only a handful in total; in my own grade and those just above and just below me, I recall one Chinese boy and a total of four or five Jewish students. In my mind, they all belonged to our white culture because I could not imagine any other.

In fact, I could not have imagined Cullum and Porter's description. I remember an occasion when I was in my late teens, meeting an Innu person for the first time (of course, I thought of him as an Eskimo). Although I knew this person normally lived in Labrador, I was still thoroughly startled even to think of an Indigenous inhabitant anywhere in my province, so completely had I imbibed the guilt narrative of complete extermination. A dispassionate nuancing of the taken-for-granted whiteness of my culture, such as that provided by Cullum and Porter, would have been well beyond my comprehension.

Literature

In the 1970s and beyond, dramatists, stand-up comics, and novelists stepped up an ongoing quest to represent and explore the province and the city of St. John's as a setting for fictions. Joan Rusted (2011) claims that St. John's today has "a higher per capita number of published writers than any other city in Canada" (p. 91). It is now possible to look at the city through the eyes of numerous fictional characters, something that was, in the most literal sense of the term, unimaginable for me as a child.

As a Canadian province, Newfoundland participated in the 1970s revolution of government support for Canadian content in the publishing industry, on radio and television, and elsewhere. The impact was perhaps felt most strongly in the field of literature (Newfoundland music already had a secure hold on the popular imagination). Once the institutional frameworks were laid down, a creative explosion followed, sometimes referred to as the Newfoundland Renaissance.

Contemporary Newfoundland literature invites me to recognize my home place in fictions and also to rethink it from a variety of perspectives. The city of St. John's now exists, for me and other readers, as the imaginary home of many deictic centres, not our own but placed in our own setting. We are invited to reimagine our situated selves. We can now practice our own forms of the reading of validation.

Contested Descriptors

None of the discursive developments I outline here (in a far too sketchy way) moves a single city stone, yet consideration of these new analyses makes it impossible to see the place in the same way as it was perceived, by me and others, in the 1950s.

I wrote an early draft of this chapter while sitting in St. John's in The Rooms, watching the fog come and go over Signal Hill. I looked down over the city from a vantage point that did not exist before 2005 (the year this magnificent combined museum, art gallery, and archive opened on the location of the old Fort Townsend). Directly below my window lay the three sites that played a shaping role in my literate education: school, library/museum, and church. The school was demolished in the early 1980s; the library building survives but has been repurposed and largely rebuilt as a career centre. Only the church stands square and recognizable; refurbished and extended, it still carries out its original function, though the nature of its engagement with the social issues of downtown St. John's has altered over the decades.

As I looked over the old part of the city to the waterfront that has mutated so significantly since the 1950s, I saw a variety of flags flying. Like so much else of Newfoundland society, the provincial flag is contested, and I observed old and new versions, testimony to ongoing political disagreement about conditions of governance in this province. Four flags now regularly fly in the Newfoundland landscape: the maple leaf of Canada, the Union Jack of prior allegiances, the new provincial flag designed by Christopher Pratt, and the pink, white, and green banner of an earlier Newfoundland politics. A fifth flag that used to fly regularly was the old Red Ensign that preceded the Canadian flag. A sixth, one that I have never seen on a flagpole, was the Newfoundland Ensign, designated between 1904 and 1931. In my own lifetime, the Stars and Stripes flew over the American base located in Fort Pepperrell, north of Quidi Vidi Lake in the heart of St. John's. The symbolism most potently conveyed by all these emblems is one of fragmentation and disagreement rather than any kind of civic unity, flux rather than the fixity I initially internalized as my first view of the world. Even as I saw solidity, I absorbed elements of dispute and contestation; even as I mastered a local discourse, I was spectator to discursive negotiation and uncertainty.

Building on Bedrock

I learned that my world was fixed and solid. I learned that family routines were mostly inviolable. I learned that I could rely on my developing set of scripts and schemas that would most likely stay "true" and useful because the world was a dependable place. When my books did not represent my own worlds, I simply learned that you manage this phenomenon by setting up compartments in your brain to house and contain the discrepancies: "fiction," say, or "the States," or "school stuff."

I was not right about the world, of course, and some of the certainties I picked up were actively harmful. We do not have access to the Murk of other people; as Johnston (2011) tells us, even the caretakers most intimately involved with small children must resort to "misremembrance, embellishment and outright fiction" (p. 36) when asked to account for somebody else's childhood experiences. I wonder if the earliest learning of today's children inevitably involves juggling contingencies, or if secure children still sort out schemas that posit the world as a singular, true, and certain place, at least to begin with.

I have learned contingency, learned to enjoy flux and contradiction, learned to revel in the dance of signifiers. But this project has revealed to me that some of the old certainties still lurk within the contingent stew of assumptions in my head, lying dormant or interacting with the correctives I have attempted to introduce over the years.

The general effect of all these changes is surprisingly apropos, given the focus of this study: it is *unsettling*. After all my childhood efforts to claim my territory, it turns out I did not understand what I was reaching for, not because I was a child but because everybody's understanding was in flux, whether they knew it or not. Yet the old suppositions inflect my current thinking; at the same time, my access to my early reading experiences is possible only through the lens of what I know, believe, and take for granted today. To what extent am I still limited by the boundaries and edges I originally established to the world as I understood it? For all the length and complexity of my work on this project, I do not feel I have a reliable answer to that important question.

DISTRICTS

DISTRICTS, says Lynch (1960), are "relatively large...areas which the observer can mentally go inside of, and which have some common character. They can be recognized internally, and occasionally can be used as external reference as a person goes by or toward them" (p. 66). My use of this term here is a stretch, but I want to take advantage of that identifiable common character to explore questions raised by the role of a variety of institutions that affected my developing powers.

This project would be deceptive if it simply portrayed a literacy growing out of the interrelationships between a girl, her books, and her landscape. My literate life was also shaped by human decisions, committee meetings, fundraising activities, and hard physical, intellectual, and social labour, all expressed through particular institutions.

Jack Zipes (2001) describes some of the frontline players whose decisions factor into how children encounter their texts, though he confines himself to children's literature, a field smaller than the fuller stage I address in this project: "The field of children's literature must include the interrelationships between children, teachers, librarians, parents, publishers, bookstore owners, vendors, business corporations, the mass media, and their various practices of producing and consuming books intended for the young as commodities" (pp. 71–72).

The decision makers I investigate in this section are largely local, but of course I acknowledge a much broader circle outside of Newfoundland altogether, along the lines of Zipes's list. Brandt and Clinton (2002) express some of the complexity of this arena: "the achievements of literacy appeared as a delicate interplay of social, cultural, economic, political, and even geographic forces" (p. 340). In this section, I examine some of these forces as they manifested themselves in my local setting.

St. John's is a sophisticated city today, but much of its history is bleak. An uncertain and often undemocratic political and social environment, a hostile climate, a constant shortage of money, the significant barriers caused by geographic isolation, and the repetitive destruction of sweeping fires compounded the complexities that face any polity, and led to a recurring theme of "one step forward, two steps back." To take just one simple example, the resolution and determination that kept people fundraising over and over again, simply to get back to what they had achieved before the last fire destroyed it all, is nothing short of awe-inspiring. St. John's was for a long time an austere city, cramped by poverty and remoteness, but it was rich in a kind of dogged ambition. Its people clearly pursued their spiritual and cultural aspirations with enormous enterprise and energy, even as the limitations imposed by colonial forms of government and the inequities (and iniquities) of a fishing economy based on barter rather than cash restricted the scope of democratic expression in Newfoundland.

The frame narrative of want, hard work, and dedication is reiterated over and over, especially in the face of those recurrent fires. At the same time, the ability of Newfoundlanders to run their own affairs was severely limited by the colonial government. Needing some form of social regulation, the city and the larger territory of the island turned to hybrid compromises that gave more unofficial "parochial" authority to the churches than would be tolerated in many jurisdictions. Paul Moore (2007), for example, describes the conditions in St. John's at the turn of the twentieth century, citing

> *a continual tight rein on the municipal authority on the part of the colonial government. St. John's had a tax rate far below cities of similar size in Canada and delivered far fewer services and of inferior quality accordingly. Council did not have the ability to run a deficit or raise funds through bonds, and could not decide its own tax rate against absentee landlords in Britain. It had little ability to write its own bylaws....[P]arochialism [i.e., church-related governance]...was an outcome of colonial policy. The City Council*

was not allowed to introduce rational, modern bureaucratic measures. The city, its people and its institutions, of course pursued parochial means of regulation instead. (p. 465)

In this chapter, I do not attempt to do justice to the detailed histories of the institutions I invoke; my main purpose is to provide a gloss to help emphasize that the organizations that scaffolded my childhood literacy did not arrive as "givens" in the world, fully formed and already functioning. They were developed by human beings who deliberately set out to support certain kinds of education, certain ideological and cultural powers of literacy. As always, I can easily make the general point; in this brief chapter I cite a few of the particularities of my own time and place to ground the generalizations in specific local examples.

The idiosyncrasies of Newfoundland history make some institutional frameworks more visible than they might be in more normatively constructed communities elsewhere in the English-speaking world. But the same issues frame literate development even in the most mainstream of situations, though they may be more taken for granted and less distinctive. Newfoundland here usefully provides an exception that proves the rule, and thus helpfully clarifies the role of the rule in the first place.

At a number of points in the history of the British Empire, Newfoundlanders were treated as disdainfully as many Indigenous populations in other parts of the empire, deprived of a democratic voice and excluded from the decisions that affected their livelihood. Sometimes, the urban voices of St. John's dominated to a greater extent, for example in the economic system of truck and barter that made the fish merchants rich and deprived the outport inhabitants of any access to a cash economy. Sometimes, the city elites were also silenced, as in the imposition of London rule through the Commission of Government between 1934 and 1949. It is a distinctive story, eccentric in places, but its very uniqueness makes the framing structures of local literacies all the more readily visible—an asset for this once-over-lightly section of my project.

If any map analogy is appropriate in this section, it may be a Google map dotted with snapshots. I will zoom in on an assortment of these shots for a closer look at key literacy agencies in the city, but there will be real limits (of size and scale and of my own expertise) in how much detail can be supplied. As with the single snapshot on the map, the effect may be frustrating as well as illuminating.

In this section, I explore a handful of major cultural institutions that inflected my own childhood and shaped my literacies: library, museum, church and Sunday school, school, movie theatres, radio, television, and newspapers. A larger study of the institutional pressures on a single child's literacy would be valuable and fascinating, but I am simply pointing out some telling examples, not developing a complete ecological analysis. These recognizable "districts" of my daily life supplied important forms of structure for the development of my own particular and local literacies.

17
Institutions of Literacy
Cultivating

The Library

IN 1936 St. John's opened the Gosling Memorial Library on Duckworth Street near the courthouse. The building was located near the site of the Athenaeum, a lavish and elegant cultural centre of the previous century that, before its destruction in the 1892 Great Fire, provided the civic amenities of a library, reading rooms, and an auditorium seating one thousand.

After the catastrophe of the 1892 fire, the city was effectively without a library for decades. According to a historical pamphlet published by the Public Libraries Board in 1957, the initial collection of the library in 1936 came mainly from gifts. Adding purchases made by the Public Libraries Board, the grand total on opening was 17,000 volumes. By 1957, when I was a regular user, the library's collection totalled approximately 230,000 volumes for the whole system (Public Libraries Board, 1957, p. 2).

The Boys' and Girls' Library occupied the basement. Its windows faced an alleyway, so it was a dark room, but its welcome to a book-loving child was bright. I spent many productive hours in this room and regarded the librarians as allies.

In 1936 the library budget stood at $11,000 compared to 1957 funding of $125,000 (Public Libraries Board, 1957, p. 2); circulation totals were 53,000 in 1936 and "over half a million" by 1957 (p. 3). In 1936 there were a thousand books for young people; by 1957, "more than a hundred thousand" books (p. 3).

The labour entailed in building and servicing a library is captured in some of the documentation of the time. The Acquisitions Register for the children's library, alas, survives only for 1936–1939. (St. John's librarians

REMARKS	Accession Number	AUTHOR	TITLE	VOL.	PUBLISHER	YEAR	SOURCE	COST	
W823	26 26	James	Young Cowboy		Scribners	1936	Scribner	1.50	
	26 27	Platt	Stories of the Scottish Border		Harrap	1935	Foyles	2/6	
W140	26 28	Molesworth	The Cuckoo Clock		Macm.	1933	Macm		
W411	26 29	Chance	Our Princesses and their Dogs		Murray	1937	Bairds	.75	
	26 30	"	"	" C-2	"	"	"		W.543
	26 31	"	"	" C-3	"	"	"		W.544
	26 32	"	"	" C-4	"	"	"		W.545
	26 33	"	"	" C-5	"	"	"		W.546
W477	226 34	"	"	" C-6	"	"	"		
	26 35								
W447	26 36		The A.B.C. Guide to the Coronation		Hutchinson	1937	"	.80	
W448	2637		" " " "		"	"	"	.20	
	26 38		Coronation Book / King George VI's & Queen Elizabeth's		Shaw	"	"	.40	
	26 39		"	" C-2	"	"	"		
	26 40		"	" C-3	"	"	"		
	26 41		"	" C-4	"	"	"		
	26 42	Mee	Salute the King		Hodder	"	"	1.00	
	26 43	"	"	C-2	"	"	"		
	2644	"	"	C-3	"	"	"		
	2645	Coatsworth	Sword of the Wilderness		Macm.	1936	Scribner	$2.00	
	2646	Bishop	The Flying Squad		Harrap	1930	Foyles Murray	2/6	
May 28	2647	Thayer	George Washington		Milford	bd	Foyles	1/6	
	2648	Gardner	Greek Art and Architecture		O.U.P	1922	"	2/6	
	2649	Barrie	Peter Pan in Kensington Gardens		Hodder	nd	St.John's "	10/6	
	26 50	Smallwood(ed.)	Book of Newfoundland. V.1		Bk. Pub.	1937	Public Wks.	G	

∧ *A page from the Acquisitions Register of the Gosling Memorial Library, dated April 22, 1937, obtained at the A.C. Hunter Branch of the Newfoundland and Labrador Public Library in St. John's.*

[Courtesy NLPL Fonds, 7.05 NL Collection, Provincial Resource Library]

surmise that from the 1940s onward, acquisitions information was added to the back of each book's catalogue card, but the catalogue itself was later destroyed.) The early pages of this register offer a vivid glimpse of Newfoundland's status as neither wholly British nor completely North American; in the page I include from April 22, 1937, it is worth noting that the list of prices moves promiscuously between pounds sterling and at least one dollar economy, possibly two (US and Canadian).

Ironically, *Our Princesses and their Dogs* and books about King George's coronation are paid for in dollars, while the book about George Washington is charged in shillings and pence. At the bottom of the page, we see "G" (for Gift) in the price column, for a donation of Volume 1 of Joseph Smallwood's encyclopaedic *Book of Newfoundland*, acquired from the Department of

∧ *The Circulation Record*
for the Boys' and Girls'
Library from the sample
month of November
1961, obtained at the
A.C. Hunter Branch of
the Newfoundland and
Labrador Public Library.

[*Courtesy* NLPL *Fonds,*
7.02 NL *Collection, Provincial*
Resource Library]

Public Works twelve years before Smallwood became premier of the new province.

Other records demonstrate the active work that went into making the library function. Circulation records from the Boys' and Girls' Library in November 1961 show a detailed breakdown of the month's borrowings, recorded daily by hand. Although the individual figures are not themselves significant for my work here, I am very interested in the level of detail that these statistics encompass.

The days of the month are listed down the left-hand side; the columns record borrowings for the day under major subject headings. For example, reading across the columns for Saturday, November 18, 10 General Works went out, 1 on Philosophy, 0 on Religion, 47 Social Sciences titles, 9 Linguistics titles, 4 Science books, 33 titles from the Applied Sciences, 5 titles from Arts and Recreation, 10 works of Literature, 5 History books, 1 book on Geography and Travel, 0 Biographies, 6 Periodicals, 7 Pamphlets, and 4 general Non-Fiction. Eight works of print fiction also circulated that day. The bottom rows record Registrations, Re-registrations, Transfers & Expiries, Total Borrowers, Major Questions, Minor Questions (these would be reference questions), Major Mends, and Minor Mends, and Notices—all entered daily.

The numbers may vary substantially from one month to another; what does not alter is the meticulous daily recording of salient transactions: one almost invisible substrate to the structuring and support of literacy in St. John's during my time.

The provision of library services to the whole province in the 1950s was a huge challenge, too large and significant for me to address here. Jessie Mifflen, an intrepid local librarian, served the outport population for many decades, beginning in the 1940s. She chronicled the numerous and lively demands on a "library missionary" as she was once described (Mifflen, 2008, p. 60) in a variety of columns and memoirs collected into a single volume in 2008. She describes library school education in Toronto, highlighting how external norms were imported into St. John's, and adding a local twist:

> *My career there was uneventful. I didn't return home bearing my blushing honours thick upon me, but at least I had received the pertinent degree, and in the process had learned enough to know that I should assume an expression of horror when anyone offered to make a gift of* Bobbsey Twins *or* Hardy Boys *books to the library. Not that there were likely to be many such offers, for most Newfoundlanders weren't very affluent in those days and couldn't afford to buy books for themselves, much less give them to libraries. (p. 68)*

Another significant library personality briefly appeared in St. John's in 1958 and 1959. Eric Moon, a longtime editor of *Library Journal* was well-known, first in Britain and later in the United States, for his activism in the cause of librarianship. He transited between one country and the other via a short stint as director of public library services and secretary-treasurer of the Newfoundland Public Libraries Board (Kister, 2002, p. 114).

Moon's outsider point of view provides interesting insight into both the library system and the City of St. John's at that time, and reflects the province's lack of resources.

> *During Moon's brief tenure as Newfoundland's top public librarian, he had a budget approaching $150,000 per annum (not reindeer feed in those days), a book collection in excess of a quarter of a million volumes, and an annual circulation of three quarters of a million. Sounds pretty good, eh? But looked at through Moon's professional eyes, the system was sadly understocked, underfunded, and underutilized: there was only half a book in the collec-*

tion for each resident, only one and a half books circulated each year per resident, and the province spent only about $0.30 each year per resident on library service. Library facilities, moreover, were generally inadequate and the Gosling was strained almost to the breaking point. (Kister, 2002, pp. 117–118)

Moon struggled to cope with the limitations of the library system, and also with the provincial restrictions of life in St. John's (he couldn't even enliven the strictures of daily life with an extramarital fling, he complained, because "Any indiscretion would have been known the next day" [p. 123]). One option did offer bright opportunities: "Given staff, budget, and plant limitations, the province's public libraries normally provided only the most rudimentary services, such as circulating books, answering basic refer-ence questions, and offering regular children's story hours and film shows. One area where the library did stand out was its extensive use of radio as a medium to bring the world of books and knowledge to the people of Newfoundland" (p. 116). I never heard a library broadcast, but I certainly internalized the library ethos of welcoming readers even in the face of strained resources. I would have been glad to encounter a bigger collection, but it was not a possibility that even occurred to me.

Of course, I gave no thought to the principles of selection and cura-tion that organized the Gosling Library's collection for boys and girls. I do not know the extent to which Newfoundland librarians participated in Canadian discussions about appropriate materials for children and the importance of good literature and Canadian content (Edwards, 2012). What I do know is that by 1959 at the latest, our library took part in Young Canada's Book Week (YCBW), designed "to stimulate 'a demand for good reading among young Canadians'" (Edwards, 2012, p. 186). That year, I participated in a YCBW contest and collected my prize (*Farmer Boy* by Laura Ingalls Wilder) on my eleventh birthday (which is why I am so certain about the date). I remember being stumped for one or two answers on the quiz and being directed by my mother to *The Book of Knowledge*, the nearest thing to *Coles Notes* that our house possessed.

The discussions of the Canadian librarians included many complex questions, and Gail Edwards (2012) does a good job of exploring the signifi-cance of institutional decisions informed by personal effort and opinion:

The idea of the common culture of Canadian childhood was central to children's librarians' understanding of the circulation of texts and to their own expert claims. The Bulletin [of the Canadian Association of Children's Librarians] *created a discursive space in which professional norms and attitudes about library services to children could be reinforced through the construction of a powerful collective identity. The uninflected and unaware "we" in the pages of the* Bulletin *was based on an assumption that members shared a similar professional education, agreed on basic standards of evaluation, and were actively engaged in promoting the canon in their own library through collection development and library programmes, even as regional disparity and interpersonal tensions challenged the claims to professional universality.*

Canon formation took on new urgency in the post-war period, as anxieties about normal childhood stimulated an intense debate about the role of literature in developing informed young citizens. (p. 140)

None of these concerns remotely troubled me as I picked up my prize on a cold, damp, and foggy birthday in 1959. Nor do I now have access to the priorities that guided the actions of my own local librarians. Given the constraints of their very limited budgets, they may have regarded this whole conversation as a luxury for rich libraries rather than a practical guide to useful selection in their own straitened setting. Or they may have balked at the very ethos of Canadianness in the discussion overall, and opted for American and British materials as a form of passive resistance to a polity that did not yet feel like their own. It would certainly have been possible to argue that books set in the mainland of Canada would not feel any more "local" than these imports to Newfoundland children. I simply have no way of telling how my librarians established their selection criteria.

My prize, it is worth noting, was an American book—but that fact may simply reflect the books for sale that November on the shelves of Dicks, the local book store. Individual and institutional priorities alike would sometimes founder on the hard facts of simple availability. I am sure that there was a degree of what Edwards calls "the persistence of professional discourse" (p. 135) among the librarians making decisions for me and other children in St. John's, but I am not sure how that discourse was framed in Newfoundland in the first decade of Confederation.

The Museum

After the destruction of the Athenaeum at the end of the nineteenth century, there were spasmodic efforts over the next few decades to recreate a proper museum for Newfoundland, but all efforts foundered with the declaration of direct rule from London:

> In March 1934, the new Commission of Government placed the Museum under the Commissioner of Public Utilities. Not long after, the institution was totally shut down, and its artifacts were variously dispersed and stored....[W]ithout a doubt, the Commission of Government years, during the late 1930s and the 1940s, were the darkest in the Museum's long history. An unfortunate combination of factors, including incompetent storage arrangements, a disastrous fire, and outright disposal of artifacts, decimated the collections. (Maunder, 1991, n.p.)

Collecting and sorting these lost and damaged artifacts was a huge challenge, and, although individuals and the local newspapers pressed for action, there was much institutional delay. Eventually, however, the museum reopened its doors to the public in January 1957, not long after my eighth birthday. It was located on the top floor of the library building, and my friend and I would often visit, after our Saturday morning trip to the library. I remember cabinets full of Beothuk artifacts and those skeletons. There was a glassed-in room representing an eighteenth-century kitchen that always struck me for the absence of any kind of comfortable chair. There was a model of the town of Corner Brook, complete with a tiny paper mill.

Arthur Fox, writing in Volume IV of Smallwood's *Book of Newfoundland* in 1967, provides a more complete account of what was salvaged and displayed:

> *Included in the display of exhibits are pictures of old St. John's; models of a Viking ship, John Cabot's ship* MATTHEW, *Sir Humphrey Gilbert's ship* SQUIRREL, *and the cable ship* GREAT EASTERN; *models of Newfoundland boats and schooners; a typical Newfoundland kitchen of eighteenth century vintage; furniture, pulp and paper, sealing and whaling, and codfishery sections; kayaks and canoes; early Newfoundland maps and charts; pictures and portraits of people who played a part in Newfoundland's history; paintings of Vikings landing on Markland, John Cabot sighting Cape Bonavista, Sir Humphrey Gilbert setting up the first British Colonial Government (at St. John's),* S.S. GREAT EASTERN *landing first transatlantic cable at Heart's Content, and Marconi receiving the first wireless signals at Cabot Tower; the propellers of the plane in which Alcock and Brown made the first transatlantic flight; as well as Beothuck, Micmac and Nascopi Indian relics, and many cases of folklore and other exhibits. (p. 193)*

The Provincial Museum is now housed in The Rooms, and the objects and artifacts are laid out more organically and appealingly; gone are the rows of matching glass cabinets.

The Rooms is also home to the Provincial Archives where, to my great delight, I found a labelled photograph of that glassed-in kitchen, along with the key to the artifacts on display. To my adult eye, it looks snug enough (though the chairs certainly are forbiddingly upright and hard).

The museum's history is a strange mixture of the energy and skill that originally fuelled the nineteenth-century collecting, cataloguing, and labelling of a broad variety of artifacts, succeeded by the criminally indifferent

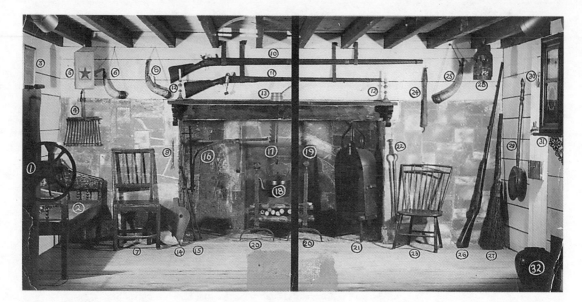

∧ *The glassed-in room displaying the interior of an eighteenth-century Newfoundland kitchen.*

[*Courtesy The Rooms Provincial Archives Division, c 1-181*]

sabotage of the Commission of Government that dismantled the collection and stored items so carelessly that only some could be salvaged. At the time of my exposure to this collection, order had been restored, and my perception of the museum included a sense of almost stifling regulation and permanence. To my elders, this pinning down of the items relating to a complex and arduous history must have been an enormous relief.

The Church

Gower Street United Church began its existence in 1815 as the urban mother church of Newfoundland Methodism. Fire destroyed the first building within a year. The second church opened only ten months later and lasted for forty years. In 1856 the congregation built a bigger church; this replacement building was destroyed in the 1892 fire, along with "1,527 homes and 150 stores and ships" (Gower Street United Church, n.p.). The current church was built after that catastrophe and opened in 1896.

The role of a church in a context of changing political structures is complicated, and I will not provide a full history of those elaborations here. David Pitt (1990), the church's historian, comments on the fact that the Newfoundland Methodists affiliated with the Methodist Church of Canada in 1873, suggesting that, even in those early days, Methodists were proponents of political union with Canada as well (p. 95). Further connections with Canada were advanced in 1925 when the United Church of Canada formed out of Methodist, Presbyterian, and Congregationalist denominations, and Gower Street Church and the rest of the Newfoundland

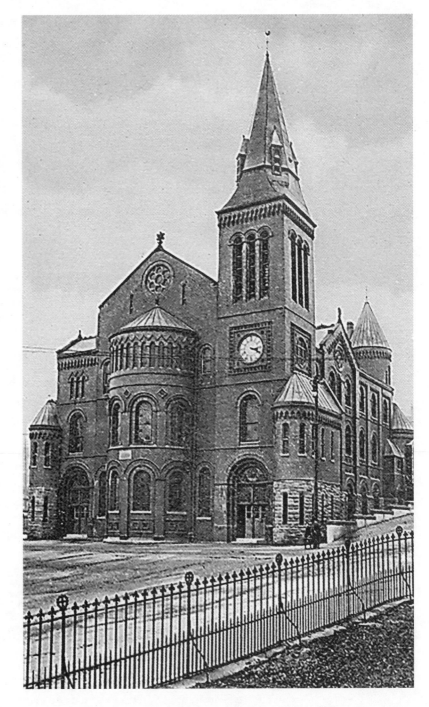

Methodists followed suit. (A fascinating example of the ways in which cultural institutions intertwine themselves in the fabric of a society lies in the history of The Ryerson Press of Toronto. Founded by the Methodists to publish religious materials, the press was given its new name in 1919 and became an active player in the development of Canadian publishing, both literary materials and school textbooks [Friskney, 2007, 381–383]. There is not room here to explore this bypath further, but it is worth marking the complex texture of cultural decisions—both those made with deliberate consideration and those that fall out as byproducts of other priorities.)

Pitt's account of the Gower congregation's activities of 1921 provides an interesting snapshot of the range of activities of this particular church. The year began with a public row over Prohibition, a cause dearer to the hearts of many Methodists than to those of some other Newfoundlanders. Beyond that local skirmish, however, lay many institutional decisions, and the importance of hardworking volunteers is very clear in this account.

> *But there were other pressing matters for the Board to deal with in
> 1921: a series of special services under the auspices of the International
> Brotherhood Association, the proceeds of collections being divided between
> the Brotherhood and the Famine of Europe Fund; a communication from the
> General Conference of the Church that the ordination of women be voted
> on (it was and passed handily); heating problems in the church requiring
> the purchase of a new plant (an extra $4000.00 debt); repairs to the church
> spire, which had caused increasing concern of late; a gravely depleted Poor
> Fund at a time when demands on it were heavier than ever (the recently
> formed Committee on Evangelism and Social Service was handed the
> problem and seems to have solved it after much hard work and individual
> canvassing). But the major event of the year was the Silver Jubilee of the
> opening in 1896 of the church building. (Pitt, 1990, p. 163)*

That vote in favour of the ordination of women in 1921 was just one marker of a progressive stance in gender issues. In 1923 women were admitted to church boards as regular members "equal in all the privileges and responsibilities" (Pitt, 1990, p. 165). In the event, however, it proved difficult to find women to stand, or to attend meetings regularly if elected, and Pitt says the church continued to be dominated by men into the 1950s (p. 195). Nevertheless, the structures were laid down and attitudes affected—including my own, by a kind of osmosis.

Church Literacies

The inexplicable survival among the family papers of a single copy of the weekly order of service (for Sunday, December 30, 1956) allows me to

Church Calendar

SUNDAY:
Public Worship, 11 a.m., and 7 p.m.
Nursery, 11 a.m. in Common Room, Children 2 and 3 years.
Sunday School and Bible Classes, 2.30 p.m.
Mission Band, third Sunday of each month at morning service.

MONDAY:
Tyro Boys at 7.15 p.m. (weekly).
Junior Choir at 7.15 p.m. (weekly).
Young People's Union at 8 p.m. (weekly).

TUESDAY:
Tuxis Boys at 7.15 p.m. (weekly).
Evening Auxiliary of W.M.S. (first Tuesday in each month) 8 p.m.
Senior Auxiliary of the W.M.S., 3.15 p.m. (1st Tuesday each month)
Mothers' Auxiliary (3rd Tuesday in the Common Room) 8 p.m.
Mission Circle (3rd Tuesday of the month) 8 p.m.
Men's Service Club (2nd Tuesday in each month—October to April)

THURSDAY:
Sigma-C Boys at 7.15 p.m. (weekly).
Choir Rehearsal, 8 p.m.

FRIDAY:
Women's Association (once monthly, October to April).
Explorers, 7.00 p.m., weekly.
C.G.I.T., 6.45 p.m. (weekly).

CHURCH OFFICIARY

Rev. L. A. D. Curtis, B.A., B.D.	Clerk of Session
Mr. D. W. K. Dawe, Q.C.	Secretary Official Board
Mr. Charles L. Roberts	Treasurer
Hon. Harold Macpherson	Honorary Chairman, Board of Stewards
Dr. H. Roberts	Chairman, Board of Stewards
Mr. Eric Knight	Secretary, Board of Stewards
Mr. H. K. Wyatt	Envelope Secretary
Mr. Isaac Bourne	Chapel Steward
Mr. Walter Grouchy	Treasurer M. and M. Fund
Mr. Charles Burden	Sexton

HEADS OF SOCIETIES

Honorary Superintendent Sunday School	Mr. W. H. Peters
Superintendent of Sunday School	Mr. Isaac Davis
Senior Auxiliary of W.M.S.	Mrs. Lewis Bartlett
Evening Auxiliary of W.M.S.	Mrs. D. W. K. Dawe
Mothers' Auxiliary	Mrs. Eric Benson
Mission Circle	Miss Joyce Bishop
Mission Band Superintendent	Mrs. L. Winsor
Baby Band Superintendent	Mrs. H. J. Peet
Woman's Association	Mrs. R. M. French
Men's Service Club	Mr. S. Short
Young People's Union	Mr. Cecil Tiller
Convener Flower Committee	Mrs. Donald Brett (Dial 7585F)
Junior Congregation	Mrs. J. Norman
Tuxis	Mr. A. E. Heselwood
Sigma C	Mr. Graham Snow
Tyro Boys	Mr. L. Smith
C.G.I.T.	Miss M. Blake
Explorers	Miss V. Bourne

Change Of Address	Newcomers Desire To Unite With Church	Desire Envelopes	Special Call Requested, Sickness, etc.	Pupils For Church School

Name ....

Address ....

Gower Street United Church
St. John's, Newfoundland

Minister:
REV. FRANCIS E. VIPOND, B.A., B.D.

Director of Christian Education:
MR. ALLAN E. HESELWOOD.

Organist and Choir Director:
MR. DOUGLAS OSMOND, L.R.A.M.

Let the people on entering God's House, in reverent silence direct their thoughts towards God, fervent in prayer, and expectant of His Holy Word.

SUNDAY, DECEMBER 30, 1956

MORNING WORSHIP

ELEVEN O'CLOCK

(The congregation will rise as the Choir enters)

ORGAN PRELUDE—"Prelude No. 2" .... Rinck
CALL TO WORSHIP.
INVOCATION.
LORD'S PRAYER (in unison)
HYMN 446—"O God of Bethel, by Whose Hand" .... P. Doddridge
PRAYER OF CONFESSION.
RESPONSIVE READING—Psalm Selection—Hymnary 720.
GLORIA—(Tune 734-2). The congregation is invited to join in the Gloria
SCRIPTURE.
PRAYER OF THANKSGIVING.
PRAYER OF DEDICATION AND OFFERING.
OFFERTORY—"Andante Con Moto" .... Calkin
GROUP OF CHRISTMAS ANTHEMS...Adaptions by Ringwald and Shaw
ANNOUNCEMENTS.
HYMN 596—"Father, Lead Me Day by Day" .... J. P. Hopps
PRAYER (Congregation will please remain standing at the close of the Hymn for Prayer, after which the Junior Congregation will retire)
SERMON—"THE CHRISTIAN FAITH IS TRUE"...Rev. F. E. Vipond
PRAYER OF INTERCESSION.
HYMN 572—"Sing to The Great Jehovah's Praise" .... C. Wesley
BENEDICTION—(Choral Benediction)
ORGAN POSTLUDE—"To God on High" .... Mendelssohn

EVENING WORSHIP

SEVEN O'CLOCK

(The congregation will please rise as the Choir enters)

INVOCATION.
LORD'S PRAYER (in unison)
HYMN 311—"O Love That Wilt Not Let Me Go" .... G. Matheson
SCRIPTURE.
PASTORAL PRAYER.
PRAYER OF DEDICATION AND OFFERING.
OFFERTORY—"I Waited for The Lord" .... Mendelssohn
GROUP OF CHRISTMAS ANTHEMS...Arranged by Richard Kountz
ANNOUNCEMENTS.
HYMN 478—"Saviour, Thy Dying Love" .... S. D. Phelps
SERMON—"RESPECT FOR PERSONS AND PROPERTY"
.... Rev. F. E. Vipond

PRAYER AND CHORAL PRAYER.
HYMN 270—"Just As I Am, Without One Plea" .... C. Elliott
BENEDICTION—(Choral Amen—Tune 770-3)
ORGAN POSTLUDE—"Postlude in D Major" .... Haydn

And the people shall before departing intreat God thus, or in words of their own choosing: "O Lord my God, go with me as I leave this house of Prayer, being mindful of my vows and Thy faithfulness; may my manner of life be worthy of the Gospel." Amen.

NEW YEAR GREETINGS

The Minister desires to express to our people his fervent wish that all may experience in 1957 a rewarding sense of God's guidance and a rich measure of happiness.

The Church at Work

TO-DAY:
11.00—Worship Service broadcast VOWR.
2.30—Sunday School, Senior Study Class and Young People's Bible Class.
6.45—Song Service followed by Evening Worship. The eighth sermon in the series on the Ten Commandments, the title being "RESPECT FOR PERSONS AND PROPERTY." Broadcast VOCM.

MONDAY, December 31:
11.15 p.m.—Watch Night Service will be held in this Church.

TUESDAY, January 1:
3.00 to 5.30 p.m.—The United Church of Canada will sponsor a reception at Emmanuel House.

WEDNESDAY, January 2:
8.00—Special Official Board Meeting will be held in Classroom 4.

THURSDAY, January 3:
8.00—The Choir will practise in the Common Room.

FRIDAY, January 4:
8.00—Executive Meeting of the Christian Education Committee will be held in the Church Office.

The Week of Prayer Services will be held from Monday, January 7th, to Friday, January 12th, inclusive. In the following Churches:
Monday.—Salvation Army Temple.
Tuesday—Cochrane Street Church.
Wednesday—St. Andrew's Presbyterian.
Thursday—St. Mary's Anglican.
Friday—Gower Street Church.
Let us attend as many of these Services as possible.

Ushers for the month of January will be: Messrs. E. White, C. Davis, R. Burke, J. C. Moores, D. Woolridge and George Cook.

Any young persons not already connected with a mid-week group in Gower Street Church are invited to—
Explorers—Friday—7 p.m. in Memorial Hall Gym.
C.G.I.T.—Friday—7 p.m. in Memorial Hall.
Tyro—Monday—7 p.m. in Memorial Hall Gym.
Sigma-C—Thursday—7.15 p.m. in Memorial Hall Gym.
Tuxis—Tuesday—7.15 p.m. in Memorial Hall Gym.
Young People's Union—Monday—8 p.m. in Common Room.
(For further information see page 4 of bulletin)

The organizations of the Church are asked to give their annual reports to Rev. L. A. D. Curtis at the earliest possible moment in the New Year so that he may prepare a unified report for the Annual Congregational meeting. Please include the names of officers for the new year in all reports.

It will be appreciated by the Church Office (Phone 3989) if you will advise immediately of any change of address.

explore elements of the church infrastructure and bureaucracy that I entirely took for granted at the age of eight.

A similar leaflet was handed out every Sunday; it contributed to my sense that the world proceeded through forms of an utterly reliable *orderliness*. Sunday worship at 11:00 A.M. and 7:00 P.M. Thursday night choir practice. Tyro and Tuxis and Sigma-C Boys, Explorers for girls and Canadian Girls in Training (I never joined), Mothers' Auxiliary, Mission Circle, Women's Missionary Society, Men's Service Club. These organizations all had convenors or heads, and reported to the annual congregational meeting.

Much of this little document simply reflects the stability of ongoing life. The minister, Francis Vipond, was offering a running series on the Ten Commandments in the evening service; by December 30, he had worked his way up to the eighth, in a sermon entitled "Respect for Persons and Property." The ushers for the month of January are listed: all men. The first women ushers appeared in 1977 (Pitt, 1990, p. 192). (Before my time, ushers wore morning dress for their Sunday duties [*A Time to Remember*, 1990], a reflection of Gower Street's sense of itself as the lead United Church in Newfoundland.)

Of course, church offered religious content as well as buttressing our Sundays with institutional arrangements. Elsewhere, I have explored the contribution of hymns to my spiritual and literate life, but it is simply not possible for me to do justice to the impact of listening to the King James Version of the Bible, week after week, Sunday after Sunday. During the week, in assembly at school, we listened to *Hurlbut's Story of the Bible* (Hurlbut, 1957/1932), rewritten for children, so meaning was not my first priority on Sunday; I often had some grasp of the gist. The sonorous cadences caught my attention most comprehensively; the swelling and fading rhythms of the great phrases shaped my ear.

My piety ebbed and flowed. I was sometimes seized by fervour; I was often bored and listless in church. I was always well-behaved. My mother did not quite run to the disciplinary regime of her own mother who, by family legend, wore a thimble on the middle finger of each hand underneath her white gloves, and administered a sharp rap on the head of any of her six children (three each side) who stirred out of line. But we were in no doubt that good behaviour in church was not negotiable, and the discipline of the church service was built into our framework of life understanding.

∧ *Gower Street United*
Church Choir at the
Kiwanis Music Festival
in the spring of 1958.
Choir director Douglas
Osmond is in the
foreground.

[Courtesy Gower Street United
Church Archives, reprinted by
permission of Gower Street
United Church]

Church Music

The impact of another church priority—music—was very significant for
my life at the time and, indeed, as I have lived it ever since. The church
organ was one of the finest in the city and the choir was excellent. Douglas
Osmond, our school music instructor and my own piano teacher, was in
charge of church music; he was renowned locally for having come from
outport life in Morton's Harbour to achieve an LRAM (Licentiate of the
Royal Academy of Music) in London.

The Gower Street Church choir was famous in St. John's, and in the late
1950s even recorded two LPS, one of sacred and one of secular music. Dad
sang in the bass section throughout my childhood. In the photo I include
here, he is fourth from the right in the back row. The men's choir occasionally came to our house for an extra practice, and I loved to lie in bed and
listen to them.

In 1958 the choir was at a high point; I estimate there are forty-two
singers in this photograph (Mr. Osmond, with his back to the camera, is
blocking one or two of them). At this stage it was a well-balanced group, and
a few of them were wonderfully talented. Their music was variably ambitious, but they took on some challenging work and gave me a love of choral
music that has persisted through my entire life.

> *Image from* Junior
Workbook Number 1:
Learning to Use the Bible
(1956/1954).
[*Reprinted by permission of
the United Church of Canada*]

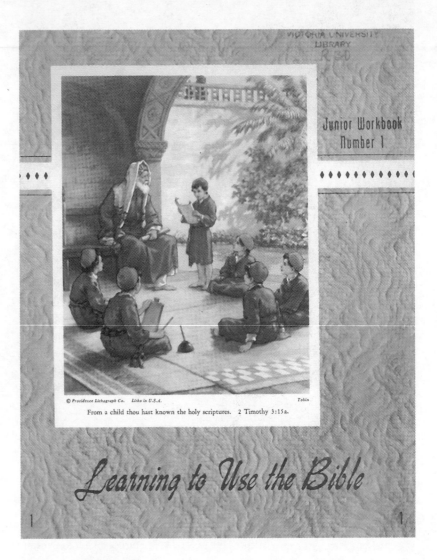

Junior Workbook
Number 1

© *Providence Lithograph Co.   Litho in U.S.A.*   *Tobin*

From a child thou hast known the holy scriptures.   2 Timothy 3:15a.

Learning to Use the Bible

The Sunday School

Sunday school at Gower Street ran from 2:30 to 3:30 on Sunday after-
noons, and any child in our family old enough to walk there and back was
dispatched after Sunday dinner.

Some of the institutional quirks of the Gower Sunday school were
charming. For example, on the Sunday following our birthday, we had to
come to the front of the group and recite a Bible verse that started with the
initial letter of our first name. I annually chanted, "Make a joyful noise unto
the Lord, all ye lands. Serve the Lord with gladness: come before his presence with singing" (Psalms 100:1–2 King James Version). It is perhaps not
a well-known fact that the Bible is short on verses beginning with M. My
friend, whose initial was B, had the full run of the Beatitudes and never had
to repeat.

About the actual lessons, I remember far less detail. We were given a weekly leaflet to take home. In the Archives of the United Church of Canada in Toronto, I found a wealth of Sunday-school curriculum materials, though not cast in leaflet form. On the covers of the Junior Workbooks, I found intensely familiar images, and I am sure some of them featured on our leaflets.

No doubt at least one intent of the picture on the cover was to convey the idea that "kids like us" could be involved in Bible stories, both by featuring in them from time to time and by learning about them, as the boys are doing in this image. This picture successfully conveys most of the elements I now remember from my Sunday-school leaflets: the children were often all boys; they wore strange clothes and frequently had no shoes; the men had beards (very unusual in St. John's in the 1950s) and dressed even more exotically than the boys; and the houses all had flat roofs (which made them excellent candidates for crafts involving shoe boxes that I liked very much). Some awareness of reading from scrolls (also a regular craft feature, often involving Popsicle sticks) also seeped into my consciousness via this route. It is not what you would call a spiritual list. Of course, I also learned many stories, one factor in the solid cultural repertoire of Bible lore that I could bring to all my other reading; and I certainly read the leaflet every week just because it was new reading fodder in the house.

None of the official church archives could supply a sample of a Sunday-school pamphlet, but a simple letter in the church newsletter turned up a parishioner who had a large collection of the leaflets brought home each week by her daughter, a child I knew. Susie Noseworthy and her daughter Grace Glastonbury sent me a scan of the whole set. Most of them are aimed at the "beginner child" and the written material is addressed to parents, but there are a couple from the *Primary Bible Lessons* series, which is the one I remember. One tells the story of Joseph and his brothers in accessible language: "Joseph had not realized how much trouble that coat was going to cause him, or how his brothers disliked him for being their father's favourite" (Brillinger, n.d.). The front picture shows "Joseph being sold to strangers." The back page, in complete contrast, shows an outline of a very conventional North American house, with the instruction, "Finish this house so that it will look like a home"—perhaps as an effort to mitigate the harshness of the rest of the story. There is a concluding "Verse to Remember: Love one another with brotherly affection. Romans 12:10a." The kind of brotherly affection on show in the story might not be something to emulate, but the general idea is clear.

In the main, I took Sunday school very much for granted. I neither liked it nor greatly disliked it. It was simply part of the pattern of the week. Some days were more interesting than others.

The institutional efforts of many volunteers were required to make Sunday school part of the weekly routine. The instructors reported to the Sunday school superintendent, who made a report to the church board. The national organization collected data, developed curriculum, set up a variety of support structures, and conducted national surveys on topics such as the recruitment of Sunday-school teachers (United Church, 1956). The infrastructure underpinning our Sunday afternoon hour was clearly substantial.

Locally, there were chains of accountability as well. In 1956 the Sunday-school superintendent reported to the board that, since the children did not seem to be attending very diligently to their lessons, a quiz of boys versus girls would be instituted at the end of each session to spur competitive instincts where spiritual ones had not quite sufficed. In such small but telling ways were our lives managed for us.

The School

The school system of Prince of Wales College covered the full range of grades offered in Newfoundland in the 1950s, Kindergarten to Grade 11 (to offer Grade 12 was beyond the province's means at that time). The grades were distributed across several sites. Just as Gower Street considered itself the premiere United Church in the province, so Prince of Wales College regarded itself as the elite institution among the United Church school systems (including a second system in St. John's, also with its own board; the utter fragmentation of educational organization in those poverty-stricken times is hard to comprehend today).

Holloway School, in all its towering bulk, housed children from Grade 2 to Grade 5. When I think of being a schoolchild, Holloway is always my default mental setting. It was the most historic of our school buildings. The site also included a residence for students coming in from the outports to study at the College.

Life at Holloway School was very strictly regimented. There were three classes at each grade level: a girls' class, a boys' class, and a mixed class. I was in the girls' class and almost never crossed over into the boys' side of the school unless sent on an errand (to the best of my recollection today,

the mixed classrooms were physically situated in the middle of the school on the dividing line). Other city and provincial school systems at that time were single-sex, so our arrangements were relatively progressive. Even sequestered as we were in the girls' class, we had assembly every day with the boys, and, of course, as we got older we became more aware of their existence.

Daily assembly was important and governed by firm rules. We carried our closed hymnals into the hall every morning and stood holding them in our two hands at a 45° angle from our ribcages. This refinement of regimentation seems unduly repressive from today's perspective, but, so soon after the Second World War and the Korean War, military models seeped into some very small details of our schooling.

This rule offered one example of how to deal with the questions raised by Kerryn Dixon (2011) about the schooled body:

> *What is the connection between schooling and the body? Managing children's undisciplined bodies that wriggle and chat and laugh and play is one of the big challenges in early primary education....*
>
> *Schools are training grounds. Children undergo training to function in the school environment itself, and are trained to function in the broader world. Much of this training is directed at the body....If we think about our own schooling and teachers' exhortations to stand straight, sit still, pay attention, write neatly, tuck in escaped shirts, pull up socks, stop talking,*

running, hitting, screaming, sniffing, swearing, spitting, chewing, and so on, these are all directed at the body. (p. 2)

There was corporal punishment in our school system, though it was unusual for a girl to be strapped. The implicit threat of this institutionalized violence overlay our schooled docility, as we learned to manage our unruly bodies and channel our energy into our singing. Regimentation marked every assembly in Pitts Memorial Hall. To us, of course, it was simply the way you did school.

The repetitiveness of the daily regime meant the days piled up more like compost than like a garden full of individual flowers. School life was dull, but I didn't know any different, and I got a reasonable education by the colonial standards of the day. I very much doubt that I would have avoided endemic racism anywhere in the English-speaking world at that time. The dreariness of the daily handwriting practices in our copies of *Maclean's Compendium* and the relentless seatwork of the *Think and Do* books were reproduced in many institutions, along with rituals such as graduating to a fountain pen (only washable blue ink permitted) in Grade 3. But our music and art and gym classes were seen as necessities rather than optional luxuries (I am not sure the same could be said of many school systems in Newfoundland in the 1950s). We had our moments of inspiration (more of mine came in art class than anywhere else), and we learned the fundamentals thoroughly, especially in English and arithmetic. By junior high we were involved in foreign languages and the sciences. We absorbed a school ethos of hard work and doing your best. Many of the outstanding teachers in the system worked at the high-school end of things, so I missed them by leaving town, but I gained a great deal that I still value from Prince of Wales College.

A 1905 picture places the Holloway School site in relation to the city landmarks and districts. The building with the ladder on the roof and the three dormer windows, in the centre left foreground of the photo, is the residence of the Methodist College (later Prince of Wales), where out-of-town students lived. The wide street running in front of the two buildings is Long's Hill, and it is much less flat than it appears here. Gower Street Church is at the bottom of Long's Hill. The harbour, the Narrows, Signal Hill, and Cabot Tower were all visible from the school's vantage point.

I placed myself in relation to world events from this site, and not just in my classroom work. From the windows of the residence, I watched the local parade to celebrate the Queen's coronation in 1953; I still remember the radiator in the front window reaching just below my chin. For many years I simply assumed that I had seen the Queen herself on that occasion. I was much older when it struck me out of the blue one day that Her Majesty would have been in London, not on Long's Hill. Once again the real action had been elsewhere.

The United Church system offered the only co-educational program in the city, and the upper grades mixed girls and boys in every class. Its conflicted ideas about the education of girls, however, were common to all the "top" schools in St. John's. Marilyn Porter (2014) sums up some of the contradictions:

> *On the one hand, the schools under discussion exemplified the ideals of education for all and the provision of an equally excellent education for girls as boys; on the other hand, girls were also being prepared to be mothers in a particular religious tradition, as well as to be social helpmeets to their middle- and upper-class husbands. (p. 148)*

Porter expands on these confusions through an examination of school publications over the period of 1900 to 1950 (I recognize most of this perspective as lasting well into the 1950s). She observes

> *a generation of girls trying to understand these changes [resulting from the social impact of the wars and the consequent loosening of restrictions on girls' activities] and incorporate them into their thinking. But the competing and conflicting agendas of these schools—to educate fully competent women, able to participate in the world, but also to ensure that the next generation of mothers would perpetuate the social and gender orders—did not change. The denominational identity of the schools enforced a particular religious view of both class and gender....The governing bodies of all schools remained dominated by male clergy until the end of denominational schooling in Newfoundland in 1997. (p. 148)*

The contradictions of this paradoxical approach were more apparent to me on my return to St. John's at the age of fifteen after two years in Alberta's secular state system. At the time I left in 1962, I simply had a vague notion that "all of the above"—diligent effort at school, full participation in the civic order, and domesticated motherhood—would be required of me in due course.

Playground Life

Playground time was livelier than classroom time. By nature I was more of a lurker than a participant, which probably served me well as the principal's daughter, but I did imbibe the playground lore, a blend of British and local rhymes and games, with a few North American details for spice. Who knows where this counting-out rhyme came from?

> *My mother and your mother*
> *Were hanging out clothes;*
> *My mother gave your mother*
> *A punch in the nose,*
> *And guess what colour blood came out of it?*
> *R-E-D spells red*
> *And O-U-T spells out*
> *And out you must go*
> *As fast as your little legs will carry you*
> *Out!*

In the playground we skipped; we played marbles (called "alleys" in St. John's and played with a mott, a dip in the ground dug out with a revolving heel); we played mass games like Red Rover and Giant Steps (aka Grandmother's Footsteps). We played enormous games of tag. Every day a chain of girls balanced their way along the top of a little right-angled wall one stone high and one stone wide; as you successfully completed your go, you joined the lineup to do it again; if you fell off, you did exactly the same thing—a seriously low-stakes game! Christopher Pratt chose to omit this little curb from his painting of the school, possibly not registering its iconic importance to the girls' playground; the general aura of stoniness in the painting, on the other hand, is entirely correct.

An Origin Story and a Survival Story

Like Gower Street Church, the Prince of Wales school system was rooted in Methodism. The first building on the Holloway School site was the Wesleyan Academy, which opened in 1860. In 1874 it was renamed the Newfoundland Methodist College, and in 1886 a model school for teacher training was added, along with a student residence next door. All of these buildings were destroyed in the Great Fire of 1892.

At the time of the fire, Robert Edwards Holloway was the College principal, a role he held from 1874 to 1904. Ruby Gough's biography of this remarkable man (for whom my incarnation of the school was named) contains much fascinating information about the ambitions surrounding the Methodist College. She outlines something of the scale of loss represented by the Great Fire as it wiped out many hard-won investments:

> Household effects, the school registers and treasurer's books, the laboratory equipment and musical instruments—all were consumed in the enormous blaze that enveloped the buildings....
>
> The well-equipped laboratory and museum, now swept away in the blaze, were not an easily-come-by collection of equipment and materials for teaching and learning. They were the result of a succession of acquisitions over a period of eighteen years as small amounts of money were made available from time to time from the often meagre resources of the board, or when an interested board member, knowing that the funds would not be forthcoming, provided the necessary money from his own pocket. (Gough, 2005, pp. 88–89)

Holloway's dedication to the education of his pupils extended to a defence of girls' rights to learn mathematics and science as thoroughly as the daintier subjects. As an active scientist himself, and a very thoughtful educator, he brought the excitement of laboratory and field trip to the Methodist College students. He was also an early and renowned Newfoundland photographer.

By 1925, as Frederick R. Smith (1978) points out in his history of Holloway School, "The College, again well equipped and modern in all ways, contained a large hall, and offered all grades from Kindergarten to Senior Associate (first year university)" (n.p.). But fire destroyed the building once again.

> The next day a special meeting of the Board of Governors was called to deal with the situation. The Board minutes show that $92,500.00 of insurance was carried on the building but this was far from sufficient to cover the loss....
>
> As soon as news spread of the fire, letters of sympathy and offers of help started to come into the Board. Everyone wanted to help. Many people were

Annual Sale of Work and Turkey Tea

Under the auspices of the Ladies' College Aid Society and Girls' Guild of the United Church and Presbyterian Colleges. will be held in

PITTS MEMORIAL HALL

Wednesday and Thursday

Nov. 15th and 16th

Sale will be opened at 3.30 p.m. by His Worship the Mayor, H. G. R. Mews, Esq.

TURKEY TEAS—$1.25

Convenors of Tables: Mrs. J. E. Butler, Mrs. W. F. Butt, Mrs. George Marshall, Mrs. R. B. Moyse, Mrs. T. A. Richards and Mrs. G. H. Verge.

AFTERNOON TEAS—50c

Mrs. J. S. Woods, Convenor.

CHILDREN'S TEAS—25c

Miss Isabel Templeton, Convenor.

Plain and Fancy Work for Sale — Admission 10c

affected by the fire since the building acted as a center for the Ladies College Aid Society, the Girls Guild, the Methodist College Literary Institute (MCLI) and other auxiliary groups in addition to school activities. (n.p.)

These reports on the fires offer insight into the daily institutional activities of the school. The efforts to shore up yet again what had already once been achieved must have felt like a relentless and very wearisome obligation to the people who worked on restoring Methodist education once more. Around the same time as the 1925 fire, the board planned the LeMarchant Road school, Prince of Wales College. It opened in 1928, and pupils were distributed across both buildings.

One institutional arrangement mentioned above that lasted into my own day was the Ladies College Aid Society. The College Sale was a major event in November. My parents, in their memoir of their Prince of Wales years, describe it lovingly (the memoir is narrated in my father's voice, but both my parents worked on this document):

> The College Sale was an annual event put on by the Ladies College Aid Society, a group of friends of the College, who worked tirelessly to raise money for the school. They produced hand-made articles for the sale, and also laid on an absolutely splendid Tea....Each grade in the school had its own stall, and each child had the opportunity to provide something for that stall; many of these items were made during school time in the weeks preceding the sale. This input gave the students a vested interest in the proceedings, and unified the whole school, grade by grade, in a competition to see which grade would make the most money. I got to make the announcement of total sales, and which grade had come top, at the next day's assembly. (McCurdy & McCurdy, 2010/2002, p. 19)

Education as Competition

My parents' account of the way different grades competed to outsell each other at the College Sale represents a larger motif in my educational life. Competition was a paramount theme of school life.

While much of what we learned involved memorization and regurgitation, a fierce competitiveness offered one live ingredient in the daily grind. We challenged our classmates for a small number of prizes (I won a general prize every year but only once featured in the top three). The distribution of report cards was an august ceremony; most years Dad, as principal, appeared in the classroom and passed out these documents, starting with the student in first place and working his way down to the last. We also competed for provincial scholarships with other schools, and those stars who managed to come top in the province had their names mounted on a plaque in the assembly hall.

A photograph of Speech Night speaks volumes for the time, embodying a set of conventions, now lost, that display the social significance placed on academic achievement and the semiotics of its celebration. The Lieutenant-Governor of the Province and the Mayor of the City are in attendance, with their wives. The gowns, the furs, the white gloves, and the pearls all testify to the solemnity of the occasion. The vice-principal, Miss Guy, who is passing prizes to the lady in the strapless gown, is wearing her academic robes, making a different statement. Note that two local radio stations, VOWR and CJON, have microphones on the stage.

Although not acknowledged in quite such a ceremonial fashion, competition was even more unbridled when it came to sports (hockey and field hockey, soccer, basketball, curling). School-wide pep rallies at the Prince of Wales site preceded the big games, and if a team won a championship, all the schools in the system were awarded a half-holiday.

We even had a competitive little jingle about the qualities of girls in the different city school systems; it showed up in my autograph book as well as being a playground chant. I cannot think of a reasonable comment so I will simply present it. Bishop Spencer College was the girls' school of the Church of England, and Mercy Convent was the Catholic girls' school.

> Spencer girls are pretty,
> Mercy girls are smart,
> But it takes a girl from Prince of Wales
> To win a fellow's heart.

The Local School Board

The denominational system of education meant a proliferation of school boards and the Prince of Wales system had its own, a group of volunteers. As the principal's children, we had a greater cognizance of the existence of these worthies than our classmates probably did, and we were expected to be very polite in their presence. I recall many of them taking a great personal interest in the doings of the school; and the chairman of the board, Dr. Harry Roberts, actually phoned Dad every evening (reliably at 7:05, marking the official end of our family supper) to inquire about the day's doings at school. Whether Dad regarded this nightly conversation as support or surveillance has never been clear to me.

Institutional and personal issues intermingled in this and other ways, making our house something of a threshold space, an interface between home and school. The most irritating of these conditions arose with a heavy snowfall. Dad would phone the secretary of the school board to consult about closing school. Luckily this man's daughter was also in my class; we shared the opprobrium when the two men, after exchanging hearty stories about their own intrepid walks to school through gale and blizzard, declared our school open, even when other denominations closed for the day.

The Wider Education Framework

The Prince of Wales College system did not create its own syllabi or textbook selections. Newfoundland's Department of Education supplied lists of set texts, with different readers prescribed for the Catholic schools and for all the other schools. In some subject areas the department also supplied different titles for schools of three rooms and over versus one- or two-room schools.

The department administered provincial exams and issued numerical and verbal reports, on comparisons, strengths, weaknesses, and needs as represented by these exams. Department officials made speeches and drew up policy documents; the Newfoundland Teachers' Association sometimes responded. The range of thought and action needed to bring schooling to a far-flung collection of mostly very small communities, with scant history or tradition of formal education and with no great means to make radical strides in a hurry, was complex and demanding.

Cultural Institutions

Many other kinds of organization factored into my cultural life and affected the ways in which I became literate in different media. Childhood literacy is framed by many overlapping local events involving deliberate decision making. I remain convinced that the hypothesis is generally true and important; what I did not bargain on when I began this work was how idiosyncratically these decisions often played out in St. John's. Poverty of income and paucity of democratic control led to many compromise arrangements—what is noteworthy is that institutional regulation did not disappear simply because there was no regularized channel for its expression. Different solutions arose for different institutions, sometimes in ad hoc ways.

This section represents only an anecdotal sampling; a full history is far beyond my scope. It offers a glimpse of a small and paradoxical civic society. Newfoundland in the 1950s was isolated, yet also internationally connected, with many nationalities of fishermen just offshore. The population, already small in terms of raw numbers, was in effect rendered still smaller through sectarianism, but unlike many other sectarian societies, Newfoundland was largely non-violent. After Confederation, the new province was governed through a new and highly personalized political system, with a naïve, imperious, and charismatic premier. Not every choice made in these challenging times was ideal, but that fact makes the human decision making all the more visible.

My account may seem exotic and unrepresentative, but, in fact, everybody's cultural setting is shaped by human decisions even when they are far more orthodox than Newfoundland's solutions. And the consequences of decisions linger; some of the history I have managed to trace predates my own times by decades, yet the residual impact of the original compromises continued to flavour the cultural atmosphere well into my own day.

The Movie Theatres

"The first exhibition of moving pictures in Newfoundland was a demonstration of the Lumière *Cinématographe* on 13 and 14 December 1897 in the Methodist College Hall for 30 cents admission," says Paul S. Moore (2007, p. 449) in his intriguing article on early picture shows in St. John's. Ten years later, the first movie theatre opened, the Nickel Theatre in St. Patrick's Hall. Unlike other jurisdictions, St. John's did not put its movie theatres in the commercial centre of Water Street but instead took over various "pre-existing buildings run by civic and religious associations" (p. 450) (the next two movie halls opened in the Total Abstinence Hall and the Star of the Sea Hall, names that give some sense of the flavour of the local culture of the day). St. John's did not introduce new licensing regulations to manage these new technological and cultural institutions, relying instead on exhortations from the churches (the Roman Catholics were particularly active) and subjecting the movie theatres only to tax laws. Moore ascribes this tendency, at least in part, to the fact that

> in this period the St. John's municipal council was cash poor and lacked the power to tax, police, and service the city at anywhere near the level becoming normative throughout North America. At times, the colonial government even suspended the existence of an elected council altogether. It was thus not only religion contributing to the parochial character of film regulation. The municipal structure overall in Newfoundland was feeble, implying that the colonial government refused to accept bureaucratic regulation and public safety measures as the cornerstone of the people's welfare, as has been theorized for American cities. (p. 448)

Movie-going has normalized in Newfoundland since those early days, but decisions about regulation, taxing, and so on continue to be made at a local level. At more national and international levels, of course, the corporate decision making entailed in the making of a feature film is highly complex—but that is another story.

I was less surprised than I might have expected to discover that the churches were initially involved in film distribution in St. John's. Something of an aura of religious prescriptiveness lingered about movie-going even into my own time. I cannot articulate how this impression made itself felt at the time; my memories are inchoate and not really helpful. But when I read Moore's article, his account chimed with my own sense of the atmosphere that surrounded the idea of going to the movies. As with so many other nebulous elements of my island life, I felt the contrast when we moved to Edmonton.

The Bookstore

The main city bookstore was Dicks and Company. "The three-storey building provided a large showroom for books and stationery on the main

floor, with additional showroom space on the second floor and the bindery on the third" (Riggs, 2005, p. 228).

I don't remember ever getting the chance to choose books to buy in this store, though it must have happened occasionally. Books were bought *for* me on rare, ritual occasions—birthdays, Christmases, and school prize-givings—but I did not normally participate in the selection. What the Dicks staff chose to bring into the store affected my reading activities neverthe-less. Many of the books I have collected from family members still bear the Dicks sticker. That label marks the end papers of my copy of *Old Mother West Wind*, and the school prize label (for the usual "General Proficiency" rather than anything more impressive) indicates that the school drew on this resource for the enticing stack of new books on the stage table at Speech Night.

Bert Riggs's history of the company tells us that sometime in the late 1830s, a stationer and bookbinder rented space on Water Street from a sailmaker named John Dicks. Dicks's youngest son Robert took over the bookbinding and selling operation in 1840, and the bookstore was a feature of Water Street until 1983. It still exists in St. John's at a different address but has reverted to its original mandate of office supplies.

∧ *My copy of Thornton W. Burgess's* Old Mother West Wind, *marked by selection processes first exercised by Dicks and Company (whose sticker appears on the lower inner corner of the cover) and second by Holloway School.*

[Courtesy Penguin Random House]

HOLLOWAY SCHOOL
ST. JOHN'S, NFLD.

Grade 3

General Proficiency PRIZE

Awarded to

Margaret McCurdy

June 195 .   *S.G. McCurdy*

Principal

Decisions made at Dicks directly affected my literate life. It is hard to recall in this age of alternatives, but for much of my time in St. John's, if Dicks didn't sell it, it wasn't available. The material impact of Confederation on book supply may well have affected Dicks's commercial and legal relationships with wholesalers. Did they begin to acquire more titles from Toronto rather than from New York or London or Boston? That history remains to be written.

Radio

Joseph Smallwood, never one for understatement if grandiloquence was an option, said, "Radio was invented by God especially for Newfoundland, and having done it for Newfoundland, He graciously allowed it to be used in other parts of the World" (Swain, 1999, p. 17). Smallwood was (probably) joking, but no doubt radio transformed the very isolated settlements of the province and had a huge impact in St. John's as well. It was in the 1920s that radio came to Newfoundland; the story is familiar: "Capitalizing on new technologies seemed impossible, however, during the 1920s, when fundamental economic problems and a perennial fiscal shortfall preoccupied the public officials. Even basic regulatory functions seemed beyond the means of the embattled government. No Newfoundland bureaucratic apparatus regulated radio broadcasters or remedied the sources of electrical interference that impeded radio reception" (Webb, 2008, p. 17).

Once again, when government failed, the churches stepped up. In the case of radio, it was the Methodists who moved into the breach. Jeff Webb (2008) tells us, "There is an unstated assumption in many histories of radio broadcasting that privately owned stations serve their owners' interests and state-ownership is synonymous with public broadcasting, yet the church-owned 8WMC (later renamed VOWR) was in many respects Newfoundland's first public broadcaster" (p. 17).

Rev. Joseph Joyce of Wesley Methodist Church in St. John's initially set out in 1924 to find a way to broadcast church services to shut-ins. But he was not averse to wider use of his facility, and "a Newfoundland Broadcasting Committee soon began using the church transmitter to provide news, entertainment, and public service" (Webb, 2008, p. 18). The exchange between religious uplift and news and entertainment was still in operation in my time; it is noteworthy that my accidentally surviving church calendar tells me that Gower Street's morning and evening services of December 30,

1956, were both broadcast—the morning service on VOWR, still in operation with something of a religious mandate, and the evening service on VOCM, a private and secular station.

In 1932 a private station opened in St. John's—VONF, Voice of Newfoundland, owned by the Dominion Broadcasting Company, a subsidiary of the Avalon Telephone Company. In 1939 this station was absorbed by the Broadcasting Corporation of Newfoundland (BCN) and, from then on, it provided Newfoundland's first public radio programming. Ten years later, the CBC took it over, and it became part of the Canadian public radio and television network as CBN.

VONF played a crucial role in Newfoundland politics in a number of ways that I can mention only briefly. Radio was influential in the isolated communities of Newfoundland, though limited by two factors: the price of the radio itself plus the license to play it legally, and the absence or unreliability of electricity supplies, which meant that expensive power generation arrangements were also a necessity. Radio could sometimes reach mariners at sea, and it provided connection with home for the fishermen who spent long seasons off the Labrador coast. Its marine safety role gave it a special place in a maritime society.

VONF gave Joseph Smallwood a route into many Newfoundland homes via his program, *The Barrelman*, sponsored by F.M. O'Leary, a local pharmaceutical wholesaler. It later supplied Smallwood and others with another platform when it broadcast much of the 1947 convention that debated Newfoundland's future.

At the same time as it delved into formal politics, Newfoundland radio supplied a chain of contact and information for far-flung residents. The *Gerald S. Doyle News Bulletin*, sponsored by a second pharmaceutical wholesaler, rival to O'Leary, became an institution. Webb (2008) describes its very broad remit:

> The Gerald S. Doyle News Bulletin *became one of the most popular programs in Newfoundland radio history and transcended the boundaries of what was commonly accepted as "news." The term* bulletin *provides an apt metaphor. The program was somewhat like a bulletin board in a public space upon which people could post notices of upcoming events, appeals for aid, or messages they might want to pass on to others....The latter ranged from notice of the arrival of vessels, to reassurances for rural listeners that*

their loved ones were being released from hospital or had arrived in the
capital, and occasionally more tragic news such as a death. In towns that
lacked a telegraph station, in the lumber camps and at sea in fishing schoo-
ners, such messages were essential. (pp. 85–86)

Radio was used for similarly intimate purposes in another program, lasting from wartime into the 1970s. *Calling Newfoundland* was hosted for decades out of London in the UK by Margot Rhys Davies. Initially featuring personal letters and recordings of Newfoundland soldiers and sailors far from home, it later morphed into a more general message show. I recall listening to these communications, paradoxically so private and so public at the same time; they prefigured some of the contradictory intimacies of the Internet today. Radio helped Newfoundlanders to build an "imagined community" (Webb, 2008, p. 215), and such programs ensured that the imagined community of Newfoundland was populated with named and real people.

Throughout the war, VONF took its main international news feeds from two sources: the BBC and a British-based Reuters news service.

Since the Reuters service, which the BCN purchased, had been compiled for
distribution in North America, it was designed to inform North Americans
of events in Europe. Reuters did not believe it was important to tell North
Americans what was happening in their own hemisphere—information
that listeners could get from other sources. This left [VONF] in the peculiar
position of lacking good coverage of American news and having even poorer
coverage of Canadian news, even though Newfoundland was part of North
America. (Webb, 2008, p. 115)

At the same time as the news largely focused on Europe, Newfoundland was a major strategic site for the war of the North Atlantic; first Canadian and later American military personnel flooded the island. The Americans, in particular, brought their entertainment tastes with them. Newfoundlanders with good enough radio sets had long been able to pick up North American stations and expected their own local radio to keep up with American music. Webb reports many complaints from the high-minded (often of British origin) about two main concerns: the lowbrow musical program- ming offered by St. John's radio stations, based on American precedents and all too often featuring "jazz"; and the propensity for local dialects and "bad grammar" to sneak into programs that made any kind of room for local voices.

Webb's account of that pendulum swing between a British news orientation and an American entertainment repertoire, with Canada barely featuring in the mix at all, resonated with me when I read it. My memories are too vague to be more precise about how this dichotomy manifested itself in the 1950s, and Webb's account mostly ends in 1949. Still, his explanation provides a historical explanation of something that confused and annoyed me as a child: the local, the British, and the American all had their place across our culture, but the Canadian was often downplayed.

Webb makes another important point when he acknowledges that radio did not *create* an international awareness, though it certainly *shaped* it in specific ways.

> Newfoundlanders were heirs to the same Western "civilization" as their counterparts elsewhere, and their views were shaped by being part of the British Empire and their proximity to the United States. They also had always been engaged in an international economy and culture. Radio broadcasting was a twentieth-century technology that developed in conjunction with consumer capitalism, so a facile reading might juxtapose a hypothetical isolated pre-modern Newfoundland culture with the modernity of North American business once radio develops. Such a false dichotomy cannot be supported by evidence. Newfoundland popular culture had always been in dynamic conversation with forms and ideas from elsewhere in the world. Newfoundland was fully integrated into international capitalism and patterns of consumption in the 1940s; in some ways it always had been. (pp. 6–7)

Don Jamieson, later a federal cabinet minister, was one of the owners of CJON Radio, a station that came into being only with Confederation because the Commission of Government had lacked the authority to grant a license. In his memoirs, he makes a case (perhaps not entirely disinterested) that CJON introduced much more robust reporting and calling community leaders to account than had previously existed.

> Prior to CJON's debut, both the print and electronic media had taken a safe, conventional approach in its treatment of local news. Investigative

*reporting was nonexistent, and people in the news could actually count on
the kid glove treatment. Indeed, they expected it....*

*At CJON we began at once to shake up the long-standing, cosy arrange-
ment. We introduced such innovations as hourly news reports, taped voice
inserts and editorial comment. Our competition soon followed suit and,
as a result, news reporting in Newfoundland changed dramatically and
permanently....Such a great change in the media reached across the whole
spectrum of Newfoundland life, but nowhere was its influence more felt
than in politics. (Jamieson, 1989, p. 182)*

The cultural history of deference that Jamieson describes as belonging
to the pre-CJON era certainly lingered well into my time; right up to my
departure from Newfoundland in 1970, it was striking how many members
of the public considered it inappropriate to say anything critical about
Premier Smallwood.

Television

Confederation reduced restrictions on commercial broadcasting; the
new province possessed licensing powers denied to the Commission
of Government. VOCM swiftly expanded its operations, and the
Newfoundland Broadcasting Company successfully applied to start CJON.

It was customary in Canada for the first television station in a new
market to be the CBC, but the private station CJON took that honour in St.
John's in 1955. The CBC opened a television station in Corner Brook on the
west coast of Newfoundland in 1959 but did not set up a station in St. John's
until 1964. This absence reinforced a public indifference to Canadian news
and culture that our Canadian family consciously resisted; we were much
more loyal to CBC Radio than most of my friends' families, even when we
couldn't have the TV channel.

Television not only introduced a new media format and content to our
lives; like radio, it also served as a catalyst as it infiltrated the rhythms of
daily life and inflected our politics. As I've already suggested in Chapter 12,
it gave us new ways to see ourselves.

The Newspapers

We took in two daily newspapers, the morning *Daily News* and the afternoon *Evening Telegram*, both produced on giant letterpress machines. The
Telegram office was near the library, and we could hear the presses roaring

as we walked by. Newspapers assembled through typesetting accumulate odd corners of empty column inches where an article randomly fails to fill the available space, and both newspapers excelled in finding brief oddities from around the world to fill these gaps. As a consequence, we would get a short news item, very much in medias res, of some ongoing event in some obscure part of the world, a nugget that presumably filled the required number of inches. There was little content logic to these items; we would pick up a reference one day and then see nothing for weeks; that sense of the world outside as utterly random and discontinuous was an underlying motif of my awareness of current events for many years.

One of the papers also supplied a regular column of Ripley's Believe It or Not!—a kind of newsprint freak show, that, in a strange way, simply confirmed that the world out there was an outlandish place. Jill Lepore (2013) suggests that, "In Ripley, the foreign is weird and the weird is foreign" (p. 65). It was sometimes difficult to resist coming to this patronizing conclusion from the entire offerings of our newspapers on any given day.

The newspapers added some depth to the analysis of local politics but not as much as might be thought. Nix Wadden, a journalist who worked for nearly every local news outlet at some point during the 1950s, offered a pithy summary of the restrictive nature of our news world in his "Town Crier" column of August 1, 1957, which appeared in the short-lived independent *Newfoundland Weekly*. As a Progressive Conservative activist, Wadden was perhaps not completely disinterested, but his general point is substantive.

> *Did you know the* Telegram's *editorials are practically all written by the same person who writes its daily column: Harold Horwood? Did you know the* Daily News *editorials are all written by the same person who writes its daily column: Albert Perlin? Everyone knows the* Sunday Herald *is owned and operated by* CJON, *although its editorials and the bulk of its story material are written by Editor Arch Sullivan, whereas Don Jamieson dictates the editorial policy of* CJON. *Not to mention the fact that the* Western Star *at Corner Brook, Nfld.'s only other newspaper of any general influence, is owned by the* Telegram. VOCM *in St. John's indulges in no editorializing, aside from the occasional theatrical "aside" from News Announcer Denys Ferry.* CBC, *being a drain upon the Canadian taxpayer, risks no comment on the status quo. (Wadden, 2008, p. 59)*

The *Daily News* ran from February 15, 1894, until June 4, 1984. Memorial University offers a listing of Newfoundland papers that provides a brief account of the newspaper's political placement during the years of my study: "In 1948, the *Daily News* supported at least a temporary return to Responsible Government before any decision on Confederation was made. The paper supported the Progressive Conservative Party in 1949 but later became increasingly favourable toward Smallwood and the Liberals" (Memorial University Libraries, n.d., n.p.).

The *Evening Telegram* was older, having been first published on April 3, 1879. Unlike the *News*, it is still in existence; it was purchased by Thomson Newspapers in 1970 and has been owned by TC Media since 2004. The Memorial listing says, "The paper supported the Commission of Government and avoided taking sides on the question of Confederation in 1948." It soon shifted to a stronger stance:

> The Evening Telegram *published material that was critical of the Smallwood administration in the 1950's and 1960's. Although the editorials, even if sceptical, maintained a respectful tone, some of the columnists, such as Harold Horwood and Ray Guy, were less circumspect. The government countered with a series of libel suits and prosecution for breach of privilege. When the government threatened to withdraw government advertising, the* Telegram *refused to accept their advertisements any more. (Memorial University Libraries, n.d., n.p.)*

That last sentence speaks volumes about the political culture of the time.

Folk Culture

Although nobody would deny deliberate human agency in the development of folk culture, it is conventionally thought to arise in amorphous and collective ways. Newfoundland's oral culture is legendary for its richness and longevity, and includes songs, dances, stories, and the drama of the mummers (which survived in vestigial form into my time in the city, in the form of groups of unknown children calling at our house to look at the tree at Christmas time, the lingering remnants of old-style wassailing in our urban setting).

Newfoundland settlers brought their local cultural repertoires with them when they immigrated. Isolation, often even from the next outpost along the coast, kept the strains reasonably pure, and the absence of alternative entertainment kept them lively. Yet the very rustic image invoked by this description is only a partial truth.

In 1927 the same Gerald S. Doyle who sponsored the news bulletin published a book of Newfoundland songs, interleaved with advertisements for his pharmaceutical products; he distributed it for free among his outport customers.

Folklorist Neil Rosenberg (1991) describes the combination of patriotic sentiment and commercial acumen that led to the distribution of this book.

> In November 1927 Doyle published Old-Time Songs and Poetry of Newfoundland. Subtitled "Songs of Folklore, Humour, Tragedy, and History, from the Days of Our Forefathers", its seventy-two pages carried the texts to forty-three songs and poems, with brief headnotes for each text. There was no music. Interspersed among the texts were advertisements for the products sold by Doyle, in the same manner as in the annual almanacs which the Chase Company, an American firm for whom Doyle was the Newfoundland agent, had been publishing for years. The commercial side of Doyle's motivation to produce the songbook was thus inspired at least in part by this example of American advertising.
>
> This songster was the first of five editions, three of which were published during Doyle's lifetime, of what is locally called the "Doyle songbook". All editions of the small center-stapled paperback were given away by Doyle's company, and were widely distributed throughout Newfoundland. In a place where little of value could be had for free, these books were prized possessions in many households, and remain so today. The Doyle songbooks presented "key texts," creating a popular canon for Newfoundland folksongs. (p. 46)

Many of the songs Doyle chose to anthologize over the years became staples in the classic Newfoundland folk repertoire. They certainly existed before he picked them up, but his role in popularizing them is significant. Rosenberg (1991) suggests that his selections for the different editions "were used to construct a vision of the nation which reflected contemporary political events" (p. 56). They were certainly chosen with deliberation: "Doyle promoted his songster as the definitive source for Newfoundland songs by keeping the songs most widely sung (and reprinted by others) in

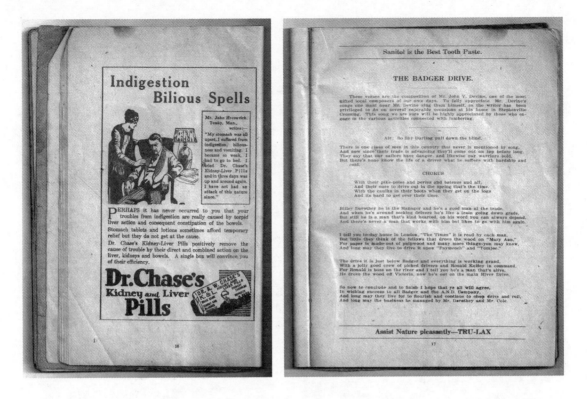

∧ *Facing pages 16–17 in*
the 1927 edition of Doyle's
Old-Time Songs and
Poetry of Newfoundland:
a typical juxtaposition
of advertising matter and
song lyrics, from a copy
preserved in a household
in Harbour Grace South
through 2011.

[Reprinted by permission of
the Doyle family]

subsequent editions, discarding songs that didn't 'catch on', and seeking new songs that might" (p. 56).

The children of Gerald S. Doyle have made an intriguing film about their father and his important role in Newfoundland history (*Regarding Our Father*, 2011). As well as drawing attention to the varied ways in which Doyle helped to shape the culture of Newfoundland over a period of many decades, this movie also features colour film of the Newfoundland outports in the early and mid-twentieth century, a rare treat. Tacitly as well as explicitly, the images and the analysis of this film offer a perspective on a lively culture in transition.

Doyle's role in the creation of a canon is not to be ignored. He also created a tradition of commercial promulgation of this material. Just before I left Newfoundland in 1970, en route to Britain, my unsentimental brother David gave me a little booklet of Newfoundland songs to take along. The volume measures four inches across by five and a half high, and contains thirty-two pages, presenting twenty-two songs. *The Fifth Edition of Newfoundland Songs* was published for free distribution by Dominion Ale. The foreword says, "The Bennett Brewing Company takes great pleasure in presenting this fifth edition of our little song book. Like our products, it is

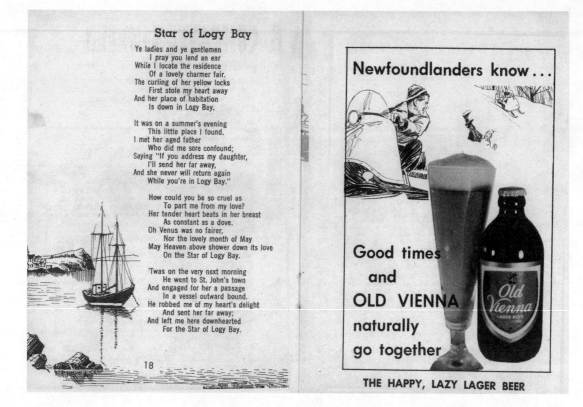

∧ *Facing pages 18–19*
in The Fifth Edition of
Newfoundland Songs.
[*Collection of the author*]

purely for your pleasure" (n.d., p. 1). The acknowledgements thank Gerald S. Doyle Ltd. for use of its song book.

Like its famous predecessor, my Dominion Ale booklet merges content and advertising. Such publications, with their mixed motivations, may be said to fertilize certain strands of the folk culture. E. David Gregory (2004) says that Newfoundland song traditions were "considerably more diverse" (p. 9) than what was reflected in the songsters. These publications indicate that the folk canon was an "assisted" phenomenon, that institutional decisions played a role in the preservation of the people's culture.

Obviously, I am setting a cautious toe into very deep waters, indeed, and I have no expertise to reach any informed conclusions. In my youth, I certainly knew the songs that Doyle rendered canonical, and others, too, but my involvement in the broad and deep traditional culture of Newfoundland was that of a city girl in a family of incomers. I took huge local pride in the lively songs and respected this element of the culture greatly.

Conclusions

To me, the creation of this chapter feels vital but reckless. It would take another research lifetime to do justice to the topics I have raised here, and I am sure that more knowledgeable local historians and scholars will take umbrage at my once-over-lightly skip through some very significant and complex topics. I apologize for those errors I have almost certainly introduced in this brief overview. But it is vital to note that the kind of mix I describe here—of cultural currents, political decisions and evasions of decision making, public and commercial resources, and the active and/or frustrated will of citizens—provides an important structural component in the developing literacy of any single, situated child. My situation did not just "grow" or develop by accident, although I am sure that no single individual or institution necessarily intended all the consequences marking the conditions in which I found myself. Emergent civic structures, arising out of technological, social, and political imperatives, shaped our cultural arrangements; in this fact, we resembled every known polity. My partial and faulty account of one jurisdiction's history raises questions about such institutional effects on any person's individual literacies.

Literacy does not develop organically out of the wilderness. It is cultivated through the agency of humans, individually and collectively. This chapter barely scratches the surface of the complex interweave of decision-making institutions that operated in one small and isolated city, and it largely ignores the broader-scale decisions made elsewhere that fed into our local existence. But it does attempt to acknowledge an element of our literate lives that is too often invisible.

CODA

[The memory cue] comes together with the fragments of remembered experience (and a lot of other knowledge and inference) to create something new. Roger Shattuck, discussing Proust, put it like this: "like our eyes, our memories must see double; these two images then converge in our minds into a single heightened reality." Our two eyes, stereoscopically aligned, allow us to see space; memory allows us to "see" time. Memories are about what happened then, but they are also about who we are now.
(Fernyhough, 2012, p. 248)

AS CHARLES FERNYHOUGH SAYS, "I am not reliving the experience so much as standing in a relation with it" (p. 248). Our two eyes give us stereoscopic vision; memory allows a kind of stereo-temporal experience—*then* inflected by *now* and vice versa.

The past that I explore in this study is illuminated for me by shafts of memory, mostly consisting of single moments. I have fleshed out these gleams to the best of my ability by revisiting the texts that feature in these transient flickers. In the most literal sense, I have "re-collected" as I recollect—bringing together as many as I can now locate of the textual artifacts that shaped those prior events. The "eye" turned on the past sees glimmers of elapsed moments; the texts, consistently laid out on page or screen, remain available to be consulted, reassessed. Unlike either my present or my past "eye," they exist in an enduring state perhaps best described as an ongoing condition of "present participle," a "suspended permanent" condition. The readings change but the words remain stable on the pages.

The present is shaped by many factors (including, no doubt, my own current locations, shifting between Alberta and Newfoundland as I work on this project). Is my contemporary experience any less formative than my childhood? My present-tense "eye" is informed by what I am reading now: books and articles and blogs and websites about acts of literacy; readings that permit me to explore how our ideas of textual interpretation may be shaped by the concept of a spatially and temporally placed and specifically embodied cognition. This current perspective works with and against a field of more constant and universal text-objects from my past.

Much of my reading today involves accessible versions of neuroscience that I am not qualified to evaluate. Such frontier work offers potentially fruitful routes into a better understanding of how we read. At the least, new ideas may shift our settled assumptions. But such a venture needs to be handled with care. The hazard of drawing extensively on such work is that my own thinking may be reduced to the limited science I am able to comprehend; my capacity to be critical is correspondingly reduced. I also risk a broader corruption. As Brian Massumi (2002) tartly warns, "People in the humanities...isolate an attractive scientific or mathematical concept and add it to the repertoire of their own disciplinary system, like an exotic pet" (p. 19).

In theory at least, my second eye, focused on the texts from my past, guards against such reductiveness. I draw on new ideas about how the mind works to the extent that it helps me make sense of the materials from my own history that I have revisited for this project. My hope is that using these texts as the pivotal point between different ways of thinking will enable me to honour the complexity of those historic materials and the challenge of reading them, in light of contemporary ideas.

In this final section of the book, I attempt a multifaceted account of how we read (the "we" of this unassuming phrase standing in for the elements of collective and universal behaviour that are shared by most readers). But I will challenge and limit that account by factoring in the singular, specific, and located ingredients of the process that occur when *I* read. My reading story only partially mirrors everybody else's; and everyone else joins the general and abstract process in equally singular ways.

18
Back to the First Place

Notes toward a Grounded Understanding of Reading

A family photo of Hughs Pond in the summer of 1957; Mrs. Duder is rowing my brother and me. I am eight; he is seven. In my mind, Mrs. Duder is timeless!

[Collection of the author]

YOU CAN'T GO HOME AGAIN. "Too bad the house is gone" (Kroetsch, 2010, p. 11). But there are traces of the scriptive invitations in the books, even when reread by an adult. And traces of the dynamic and situated awareness that once fuelled my ability to read still occasionally survive in today's landscape, reminding me of how the world opened to me in my childhood.

Of Water Lilies and Re-Cognition

In the summer of 2013, for the first time in over fifty years, I drove to Hughs Pond, the place where I learned to row a boat, instructed by Mrs. Gwen Duder, who also taught me to read. I soon found that the left and right turnings in the road to the pond were familiar from way back, both to my eyes and also to my physical sense of balance. Hughs Pond, now on the edge of the city rather than out in the country, has predictably changed from the rustic setting for a few rough cabins into a desirable residential area. The homes springing up along the edge of the pond today are large and lavish, and suburban in style, exactly as I had anticipated. I reached the end of the spur road, unsurprised, and turned around to drive back out again—and then I spotted the water lilies at the edge of the pond.

It was a stereo-temporal moment, an absolute match of then and now that discharged an electric surge of *potential* through me, a subjunctive opening of possibilities. I am not a big fan of the inserted hyphen, but this was a moment of both recognition and re-cognition.

As a child, I was very aware of water lilies as pretty and interesting. Seeing them now, I felt a sharp physical memory of how difficult it was to manage the heavy oars that clunked uncooperatively in the oarlocks with the weight of the lake pulling against us. I also suddenly recalled my young self, cherishing an image of my brother and me rowing smoothly into the lilies to pick a few for our mother, who loved wildflowers. Mrs. Duder, however, warned us to avoid those lilies at all cost. Their roots, invisible to our eyes, would entangle our oars and threaten the boat's equilibrium far beyond our feeble powers of recovery.

Absorbing that dynamic fact would alter my understanding of water lilies forever—and in the summer of 2013, I suddenly remembered that moment of learning, of adjusting my sense of my known world. Of course, since then, I have seen other water lilies. But these particular flowers, exactly where I remember them hugging the shoreline, returned me to that moment of sudden new ways of framing a known scene (water lilies as treacherous, not just beautiful), complicating a situation I thought I already understood perfectly well. The specific 2013 landscape was briefly fused with remembered potential for change. In our boat, struggling to control one oar apiece, my brother and I were already in a liminal space; the disruption to my sense of the world provided by learning about the perfidiousness of the lilies was one more shift in an arena already charged for change.

Brief as it was, this moment of remembering served as a corrective to my adult sense of the past as something singular. For children, an idea is singular only until it is rendered multiple or contradictory or confusing. Such changes are a regular feature of ordinary life, and children incorporate new knowledge in a taken-for-granted way. Returning to that place where I learned about water lilies brought me for a moment into the mental space of adjustment that I so often inhabited as a child. For a moment I felt that change of awareness in its moment of *unfolding*. It was a gleam into the Murk.

Novels capture some of that energy of change, stow it inside the covers of the book in all its latent readiness to be discharged by a reader. And in the course of our reading, we also enter a zone of necessary fluidity. Mendelsund points out that we extrapolate far ahead of the data the author provides and then fudge our extrapolating processes. He offers an example from Virginia Woolf's *To the Lighthouse*:

> *Mrs. Ramsey is speaking to her son, we are told. Is she, perhaps, seventy—and he fifty? No, we learn that he is only six. Revisions are made. And so on. If fiction were linear, we would learn to wait, in order to picture. But we don't wait. We begin imaging right out of the gate, immediately on beginning a book.*
>
> *When we remember reading books, we don't remember having made these constant little adjustments. (Mendelsund, 2014, pp. 52–53)*

By Mendelsund's account, much of our regular activity of making sense of a narrative sets up a kind of local mini-Murk. How quickly do we forget that we once—briefly—pictured James as a middle-aged man? The traces do not entirely disappear but they are somehow "Murkified"—the appearance and evaporation of initial confusions is simply part of how reading happens, and we don't notice what we are forgetting in the necessary cause of greater understanding.

It is rare to re-enter a situated moment of conceptual change as completely as I did for a second or two in 2013 at the sight of the water lilies in Hughs Pond, but the act of opening up a book read long ago is a relatively commonplace occurrence. What past energies of our own changing perspectives also inhabit the book, along with the subjunctive vitality of the fiction itself?

Lessons of Rereading

It would be possible to consider rereading as a way of re-achieving something. In contrast, my experience in rereading so many materials from my own past is that, sooner or later, the story opens up to uncertainty all over again, and I experience Gerrig's (1993) "anomalous suspense," in which "knowledge from outside a narrative world fails to influence the moment-by-moment experience of the narrative" (p. 176). My previous knowledge of the story is somehow also Murkified, and for the moment I am unable to access it.

Is the development of a local mini-Murk an essential element of immersed reading? I do not have a definitive answer to that question, but I find the question itself provocative. In order to participate in the subjunctive moment of a story, I may indeed need to forget a variety of well-established prior knowledge; I may also have to jettison my initial hypotheses about the story itself and make every effort to obliterate their ongoing impact. The activation of a mini-Murk, a local forgetting, may indeed be a habitual component of the repertoire I bring to bear on this activity.

Ingold's (2010) work on "making" helped me to understand the sense of open-endedness that is needed to re-engage fully with a fiction. He does not consider the idea of readers as "makers," but I think a case can be made that they are. "As practitioners," says Ingold, "the builder, the gardener, the cook, the alchemist and the painter are not so much imposing form on matter as bringing together diverse materials and combining or redirecting their flow in the anticipation of what might emerge" (p. 91). We do not read backward from the achievement of a fully realized artistic experience (although some-times we write about our reading as if we had done so); we read forward into the uncertainty that develops in the story being told. The practice of reading itself shares this quality; we do not impose a pre-established form on our experience of reading. Instead we weave strands of own lives into the words before us on the page and *ride* the energy that is thus created— and so, every reading is also new.

My account of reading has entailed an embodied, placed reader as an essential component of that achieved texture of a reading experience. My final challenge is to explore how contemporary scholarship can illuminate the *general* achievements of a *specified* reader and make conceptual sense of the placed physicality of reading.

Crago (2014) sums up the enigma of how we make sense of a fiction in the following terms: "What is inside us somehow merges with that comes from 'outside'—a story made up by someone we have never met—and the way this happens is the great mystery of the reading experience" (p. 148). Even as I simultaneously explore my own interior recollections and revisit a work on today's terms, as today's reader, I come up against what is *unspeakable* in this event. The challenge of description is formidable.

The Ascertainable and the Ineffable

"[T]o completely analyze what we do when we read," wrote E.B. Huey (2009/1908) more than a century ago, "would almost be the acme of a psychologist's achievements, for it would be to describe very many of the most intricate workings of the human mind, as well as to unravel the tangled story of the most remarkable specific performance that civilization has learned in all its history" (p. 4).

I present this famous quotation, not because I am vainglorious enough to consider that I have met Huey's challenge, but rather more as an apologia for the complex chapter that concludes this book. This intricate choreography of the human mind, this historic achievement of civilization—how do we explain its acquisition by an ordinary child in St. John's, Newfoundland, in the 1950s? This chapter will attempt to mark out the territory covered by such a question. I will address this challenge from several perspectives.

First comes the issue of how we may develop inside our own private minds an embodied understanding of the words on the page—the neuro-psychological question. I will move between aspects of neuroscience, components of literary theorizing, and examples from my childhood books to investigate this question.

Second, I return to the power of the subjunctive mood, that agent of "anomalous suspense" (Gerrig, 1993, p. 79) that allows us to move deictic centres, to enter the uncertainties of a fictional world as many times as we choose. I will test the powers of the subjunctive in a final visit to *The Moffats*.

Third, I take the universal state of embodiment and explore how our understanding of reading is enriched by considering the location of that body. What do we comprehend more acutely when we take account of the fact that the universals of psychological responses to particular stimuli and the abstractions of the grammar of fiction are all brought into action in a singular time and place by each individual reader? What can we learn if we add the idea of groundedness to our reception theories?

It is an ambitious agenda, but I hope that keeping a single reader in mind will help in maintaining clarity of purpose and of focus.

"From my body inwards":
A Hypothesis of Sympathetic Embodiment

Lacking introspective access to my earliest stages of comprehending both my own actual and a full range of possible worlds, I turn (with my present-tense eye) to accounts of babies expressing their own embodied reactions to the world. Shaun Gallagher quotes studies that demonstrate that babies as young as forty-two minutes old are able to imitate the actions of an adult by opening their mouths and sticking out their tongues. Neonates reliably produce this response, which is all the more remarkable when it is taken into account that they are taking in *visual* data and responding with *motor* activity—and that their visual functions are working for the first time. Gallagher (2005) speaks of "an intermodal sensory system that enables the infant to recognize a structural equivalence between itself and the other person" (p. 75).

If newborns can recognize structural equivalence between another person and themselves in the first moments of their lives, we are talking about a very potent capacity, indeed. We seem able to *invest* that structural equivalence into the figments of humanity that occupy our written universe. The automatic transfer of a sense of structural equivalence between human readers and the verbal or audio-visual illusions placed before them represents one transfer point where the energy of reading is generated out of a fusion of life and text. By the time we emerge from the Murk, many of us can recognize written personalities as virtually possessing qualities that mark our own embodied lives.

Crago calls on Freud to describe this transfer point in different terms, discussing a reader, Janet, who felt a strong identification with *The Twelve Dancing Princesses*. As I have done before with Crago's (2014) elaborate argument, I will address only a small component—but one that factors readily into my own sense of structural equivalence.

> For Janet, the words of the fairy tale contained the power that magically transformed her world; in fact, that power came from within her. Freud says that we unconsciously "put" our own psychic energy into someone or something (cathexis) and in so doing, we lend it that magic which then (in turn) casts its glamour over the mundane events and characters of our own lives. But the "lending" is not something any of us decides to do—conscious decisions are largely a function of the left hemisphere: rather, it happens automatically and instantly, when the right hemisphere responds to a simi-

larity between a new experience, and a pattern that is already familiar.
(*p. 66*)

The field of neuroscience offers potent indicators that exactly some such transfer into the text occurs, whether or not in the right hemisphere of the brain; and some literary scholars are already drawing on these ideas. The idea of mirror neurons is contested and there is a danger of a layperson using this concept too glibly. Nevertheless, it is intriguing to observe issues of reader response being addressed at the level of human physiology: "when we read a novel, our mirror neurons simulate the actions described in the novel, as if we were doing those actions ourselves" (Iacoboni, 2009, pp. 94–95). The brain thus participates in a direct way in the actions described in the story.

Kuzmičová (2012) enters this field in more detail, relating our motor capacities to our ability to immerse ourselves in a fictional work as we elicit "*presence* in the reader, the sense of having physically entered a tangible environment, of 'being there'" (p. 24). Such a sense of presence, she argues, "arises from a first-person, *enactive* process of sensorimotor simulation/ resonance, rather than from mere visualizing from the perspective of a passive, third-person observer….[O]ur enjoyment of literature is embodied" (p. 24). Such processes are activated by accounts of actions within the text. "A higher degree of spatial vividness, arousing in the reader a sense of having physically entered a tangible environment (presence), is achieved when certain forms of human bodily movement are rendered in the narra- tive, as compared to when they are not" (p. 25). Kuzmičová's explanation of spatial vividness refers directly to the involuntary capture of attention and involvement, "an assumed intensity of the fragmentary, instantaneous, and mostly extremely shortlived spatial imagery prompted by a narra- tive passage….mostly spontaneous and pre-reflective….not consciously controlled by the reader—once the reader has made the initial choice to treat the narrative conventionally as narrative literature, i.e., to immerse" (p. 26).

Elaine Scarry (1999) similarly suggests, "[I]maginary vivacity comes about by reproducing the deep structure of perception" (p. 9). She explores the importance of touch as part of creating virtual experience. Her list of conditions for creating imaginary space for the figments of our stories to inhabit correlates with Kuzmičová's account of spatial vividness.

First, solidity...is the key experience for percipient creatures; solidity relies on touch to provide access not just to material surfaces but to deep haptic experience as well. Second, solidity is difficult to reproduce in the imagination because it entails touch, the sense whose operation is most remote to us in imagining....Third, the very difficulty of achieving in the imaginary realm tactilely or haptically confirmed solidity is matched by the importance of doing so. It is impossible to create imaginary persons if one has not created a space for them....Fourth and finally, even more important than the provision of an inhabitable space for imaginary persons is the creation for the reader of a fiction's vertical floor that, by promising to stop our inward fall, permits us to enter capaciously into the projective space without fear and therefore with the lifting of inhibitions on vivacity. (Scarry, 1999, p. 14)

Scarry suggests one route into such tactile confidence is the special attention we pay when movements described in the text mirror the actions of our own eyes and hands while reading: "The imaginer, although almost wholly immobilized in the process of reading, is still performing sustained actions with her eyes (moving across the words) and hands (turning the pages)" (p. 147). Scarry details "the small gestures of fingers lifting and turning a single page....Reaching, stretching, and folding are the actual motions the hand carries out—like a spell of hand motions performed over the book—as one reads" (p. 147).

The eyes, too, are moving, and Scarry suggests, "Their actual motion is incorporated into the motion of fictional persons so that our somatic mimesis of what is happening in the book works to substantiate and vivify motions on the mental retina that are wholly imaginary" (p. 148).

Scarry's theory is that when actions of reaching, stretching, and folding are described within the created world, it allows us to imagine a more tangible reality within the fiction, and that characters themselves move their eyes in ways that we verify ("make true") with our own. Of course, differently abled readers may take alternative routes into verification, but a large majority will recognize her account.

Leaving aside the irresistible and interesting questions about e-reading that Scarry's hypothesis invites, the idea that the "spell of hand motions performed over the book" contributes to the liveliness of what we imagine is suggestive and intriguing. Its delineation of reading as a physical event is part of its appeal to me; and it certainly serves as a reminder that we must pay attention as our physical relationships to the material forms of our texts begin to mutate.

Gallagher's newborns suggest that we possess innate sophisticated powers to render our visual impressions in motor form. Kuzmičová suggests that these motor responses are involuntarily and immersively brought "into play" when we encounter verbal descriptions of action. Scarry suggests that our minds are sensitive even to the modest actions of the reading hand. It seems possible that the innateness of these mental reactions helps to explain how we can develop the potential to respond to fictional action with motor responses in our own brains so very early in our lives—if we receive the requisite exposure to such fictions.

As we build our experience of interactions between our own bodies and the textual materials we encounter, we acquire a habit of reading or viewing that our body reinforces. Our very posture as we read or view reinforces the fluidity with which we learn to move into the world of the text. Paul Connerton (1989) addresses the powers of habit, in regard to the development of skilled typing but in terms that readily transfer to the act of reading: "We know where the letters are on the typewriter as we know where one of our limbs is. We remember this through knowledge bred of familiarity in our lived space....Habit is a knowledge and a remembering in the hands and in the body; and in the cultivation of habit it is our body which 'understands'" (p. 95).

By the time I was six and a half and a fully fledged reader, I certainly oriented myself to the book in my hands as readily as if it were part of my own body. Connerton describes the impact of these habits, and I do not think it matters at all that the muscle movements of reading are small ones: "By exercise the body comes to co-ordinate an increasing range of muscular activities in an increasingly automatic way, until awareness retreats, the movement flows 'involuntarily', and there occurs a firm and practised sequence of acts which take their fluent course" (p. 94).

We know how to read with our bodies as well as with our minds. At the same time, our minds recognize the *other* bodies and minds in the stories we encounter, and we are able to activate the textual creatures through the energy of that comprehension.

Motor Response in the Murk

I cannot go back into the past and hook myself up so that my brain reflexes can be retro-measured. But I can turn once more to the strategy I have used all the way through this project and examine the texts of my youth with questions of motor response in mind. Does this approach offer the potential of insight into that mysterious time in our earliest youth when we begin to learn how to make our fictions breathe?

Well, *The Story of Margaret Field-Mouse* is certainly full of movement. On the page where Margaret is rushing home to Crocus, it is a four-legged animal kind of movement, but the physical and emotional intensity of

"You mean, in case it really is two Woozles," said Winnie-the-Pooh, and Piglet said that anyhow he had nothing to do until Friday. So off they went together.

There was a small spinney of larch trees just here, and it seemed as if the two Woozles, if that is what they were, had been going round this spinney; so round this spinney went Pooh and Piglet after them; Piglet passing the time by telling Pooh what his Grandfather Trespassers W had done to Remove Stiffness after Tracking, and how his Grandfather Trespassers W had suffered in his later years from Shortness of Breath, and other matters of interest, and Pooh wondering what a Grandfather was like, and if perhaps this was Two Grandfathers they were after now, and, if so, whether he would be allowed to take one home and keep it, and what Christopher Robin would say. And still the tracks went on in front of them. . . .

Suddenly Winnie-the-Pooh stopped, and pointed excitedly in front of him. *"Look!"*

"What?" said Piglet, with a jump. And then, to show that he hadn't been frightened, he jumped up and down once or twice in an exercising sort of way.

"The tracks!" said Pooh. *"A third animal has joined the other two!"*

"Pooh!" cried Piglet. "Do you think it is another Woozle?"

"No," said Pooh, "because it makes different marks. It is either Two Woozles and one, as it might be, Wizzle, or Two, as it might be, Wizzles and one, if so it is, Woozle. Let us continue to follow them."

So they went on, feeling just a little anxious now, in case the three animals in front of them were of Hostile Intent. And Piglet wished very much that his Grandfather T. W. were there, instead of elsewhere, and Pooh thought how nice it would be if they met Christopher Robin suddenly but quite accidentally, and only because he liked Christopher Robin so much. And then, all of a sudden, Winnie-the-Pooh stopped again, and licked the tip of his nose in a cooling manner, for he was feeling more hot and anxious than ever

in his life before. *There were four animals in front of them!*

∧ *Pooh and Piglet creating and inspecting their own footprints. Colouring supplied by an unknown McCurdy child (Milne, illus. Shepard, 1957, pp. 40-41).*
[Courtesy Penguin Random House]

Margaret's velocity stirs a sympathetic twitch in my brain to this day. And the picture we have already seen on page 133 of Margaret racing upright down the stairs and Crocus knocking over the stool to run to meet her, seems to me to be impossible to observe with a static mind.

Winnie-the-Pooh, traipsing around the bush and leaving his marks in the snow, is also invoking very clear ideas of motion. He eventually learns to *read* his own track through the action of placing his foot in it, an operation that merges movement and cognition in highly satisfying ways and foreshadows almost uncannily the title of my first written account of this project, "Reading from the Feet Up" (Mackey, 2010b).

These images also supply input for our motor responses. The relationship between what is conveyed in the pictures and what is communicated by the words is complex one, but there can be little doubt that they both tap into our nervous systems.

The notion of the motor response survives my graduation from the simpler books that are part of my experience of the Murk. It certainly clarifies the instantaneous appeal of *The Moffats*. Typing "The way Mama could

1

THE YELLOW HOUSE ON NEW DOLLAR STREET

THE WAY MAMA COULD PEEL APPLES! A FEW TURNS OF the knife and there the apple was, all skinned! Jane could not take her eyes from her mother's hands. They had a way of doing things, peeling apples, sprinkling salt, counting pennies, that fascinated her. Jane sighed. Her mother's peelings fell off in lovely long curls, while, for the life of her, Jane couldn't do any better than these thick little chunks

7

peel apples!" I can feel my mind virtually shaping my hands to hold knife and fruit. Action is married to cognition; we readily infer that this thought is in somebody else's brain. We soon learn that we are thinking with Jane, in the subjunctive with Jane, occupying Jane's deictic centre. Slobodkin's eloquent illustration reinforces the impact, but it is the words that allow us to enter into Jane's thoughts as she stares at her mother's moving hands.

Compare this opening to the start of *Anne of Green Gables*, an enormous single sentence about the brook running past Mrs. Rachel Lynde's house. Although I came to this book with great life experience of brooks, my mind has never felt any interest in simulating a brook's movements. We see Matthew's departure through the distant spectator eyes of Mrs. Lynde. Only when Matthew encounters Anne sitting tensely on the bench at Bright River is there any human muscle action for my motor instincts to step into. For me, and I suspect for many readers, that moment is when the story really begins.

The precision of the motions in the *Swallows and Amazons* books speaks for itself, as we say (and similar physical details activate the appeal of *Farmer Boy*, which I read, and the rest of the *Little House* books, which I did not). Many of the girl detectives also go in for movement on a regular basis. As for following the thread under Princess Irene's forefinger, the connection to the hand on the page is palpable.

I did not select books for detailed discussion in earlier chapters because they fit this pattern. I first read about these ideas after the manuscript of this book was nearly complete, and I selected my examples here from the titles already highlighted as especially important to me. But the goodness of fit is striking.

Right at the beginning of this study, I described myself as a kinesthetic reader, as opposed to a visualizer or an auditory reader. I have used these terms for some years to talk about personal reading preferences and behaviours with my graduate students, but I have always been uncomfortable about that *kinesthetic* label, using it only for lack of a better alternative. Now I consider it potentially a more robust descriptor. Readers often manifest a preference for one kind of response over others; it may be that a kinesthetically inclined reader would be more *moved* (the pun is irresistible) by the brain's instinctive motor responses. Or it may be that all readers, even those who respond much more visually, make that same innate connection with motor activity that is displayed by those newborns who take the *action* of sticking out their tongues on *sight* of an adult doing the same thing. My current project is not the kind of study that will allow me to do more than speculate—and of course there are successful readers who cannot themselves see, or move, so my account is certainly not all-inclusive. All I can say is that after five years of revisiting both the books and other texts of my childhood and re-exploring the physical and social arena of my developing literacy, I find the embodied explanation of sympathetic motor response highly satisfactory—for me and maybe for other readers as well—as at least one part of the missing link between my physical environment, my cognitive efforts, and the virtual worlds of my texts. In the Murk, I learned to immerse myself in a fictional universe. Looking back now, with my stereo-temporal eyes, I find Kuzmičová's explanation very *telling*. As an embodied reader, I learned how to lend essential elements of my body to my fictions in order to make them vivid enough to let me in.

The Subjunctive of the "As If"

Kuzmičová's explanation is partial, dealing mainly with elements of action. Gallagher reminds us that more is at stake. Children are capable of pretending and recognizing pretend behaviour in others by the age of two (Gallagher, 2005, p. 229). Just as our bodies may be irresistibly drawn into invigorating a fiction before us, so our minds lend themselves to the other minds in the text.

At this late stage of the book, I return to Bruner's account of the subjunctive mode of narrative as a compelling invocation of this astonishing capacity. Bruner's approach is paralleled in striking ways through the neuroscience of Vittorio Gallese, Christian Keysers, and Giacomo Rizzolatti (2004). It is worth returning to Bruner one more time for the insight he permits into the role of the text in this readerly exchange.

The subjunctive mode is a category of grammar. It is used to express non-factual suppositions about the world: fears, hopes, suspicions, and the like. Bruner (1986) says, "To be in the subjunctive mode is, then, trafficking in human possibilities rather than in settled certainties" (p. 26). The subjunctive allows us to move into the "as-if" world of things that are possible rather than things that are conclusively established.

Bruner quotes the *Oxford English Dictionary* on the meaning of subjunctive: "Designating a mood...the forms of which are employed to denote an action or state as conceived (and not as a fact) and therefore used to express a wish, command, exhortation, or a contingent, hypothetical, or prospective event" (p. 26). His interest lies in how "reality [is] rendered subjunctive by language," or, putting it in slightly different terms, how it is possible to "transform the action of the verb from being a fait accompli to being psychologically *in process*" (p. 29, emphasis added).

Some time after Bruner's 1986 publication of *Actual Minds, Possible Worlds* with its elegant account of the narrative powers of the subjunctive, neuroscientists began to explore the radical potential of mirror neurons. I am certainly not qualified to assess these studies but the parallel uses of language are extremely suggestive. Gallese, Keysers, and Rizzolatti (2004) describe mirror neurons in the following terms:

> We will posit that, in our brain, there are neural mechanisms (mirror mechanisms) that allow us to directly understand the meaning of the actions and emotions of others by internally replicating ("simulating") them without any explicit reflective mediation....[T]he fundamental mechanism that allows us a direct experiential grasp of the mind of others is not conceptual reasoning but direct simulation of the observed events through the mirror mechanism....[W]hen we see someone performing an action, besides the activation of various visual areas [of our brain], there is a concurrent activation of part of the same motor circuits that are recruited when we ourselves perform that action. Although we do not overtly reproduce the observed action, part of our motor system becomes active "as if" we were executing that very same action that we are observing. (pp. 396–397)

The "as if" governs the subjunctive verb in this sentence—"as if we *were*" (emphasis added).

Gallese, Keysers, and Rizzolatti suggest that we simulate emotional response in the same way that we simulate motor action. "The human brain," they say, "is endowed with structures that are active both during the first- and third-person experience of actions and emotions" (p. 400). If this account is reliable, it would not be much of a leap to suggest further that we are fundamentally equipped to invest our first-person understanding into the third-person account of a fiction. The overlapping concepts of simulation and subjunctive do seem to point to a transactional arrangement by which this sympathetic transfer of vitality can occur. The involuntary nature of such a connection also rings true (as does the idea of its refusal, an alternative response also not controllable—I cannot force myself to make vivid human connections to Dick and Jane). The irresistibility of our responses possibly helps to explain why we find it so difficult to articulate what happens as we read.

I am at my scientific limit with this argument, able only to report and not to critique. I will turn with some relief, therefore, back to a children's fiction that lets me explore these concepts in more concrete terms.

Into the Mind of Another

The Moffats was my favourite book for some years, so, for a final time, I open its first page for a test run of the potential synergy of mental connections between motor and emotional simulation and subjunctive entry into human possibilities. What responses does *The Moffats* script for its readers? Here is the first paragraph.

> *The way Mama could peel apples! A few turns of the knife and there the apple was, all skinned! Jane could not take her eyes from her mother's hands. They had a way of doing things, peeling apples, sprinkling salt, counting pennies, that fascinated her. Jane sighed. Her mother's peelings fell off in lovely long curls, while, for the life of her, Jane couldn't do any better than these thick little chunks which she popped into her mouth. Moreover it took her as long to peel one apple as for Mama to do five or six. Would she ever get so she could do as well?* (Estes, 1941/1959, pp. 7–8)

This paragraph illustrates both motor and subjunctive investment in very clear-cut ways. The physicality of that first paragraph remains vivid to me; I lend my motor awareness of the specified manual actions to Mama's sensuous control of the apple peeling, and I register the sharp physical disappointment of the incompetent jerks that produce Janey's "thick little chunks" (my own experience of apple peeling definitely matched hers at the time I first read the book). Furthermore, Mama's long curling apple peelings curve under the hand like Scarry's turning book page.

The role of the subjunctive is also clear, though implicit, in this paragraph. Jane wishes that....She regrets that....She harbours ambitions that.... Just as I moved mentally into the hand motions of apple peeling, so I moved into the humble dissatisfactions of a childish yearning for competence. I inhabited Jane.

And Jane inhabited me. For my entire life, I have never peeled an apple without attempting to reproduce Mama's elegant skill, though I am quick to give up at the first inept turn of the knife. I have always owned that wish to emulate not just Mama's achievement but Mama's nonchalance; a little edge of Jane's take on the world inflects my own to this day. In terms of "trafficking in human possibilities" (Bruner, 1986, p. 26), I so far absorbed Jane's possibilities that in some small ways they shaped—not my own, directly, perhaps, but at least how I perceived my own. Estes's words pointed, underlined, highlighted, emphasized small daily elements that I noticed in my own life, and gave me some externalized ways to think about them.

Maria Nikolajeva (2014), in her study of cognitive approaches to children's literature, discusses the significance of free indirect discourse as a challenge that enhances children's developing mind-reading capacities (p. 92). Estes makes skilful use of this mode of narration, and it seems to me that part of the enormous enjoyment I associate with her books comes out of my active pleasure, from the first reading onward, in moving into somebody else's experiences and also somebody else's thoughts.

By the time I reached *The Moffats*, I was able to step effortlessly into the subjunctive world of that little family, but it was something of a willed gesture compared with the involuntary sensation of holding the knife to peel the apple. I had learned how to respond to the fictional demands of the subjunctive through my bedtime stories and my early chapter books. I learned to let go of my own actual surroundings. Dick and Jane, on the other hand, taught me that stepping into the subjunctive of the story is not automatically successful. Even as a five-year-old, I registered that I did not inhabit their pallid world. I used it only as a scaffold for technical skill development. My excitement over learning the word "said" reflected some inkling that I could soon leave them behind.

Theoretical and scientific perspectives draw on our expanding knowledge of capacities of the mind to explore how we may enliven words on the page, bring them to active life inside our heads. But, as is clear throughout this whole study, when I turn my "past-tense" eye on my childhood, I do not simply see myself as a kind of universal specimen of generic reader with an involuntary response of simulation occurring in her mind. I also see a particular, situated, local reader in a specific setting. These qualities of individual location feed into the activity of reading, that human achievement at once and paradoxically so invisible and personal, and so social and collective. In addition to exploring the generic, we must also attend to the particular.

"From my body outwards": Folding and Unfolding

The inexorable motor responses of the brain perhaps offer us a gleam into the Murk. But the more we subscribe to an embodied account of developing narrative understanding, the more carefully we must notice one inescapable fact: that body is always *somewhere*. The irresistible impulse to simulate tells only part of how a mind engages a fiction; a reader's social, political, ideological, intellectual, and cultural setting all bear on the transaction as well. The brain may well feature some universal capacities, but particular situations are multiple and diverse. And the third party in that mix, the text, is designed to transfer from one situation to another without changing its semiotic specifics as it is brought to life inside the mind of an individual, situated reader.

As it happens, all three elements in the interpretive transaction—reader, setting, text—have been described in terms of folding and unfolding. We have seen Elaine Scarry's account of the page folding under the finger and the traces of such activity involuntarily aroused in the brain. I have addressed this question of motor activation in some detail, so I will simply mention it at this point and turn in more detailed ways to the works of Kevin Leander and Gail Boldt, and Deborah Brandt and Katie Clinton.

To pursue the paradox of the collective and the particular, Leander and Boldt (2013) offer what they call a "strategic sketch" of a ten-year-old boy called Lee "doing and feeling things with manga" (p. 26). On a single Sunday, Lee read his manga, he arrayed himself with a headband and some toy daggers, he acted out gestures and sound effects, he tried poses, he checked the TV guide and the Internet to pursue supplementary materials, and he played with his friend Hunter, who turned up partway through the day. Hunter also read, and the two boys played various games based on their stories. With some short interruptions, these and other related activities lasted through a full day (pp. 26–27). Leander and Boldt suggest that the most salient feature of the day is "their bodies in persistent and largely unpremeditated motion" (p. 28). It is reductive to privilege the text-based parts of the day, say Leander and Boldt; "script-like, purposeful, or rule-governed practices were in constant interaction with actions that were spontaneous and improvisational, produced through an emergent moment-by-moment *unfolding*" (p. 29).

> Even this small sampling of activity makes evident how Lee's experience
> of the world around him is enacted through his body; text—in this case,
> manga—joins the flow or movement of multiple sensations and experiences
> as he sits, reads, performs, later searches the Internet, looks at trading
> cards, and engages in sword play....Because the body is in constant move-
> ment in an environment that is itself always in motion, the potential for

variation is almost infinite. The body is always indeterminate, in an imme-diate, unfolding relation to its own potential to vary (p. 29).

I cannot recover the extemporaneous ways in which I similarly unfolded my life around and in and out of my texts. But that energy was grounded in the environment in which and out of which I operated. The texts scripted potential responses; the limits of my local setting and awareness earthed them. The dynamic relationship between the enduring text and the fluctu-ating situation *on the ground* created a space where unfolding could occur.

Brandt and Clinton come at this space from the opposite direction, respecting the significance of how an interpretive act is rooted in the local situation but keen to ensure that the larger, fixed elements of literacy are not lost in a focus on the particular. They speak of "folding in," a phrase borrowed from Latour "that expresses ontological relationships between people and things" (Brandt & Clinton, 2002, p. 353). The thing maintains a relationship when the actors are not available, offers a permanence that specific people and situations cannot maintain on their own. "As authors of this article," they say,

> *we fold ourselves into a thing called the* Journal of Literacy Research, *which will disseminate our article and engage our readers while we are doing other things....The ability of the journal to travel and endure in one piece extends interaction across space and time, and for the advantages of that surrogacy we relinquish control....Through the concept of folding in we can restore attention to what is abstract and displaced in literate interactions without falling into autonomous myths. (p. 353)*

By acknowledging the abstract and permanent components of literacy, say Brandt and Clinton, we are enabled to compare local situations, "to consider how and how much local literacies involve importing and exporting literacy across contexts as well as the role of things in managing these movements" (pp. 353–354).

It is difficult to merge these ideas without oversimplification, but I will assay a tentative exposition: our systems of literacy allow us to *fold* our ideas, stories, knowledge *into* a textual abstraction that is relatively perma-nent and certainly portable. We unpack the texts that reach us in our own local settings, and the physical experience of stretching and *folding* the physical container of the paper is part of what raises relatively comparable responses in our individual brains; we then *unfold* the compact expression of the text into our broader local world through our cognitive, emotional, physical, and playful responses, through associating one text with another, and through connecting with local and/or broader communities of interpreters.

This congruence of vocabulary is certainly more than a coincidence, but I have probably stretched it as far as I usefully can. At a minimum, it is a reminder that the cognitive, the situated, and the abstract are all at work in any act of textual interpretation.

Porch Steps and Liminal Spaces

Lee and Hunter, exploring their manga worlds, were fully placed in their specific physical environment, as Leander and Boldt (2013) make plain:

> For example, at one point they carried their books, costume accessories, and weapons outdoors and sat reading in a porch swing. With no spoken planning, Lee stood up, grabbed a sword, and began swinging it at Hunter. Hunter dropped his book and picked up a sword, and for the next several minutes the battle moved between the porch and the front yard, with the porch steps offering a vantage point from which to make leaping lunges at one another. Just as suddenly as it began, Hunter sat down and started narrating a favorite scene, and then picked up a book and read for a few minutes while Lee continued swinging a sword and talking to Hunter and to himself. (p. 27)

This account of behaviour that is at once totally absorbed and apparently random in the way it moves between options and vehicles is grounded in a setting. The manga stories and characters, and the assorted accoutrements and weapons that the boys have gathered all script certain kinds of response and not others. The setting also offers affordances and restrictions. How many childish literary enactments are supported by a set of porch steps? The answer probably nears infinity, and it is hard to imagine a more vivid or literal representation of a liminal space. Yet each particular set of steps yields a somewhat different script through the physical limits of its design and through the social understanding of porches and steps, and who has rights to what territory, and many other specifically grounded questions. The games that were possible on our own porch steps, leading up to the side of the house from our extended gravel driveway, were different from those enabled by the steps of our friends' houses feeding directly off the sidewalks of Pennywell Road. The high steps that led to the upper level of the pavilion next to the tennis courts on the Ayre Athletic Grounds allowed for a further assortment of fictional enactments. And my grandparents' verandah in the Granville Ferry rectory was a veritable palace of potential literary space. Leander and Boldt discuss the literal use of porch steps as part of an extended text game; these physically and socially defined spaces also provide imaginative options that diffuse into literate understanding in more general ways.

Leander and Boldt suggest that literacy research risks being a subtractive process. "We subtract those things that are not so clearly about texts, making texts central to any instance of practice, perhaps because they are central to us" (Leander & Boldt, 2013, p. 41). In this case, perhaps as a counterweight to such processes, they subtract any broad consideration of the series of manga texts that Lee and Hunter inhabited on that Sunday, mentioning titles but no more. They also subtract the local and concrete details of how these boys are grounded in a particular setting. I agree with their concerns about text-centric theories of literacy, but I contend that they do not set their own lens specifically enough.

It was my intent at the start of this project to subtract radically less than other research projects do, to include all kinds of texts that normally slide under the radar, whose roles in the ongoing accretion of literate understanding receive no consideration. Nevertheless, my initial focus was undeniably text-centred; I just had a larger than usual set of texts in mind.

When I began to address my own memories of literacy, however, I found it impossible to subtract two major ingredients: my own body and psyche, and the physical, social, and cultural setting in which I learned to interpret representations of many kinds. As Leander and Boldt (2013) say, "What is carried forward is not the preexisting surface features or grammars—the meanings or identities—but rather the force and affect created by a text, an action, an idea" (p. 37). These traces of force and affect were *placed* when I first experienced them and they remain *placed* when I consider them today. Leander and Boldt do not comment on this fact, but Lee and Hunter were also situated.

At the same time that I was learning to breathe life into my fictions, I was sorting and sifting my early scripts and schemas about the world. Of necessity these were initially singular; I was quite sure that there was one correct route through much of the tangle of my daily experience (down to the detail, apparently, of throwing a tantrum if the inexorable order of "one foot, other foot" was disrupted when somebody put on my shoes). In Malouf's (1985) terms, I was learning to understand the world "from my body outwards" (p. 3), using my body and its rhythms and responses to help me make sense of that world.

But of course the world was not singular. As I became more adept as a reader, my texts taught me that fact. My body understood Jane Moffat peeling thick chunks of apple, and even breathed her to life through this understanding. But Jane lived in a small New England town in wartime; these conditions involve forms of social understanding that did not arise out of peacetime life in the urban space of Pennywell Road.

It was never an option, for me or for any other reader, to learn *enough* to master all the world's discourses, so instead I had to learn to manage the primary subjunctive of my own uncertainty. Moments of *re-learning*, like the encounter between the rowboat and the water lilies, helped me register the dynamic nature of my own world and how I needed to come to terms with a shifting understanding of it. That power to "ride" a mutating awareness of a world enabled me to make sense of the universes that unfolded in my fictions. Even after we are old enough to remember a great deal, much of such schema-adjusting activity seems to exist within its own version of the Murk. I would never have remembered that small epiphany with the water lilies had I not returned to the same place at the right time of year with a mind already full of childhood reflections. Similarly, some but not all of our sense-building memories may be restored to us when we return to a previously read book.

Reading the Readers

The ability of a placed society to participate in the abstract world of texts is also important. Among the many physical and social changes in Newfoundland over the past half-century, there has also been a radical cultural shift in participation rates and possibilities. In the 1950s, there was very little Newfoundland writing, and it felt as if no reasonable person would think that the subject of Newfoundland readers was of any interest. Today, scholars explore the roles of both writing and reading situated in this specific space.

For example, Danielle Fuller (2004) explores the importance of setting in two Newfoundland novels. "[F]ictional texts," she says, "can construct vivid imagined geographies that articulate emotions associated with particular places" (p. 25). In her study of Wayne Johnston's *The Colony of Unrequited Dreams* and Joan Clark's *Latitudes of Melt*, Fuller addresses several "place-myths" of Newfoundland:

> *One of them posits Newfoundland as "other" to urban centres such as Toronto and therefore a leisure space where city dwellers can enjoy "wilderness" pursuits far away from the stresses of life in a global city....Another persistent place-myth upholds Newfoundland's heritage and folk culture as distinctive, shaped by the hardships of life on a wind-battered rock in the midst of the Atlantic Ocean and resistant to outside cultural influences. For some Newfoundlanders, this latter myth underwrites a very significant place-bound identity....While for other Newfoundlanders this image of cultural isolation and distinctiveness is backward-looking and restrictive, to the Newfoundland tourist industry it represents a marketing opportunity....*
>
> *Newfoundlanders' resistance to and complication of such romantic and outdated notions of their home place and lifestyle come in various forms.*
> (p. 24)

As a reader in the 1950s, I know I resisted and complicated many texts, but never any that involved my "home place." My resistance arose out of alienation rather than the kind of active critique that is now made possible by familiarity and recognition. My daily actions in crossing Harvey Road on the red light to get to school would not have changed if I had read Larry Mathews's (2010) account of that junction: "By now I'm at the impossible intersection of Long's Hill, LeMarchant Road, Freshwater Road, Parade Street, and Harvey Road, a Gordian knot for pedestrians, severable by selective disregard of traffic lights and crosswalks" (pp. 164–165). (My own assessment of that junction adds a sixth street, Carters Hill, to the mix, but I would have been electrified even at this near miss!) How differently would I have looked at this knotty intersection if I had perceived its complexities as worthy of public reimagination and description in a novel?

From a different perspective, Judith Robertson, David Lewkowich, and Jennifer Rottmann (2010) explore the significance of the reader's own location as a part of the reading act, through a study of St. John's reading groups that I found when I had nearly finished this project. "Newfoundlanders have long self-identified as occupants of liminal space," they say (p. 144):

between Old and New Worlds, between being a country and being a province, and so forth. They speak of St. John's readers occupying a "*landwash, the space of perilous change between high and low tides,* [which] while representative of the ferocity of the Newfoundland shoreline, also configures as a material and metaphorical trope" of the shifting desires of the book group members they study (p. 152).

> *The fluidity of boundaries is an important characteristic of the landwash.*
> *The Atlantic Ocean, with its sounds, its smells, its birds and its mists is*
> *impossible to ignore while walking the streets of St. John's, and becomes an*
> *essential component underlying the psychic fabric of the place. More than*
> *a prison, the water acts as a passage for a reading of the world and of one's*
> *place in it. It functions as a channel for international trade but also for the*
> *drifting of thoughts, comparable to the outermost depths of any passionate*
> *and truly involved reading. It's a conduit for a sense of confinement, while*
> *also for an incomparable freedom. (p. 153)*

The articles about Newfoundland writing and reading raise interesting questions, though I am still startled when I read a phrase like Fuller's (2004) description of the island as a "marginal and heavily mediated place" (p. 46), or her reference to its "prominent place in the Canadian cultural imaginary" (p. 21)—a sharp contrast to the unlimned territory I knew in my youth.

After all the efforts I have made in this project to place myself as a reader in a very distinctive setting, I can hardly quarrel with these accounts claiming significance for Newfoundland's particularities and their impact on local readers and readings. I want to qualify this agreement, however, with the observation that for a child learning to read, *any* place is a liminal site. All readers incorporate the place of their reading into how they make sense of the text—incorporate in a very literal sense of bringing their own bodies and sites of reading to bear on the activity of bringing print to life in the mind. Newfoundland's particular distinctiveness may perhaps make the process more visible, but the local discourses of any place create their own landwash of shifting perspectives that render such reading contingent, no matter how fixed the landmarks that ground it.

Margaret Mahy (1991) has spoken of "dislocations in a true landscape" (p. 10). I look at my city today through new lenses—but that city is still, in vital ways, the lens through which I look at everything else. Mahy's paradox—the deep truth of something inherently unreliable—forms one of the dynamics that animate the act of reading. Her fault lines engender potential for unfolding.

Other Routes to Reading

Even as I report the importance of foot-knowledge of my city to my own literate awareness, I acknowledge many other ways of learning to read. The detailed attention I have paid to my own development can serve best as a way of raising questions about how different details play a role in the development of a different child. I experienced my local world on foot, often in purposive ways, but also in the more open-ended and aimless territory that Frédéric Gros (2014/2009) describes as simply *outside*: "some space that takes some time" (p. 32).

Contemporary children, for example, are far less likely than I was to walk their local streets as they learn to interpret the world and their books. "In Canada, a recent survey found that although 58% of parents walked to school when they were kids, only 28% of their children walk to school today" (2013 Active, n.p.). The continent-wide figures are even more disconcerting, with Toronto's chief city planner suggesting that only 12 per cent of North American children walk or cycle to school (quoted in Renzetti, 2014, n.p.). The National Trust in the United Kingdom has produced sobering statistics suggesting that British children's "radius of [outdoor] activity" has declined by almost 90 per cent in a single generation (Moss, 2012, p. 5). Some youngsters will watch the DVD screen in the back seats as they are driven to key locations in their local landscapes, gaining little in the way of even indirect awareness of the paths, nodes, and landmarks of their surroundings. Their ways of learning to breathe life into the printed word will necessarily differ from mine.

The abstract permanence of the inscribed word is also in flux. The always-under-revision electronic text works on a different basis from the paper books of my childhood. Many decades after my original encounters with these materials, I was able to take them from my parents' bookshelves or readily acquire substitute copies from library or bookstore, confident that they would be identical. We will need new theories to help us understand the kinds of literate materials that are provisional in their very essence, not just in the use we make of them. And of course, the physical dynamic of folding and unfolding the concretely particular paper page is also mutating, as we learn to click, or tap, or drag, or press, in order to move the text along. What intellectual changes will follow as the role of our hands in reading is so significantly altered?

Many of the details of my childhood are unfamiliar today. Our routines were predictable; the ideological and theological underpinnings of the different institutions in our lives were coherent; our home was secure; and our freedom to roam our local territory was extensive. Bedrock under-pinned my daily life, both actually and metaphorically. No doubt it was a minority—and highly privileged—experience. From a base of great security, I learned to branch out into the subjunctive and to "handle" (a sugges-tive word) imaginative accounts of worlds not known to me. Other children develop the same capacities from very different base experiences. Today's children, learning to manipulate a dancing and disappearing alphabet on a smartphone, acquire novel skills and understandings while still inside the conditions of their own Murk.

Becoming Contingent

Newfoundland supplies a dramatic case study of discursive mutation, but all children, sorting out scripts and schemas to make sense of their world, step onto a moving rather than a static platform. Children's early and hard-won distillation of complexity down to singular and transferrable units of understanding is informed and distorted by mutability even as it is achieved. Even as young people grasp at local and embodied awareness, they participate in forms of knowledge that are contingent and transient.

I had a singular sense of my world. I was wrong. But at the time of learning, at that particular trajectory through that particular space, the singularity I perceived served in some ways as a useful tool, a secure and portable understanding that I relied on to help me make sense of my texts. At the same time, I suspect that my certainties also limited me. Children more aware of the contingencies of the world might hold the advantage.

For me, the Nova Scotia experience bolstered an awareness that the givens of my St. John's life might not be the only conditions of the world. No doubt many of my classmates balanced between their urban lives and the outport settings they met while visiting their extended families. For all of us, no matter how singular and monolithic or discordant and confusing our life experiences, our encounters with materials that did not match our lived realities introduced further plurality into our mental constructs.

Initially I learned to stand firm in my bedroom on Pennywell Road, extracting some sensible fixed forms for understanding my environment out of the swirl of my early awareness. But it was not long before I knew that the necessary stance was one of achieving balance between conflicting accounts of what it meant and felt like to be alive in the world. My mental activation of motor response to fictional actions was perhaps instinctive, involuntary, and universal, but my physical and temporal location was always already both specified and in transition. The permanence was lodged in the materials, and especially in the books. Magazines and Sunday-school leaflets arrived and disappeared, radio and television vanished in the moment of appearance; but even when my borrowed books were returned to their owners, I knew they were still *there* in a larger sense. That "there-ness" is one element of reading that is currently in transition, to an unquantifiable degree and to unknown destinations. At the same time, of course, the moving image is travelling in the opposite direction; I can now hold the DVD copy of my transient television program in my two hands; it has (at least for the current moment) acquired "there-ness" and become repeatable, in stark contrast to its ephemeral nature in my youth. When those TV shows take up a home in the cloud, their qualities of "there-ness" will alter again; they will be repeatable but not holdable. How do these changes affect the ways we think?

The shifting discourses that mark Newfoundland's very contingent history and geography dramatize the need for a sense of balance. My childhood allowed me to stand steady before I needed to learn to straddle conflicting descriptions of the world. Despite not really "belonging" to Newfoundland, according to many local perspectives, in all important ways, I was secure.

Many children take on a strong sense of unreliability much earlier than I did, learning, perhaps even during their time in the Murk, that they do not belong to the side of the discursive "winners." Shirley Brice Heath's classic *Ways with Words* (1983) describes some of those conflicts in terms of ethnicity and class. I observed deep disjunctures affecting their relationship with school among those of my classmates, for example, who would not sacrifice their mother dialect for the strictures of the *Think and Do* book's grammar rules on subject-verb agreement. I witnessed the impact of many forms of belonging and not belonging for years before I began remotely to understand them.

As a bookish child in a bookish family, I had an untroubled start to my literate existence. I had access to enough material to support a full reading life, and I eagerly embarked on it even before I emerged from the Murk. For twelve years, I lived in the same place and did not have to process the impact of further migration.

For all these reasons and many more, my reading history cannot serve as any kind of general pattern. Why then, apart from a self-indulgent fascination with my past, have I devoted so much effort to the acquisition and reinspection of my childhood resources?

Rereading

It is probably not surprising that I was able to find a quote suggesting that rereading is also a kind of unfolding. Allegra Goodman (2005), talking about rereading *Pride and Prejudice* says,

> *I think unfolding is what rereading is about. Like pleated fabric, the text reveals different parts of its pattern at different times. And yet every time the text unfolds, in the library, or in bed, or upon the grass, the reader adds new wrinkles. Memory and experience press themselves into each reading so that each encounter informs the next....I return to it...because of the memories and wishes I've folded in its pages—because on every reading I see old things in it. (p. 164)*

A metaphor that suggests I have folded some of my own past inside the pages of the books I read as a child certainly rings true at this stage of the project. And in those pages, as Rebecca Mead (2014) (drawing on the insights of George Eliot) suggests, I have found "an opportunity to be in touch again with the intensity and imagination of beginnings. It is a discovery, later in life, of what remains with me" (p. 253).

Undoubtedly this experience is and remains a personal one, no matter how many details I make public in this book. I hope that by making connections with the work of reading scholars in many disciplines, I have transmuted the personal qualities of this experience into a broader understanding of how reading works.

Mapping a Shifting World

My own specific details are unique, and so are everyone's. My case is that the particulars, whatever they are, are themselves important. Reception is always and necessarily earthed. We do not learn to read in the abstract, though the abstract nature of print makes it tempting to think in such terms. We learn to read in grounded, individual, and local times and spaces. We learn to read with our minds and bodies and with the social understanding we develop out of our own locations and circumstances. We join the world of abstract textuality through the specific materials that are available to us in our local settings. I cannot describe these vital particularities in any terms but my own; everybody learns through their own details.

We internalize the words on the page in the cadences and spoken rhythms of our home languages. We bring homegrown scripts and schemas to bear on the scenarios on page or screen. Our intertextual juxtapositions, often fleeting and fragmentary, are idiosyncratic and probably not reproducible in full detail by anyone else (nor can we recall a complete set, even for ourselves). Our textual lives merge abstract, embodied, and placed understanding and forgetting.

Of all the media at our disposal, print still best enables this kind of mental fusion. Audio and video import external rather than local cadences; actors and audio narrators breathe for themselves rather than relying on the reader's breath and pulse to bring them to life. Reading, says Harold Brodkey (1985), is the most intimate human act because of "the prolonged (or intense) exposure of one mind to another" (p. A1). Those interacting minds draw on common bodily understanding to help make the connection. Reading, as well as being an act of intimate communication with *elsewhere*, is thus simultaneously rendered local. Even as adults, we enact and play our understanding on local ground. Mendelsund (2014) explains this experience as a performance:

> *Once a reading of a book is under way, and we sink into the experience, a performance of a sort begins...*
>
> *We perform a book—we perform a reading of a book. We perform a book, and we attend the performance.*
>
> *(As readers, we are both the conductor and the orchestra, as well as the audience). (p. 160, ellipsis in original)*

Mapmaking

Our developing literacy is idiosyncratic and unique as well as embodied and universal. It is, in this sense, impossible to tell a general story; at the same time every unique story is thus general in the truth of its uniqueness. To map what happens as we respond to textual constructions is at best a partial enterprise; yet I believe there is merit in creating even an incomplete map. The process of mapping itself illuminates the territory.

Bruner (1986) talks about the use of maps, even maps that do not necessarily match up to the landscape being traversed but that still serve a function.

> As...readers read, as they begin to construct a virtual text of their own, it is as if they were embarking on a journey without maps—and yet, they possess a stock of maps that might give hints, and besides, they know a lot about journeys and about mapmaking. First impressions of the new terrain are, of course, based on older journeys already taken. In time, the new journey becomes a thing in itself, however much its initial shape was borrowed from the past. The virtual text becomes a story of its own, its very strangeness only a contrast with the reader's sense of the ordinary. The fictional landscape, finally, must be given a "reality" of its own—the ontological step. (pp. 36-37)

Roger Shattuck (1983/1962), speaking of reading Proust, uses an image of maps that relate to the landscape in even more tenuous and mysterious ways.

> To read Proust is like looking at a map on which one sees clearly the names of all the cities and rivers and principal provinces, but not the name of the country itself; and not until much later, when one's eyes have finally relaxed, renouncing the possibility of ever discovering that information on the map, does one suddenly perceive, large as life and as if by chance, the name written in bold letters over the entire surface of the area; and then that name, which was so hard to see when one was looking right at it, turns out to be not unknown but only forgotten—one of the places read about in childhood and associated with miraculous trees bearing bread and dates, and animals with monstrous but very useful tails and noses, yet a country never visited and never mentioned in the everyday version of the world's events. (p. 4)

Both Bruner and Shattuck seem to be describing a variable and kaleido-scopic map that relates—sort of, sometimes, somehow—to known and imagined landscapes, shifting in and out of familiarity depending on the reader's point of view, depth of focus, current awareness, and sudden unexpected ability to see things differently. A neat map is simply wrong; a completely amorphous map is a contradiction in terms. We unfold a map to use it, but a map that is itself unfolding contains the scripted energy of the textual world.

Digital mapmaking opens up possibilities for aggregating singular experiences in ways that may help us manage the riot of individual experiences that is the logical outcome of my approach to valuing everyone's individual reading history. Presner, Shepard, and Kawano (2014), discussing the potential of thick mapping, describe it as

> the processes of collecting, aggregating, and visualizing ever more layers of geographic or place-specific data. Thick maps...embody temporal and historical dynamics through a multiplicity of layered narratives, sources, and even representational practices....Thickness means extensibility and polyvocality: diachronic and synchronic, temporally layered, and polyvalent ways of authoring, knowing, and making meaning. (pp. 17–18)

Across my thick map of my own childhood literacy, sprawling and shaggy, with its paradoxically singular focus on one particular reader, I have labelled paths, nodes, landmarks, edges, and districts. I hope that the "bold letters" of a larger understanding of this vast territory are discernible. Each of us, in our individual ways, knows "a lot about journeys and about mapmaking," and it would be exciting to find new ways of layering and analyzing the individual experiences of many readers. Acknowledging the limits of how we may ever hope to comprehend the reading of another person, we may still explore what insights these partial and personal maps can offer to a larger understanding.

References

2013 Active Healthy Kids Canada. (2013). *Are we driving our kids to unhealthy habits? Report card on physical activity for children and youth*. Retrieved June 3, 2013, from www.activehealthykids.ca.

Albrecht-Crane, Christa, & Cutchins, Dennis. (2010). *Adaptation studies: New approaches*. Madison, NJ: Fairleigh Dickinson University Press.

Bakhtin, M.M. (1981). *The dialogic imagination: Four essays*. M. Holquist (Ed.). C. Emerson & M. Holquist (Trans.). Austin: University of Texas Press.

Bartlett, Steve. (2011, May 19). What a blast! *The Telegram*. Retrieved May 10, 2013, from http://www.thetelegram.com/News/Local/2011-05-19/article-2518701/What-a-blast!/1.

Barton, David, & Hamilton, Mary. (1998). *Local literacies: Reading and writing in one community*. London: Routledge.

Bearne, Eve. (2009). And what do you think happened next? In M. Styles & E. Arizpe (Eds.), *Acts of reading: Teachers, text and childhood* (219–231). Stoke-on-Trent: Trentham Books.

Beaver Brook Branch of the Women's Institutes of Nova Scotia. (1959). "A History of Beaver Brook, 1760–1959." Chignecto Project Electronic Edition, January 1999. Retrieved January 3, 2013, from http://www.canadagenweb.org/archives/ns/bbrook.txt.

Beavin, Kristi. (2003, February 15). Review of audiobook of *The Moffats*. *Booklist*, 1094.

Beckwith, John. (1988, Summer). Tunebooks and hymnals in Canada, 1801–1939. *American Music, 6*(2), 193–234.

Bennett, Alan. (1995/1994). *Writing home*. London: Faber & Faber.

Birkerts, Sven. (1994). *The Gutenberg elegies: The fate of reading in an electronic age*. New York: Faber & Faber.

Bernstein, Robin. (2011). *Racial innocence: Performing American childhood from slavery to civil rights*. New York: NYU Press.

Boston notes. (1906, October 6). *The New York Times*. Retrieved August 16, 2011, from http://query.nytimes.com/mem/archive-free/pdf?res=F00A1EFE3D5512738DDDAF0894D8415B868CF1D3.

Bowen, Elizabeth. (1986). *The mulberry tree*. H. Lee (Ed.). London: Virago.

Brandt, Deborah. (1995, October). Accumulating literacy: Writing and learning to write in the twentieth century. *College English, 57*(6), 649–668.

Brandt, Deborah, & Clinton, Katie. (2002). Limits of the local: Expanding perspectives on literacy as a social practice. *Journal of Literacy Research, 34*(3), 337–356.

Brillinger, Marion M. (n.d.). Joseph and his brothers. In *Primary Bible lessons: A Bible family and God's love* (Part 11, Unit 11C, April, May, June. Leaflet). Toronto: United Church of Canada.

Britzman, Deborah P. (1995, Spring). Is there a queer pedagogy? Or, stop reading straight. *Educational Theory, 45*(2), 151–165.

Brodkey, Harold. (1985, November 24). Reading, the most dangerous game. *The New York Times*, A1.

Brooker-Gross, Susan R. (1981, February). Landscape and social values in popular children's literature: Nancy Drew mysteries. *Journal of Geography, 80*(2), 59–64.

Bruner, Jerome. (1986). *Actual minds, possible worlds*. Cambridge, MA: Harvard University Press.

Bruner, Jerome. (1996). *The culture of education*. Cambridge, MA: Harvard University Press.

Buckridge, Patrick. (2006). Generations of books: A Tasmanian family library, 1816–1994. *Library Quarterly, 76*(4), 388–402.

Burbules, Nicholas C. (2006). Rethinking the virtual. In J. Weiss, J. Nolan, J. Hunsinger, & P. Trifonas (Eds.), *The international handbook of virtual learning environments*. Dordrecht, The Netherlands: Springer, 37–58.

Buzbee, Lewis. (2006). *The yellow-lighted bookshop*. Saint Paul, MN: Graywolf Press.

Chittenden, Edward, & Salinger, Terry, with Anne M. Bussis. (2001). *Inquiry into meaning: An investigation of learning to read*. Rev. edition. New York: Teachers College Press.

Clapp-Itnyre, Alisa. (2010). Nineteenth-century British children's hymnody: Re-tuning the history of childhood with chords and verses. *Children's Literature Association Quarterly, 35*(2), 144–175.

Cliff Hodges, Gabrielle, Nikolajeva, Maria, & Taylor, Liz. (2010, September). Three walks through fictional fens: Multidisciplinary perspectives on *Gaffer Samson's Luck*. *Children's Literature in Education, 41*(3), 189–206.

Cochran-Smith, Marilyn. (1984). *The making of a reader: Language and learning for the human services professions*. Norwood, NJ: Ablex.

Collins, Billy. (2002). *Sailing alone around the room: New and selected poems*. New York: Random House.

Collins, Christopher. (1991). *Literature and the mind's eye: Literature and the psychology of imagination*. Philadelphia: University of Pennsylvania Press.

Colony of Avalon Foundation. (2013/1999). David Kirke and the Pool Plantation. *Heritage Newfoundland and Labrador*. Retrieved August 28, 2015, from http://www.heritage.nf.ca/articles/exploration/david-kirke-and-pool-plantation.php.

Connerton, Paul. (1989). *How societies remember*. Cambridge: Cambridge University Press.

Crago, Hugh. (2014). *Entranced by story: Brain, tale and teller, from infancy to old age*. New York: Routledge.

Crago, Maureen, & Crago, Hugh. (1983). *Prelude to literacy: A preschool child's encounter with picture and story*. Carbondale, IL: Southern Illinois University Press.

Crane, Mary Thomas. (2009, Fall). Surface, depth, and the spatial imaginary: A cognitive reading of the political unconscious. *Representations, 108*(1), 76–97.

Crummey, Michael. (2013). *Under the keel: Poems*. Toronto: House of Anansi Press.

Cuddy-Keane, Melba. (2010). Narration, navigation, and non-conscious thought: Neuroscientific and literary approaches to the thinking body. *University of Toronto Quarterly, 79*(2), 680–701.

Cullum, Linda, & Porter, Marilyn. (2014). Creating this place: An introduction. In L. Cullum & M. Porter (Eds.), *Creating this place: Women, family, and class in St. John's, 1900–1950* (3–24). Montreal: McGill-Queen's University Press.

Darwin, Charles. (1859). *On the origin of species by means of natural selection or the preservation of favoured races in the struggle for life*. London: John Murray.

de Certeau, Michel. (1984). *The practice of everyday life*. S. Rendall (Trans.). Berkeley: University of California Press.

Dehaene, Stanislas. (2009). *Reading in the brain: The science and evolution of a human invention*. New York: Viking.

DeNora, Tia. (2000). *Music in everyday life*. Cambridge: Cambridge University Press.

Dickinson, Peter. (1970). A defence of rubbish. *Children's Literature in Education, 1*(3), 7–10.

Dixon, Kerryn. (2011). *Literacy, power, and the schooled body: Learning in time and space*. New York: Routledge.

Doyle, Marjorie. (2013). *A Doyle reader: Writings from home and away*. Portugal Cove–St. Phillips, NL: Boulder Publications.

Duley, Margot I. (2014). Armine Nutting Gosling: A full and useful life. In L. Cullum & M. Porter (Eds.), *Creating this place: Women, family, and class in St. John's, 1900–1950* (114–145). Montreal: McGill-Queen's University Press.

Eco, Umberto, & Carrière, Jean-Claude. (2011). *This is not the end of the book: A conversation curated by Jean-Phillipe de Tonnac*. Polly McLean (Trans.). London: Harvill Secker.

Edwards, Gail. (2012, June). "Good reading among young Canadians" (c. 1900–1950): The Canadian Association of Children's Librarians, Young Canada's Book Week, and the persistence of professional discourse. *Library and Information History, 28*(2), 135–149.

Fardy, B.D. (2005). *Ferryland: The colony of Avalonia*. St. John's: Flanker Press.

Fer, Briony. (2008). Color manual. In A. Temkin (Ed.), *Color chart: Reinventing color, 1950 to today* (28–38). New York: Museum of Modern Art.

Fernyhough, Charles. (2012). *Pieces of light: How the new science of memory illuminates the stories we tell about our pasts*. New York: HarperCollins.

Ford, Tim. (2005). Carolyn Haywood. *Pennsylvania Center for the Book*. Retrieved April 7, 2012, from http://pabook.libraries.psu.edu/palitmap/bios/Haywood_Carolyn.html.

Foster, Shirley, & Simons, Judy. (1995). *What Katy read: Feminist re-readings of "classic" stories for girls*. Basingstoke: Macmillan.

Fox, Arthur. (1967). The Athenaeum and the Museum. In J.R. Smallwood (Ed.), *The Book of Newfoundland* (Volume IV, 190–193). St. John's: Newfoundland Book Publishers.

Freire, Paulo, & Macedo, Donaldo. (1987). *Literacy: Reading the word and the world*. Westport, CT: Bergin & Garvey.

Friedan, Betty. (1964/1963). *The feminine mystique*. New York: Dell.

Friesen, Joe. (2014, April 14). How one in five Newfoundlanders embraced an Aboriginal heritage. *The Globe and Mail*, A1, A8.

Friskney, Janet B. (2007). From Methodist literary culture to Canadian literary culture: The United Church Publishing House/The Ryerson Press, 1829–1970. In S. Eliot, A. Nash, & I. Willison (Eds.), *Literary cultures and the material book* (379–385). British Library Studies in the History of the Book. London: The British Library.

Fuller, Danielle. (2004, Spring). Strange terrain: Reproducing and resisting place-myths in two contemporary fictions of Newfoundland. *Essays on Canadian Writing, 82*, 21–50.

Gaiman, Neil. (2013). *The ocean at the end of the lane*. New York: William Morrow/HarperCollins.

Gallagher, Shaun. (2005). *How the body shapes the mind*. Oxford: Clarendon Press.

Gallese, Vittorio, Keysers, Christian, & Rizzolatti, Giacomo. (2004, September). A unifying view of the basis of social cognition. TRENDS *in Cognitive Sciences, 8*(9), 396–403.

Garfield, Simon. (2013). *On the map: A mind-expanding exploration of the way the world looks*. New York: Gotham Books.

Gelernter, David. (1994). *The muse in the machine: Computerizing the poetry of human thought*. New York: Free Press.

Genette, Gérard. (1980). *Narrative discourse*. J.E. Lewin (Trans.). Oxford: Basil Blackwell.

Geri. *Bernardine* (review). Loving the Classics. Retrieved February 3, 2013, from http://www.lovingtheclassics.com/decade/1950s-movies/bernardine-1957.html.

Gerrig, Richard J. (1993). *Experiencing narrative worlds: On the psychological activities of reading*. New Haven, CT: Westview Press.

Gill, Rosalind. (2013, November). Sense of place: "Self-creativity and co-creativity." *EarthLines: The Culture of Nature, 7*, 34–39.

Girl Detective. Mignon Eberhart: Death and the maiden (n.d.). *Girl-detective*. Retrieved December 8, 2012, from http://www.girl-detective.net/eberhart.html.

Goodman, Allegra. (2005). Pemberley previsited: *Pride and Prejudice* by Jane Austen. In A. Fadiman (Ed.), *Rereadings: Seventeen writers revisit books they love* (155–164). New York: Farrar, Straus and Giroux.

Gough, Ruby L. (2005). *Robert Edwards Holloway: Newfoundland educator, scientist, photographer, 1874–1904*. Montreal: McGill-Queen's University Press.

Gower Street United Church: A short history. Retrieved May 5, 2013, from http://ez-host2.com/tp40/page.asp?ID=137443.

Gregory, E. David. (2004). Vernacular song, cultural identity, and nationalism in Newfoundland, 1920–1955. *History of Intellectual Culture, 4*(1), 1–22.

Gros, Frédéric. (2014/2009). *A philosophy of walking*. John Howe (Trans.). London: Verso.

Heath, Shirley Brice. (1983). *Ways with words: Language, life, and work in communities and classrooms*. Cambridge: Cambridge University Press.

Hild, Martha Hickman. (2012). *Geology of Newfoundland: Touring through time at 48 scenic sites*. Portugal Cove–St. Phillips, NL: Boulder Publications.

Hodge, Bob, & Tripp, David. (1986). *Children and television: A semiotic approach*. Cambridge: Polity Press.

Hodgins, Jack. (2001). *A passion for narrative: A guide for writing fiction*. Rev. edition. Toronto: McClelland & Stewart.

Hogan, Patrick Colm. (2003). *Cognitive science, literature, and the arts: A guide for humanists*. New York: Routledge.

Howdy Doody. Wikipedia. Retrieved November 29, 2010, from http://en.wikipedia.org/wiki/ Howdy_Doody.

Huey, E.B. (2009/1908). *The psychology and pedagogy of reading*. Newark, DE: International Reading Association.

Hutcheon, Linda. (2006). *A theory of adaptation*. New York: Routledge.

Iacoboní, Marco. (2009). *Mirroring people: The science of empathy and how we connect with others*. New York: Picador.

Ingold, Tim. (2004). Culture on the ground: The world perceived through the feet. *Journal of Material Culture, 9*(3), 315–340.

Ingold, Tim. (2010). The textility of making. *Cambridge Journal of Economics, 34*, 91–102.

Iser, Wolfgang. (1978). *The act of reading: A theory of aesthetic response*. Baltimore: Johns Hopkins University Press.

Jamieson, Don. (1989). *No place for fools: The political memoirs of Don Jamieson, Volume 1*. Carmelita McGrath (Ed.). St. John's: Breakwater Books.

Jauss, Hans Robert, & Benzinger, Elizabeth. (1970, Autumn). Literary history as a challenge to literary theory. *New Literary History, 2*(1), 7–37.

Jefferson, Philip Clarke. (2002). *Clarke connections: Stories of kinfolk on the Kennetcook in Nova Scotia*. Unpublished manuscript.

Johnston, Wayne. (2014/2013). *The son of a certain woman*. Toronto: Vintage Canada.

Johnston, Wayne. (2011). *A world elsewhere*. Toronto: Alfred A. Knopf Canada.

Junior workbook number 1: Learning to use the Bible. (1956/1954). Toronto: Published cooperatively by The United Church Publishing House and the Baptist Publications Committee of Canada.

Just himself: The story of Don Jamieson. (2011). Written and directed by Joshua Jamieson. Odd Sock Films. DVD. Vaughan, ON: Visual Education Centre.

Kister, Kenneth F. (2002). *Eric Moon: The life and library times*. Jefferson, NC: McFarland.

Kohl, Herbert. (1995). *Should we burn Babar? Essays on children's literature and the power of stories*. New York: New Press.

Krips, Valerie. (2000). *The presence of the past: Memory, heritage, and childhood in postwar Britain*. New York: Garland.

Kroetsch, Robert. (2010). *Too bad: Sketches toward a self-portrait*. Edmonton: University of Alberta Press.

Kuzmičová, Anežka. (2012). Presence in the reading of literary narrative: A case for motor enactment. *Semiotica, 189*(1/4), 23–48.

Langford, Sondra Gordon. (1991, November/December). A second look: "Rufus M." *Horn Book Magazine, 67*(6), n.p.

Laurence, Margaret. (2003). Where the world began. In N.F. Stovel (Ed.), *Heart of a stranger* (2nd ed., 169–174). Edmonton: University of Alberta Press.

Laurence, Margaret. (1969). *The fire-dwellers*. Toronto: McClelland & Stewart, New Canadian Library.

Leander, Kevin, & Boldt, Gail. (2013, March). Rereading 'A pedagogy of multiliteracies': Bodies, texts, and emergence. *Journal of Literacy Research, 45*(1), 22–46.

Leonhardt, Mary. (1996). *Keeping kids reading: How to raise avid readers in the video age*. New York: Three Rivers Press.

Lepore, Jill. (2013, June 3). The oddyssey: Robert Ripley and his world. *The New Yorker*, 62–66.

List of Dick Tracy characters. Wikipedia. Retrieved March 20, 2011, from http://en.wikipedia.org/wiki/List_of_Dick_Tracy_characters.

Leviton, Daniel J. (2006). *This is your brain on music: The science of a human obsession*. New York: Dutton.

Lively, Penelope. (2012). *How it all began*. New York: Penguin.

Lloyd, Rebecca J. (2011). Awakening movement consciousness in the physical landscapes of literacy: Leaving, reading and being moved by one's trace. *Phenomenology and Practice, 5*(2), 70–92.

Luhrmann, T.M. (2014, September 5). Can't place that smell? You must be American: How culture shapes our senses. *The New York Times*, SR6.

Lynch, Kevin. (1960). *The image of the city*. Cambridge, MA: MIT Press.

Macfarlane, David. (1991). *The danger tree: Memory, war, and the search for a family's past*. Toronto: Macfarlane, Walter and Ross.

Mackey, Margaret. (1991, July). Developing readers: Lessons from Agatha Christie. *Reading, 25*(2), 25–30.

Mackey, Margaret. (1993). Many spaces: Some limitations of single readings. *Children's Literature in Education, 24*(3), 147–163.

Mackey, Margaret. (2006). Serial monogamy: Extended fictions and the television revolution. *Children's Literature in Education: An International Quarterly, 37*(2), 149–161.

Mackey, Margaret. (2007). *Mapping recreational literacies: Contemporary adults at play*. New York: Peter Lang.

Mackey, Margaret. (2010a). A multimodal history of learning to read. Presentation at the United Kingdom Literacy Association annual conference. Winchester, UK.

Mackey, Margaret. (2010b). Reading from the feet up: The local work of literacy. *Children's Literature in Education: An International Quarterly, 41*(4), 323–339.

Mackey, Margaret. (2011). The embedded and embodied literacies of an early reader. *Children's Literature in Education: An International Quarterly, 42*(4), 289–307.

Mackey, Margaret. (2012). Grounding our perspectives on children's literature. Gryphon Lecture. Children's Center for the Book, University of Illinois, Urbana-Champaign.

Mackey, Margaret. (2015). Standing on a rainbow: Reading in place, position, and time. In R. Panofsky & K. Kellett (Eds.), *Cultural mapping and the digital sphere: Place and Space*. Edmonton: University of Alberta Press, 263–278.

Mackey, Margaret, Vermeer, Leslie, Storie, Dale, & DeBlois, Elizabeth. (2012). The constancy of the school "canon": A survey of texts used in grade 10 English language arts in 2006 and 1996. *Language and Literacy: A Canadian E-Journal, 14*(1), 26–58.

Mahy, Margaret. (1991, Winter). A dissolving ghost. *Sport, 7,* 5–24.

Maine, Fiona, & Waller, Alison. (2011). *Swallows and Amazons* forever: How adults and children engage in reading a classic text. *Children's Literature in Education: An International Quarterly, 42,* 354–371.

Major, Alice. (2011). *Intersecting sets: A poet looks at science.* Edmonton: University of Alberta Press.

Major, Kevin. (2001). *As near to heaven by sea: A history of Newfoundland and Labrador.* Toronto: Penguin Canada.

Malouf, David. (1985). A first place: The mapping of a world. *Southerly: A Review of Australian Literature, 45*(1), 3–10.

Mandler, Jean. M. (1992, October). How to build a baby: II. Conceptual primitives. *Psychological Review, 99*(4), 387–604.

Massey, Doreen. (2005). *For space.* Los Angeles: Sage.

Massumi, Brian. (2002). *Parables for the virtual: Movement, affect, sensation.* Durham, NC: Duke University Press.

Mathews, Larry. (2010). *The artificial Newfoundlander.* St. John's: Breakwater.

Maunder, John. (1991). Museum notes—The Newfoundland Museum: Origins and development. The Rooms. Retrieved August 5, 2011, from http://www.therooms.ca/museum/mnotes2.asp.

McClure, Wendy. (2012). *The Wilder life: My adventures in the lost world of* Little House on the Prairie. New York: Riverhead Books.

McCulloch, Fiona. (2006, Spring). "A strange race of beings": Undermining innocence in *The Princess and the Goblin. Scottish Studies Review, 7*(1), 53–67.

McCurdy, Sherburne, & McCurdy, Elizabeth. (2010/2002). *The Prince of Wales memoirs, 1950–1962.* Unpublished manuscript.

Mead, Rebecca. (2014). *My life in Middlemarch.* New York: Crown Publishers.

Meek, Margaret. (1988). *How texts teach what readers learn.* Stroud, UK: Thimble Press.

Memorial University Libraries. Newspapers. Retrieved June 5, 2013, from (for the *Daily News*) http://www.library.mun.ca/cns/nlnews/title/df/ and (for the *Evening Telegram*) http://www.library.mun.ca/cns/nlnews/title/s-w/.

Mendelsund, Peter. (2014). *What we see when we read: A phenomenology with illustrations.* New York: Vintage.

Mifflen, Jessie. (2008). *Journey to yesterday: The collected works of Jessie Mifflen.* St. John's: DRC Publishing.

Mitchell, Claudia, & Reid-Walsh, Jacqueline. (2002). *Researching children's popular culture: The cultural spaces of childhood.* London: Routledge.

Moore, Paul S. (2007). Early picture shows at the fulcrum of modern and parochial St. John's, Newfoundland. *Newfoundland and Labrador Studies, 22*(2), 447–471.

Moores, Shaun. (2005). *Media/theory: Thinking about media and communications.* London: Routledge.

Morgan, Bernice. (2003). The culture of place. *Newfoundland and Labrador Studies, 19*(2), 373–377.

Morgan, Bonnie. (2014). Activist Anglicans and rectors' wives: The impact of class and gender on women's church work in St John's. In L. Cullum & M. Porter (Eds.), *Creating this place: Women, family, and class in St. John's, 1900–1950* (25–46). Montreal: McGill-Queen's University Press.

Moss, Stephen. (2012). *Natural childhood*. Swindon, UK: The National Trust. Retrieved from http://www.nationaltrust.org.uk/document-1355766991839/.

Munro, Alice. (2011, September 11). "Dear life." *The New Yorker*, 40–47.

Murray, Hilda Chaulk. (2002). *Cows don't know it's Sunday*. St. John's: Institute of Social and Economic Research.

Nardi, Bonnie. (2008, December). Mixed realities: Information spaces then and now. *Information Research, 13*(4), paper 354. Retrieved May 4, 2010, from http://InformationR.net/ir/13-4/paper354.html.

Neary, Peter, & O'Flaherty, Patrick (Eds.). (1974). *By great waters: A Newfoundland and Labrador anthology*. M. Bliss (Ed.), The Social History of Canada. Toronto: University of Toronto Press.

Newfoundland. (2013). *Canada History*. Retrieved March 5, 2014, from http://www.canadahistory.com/sections/war/WW%20I/Newfoundland.html.

Nikolajeva, Maria. (2014). *Reading for learning: Cognitive approaches to children's literature*. Amsterdam: John Benjamins.

Nikolajeva, Maria. (2013). Beyond happily ever after: The aesthetic dilemma of multivolume fiction for children. In B. Lefebvre (Ed.), *Textual transformations in children's literature: Adaptations, translations, reconsiderations*. New York: Routledge.

No great future: Government sponsored resettlement in Newfoundland and Labrador since Confederation. (2004). Maritime History Archive. Retrieved March 5, 2014, from https://www.mun.ca/mha/resettlement/.

Nodelman, Perry. (2008). *The hidden adult: Defining children's literature*. Baltimore, MD: Johns Hopkins University Press.

Nodelman, Perry. (1981, December). How typical children read typical books. *Children's Literature in Education, 12*(4), 177–185.

Now I lay me down to sleep. Wikipedia. Retrieved May 13, 2012, from http://en.wikipedia.org/wiki/Now_I_Lay_Me_Down_to_Sleep.

O'Brien, Geoffrey. (2004). *Sonata for jukebox: Pop music, memory, and the imagined life*. New York: Counterpoint.

O'Neill, Paul. (2008). *The oldest city: The story of St. John's, Newfoundland*. Portugal Cove-St. Phillips, NL: Boulder Publications.

Paul, Annie Murphy. (2012, March 17). Your brain on fiction. *The New York Times*. Retrieved March 30, 2012, from www.nytimes.com/2012/03/18/opinion/sunday/the-neuroscience-of-your-brain-on-fiction.html?_r=3&pagewanted=1.

Pennycook, Alistair. (2010). *Language as a local practice*. London: Routledge.

Pitt, David G. (1990). *Windows of agates: The life and times of Gower Street Church, St. John's, Newfoundland 1815–1990*. Rev. ed. St. John's: Jesperson Press.

Porter, Helen Fogwill. (1988). *january, february, june or july*. St. John's: Breakwater Books.

Porter, Marilyn. (2014). "She knows who she is": Educating girls to their place in society. In L. Cullum & M. Porter (Eds.), *Creating this place: Women, family, and class in St. John's, 1900–1950* (146–178). Montreal: McGill-Queen's University Press.

Presner, Todd, Shepard, David, & Kawano, Yoh. (2014). *HyperCities: Thick mapping in the digital humanities*. Cambridge, MA: Harvard University Press.

The Public Libraries Board, Gosling Memorial Library. (1957). *21 years of library service in Newfoundland, 1936–1957*. St. John's: Public Libraries Board.

Regarding our father: The life and times of Gerald S. Doyle. (2011). John W. Doyle and Marjorie Doyle. DVD. St. John's: Rink Rat Productions in association with the Canadian Broadcasting Corporation.

Reid, Mark. (2009, June). Reframing literacy: A film pitch for the 21st century. *English Drama Media, 14*, 19–23.

Renzetti, Elizabeth. (2014, February 24). Urban walking is a legal high, so why are cities cruel to pedestrians? *The Globe and Mail*. Retrieved February 24, 2014, from http://www.theglobeandmail.com/globe-debate/cities-should-worship-the-ground-we-walk-on/article17028062/.

Riggs, Bert. (2005). Case study: At the sign of the book: Dicks and Company of St. John's. In Y. Lamond, P.L. Fleming, & F.A. Black (Eds.), *History of the book in Canada, Volume II, 1840–1918* (226–229). Toronto: University of Toronto Press.

Robertson, Judith P., Lewkowich, David, & Rottmann, Jennifer. (2010). Saltwater chronicles: Reading representational spaces in selected book clubs in St. John's, Newfoundland. *Island Studies Journal, 5*(2), 141–164.

Rosen, Harold. (1996). Autobiographical memory. *Changing English, 3*(1), 21–34.

Rosenberg, Neil V. (1991). The Gerald S. Doyle Songsters and the politics of Newfoundland folksong. *Canadian Folklore Canadien, 13*(1), 45–57.

Rosenblatt, Louise. (1978). *The reader, the text, the poem: The transactional theory of the literary work*. Carbondale, IL: Southern Illinois University Press.

Ross, Catherine Sheldrick. (1995). "If they read Nancy Drew, so what?": Series book readers talk back. *Library and Information Science Research, 17*, 201–236.

Rusted, Joan. (2011). *St. John's: A brief history*. St. John's: Breakwater Books.

Ryan, Marie-Laure. (2006). *Avatars of story*. Electronic Mediations, Book 17. M. Poster Hayles & S. Weber (Eds.). Minneapolis: University of Minnesota Press.

Sarland, Charles. (1991). *Young people reading: Culture and response*. In A. Adams (Gen. Ed.), *English, Language, and Education* series. Milton Keynes: Open University Press.

Scarry, Elaine. (1999). *Dreaming by the book*. New York: Farrar, Strauss and Giroux.

Schmitz, Terri. (2001, September/October). Characters you can count on. *Horn Book Magazine, 77*(5), 557–567.

Schwebel, Sara L. (2011). *Child-sized history: Fictions of the past in US classrooms*. Nashville, TN: Vanderbilt University Press.

Scollon, Ron, & Scollon, Suzie Wong. (2003). *Discourses in place: Language in the material world*. London: Routledge.

Segal, Erwin M. (1995). Narrative comprehension and the role of deictic shift theory. In J.F. Duchan, G.A. Bruder, & L.E. Hewitt (Eds.), *Deixis in narrative: A cognitive science perspective* (3-17). Hillsdale, NJ: Lawrence Erlbaum Associates.

Shattuck, Roger. (1983/1962). *Proust's binoculars: A study of memory, time and recognition in À La Recherche du Temps Perdu*. Princeton, NJ: Princeton University Press.

Silcox, Donald P., & Weiler, Meriké. (1982). *Christopher Pratt*. Scarborough, ON: Prentice-Hall.

Simons, Paula. (2002, April 2). After shovelling snow on Easter, now we look forward to brown grass, mud puddles, potholes, melting dog poop. *Edmonton Journal*, B1.

Sipe, Lawrence R. (2008). *Storytime: Young children's literary understanding in the classroom*. New York: Teachers College Press.

Smith, Frank. (1987). *Joining the literacy club: Further essays into education*. Portsmouth, NH: Heinemann.

Smith, Frederick R. (1978). The early history and formation of Holloway School. Pamphlet. OCLC 456753656.

Smith, Michael, & Wilhelm, Jeffrey D. (2004). "I just like being good at it": The importance of competence in the literate lives of young men. *Journal of Adolescent & Adult Literacy, 47*(6), 454-461.

Spacks, Patricia Meyer. (2011). *On rereading*. Cambridge, MA: Belknap Press/Harvard University Press.

St. John's, Newfoundland and Labrador: Climate. Wikipedia. Retrieved August 6, 2012, from http://en.wikipedia.org/wiki/St._John%27s,_Newfoundland_and_Labrador#Climate.

Stephens, John, & McCallum, Robyn. (2013/1998). *Retelling stories, framing culture: Traditional story and metanarratives in children's literature*. New York: Routledge.

Stockwell, Peter. (2002). *Cognitive poetics: An introduction*. London: Routledge.

Sutherland, Robin. (2007). Introduction. In Grace McLeod Rogers, *Joan at Halfway* (vii-xvi). Halifax: Formac.

Swain, Hector K. (1999). *VOWR: The unfolding dream*. St. John's: Creative Publishers.

Temkin, Ann. (2008). Color shift. In A. Temkin (Ed.), *Color chart: Reinventing color, 1950 to today* (16-27). New York: Museum of Modern Art.

The twentieth century (TV series). Wikipedia. Retrieved February 16, 2013, from http://en.wikipedia.org/wiki/The_Twentieth_Century_(TV_series).

Thomas, Nicholas. (1987, October). Accessible adventure in "Swallows and Amazons." *Anthropology Today, 3*(5), 8-11.

A time to remember. (1990). Shirley Newhook interviewing Miss Lima Davis and Miss Ida Duder. Gower Seniors Club Project 1990. 175th Anniversary—Gower Street United Church. Audiotape.

Trites, Roberta Seelinger. (2014). *Literary conceptualizations of growth: Metaphors and cognition in adolescent literature*. Amsterdam: John Benjamins.

United Church of Canada Board of Christian Education. (1956, April). Reports. Section R6. Loc. No. 83.051C. Box-File 10-2. Toronto: United Church of Canada Archives.

Vandenberg, Brian. (1998). Real and not real: A vital developmental dichotomy. In Olivia N. Saracho & Bernard Spodek (Eds.), *Multiple perspectives on play in early childhood education* (295–304). Early Childhood Education: Inquiries and Insights. New York: State University of New York Press.

van Dijck, José. (2007). *Mediated memories in the digital age*. Stanford, CA: Stanford University Press.

Vygotsky, L.S. (1978). *Mind in society: The development of higher psychological processes*. M. Cole, V. John-Steiner, S. Scribner, & E. Souberman (Eds.). Cambridge, MA: Harvard University Press.

Wadden, Nix. (2008). *Yesterday's news*. St. John's: DRC Publishing.

Wagamese, Richard. (2014). *Medicine walk*. Toronto: McClelland & Stewart.

Webb, Jeff A. (2008). *The voice of Newfoundland: A social history of the Broadcasting Corporation of Newfoundland, 1939–1949*. Toronto: University of Toronto Press.

Weber, Sandra, & Mitchell, Claudia. (2004). Dress stories. In S. Weber & C. Mitchell (Eds.), *Not just any dress: Narratives of memory, body, and identity*. New York: Peter Lang.

Welchan, Imelda. (1999). Adaptations: The contemporary dilemmas. In D. Cartmell & I. Welchan (Eds.), *Adaptations: From text to screen, screen to text* (3–18). London: Routledge.

White, Jennifer. The Beverly Gray mystery stories. *Series books for girls...and a few for boys*. Retrieved March 13, 2012, from http://www.series-books.com/beverlygray/beverlygray.html.

White, Raymond E. (2005). *King of the cowboys, queen of the west: Roy Rogers and Dale Evans*. Madison: University of Wisconsin Press/Popular Press.

Whitman, Walt. (1892). *Song of myself*. Retrieved from http://www.poetryfoundation.org/poem/174745.

Williams, Raymond. (1974). *Television: Technology and cultural form*. London: Fontana.

Wolf, Maryanne. (2007). *Proust and the squid: The story and science of the reading brain*. C. Stoodley (Illus.). New York: HarperCollins.

Wolf, Shelby Anne, & Heath, Shirley Brice. (1992). *The braid of literature: Children's worlds of reading*. Cambridge, MA: Harvard University Press.

Wordsworth, William. (1960/1802). Preface to lyrical ballads. In T. Hutchinson (Ed.), E. de Selincourt (Rev. Ed.), *The poetical works of Wordsworth* (734–741). London: Oxford University Press.

Wyile, Herb. (2011). *Anne of Tim Hortons: Globalization and the reshaping of Atlantic-Canadian literature*. Waterloo, ON: Wilfrid Laurier University Press.

Wynne-Jones, Tim. (1998). The survival of the book. *Signal: Approaches to Children's Books, 87*, 160–166.

Yeo, Leslie. (1998). *A thousand and one first nights*. Canadian Theatre History Series #2, Denis Johnston (Ed.). Oakville, ON: Mosaic Press.

Zipes, Jack. (2001). *Sticks and stones: The troublesome success of children's literature from Slovenly Peter to Harry Potter*. New York: Routledge.

Children's Titles

Andersen, Hans Christian. (1845). The little match girl. Jean Hersholt (Trans.). Retrieved from The Hans Christian Andersen Centre at http://www.andersen.sdu.dk/vaerk/hersholt/TheLittleMatchGirl_e.html.

Bee, Clair. (1949). *Strike three! A Chip Hilton sports story*. London: Grosset & Dunlap.

Blank, Clair. (1935). *Beverly Gray's career*. New York: Grosset & Dunlap.

Blank, Clair. (1936). *Beverly Gray on a world cruise*. New York: Grosset & Dunlap.

Blank, Clair. (1937). *Beverly Gray in the Orient*. New York: Grosset & Dunlap.

Blank, Clair. (1938). *Beverly Gray on a treasure hunt*. New York: Grosset & Dunlap.

Blank, Clair. (1942). *Beverly Gray's quest*. New York: Grosset & Dunlap.

Boyd, Irene. (n.d.). A day in the forest. In *Ripping stories for girls* (n.p.). London: Blackie & Son.

Boylston, Helen Dore. (1939). *Sue Barton: student nurse*. London: Bodley Head.

Brink, Carol Ryrie. (1990/1935). *Caddie Woodlawn*. Trina Schart Human (Illus.). New York: Aladdin.

Brown, Mrs. J.T. (n.d.). A short cut to Australia. In *The Bumper Book for Children* (65–77). London: Thomas Nelson & Sons.

The Bumper book for children. (n.d.) London: Thomas Nelson & Sons.

Burgess, Thornton W. (1910). *Old Mother West Wind*. George Kerr (Illus.). New York: Grosset & Dunlap.

Burgess, Thornton W. (1912). *Old Mother West Wind's animal friends*. George Kerr (Illus.). New York: Grosset & Dunlap.

Burgess, Thornton W. (1924). *Billy Mink*. Harrison Cady (Illus.). New York: Grosset & Dunlap.

Burgess, Thornton W. (1943). *The adventures of Chatterer the Red Squirrel*. Toronto: McClelland & Stewart.

Cam. (1950/1946). *The story of Margaret Field-Mouse*. Oxford: John Lane The Bodley Head.

Chandler, Olive. (n.d.). The captain and Jeremy. In *The Bumper Book for Children* (14–18). London: Thomas Nelson & Sons.

Cleary, Beverly. (1988/1984). *Ramona forever*. London: Puffin.

Crossland, John R., & Parrish, J.M. (Eds.). (1933). *The children's wonder book*. London: Odhams Press.

de Brunhoff, Jean. (2008/1940). *Babar and Father Christmas*. In *The Babar collection: Five classic tales*. London: Egmont.

Decker, Duane. (1947). *Good field, no hit*. New York: M.S. Mill.

Decker, Duane. (1958). *Long ball to left field*. New York: William Morrow.

Dixon, Franklin W. (1927). *The tower treasure*. New York: Grosset & Dunlap.

Estes, Eleanor. (1959/1941). *The Moffats*. Louis Slobodkin (Illus.). London: Bodley Head.

Estes, Eleanor. (1972/1942). *The Middle Moffat*. Louis Slobodkin (Illus.). Leicester: Knight Books.

Estes, Eleanor. (1943). *Rufus M*. Louis Slobodkin (Illus.). San Diego: Harcourt Brace Jovanovich.

Estes, Eleanor. (2001/1983). *The Moffat Museum*. E. Estes (Illus.). San Diego: Odyssey/Harcourt Young Classic.

Field, Rachel. (1944). *Prayer for a child*. Elizabeth Orton Jones (Illus.). New York: Macmillan.

Friskey, Margaret. (1940). *Seven diving ducks*. Lucia Patton (Illus.). Philadelphia: David McKay Company.

Gipson, Morrell. (2000/1950). *Mr. Bear Squash-You-All-Flat*. Angela (Illus.). Gary Larson (Afterword). First published by Wonder Books. Cynthiana, KY: Purple House Press.

Grahame, Kenneth. (1961/1908). *The wind in the willows*. E.H. Shepard (Illus.). New York: Charles Scribner's Sons.

Grimms' Fairy Tales. (1945). Mrs. E.V. Lucas, L. Crane, & M. Edwardes (Trans.), F. Kredel (Illus.). New York: Grosset & Dunlap.

Haywood, Carolyn. (1939). *"B" is for Betsy*. New York: Harcourt Brace.

Heward, Constance. (1972/1920). *Ameliaranne and the green umbrella*. Beatrice Pearse (Illus.). London: George G. Harrap.

Hill, Lorna. (1988/1950). *A dream of Sadler's Wells*. London: Pan Piper.

Hope, Laura Lee. (1950). *The Bobbsey twins: Merry days indoors and out*. Janet Laura Scott (Illus.). Racine, WI: Whitman Publishing Company.

Hughes, Shirley. (1981). *Lucy and Tom's Christmas*. London: Victor Gollancz.

Jackson, Kathryn. (1958/1952). *Nurse Nancy*. Corinne Malvern (Illus.). New York: Little Golden Book.

Jones, Jessie Orton (Ed.) (1949). *Small rain: Verses from the Bible*. Elizabeth Orton Jones (Illus.). New York: Viking Press.

Keene, Carolyn. (1930). *The secret of the old clock*. New York: Grosset & Dunlap.

MacDonald, George. (1949/1872). *The princess and the goblin*. Charles Folkard (Illus.). London: J.M. Dent & Sons.

Martin, Marcia. (1952). *Waiting for Santa Claus (Christmas is coming)*. Alison Cummings (Illus.). New York: Wonder Books.

McCormick, Wilfred. (1951). *Grand-slam homer. A Bronc Burnett story*. New York: Grosset & Dunlap.

Milne, A.A. (1957). *The world of Pooh*. E.H. Shepard (Illus.). Toronto: McClelland & Stewart.

Montgomery, L.M. (1975/1909). *Anne of Green Gables*. Harmondsworth: Penguin Peacock.

Montgomery, L.M. (1985/1925). *Emily of New Moon*. Toronto: Seal Books/McClelland-Bantam.

Montgomery, L.M. (1980/1927). *Emily's quest*. Toronto: McClelland & Stewart.

Montgomery, L.M. (1988/1933). *Pat of Silver Bush*. Toronto: Seal Books/McClelland-Bantam.

Montgomery, L.M. (1988/1935). *Mistress Pat*. Toronto: Seal Books/McClelland-Bantam.

Norton, Mary. (1986/1952). *The Borrowers*. Diana Stanley (Illus.). Harmondsworth: Puffin.

Norton, Mary. (1953, June/July, August/September). *The Borrowers*. Erik Blegvad (Illus.). Serialized in *Woman's Day*.

Oxenham, Elise J. (1914). *The girls of the Hamlet Club*. London: W. & R. Chambers.

Oxenham, Elsie J. (1959). *Two queens at the abbey*. London: Collins.

Phillips, Lydia. (1902). *The children of Brookfield Hall*. London: Religious Tract Society.

Porter, Eleanor H. (1940/1913). *Pollyanna*. New York: Grosset & Dunlap.

Porter, Eleanor H. (1987/1927). *Pollyanna grows up*. Harmondsworth: Puffin Books.

Ransome, Arthur. (1962/1930). *Swallows and Amazons*. A. Ransome (Illus.). Harmondsworth: Puffin Books.

Ransome, Arthur. (2001/1940). *Swallowdale*. A. Ransome (Illus.). London: Red Fox.

Sidney, Margaret. (1955). *Five little Peppers and how they grew*. Sari (Illus.). Racine, WI: Whitman Publishing Company.

Smith, Harriet Lummis. (1924). *Pollyanna of the orange blossoms*. New York: Grosset & Dunlap.

Spier, Peter. (1981). *People*. Tadworth, Surrey: World's Work Ltd./Windmill Press.

Spyri, Johanna. (2002/1880–81). *Heidi*. Angelo Rinaldi (Illus.). Foreword by Beverly Cleary. Eileen Hall (Trans.). London: Kingfisher.

Thorndyke, Helen Louise. (1923a). *Honey Bunch: Just a little girl*. New York: Grosset & Dunlap.

Thorndyke, Helen Louise. (1923b). *Honey Bunch: Her first visit to the city*. New York: Grosset & Dunlap.

Thorndyke, Helen Louise. (1946). *Honey Bunch: Her first winter at Snowtop*. New York: Grosset & Dunlap.

Travers, P.L. (1965/1934). *Mary Poppins*. Mary Shepard (Illus.). London: Collins.

Wells, Carolyn. (1909). *Marjorie's new friend*. New York: Grosset & Dunlap.

Wells, Carolyn. (1911). *Marjorie's Maytime*. New York: Grosset & Dunlap.

Wiggin, Kate Douglas. (1888/1886). *The Birds' Christmas carol*. Boston: Houghton Mifflin.

Wilde, Irma. (1976/1951). *Merry Christmas Mr. Snowman (The snowman's Christmas present)*. New York: Wonder Books.

Wilder, Laura Ingalls. (1933). *Farmer boy*. Helen Sewell (Illus.). Eau Claire, WI: Cadmus Books/E.M. Hale and Company.

Wilder, Laura Ingalls. (1968/1940). *The long winter*. Garth Williams (Illus.). New York: HarperTrophy.

Adult Titles

Carroll, Gladys Hasty. (1947). *While the angels sing*. New York: Macmillan.

Comstock, Harriet T. (1933/1902). *Tower or throne? A romance of Queen Elizabeth's girlhood*. London: George G. Harrap.

de la Roche, Mazo. (2006/1927). *Jalna*. Toronto: Dundurn Press.

Delafield, E.M. (1993/1947). *The diary of a provincial lady*. London: Virago.

Eberhart, Mignon G. (1959). *Melora*. New York: Random House.

Gilbreth, Frank B. Jr., & Carey, Ernestine Gilbreth. (2002/1948). *Cheaper by the dozen*. New York: Perennial Classics.

Gilbreth, Frank B. Jr., & Carey, Ernestine Gilbreth. (1950). *Belles on their toes*. New York: Thomas Y. Crowell.

Innis, Mary Quayle. (1943). *Stand on a rainbow*. Toronto: Wm. Collins & Co.

Milton, John. (1912). *The poetical works of John Milton*. Oxford Edition. Rev. H.C. Beeching (Ed.). London: Henry Frowde, Oxford University Press.

Rogers, Grace McLeod. (1919). *Joan at Halfway*. Toronto: McClelland & Stewart.

Skinner, Cornelia Otis, & Kimbrough, Emily. (1944). *Our hearts were young and gay*. Toronto: Dodd, Mead & Company.

Smith, Dodie. (1948). *I capture the castle*. An Atlantic Monthly Press Book. Boston: Little, Brown and Company.

Tennyson, Lord Alfred. (n.d.). *The poetical works of Alfred, Lord*. Arthur Waugh (Ed.). London: Collins.

Wilson, Theodora Wilson. (1910). *The islanders*. London: Blackie & Son.

Miscellaneous Materials

Bartók, Béla. (n.d.). *Little pieces for children: Book 1, for solo piano*. Boca Raton, FL: Well-Tempered Press.

Betty Crocker's Guide to Easy Entertaining. (1959). Peter Spier (Illus.). New York: Golden Press.

The Canadian youth hymnal. (1939). Committee of the General Council of the United Church of Canada (Compilers). Toronto: United Church Publishing House.

Collins, Max Allan, & Locher, Dick (Eds.). (1991). *Dick Tracy's fiendish foes! A 60th Anniversary Celebration*. New York: St. Martin's Press.

Disney, Dorothy Cameron. (1959, October). The marriage that could not be saved. *Ladies' Home Journal, LXXVI*(10), 82, 182, 184–186.

Doyle, Gerald S. (1927, November). *The old time songs and poetry of Newfoundland*. Printed by the publishers of "The Family Fireside."

Farmer, Fannie Merritt. (1941/1896). *The Boston Cooking School cook book*. Toronto: McClelland & Stewart.

Ficarra, J. (Ed.). (2012). *Totally MAD: 60 years of humor, satire, stupidity and stupidity*. New York: Time Home Entertainment.

The fifth edition of Newfoundland songs. (n.d.). Presented for Free Distribution by Dominion Ale.

Godden, Rumer. (1957, December). The story of Holly and Ivy. *Ladies' Home Journal, LXXIV*(12), 42–43, 156–160.

Grant, Robert. O worship the King. *The hymnary of the United Church of Canada*. (1930). #21.

Hart, Bet. (1959, May). How to dress well on practically nothing. *Ladies' Home Journal, LXXVI*(5), 109.

Hayes, Joyce. (1959, May). How to bring up four children on $100 a month. *Ladies' Home Journal, LXXVI*(5), 157–159, 166, 168.

Hays, Wilma Pitchford. (1958, November). Paying for the Indian corn. *Jack and Jill*, 9–14.

Hurlbut, Jesse Lyman. (1957). *Hurlbut's story of the Bible for young and old*. 5th ed. R.P. Coleman and S. Savage (Illus.). Philadelphia: John C. Winston Company.

The hymnary of the United Church of Canada. (1930). Authorized by the General Council. Toronto: The United Church Publishing House.

A Jack and Jill TV prevue: Scenes from Shirley Temple's storybook "Mother Goose." (1959, December). *Jack and Jill, 22*(2), 10–13.

Kindergarten of the air. CBC Radio.

Lyte, Henry Francis. Praise, my soul, the King of Heaven. *The hymnary of the United Church of Canada*. (1930). #17.

The McCurdy News. (1960, May 15). Newsletter.

The McCurdy News. (1961, August 6). Newsletter.

McGinley, Phyllis. (1956, December). The year without a Santa Claus. *Good Housekeeping*, *143*(6), 93–99.

McLoughlin, E.V. (Ed.). (1955). *The book of knowledge: The children's encyclopedia*. Vols. 9 and 11. New York: The Grolier Society.

Moon, Andrea. (2005). The instrument song. *I Love Music*. Audio CD. http://www.songsforteaching.com/store/music-appreciation-songs-cd-pr-1106.html.

Patons Craft Book No. C.5. (n.d.). Australia: Patons and Baldwin.

The Pow-Wow. (1961, June 22). Volume 5, Number 1. Newsletter.

The Pow-Wow. (1962, April 6). Volume 1, Number 6. Newsletter.

Schulte, Karl (Ed.). (1952). *Christmas carols*. F.D. Lohman (Illus.). Racine, WI: Whitman Publishing Company.

Smith, Walter Chalmers. Immortal, invisible, God only wise. *The hymnary of the United Church of Canada*. (1930). #34.

Tennyson, Alfred. (1908/1889). "Crossing the Bar." Music by F.W. Wegenast. Toronto: Whaley, Royce & Co.

"Things to Make." (1959, August). *Jack and Jill*, 11.

Thompson, John. (1994). *Teaching little fingers to play*. Florency, KY: Willis Music Company.

Vintage valentines: Flocked valentines to punch out and assemble. (2006). New York: Random House/Golden Books.

Younger, Joan. (1960, January). Our baby was born at home. *Ladies' Home Journal*, LXXVII(1), 111–116.

School Textbooks

Ambler, S.O., & Coatman, Th. (1936). *The stream of time: A history series for juniors*. Book I. London: Cassell & Company.

Atwood, Wallace W., & Thomas, Helen Goss. (1943). *Visits in other lands*. Boston: Ginn and Company.

Briffett, Frances. (1954). *The story of Newfoundland and Labrador*. P.R. Blakeley & M.C. Vernon (Eds.). Toronto: J.M. Dent & Sons (Canada).

Manuel, Edith M. (n.d., 15th impression 1960). *Newfoundland, our province*. Exeter, UK: A. Wheaton.

Schoolland, Marian. (1956). Pictures in the snow. In W.S. Gray, M. Monroe, A.S. Artley, & M.H. Arbuthnot (Eds.), *The new more streets and roads* (6–12). Chicago: Scott, Foresman.

Stoddard, Alexander, J., Bailey, Matilda, & Lewis, William Dodge. (n.d.). *English: Grade 3*. 2nd ed. Toronto: W.J. Gage.

Stong, Phil. (1942). The young cowboy. In W.S. Gray & M.H. Arbuthnot (Eds.), *More streets and roads* (81–90). Chicago: Scott, Foresman.

Television Programs

Ambush canyon. *Annie Oakley*. 10 Episodes. DVD. TV Classic Westerns. La Cross, WI: Platinum Disc Corporation, 2003.

Bad neighbors. (1954, November 21). *The Roy Rogers show*, Volume One. DVD. Critics Choice Video, 2004.

The best of The Burns and Allen show. (n.d.). DVD. New York: GoodTimes.

Enter the Lone Ranger. *The Lone Ranger*. 6 Episodes. DVD. TV Classic Westerns. La Cross, WI: Platinum Disc Corporation, 2003.

The mink coat. (1955, February 13). *Father knows best*, Season One. DVD. Los Angeles: Shout! Factory, 2008.

Strangers. (1954, December 5). *The Roy Rogers show*, Volume One. DVD. Critics Choice Video, 2004.

The twentieth century. (1957–1966). Written by Earle Luby. Narrated by Walter Cronkite. CBS.

Movies

Bernadine. (1957). Dir. Harry Levin. Twentieth Century Fox. DVD. Northampton, MA: Pressplayhouse.

Bush Christmas. (1947). Dir. Ralph Smart. DVD. Culver City, CA: Sony Pictures Home Entertainment, 2005.

Heidi. (1937). Dir. Allan Dwan. DVD. Beverly Hills: Twentieth Century Fox Home Entertainment, 2005.

Pollyanna. (1960). Dir. David Swift. DVD. Vault Disney Collection. Burbank: Buena Vista Home Entertainment, n.d.

Raintree county. (1957). Dir. Edward Dmytryk. DVD. Metro-Goldwyn-Mayer. The Castaways Pictures, n.d.

Permissions

p. 191. *The Borrowers*

p. 312, *Vintage Valentines*

pp. 316–317, 333, *Bush Christmas*

p. 355, *Jack and Jill*

Text

The author would like to thank Springer for the use of material previously published in *Children's Literature in Education: An International Quarterly*, as follows:

Springer, *Children's Literature in Education*, "Reading from the Feet Up: The Local Work of Literacy." Volume 41, Issue 4, 2010, pp. 323–339. Margaret Mackey, © Springer Science+Business Media, LLC 2010. With kind permission of Springer Science+Business Media.

Springer, *Children's Literature in Education*, "The Embedded and Embodied Literacies of a Young Reader." Volume 42, Issue 4, 2011, pp. 289–307. Margaret Mackey, © Springer Science+Business Media, LLC 2011. With kind permission of Springer Science+Business Media.

Springer, *Children's Literature in Education*, "The Emergent Reader's Working Kit of Stereotypes." Volume 44, Issue 2, 2013, pp. 87–103. Margaret Mackey, © Springer Science+Business Media, LLC 2012. With kind permission of Springer Science+Business Media.

Index

negative impacts of dissatisfaction, 330

neuroscience and reader's emotional responses, 493, 495

rejection of stereotypes, 151

story as not worth the effort, 207

unmemorable texts, 228–30, *229*

texts: *Dick and Jane* basic readers, 134–35, 137, 139, 493, 495; *Honey Bunch* series, 151; *Melora*, 228–30, *229*; *Raintree County* (movie), 330; *Tower or Throne?*, 374–77

Dixon, Kerryn, 449–50

dolls

about, 53, 56–57, 152

dolls' beds, 56, 124, *126*

dolls' clothes by MM, 153, 293–94, *294*

femininity and, 56–57, 153

picture books, 124, *126*

scriptive things, 53–54

dolls, paper

femininity of, 57, 152, 153

in women's magazines, 215, 218–20, *219*

domestic libraries. *See* family library

domestic literacies. *See* applied literacy and everyday life

domestic stories, MM's preferences for, 110, 129–30, 131, 152, 162, 188, 191

Don Messer's Jubilee (TV show), 318

Doyle, Gerald S., 464–65, 470–73, 471–72

Doyle, Marjorie, 31–32

A Dream of Sadler's Wells (Hill), 161, 164–65

du Maurier, Daphne, 220, 228

Duder, Mrs. Gwen, *274*, 381, *478*, 479–80

Eberhart, Mignon, 228–30, *229*

Eco, Umberto, 76

The Ed Sullivan Show (TV show), 339

Edmonton and MM's life

everyday life, 391, 452

gap between text and lived experience, 148

move to Edmonton, 13, 403

time zones and TV viewing, 308, 339

Education, Department of, 387, 417, 456, 458

See also school systems

education of MM, reading. *See* Mackey, Margaret, learning to read

education of MM, school life. *See* Holloway School; Mackey, Margaret, school life; Prince of Wales College

education of MM, writing. *See* Mackey, Margaret, handwriting; Mackey, Margaret, writing

Edwards, Gail, 436–37

Egypt, in texts, 168, 170

embodied reading

about, 2, 3–6, 12, 484–87, 491–92, 495–96

eye and hand motions, 486–87

first place of childhood, 52–53

habits, 487

kinesthetic learners, 16, 491

reader's emotional responses, 493–95

reader's motor responses, 485–87, 494–95

recognition of structural equivalences, 484–87, 491

schema for navigation of mental space, 60

sensory perception, 13

situated bodies, 495–96

spatial vividness, 485–86

subjunctive mode of narrative, 492–95

sympathetic embodiment, 484–87, 491–92

touch by hands and feet, 60–62, 485–87

vertical floor, 486

visceral clues of previous reading, 25–26, 171

walking and, 59–60

texts: *Anne of Green Gables* series, 490–91; *Moffat* books, 489–90, *490*, 494–95, 500; sketch of Lee and manga (Japanese comics), 496–99; *The Story of Margaret Field-Mouse*, 488, 488–89; *Winnie-the-Pooh*, Woozle hunt, 489, *489*

See also situated reading; walking and foot-knowledge

Emily of New Moon (Montgomery), 255–57

Emily trilogy (Montgomery), 255–58

Emily's Quest (Montgomery), 251–52, 255–58

emotions

affect linking of life and texts, 99–100

empathy and difference, 154

MM's reading style, 23, 24

neuroscience and reading, 10, 493

reading for story's emotional core, 207

subjunctive mode of narrative, 493

texts: "Killer Ducks" incident, 98–99; *Moffat* books, 494, 500

Innis, Mary Quayle, 221, 224, 372

instability in discourse. *See* contingent discourses

"The Instrument Song", 71

intertextuality and MM's life

about, 394

Christian culture, 300–01

gaps and blanks of texts, 396

intertextual and intermedial crossovers, 289, 323–26, 341, 353–54, 360–61

literary canon, 211–12

schemas and scripts, 160

white, middle-class American life in media, 326, 328

working stereotypes, 158–60

texts: baby cards, 241, *242*; *The Children's Wonder Book*, 209–14, *210*; circuses, 159–60; cowboy stories, 323–25; hymns, 299; MAD *Magazine*, 225, *226*; MM's cowboy story, 349–52, *351–52*; sleepwalking, 335–36; Thanksgiving, 158–59; toy cars, 329

Iser, Wolfgang, 396

The Islanders (Wilson Wilson), 359–60

Jack and Jill (magazine)

about, 214–15

Aboriginal peoples in, 354–55, *355*

American culture, 159, 214–15, 355–56

arts and crafts, 214

children's writing, 214

December issues, 281, 283–84

implied reader, 354

television programs, 159, 283

working stereotypes, 159

Jackson, Kathryn, 124

Jalna series (de la Roche), 226–27, 231

James, William, 10

Jamieson, Don, 30–31, 326–27, 399–400, 466–67

january, february, june or july (Porter), 176

Jauss, Hans, 62, 82

Jefferson, John (MM's uncle), 76, 78

Jefferson, Philip Clarke (MM's uncle), 77–78

Jefferson, Rev. and Mrs. W.E. (MM's maternal grandparents)

Beaver Brook farmhouse, 75–77

discipline of children, 444

MM's solo visit, 250–63, 499, 504

Joan at Halfway (Rogers), 251–52, 258–60

Johnston, Wayne, 37–38, 44, 106–07, 117, 422, 501

Jones, Orton and Jessie Orton, 124

Joyce, Joseph, 463

Judy Bolton series (Sutton), 143, 161, 162, 173

Junior Workbooks for *Learning to Use the Bible*, 446, 447

Just Himself (movie), 327

Kawano, Yoh, 64–65, 509

Keene, Carolyn. See *Nancy Drew Mystery Stories*

Keysers, Christian, 492–93

Kindergarten of the Air (radio), 65–67, 323, 389

King of the Golden River (Ruskin), 211

Kipling, Rudyard, 209

Kirke, Sir David and Lady Sara, 369–70

knitting. *See* sewing and knitting

Krips, Valerie, 5, 198

Kroetsch, Robert, 17, 479

Künstlerroman, 256

Kuzmičová, Anežka, 485, 487, 492

Labrador

contingent discourses, 416, 419–20

history of, 28, 416

race and ethnicity, 419–20

See also Newfoundland and Labrador

Ladies College Aid Society, *455*, 455–56

Ladies' Home Journal (magazine), 204–05, 215–17, 281–83, *282*, 326

Lamb, Charles, 211

landscapes

fictional and physical, 89, *92*, 92–94, 187–88

fluidity of boundaries, 502

gaps between text and lived experience, 149

as metaphor for reading, 508–09

MM's writing and, 384–86

pastoral settings, 97

"place-myths," 501

reader's perspective as added element, 97–99

reading of validation, 176–77

society's self-image in, 97

stereotypes on popular fiction, 97

United States as assumed setting, 359

Emily trilogy, 251–52, 255–58

influence on MM's writing, 384–86

Mistress Pat, 382–83

Pat of Silver Bush, 200, 382–83

writing style, 256–57, 382–83

yearning for home, 256–58, 382–83

See also *Anne of Green Gables* series; *Emily's Quest*

Moon, Eric, 435–36

Moore, Paul, 427–28, 459–60

Moores, Shaun, 21, 89, 317

More Streets and Roads (Gr. 3), 352–54, *353*

See also *Dick and Jane* basic readers

Morgan, Bernice, 34

movies

about, 288, 328–30

adapted texts, 334–39

dissatisfaction with, 330

foreshadowings, 332

Hutcheon's "knowing viewer," 334–35, 337–38

implied viewer, 334, 335

intertextual and intermedial crossovers, 289, 323, 329, 353–54, 360–61

local theatres, 338, 459–60

MM's lack of experience with, 288, 317, 328, 338, 339

schemas, 339

voice-overs, 331–32

white, middle-class American life in, 328

texts: *Bernadine*, 328–29; *Bush Christmas*, 331–34, *333*; *Heidi*, 334–38; *Pollyanna*, 334–39, *336–37*; *Raintree County*, 329–30

Mr. Bear Squash-You-All-Flat (Gipson), 108–11, *109*, 113–16, 129

Munro, Alice, 93

the Murk (before memory)

about, 106–08

Christmas stories, 268

deictic shifting, 112–13, 116

flux of memory and Murk, 117–18

God and Baby Jesus, 108

identity as girl, 108

inability to access others' Murk, 422

learning to read, 134–38

MM's earliest memory, 105

motor responses as glimpse into, 495–96

reading as mini-Murk, 481

recognition of structural equivalence, 484

situated bodies, 495–96

stories, 108–11

subjunctive mode of narrative, 113–16

theory of mind, 111–12

museums

The Rooms, 417, 421, 439

Signal Hill geological museum, 415

See also Newfoundland Museum

music

about, 69–72

brain structures and, 280–81

Christmas music, 266, 275, 275–81, 278–79

concert attendance, 71–72

family performances, 69

folksongs, 470–73, *471–72*

hit parade songs, 298

MM's love of choral music, 445

musical awareness, 70–72

nostalgia and age of recording, 17

orchestra instruments, 70–71

school boys band, 401

sheet music, 69–70, 71, *275*, 276

See also piano; songs and singing

The Musical Clock (radio), 399

mysteries

adult mysteries, 223–24

Melora, 228–30, *229*

reading skills development, 224, 231

See also *Nancy Drew Mystery Stories* (Keene)

myths and legends

The Book of Knowledge, 301

children's magazines, 214

The Children's Wonder Book, 209–14, *210*, 230

name of child

first word learned in childhood reading, 238

literacy marker, 237–38

MM's love of name in *The Story of Margaret Field-Mouse*, 131, 132–33, 134

Sunday school alphabet activities, 446

schools attended by MM. *See* Holloway School; Prince of
    Wales College
school systems
    about, 33, 448–52
    Catholic schools, 309, 457, 458
    co-educational classes, 152
    contemporary school systems, 417
    contingent discourses, 417
    corporal punishment, 450
    denominational systems, 33, 387, 417, 451–52, 457, 458
    exams, 458
    gender roles, 152, 451–52
    gender separation, 448–49, 451
    history of, 417, 453–56
    interschool sports leagues, 309
    provincial competitions, 456
    race and ethnicity, 419–20
    scholarships, 456
    school boards, 458
    school uniforms, 53
    United Church schools, 448–52
    See also Department of Education, Newfoundland
school textbooks
    contingent discourses, 413–23
    dullness of, 370–73, 376, 387
    English language (Gr. 3), 343–47, *344*
    funding for, 387
    gaps between text and lived experience, 149
    gaps between textbooks and recreational reading, 382,
        384, 386
    geography (Gr. 3–4), 89, *90–91*, 169, 397, *397*
    geography (Gr. 6), 169, 383–84
    history (Gr. 5), 342–43, 370–73, 376
    lack of local perspective, 346, 387
    as male story, 371
    provincial lists, 458
    racism, 343–47, *344*
    settler culture, 342–47, *344*
    See also *Dick and Jane* basic readers
Schulte, Karl, *275*, 276
Schwebel, Sara, 92
science and nature study
    The Book of Knowledge, 301–02

contingent discourses, 413
    family interest, 382
    gaps between text and lived experience, 149
    nature study, 149, 302, 386–87
    snowflakes and intertextuality, 395–96
Scollon, Ron and Suzie Wong, 79
Scott Foresman basic readers. See *Dick and Jane* basic
        readers
scrapbooks, 153, 191–92, *402*, 402–03, 408–09
scripts
    about, 78–79, 178, 306
    analytical questions on, 306
    contingent discourses, 422–23
    interior of a child thinker, 177–78
    intertextuality, 160
    literacy and, 507
    scriptive things, 53–54, 306, 496, 498–99
    working stereotypes, 160
    texts: books, 53–54; Christmas concerts, 275; dolls, 53–54;
        hockey coins, *305*, 306–07; hockey table games, 304–
        06, *305*; Lee and manga stories, 498; *Moffat* books,
        177–82; visits to relatives, 79
    See also schemas
seasons and climate
    about, 64, 390–91, 416
    clothing, 155
    contingent discourses, 416
    gap between text and lived experience, 391, 395–98
    intertextuality, 394–96
    part of space and time, 64, 389–90
    schemas, 390–91
    seasonal time, 389–93, *392*
    spring, 382–83, 390–92, *392*
    summer, 390
    winter, 390–92, *392*, 394–99, *398*
    texts: basic readers (Gr. 3), 397, *398*; geography textbook
        (Gr. 3), 397, *397*; *Honey Bunch: Her First Winter at
        Snowtop*, 394–96; *The Long Winter*, 398–99
Second World War, 31, 465
The Secret Garden (Burnett), 209
The Secret of the Old Clock (Keene), 165
Segal, Erwin, 112
sentimentality, 224

Other Titles from The University of Alberta Press

Who Needs Books?

Reading in the Digital Age

LYNN COADY

Introduction by PAUL KENNEDY

72 pages | Foreword/liminaire, introduction, notes

Copublished with Canadian Literature Centre/
Centre de littérature canadienne

CLC Kreisel Lecture Series

978-1-77212-124-7 | $10.95 (T) paper

978-1-77212-120-9 | $8.99 (T) EPUB

978-1-77212-142-1 | $8.99 (T) Amazon Kindle

978-1-77212-143-8 | $8.99 (T) PDF

Canadian Literature | Essay

Magazines, Travel, and Middlebrow Culture

Canadian Periodicals in English and French, 1925–1960

FAYE HAMMILL & MICHELLE SMITH

256 pages | 32 colour photographs, bibliography, notes, index

Copublished with Liverpool University Press

978-1-77212-083-7 | $49.95 (T) paper

Cultural Studies | Travel

In Bed with the Word

Reading, Spirituality, and Cultural Politics

DANIEL COLEMAN

160 pages | Selected bibliography, index

978-0-88864-507-4 | $19.95 (T) paper

978-0-88864-647-7 | $15.99 (T) EPUB

978-0-88864-668-2 | $15.99 (T) Amazon Kindle

Literature | Criticism | Memoir